THE NEW
INTERNATIONAL
ECONOMICS

INTER

Jan S. Hogendorn COLBY COLLEGE

THE NEW NATIONAL ECONOMICS

Wilson B. Brown   NORTHERN ILLINOIS UNIVERSITY

ADDISON-WESLEY PUBLISHING COMPANY

READING, MASSACHUSETTS • MENLO PARK, CALIFORNIA • LONDON
AMSTERDAM • DON MILLS, ONTARIO • SYDNEY

This book is in the
ADDISON-WESLEY SERIES IN ECONOMICS

Library of Congress Cataloging in Publication Data

Hogendorn, Jan S
  The new international economics.

  Includes index.
  1. International economic relations.
I. Brown, Wilson B., 1938-   II. Title.
HF1411.H55   382.1   78-67951
ISBN 0-201-02824-7

ISBN 0-201-02824-7
ABCDEFGHIJ-HA-79

PREFACE AND ACKNOWLEDGMENTS

We have written this book with the aims of tying the basic international economics course more closely to the modern economic environment, and of enabling the reader to understand both theory and the manner in which theory can be applied to analysis of international economic problems. These aims reflect our own views regarding the uses of economics and also our approach to the teaching of international economics. The vast majority of students experience only one course in international economics before they go on to pursue careers in business, government, or the professions. This fact encouraged our quest in this book for a selection of material that was sufficiently advanced to sustain analytical skills, yet important in more than simply a theoretical sense. The book thus changes to some degree both the corpus of material presented in the standard course and the presentation itself. It integrates, for example, floating exchange rates, Eurodollars, and national income approaches into the macroeconomic analysis, and imperfect competition and new trade theories into the microeconomic. The presentation itself lays stress on the institutional and economic environment in which theory developed, tracing, for instance, the history of exchange rate systems,

Eurodollars, and tariff policies. Not only does this background provide relevant factual material, adding interest and depth to the book, but it makes the theory easier to learn and is, at least in our own classes, pedagogically effective.

In the process of adding new material and attempting to do justice to the traditional material, the book necessarily grew longer than originally envisaged. We have been careful throughout to allow for teaching flexibility, isolating certain subjects in separate chapters or subheadings (but using only one appendix). Thus the instructor who does not wish to spend a week on offer curves, or who feels that multinational firms are rather peripheral, can omit those sections or assign them as supplemental reading. In so doing he or she would find that subsequent analysis in the book is not based on the omitted material. Indeed, there seemed so much disagreement among our readers about whether macroeconomics should precede or follow the microeconomic section that we left it possible to move directly from the introductory chapter to Chapter 10, thus putting trade theory first. In our own teaching, however, we have always found it more effective to start with the macroeconomic side. The material there, essentially an expansion of banking and national income approaches, is closer to the student's basic principles background and more concrete to the student than the general equilibrium analysis that accompanies trade theory. To aid in such choices of material, we have prepared a "core" curriculum, stressing the building block parts of the text and the core knowledge. Instructors can then decide for themselves how much and which parts of the remaining text to use.

This book has been in many senses a labor of love on a subject that has had unending interest for us both. Virtually every chapter is a joint effort, and several have been recast and rewritten many times – far beyond, it seemed, the call of duty. Without each other's continued support, enthusiasm, insight, and considerable experience, we doubt the book could have been done at all.

We owe thanks to many people: to numerous of our teachers, who may recognize their influence in various passages; to students at Colby College, Northern Illinois University, and Chiang Mai University in Thailand, who struggled with typescript versions as we tested chapters in class; and to a number of anonymous colleagues, who provided (sometimes rather pointed) reviews of sample chapters. We would like to thank Jennifer Brown, who turned her considerable editorial talents to many of the chapters in various drafting stages; Chester Wasson and Robert Dodge, who contributed much to our knowledge of product life-cycle theory and encouraged us in the project; and Richard Shreve, who first explained learning curve theory and its importance.

Thanks are also due to Colby College for financial assistance; to P. Lynn Stuart, Judy Fairclough, and Lynne Graybeale, who worked on the manuscript over a period of two years as editorial assistants; and to Diana Small for the typing. We would also like to thank the staff at Addison-Wesley, in particular Marshall Aronson, Linda Bedell, and Melissa Hodgson, whose patient and painstaking editing is gratefully acknowledged.

East Vassalboro, Maine   J.S.H.
1979   W.B.B.

CONTENTS

1

INTRODUCTION: THE STUDY OF INTERNATIONAL ECONOMICS

The study of international economics is the oldest branch of the discipline. The first acceptable figures for gross national product date from the 1930s, but foreign trade data can be traced back to medieval times. English statistics, for instance, date back to 1355, in the reign of Edward III. Agents of the crown or city state could tax and measure foreign trade funneled through relatively few ports or highways. Domestic trade, however, was far too various and complicated to control. For the same reasons, economists today find that in many less developed countries trade statistics are reliable while many other figures are not.[1]

Trade among kingdoms and empires is of great antiquity. Some of the earliest evidence we have dates from the Bronze Age three thousand years before Christ: A merchant ship laden with, not surprisingly, bronze, heading for some Asia Minor port, sank off the coast of Turkey and lay submerged nearly five thousand years. Some two thousand years later, trade agreements between kingdoms were being made, as evidenced in the biblical story of Solomon's temple.

> And Hiram sent to Solomon saying, I have considered the things which thou sentest to me for: and I will do all thy desire concerning timber of cedar, and concerning timber of fir. My servants shall bring them down from Lebanon unto the sea: and I will convey them by sea in floats unto the place that thou shalt appoint me.
>
> . . . So Hiram gave Solomon cedar trees and fir trees, according to all his desire. And Solomon gave Hiram twenty thousand measures of wheat for food to his household and twenty measures of pure oil: thus gave Solomon to Hiram year by year.[2]

This is not the last time that oil and wheat have figured in trade agreements.

Ancient times saw not only extensive trade but also problems of currency exchange. Currency changers were common throughout the ancient world; indeed, it was foreign exchange traders whom Christ drove out of the temple (for profaning the temple, not for changing currency). Kingdoms used a variety of metals for coinage—gold and silver, electrum (a gold-silver alloy), copper, bronze, and even iron, though gold and silver came to predominate. The prices of gold and silver varied considerably against each other as the demand and supply of the two changed over the centuries. Consequently, the values of coins made of each metal varied. In addition, rulers frequently debased their coins, manufacturing them from less precious metal than their markings indicated. Cleopatra and her father unleashed a serious inflation in Egypt, as did Nero (who rebuilt Rome after the fire with his profits) and many of the late Roman emperors. In Egypt, the value of a pound of gold increased from some 1,125 denarii in AD 179, to 3000 denarii by AD 191, and to over 3 billion denarii by the end of the third century. The currency problems of recent years, it appears, are hardly new. Even such seemingly modern and sophisticated devices as forward exchange rates (Chapter 4) and the use of "units of account" to denominate debt date back at least to medieval times.[3]

From ancient times there have been fundamental differences between economic activities *within* a country and activities *between* countries. Not only were there differences of custom, consumption, and production, but trade was taxed and currency problems arose. With modern states, the ancient problems persist, but they have been joined by others. The modern state is considerably more powerful than its earlier counterpart; even the most liberal democracy regulates its commerce with an efficiency and uniformity that would be the envy of any ancient emperor. Hence every modern nation presents the traveler or businessperson with a different and often bewildering array of commercial regulations, taxes, subsidies, controls on migration, and the like, with far-reaching and often subtle effects.

International economics has traditionally dealt with differences among nations—both the "natural" differences and those created by the states with their various regulations. The exportation of American oranges to Canada in exchange for paper reflects natural differences in environment. The extensive exportation of Canadian earthworms from Toronto to Chicago bait stores may reflect the superior qualities of Canadian earthworms and—more importantly—the willingness of various ethnic groups in Canada to pick up spare cash some evenings on nearby farms or golf courses.[4] Such natural differences tend to coincide with national boundaries. Nations lie in differing climatological regions, and borders often follow the edges of the regions. Oceans, seas, jungles, deserts, and mountain ranges not only form militarily defensible lines, but more or less incidentally serve to hold a nation within climatological boundaries.

Often too, national borders serve to delineate cultural differences, as cultural groups have struggled to preserve themselves. Religions change with the crossing of a border, as from Israel to Jordan or Pakistan to India. Languages switch—and woe to the international seller who fails to penetrate the nuances of another language and, for instance, ends up calling a pen "terrifying" instead of "terrific," or describes a baby food as food (made) *of* instead of *for* babies.[5] Attitudes toward thrift and credit differ. Even nations that seem similar may have strikingly different tastes in food. A visitor from Detroit to a supermarket in Windsor, Ontario, just a mile or two across the border, for example, finds different flavors in cookies and coffees, plus a number of dessert items, such as cooked pudding mixes and butter tarts, that are not found on the American side of the border.

Although the effects of regional and cultural differences form part of the study of international economics, they are often not as important as the effects of differing sets of rules and regulations. National boundaries sometimes cut artificially through cultural groups—African boundaries, for instance, reflect colonial arrangements, not tribal locations. Or the boundaries, set at some distant conference table, follow parallels of latitude or longitude that have no geographical logic. In such situations, regional or cultural differences fail to explain international differences. One is hard put, for instance, to explain such phenomena as the one shown in the accompanying photograph of prairie land along the United States-Canadian border. The artificial border along the 45th parallel is clearly delineated in differing land-use patterns. Surely wheat grows just as well on both sides of the border and the wind blows just as cold in the winter, but the farms stop at the Canadian border. International economists could discount regional physiographic differences and to a considerable extent cultural differences in analyzing causes of these contrasts. Rather they would examine differences in tax rates and bases, in subsidies in rail systems and freight rates, or in tax treatment of unfarmed land. The lounge of the Dundee Line Hotel, spanning the border between New York and Quebec, is easier to explain; the bar and cash register are in Quebec, where the business and liquor taxes are lower, while the nonrevenue-generating pool table lies mostly in New York. Of course, during Prohibition in the United States, there were even more compelling reasons for keeping the bar in Canada.

As the two Canadian-American examples suggest, each nation has different codes or rules that distinguish its economy from those of its neighbors. Taxes may be based principally on income in one nation and on value added in another. One nation may subsidize farming, another industry. Pollution, safety, labeling, and branding requirements differ enormously—and often for no better reason than that they have evolved separately. Habits that are basically customary become sanctioned by law, such as which side of the road to drive on. A motorist traveling in West Africa from the Niger Republic to

Senegal in the 1960s started on the right side of the road in the Niger Republic, shifted to the left for Nigeria, then right for Dahomey and Togo, left for Ghana, right for the Ivory Coast and Liberia, left for Sierra Leone, right for Guinea, left for Gambia, and right again in Senegal—all this in a trip shorter than that from Denver to Boston. This reflected not logic, but what areas had or had not been British colonies.

National laws also tend to isolate each nation from its neighbors, making a considerable difference in the way trade is conducted *within* a country and *between* countries. Within the United States, for example, labor, management, and capital move freely—and great movements these can be, as with pioneers to the frontier, blacks to northern cities, or businesses to the so-called Sunbelt.[6] In Europe one finds the Welsh moving to London, provincial French to Paris, or Germans to Bavaria. Capital moves too. New textile plants are built in the American South, leaving old ones idle in New England; electronics firms have moved to the circumferential highway around Boston; and capital raised through the sale of stocks and bonds sold in any area of the United States can serve to finance operations in any other area.

Between countries the situation is different. In the United States, Ellis Island, the point of entry for millions of immigrants for over a century, is a museum, and immigration has slowed to a trickle. Canada and Australia, which until recently had virtually open doors for (white at least) immigrants, now have them open just a crack. Today it seems that more often than not what movement there is results from forced emigration. Recession and slow growth in Europe have caused many of the Turks and Yugoslavs who had swelled the labor force in Germany to return home. Nationalistic and racial feelings have led to the expulsion of Indians from Uganda and Chinese from Burma and Ceylon, and these populations have been given only a grudging, if dutiful, reception by their new hosts. Even the tourist must often spend hours or days in search of the elusive entry visa. This contrasts sharply with previous centuries: Early nineteenth-century Germany, for instance, was not a single state but several dozen small states; nonetheless, travel and immigration were free as none of the states required an entry visa. (The widespread use of visas is relatively new.) The same area today is occupied by West Germany, East Germany, Poland, and a small part of the Soviet Union; even tourist travel is difficult.

Movements of capital are also restricted by modern governments, although restriction is exceedingly difficult and often unsuccessful. Just ask the finance minister of a government trying to stem the outflow of capital during a period of political instability. Restrictions are tried nonetheless. Many nations require a business or individual to have government permission before sending money abroad. Or there are tax incentives for investing domestically rather than abroad. Several nations restrict the inflow of capital; the Swiss actually charge foreigners a fee instead of paying them interest on their Swiss accounts. Many countries limit any capital movements associated with a controlling ownership of national resources or even national companies. A firm may be able to move many miles from New York to Alabama without any trouble, but if it went just a few miles to Quebec it would very likely have to beg permission from the Canadian government. In Japan, Mexico, and the Andean Pact countries, foreign firms cannot invest unless they share ownership with domestic citizens. Communist countries, of course, prohibit foreign private ownership on principle.

Transport costs alone often make international trade more difficult. The distances involved are often longer. More important, perhaps, is that there are not customs stations just anywhere. The map on the next page shows the lack of connections between the United States and Canadian railway systems along the border from Winnipeg, Manitoba to Havre, Montana, a rail distance of over five hundred miles. International documentation, too, is often considerably longer and more complicated than the domestic.

These many national differences can create large practical difficulties. Consider American exporters who want to export electrical appliances to Europe. They have first to cope with product specifications that are different.

Inches must be changed to centimeters, gallons to liters, and so on. There are different safety requirements for wiring and grounding. Nor should they forget that Europe is on a 220 volt system; American 110 volt appliances behave strangely when plugged into the European systems.[7] Even the gauges and threadings of nuts and bolts may differ. Not only that, but they have to worry about the labeling and the instruction booklet. (The Italian manufacturer who directed Americans to be sure the freezer was "earthed" can expect to cause some puzzlement.) If they do their own advertising or distribution there are many more headaches.

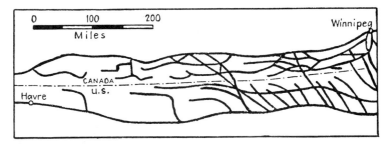

From August Lösch, "Die räumliche Ordnung der Wirtschaft," Fig. 80, p. 292, Gustav Fischer Verlag, Jena, 1940.

The rules of international economic policy are also often much rougher than at home. Politicians whose economic policy suggestions may be fully sensible at home find that the same policies do not work in an international world of tariffs, import quotas, foreign exchange restrictions, and the like. Often these international restrictions would be politically intolerable if perpetrated against citizens in the home country. It might be politically possible for the United States to restrict the investment of its firms abroad, but it could not force a firm to stay in New York and not move to Texas. Texans vote in the United States, the foreign beneficiaries of the investment do not. Similarly, when the United States government blocks grain sales to foreign countries, it does not have to worry about angry foreign consumers.

With all these differences noted, we must still remember the very important pressures reducing national differences. The heyday of high tariffs, capital restrictions, and "go-it-alone" politics was in the second quarter of this century. The third quarter saw dramatic declines in tariff barriers, reductions of capital controls, and attempts at international standardization of safety, health, and labeling requirements. It saw enormous capital movements on a scale never before witnessed—whether or not desired by governments. Transportation rates declined sharply and speed of delivery rose with the introduction of large, highly automated ships capable of unloading their cargoes in a single day. (Indeed, the problem today is to store and move the cargo that has been unloaded. Thus the New York City piers are rotting, while the New Jersey ports of Newark and Elizabeth, with their enormous "meadows" of marsh that can be used for storage, have virtually all the business.) With rising fuel costs, too, ocean transport becomes relatively cheaper than land. Once a boat is loaded, the marginal cost of sailing another one hundred miles is very low. Astonishingly, it is cheaper today to move cars from Japan to California than it is to get them there from Detroit.

National tastes, too, appear to be converging. As large parts of the developed world come to enjoy high per capita incomes and high levels of education, they develop many similar desires. The spread of moving pictures, magazines, television programs, books, and the extensive interpersonal contact of people presses toward a certain uniformity in taste. The once uniquely Western business suit, for instance, is well-nigh ubiquitous among business leaders and government people. Blue jeans and Coca-Cola seem as popular in Japan and France as in the United States. Mechanization has brought with it its own physical demands, lending a certain sameness to cities and factories everywhere. Except for some surface styling, an elevator is an elevator, a petrochemical factory just that; even automobiles vary little from country to country.

The third quarter of the century has also seen the rise of a tremendous amount of nongovernmental cross-border activity—what has come to be called *transnational* activity, as opposed to "international" activities involving relations between governments. The ready communications of satellite and fast jets put people into contact with an ease never before imagined. IBM, for instance, has all of its European operations tied together on telephone lines such that one computer can send to any other detailed plans and specifications on any project. It is not unusual, too, for an executive to fly across the Atlantic to meet with other executives in some airport hotel for a few hours and then fly back. As a result of this easy communication, there has been a mushrooming growth of all kinds of transnational contacts—charities like Foster Parents, service groups like the Rotary, myriads of professional groups of engineers, architects, and economists, interest groups like the Audubon Society and, not least, those profit-making enterprises known as multinational corporations. Solomon's temple today might have been built by international contractors from Rome, designed by an architect found through the International Architects Association, and constructed of wood supplied by some international conglomerate.

Falling trade barriers, rapid capital movements, increasingly similar tastes and incomes, and more day-to-day contact has led to a world in which international economic activities touch almost every individual. International trade is larger both in absolute terms and in percentage of national income than it has been in this century (and possibly ever). Foreign corporations penetrate the

United States market in increasing numbers, just as American corporations operate abroad. One simply cannot go through a day without being touched by some aspect of international economics. It was, in fact, just this morning that Mr. Peoria woke up to his Sony clock radio (Japanese-made), glanced at his Sessions clock (made by an American subsidiary of Philips Lamp Works of Holland) in the hall, grabbed his Norelco razor (another Philips subsidiary), pulled on his Korean-made shirt washed in Surf (made by Lever Brothers, a subsidiary of the British-Dutch Unilever), drank his Maxim coffee (freeze-dried in Germany by General Foods from beans grown in many places), hopped into his (Canadian-made) Pinto with his new Michelin (French) tires, and roared off to work, burning his Arabian oil refined by Shell Oil (a British-Dutch firm). Fortunately for the United States, he was headed for Caterpillar, which is an extensive exporter and brings home substantial earnings from its foreign operations.

International economics, it appears, affects all our lives. Thus it is an important branch of economics, not only for its antiquity, but because it analyzes many problems that are unique to trade between national entities. This book serves as an introduction to the field. It provides a view of the practice as well as of the theory of the subject, to prepare the reader for further encounters with the ins and outs of international finance and trade. The theories and economic models in the book are numerous, but also, the authors trust, useful. But the book is not intended to be wall-to-wall theory; rather, it seeks to use the necessary descriptive material to build the theory and to give the reader a sound institutional and analytical base.

Notes

1. Virtually all of Peru's imports, for instance, come through the port of Callao, near Lima. A few other ports serve for exports, but there are few good harbors. Only one road, the Pan-American Highway, connects Peru with Ecuador and Chile and there is only one railway connection (with Bolivia, by rail-barge across Lake Titicaca); finally, there is the Amazonian port of Iquitos. All of these are easily watched. While goods can be smuggled around these ports of entry, they can be moved only in small lots, which makes economic sense only for gold or drugs.
2. Norman Crump, *The ABC of the Foreign Exchanges* (London: Macmillan, 1965) quotes this from I Kings 5:8-11. This book stands as an example of the age of international economics; still in print and used in modern courses, it was first published in 1892 and has been revised thirteen times.
3. See Paul Einzig, *The History of Foreign Exchange* (London: Macmillan, 1964), Chapters 1-6.
4. Michael Levas, "Pricing in the Fishbait Industry" (seminar paper, Department of Marketing, Northern Illinois University), unpublished.
5. Mussolini thought he spoke good German. He didn't. His insistence on speaking it with Hitler, and continually misunderstanding top-secret private discussions, was

one reason for Italy's poor military performance in World War II. Many blunders of language are committed every day in the world of international trade. The car names Matador and Nova, for instance, mean "Killer" and "Doesn't Go" in Spanish, while ENCO, the name EXXON was first thinking of adopting, means "Stalled Car" in Japanese. Even in the same language there are problems. Two corporate negotiating teams from the United States and Great Britain wasted a whole day arguing whether to "table" a motion only to discover late in the day that "table" in British means to consider the motion right away while in American it means to consider it at some future date.

6. Not to say that states in the United States have not at times attempted to halt immigration. California tried to do so, but with little success, in the Great Depression.

7. One of the authors once attended a spectacular Christmas party in London. An American plugged in a new string of imported Christmas tree bulbs. They were designed for 110 volts but the circuit was 220 volts. The bulbs popped like firecrackers.

PART I

MONEY AND PRICES IN
AN INTERNATIONAL SETTING

CHAPTER **2**

MONEY
AND EXCHANGE RATES

Just as every modern nation, large or small, must have its own flag, each must have its own currency—be it a famous one such as the American dollar, British pound sterling, French franc, German mark, Japanese yen, Swiss franc, Dutch guilder, and Italian lira, or an exotic one like the Zambian kwacha, Bangladesh taka, Burmese kyat, Gambian dalasi, Albanian lek, Mauritanian ouguiya, and Panamanian balboa. The national currency is *legal tender* within the country's borders, and all prices, wages, and debts are expressed in it. (Admittedly, in some small countries foreign currency does circulate, for example, the dollar in Liberia, where the real Liberian national currency is seldom seen. Also, accounts are often expressed in dollar terms for convenience. But foreign currency is seldom legal tender outside the issuing country's borders.)

Because of the great multiplicity of monies—over a hundred as of 1979—every tourist crossing a border must visit a currency exchange, every businessperson making a payment must transfer funds from a checking account in one currency to an account in another currency, and every economist seeking to compare prices or national income in two different countries must cope with the problem of different monies.

Our task in the several chapters that follow is to examine the mechanisms involved in exchanging one currency for another. The manner in which exchange rates between currencies are established is not particularly simple in either its practical mechanics or its theoretical implications. But it is a central

13

problem in modern economics because it links one country's domestic economy with the rest of the world. Accordingly, the setting of exchange rates will be a recurrent theme in this book.

Transferring Money between Countries

How do exchange rates become established? To answer this question, consider the following typical transaction in the world of international business. This example demonstrates the complexities of international money and banking, and shows how such transactions influence the foreign exchange market. These exchanges of currency, of which many millions occur every day, are themselves the means by which exchange rates are set.

Suppose that an American firm, Knight Stillman Distributors, Inc., a wholesale liquor dealer, wishes to purchase fifty barrels of "Auld Reekie" Scotch whisky direct from the Reekie distillery in Edinburgh. Immediately there is a problem. The price of the whisky is quoted in British pounds sterling (£) at £200 for a fifty-gallon barrel, and the invoice on the shipment reads £10,000. Mr. Stillman's dilemma is that he has dollars in his company's bank account, not pounds sterling. Even if he is a tenderfoot among travelers, he is doubtless aware that thousands of people make their living by exchanging currencies. In fact, nothing is a more familiar sight in Europe than the little kiosks marked "Change/Cambio/Wechsel" where small exchanges can be made. But Mr. Stillman is not in Europe, and even if he were his attempt to acquire £10,000 would strain the resources of any small dealer.

What then does he do? One fairly obvious solution is to check the financial pages of the *Wall Street Journal* to see what the pound costs in terms of dollars this morning. Say the paper gives the rate as £1.00 = $2.0591 (such rates are commonly carried out to a hundredth of a cent). Stillman could then presumably send off a dollar check or bank draft for $20,591 to the Reekie distillery, thus settling the bill. Alas, a moment's thought shows this to be unwise. Even in tranquil times, the dollar/pound exchange rate may move up or down by several tenths of a percent during the day. Hence the check for $20,591 may be worth a little more or a little less to the Reekie Company when Her Majesty's Post Office delivers it to its offices in Edinburgh. If it has lost on the transaction, the Reekie Company will be annoyed and send a dunning cablegram. Should the rate go against the Stillman Company, it probably will hear nothing more of the matter. Reekie's gain is Stillman's loss.

If Stillman is to send the precise amount and avoid such difficulties, it must send a check denominated in pounds sterling. Sending such a check involves the firm in the daily activities of the international banking system, in one of the following ways:

1. It could write a check in sterling on an account it had previously established at a British bank—Barclay's, for example, presently Britain's largest.

Whenever there is a frequent need to do business in another country, firms or individuals commonly establish checking accounts in foreign banks from which to make payments. (Both authors of this book have bank accounts abroad—it eases enormously the problem of buying books, subscribing to journals, paying bills run up by research and holidays, and so on.) After an outpayment is made from the sterling account, the funds can be replenished by sending Barclay's a check drawn in dollars. Barclay's will then credit the check to the sterling account at whatever the exchange rate happens to be when Barclay's receives the check.

2.   A second and much faster method would be for Stillman to cable (telephone) Barclay's to transfer pounds from its account to that of the Reekie Company. These cable or telephone transfers are an increasingly common means for effecting payment.

3.   Lacking a foreign account, Stillman could buy a *cashier's check* in pounds sterling from its bank in the United States, say the First National Bank of Boston. First National would debit Stillman the dollar equivalent at today's rate for the £10,000 cashier's check, and would write the check on an account it holds at a British bank. This transaction could also be accomplished by cable if speed were a requirement.

4.   Finally, Stillman could use a *bill of exchange* to make payment. The international use of such bills is said to have originated in the thirteenth and fourteenth centuries, when Jews were trying to salvage some of their property that had to be left behind when they were expelled from France. This method of payment has the longest history and would have been the standard means had our transaction taken place during the nineteenth century. It is also one of the more complicated means of transfer. Bills of exchange are still used to some extent and work much like checks. Basically they are orders written by the paying party (Stillman) to some third party in Britain to pay the Reekie Company £10,000. Had this transaction been by check, the payments would have been immediate and the third party would have been a bank—Stillman (first party) would order Barclay's Bank (third party) to pay Reekie (second party). A bill of exchange, however, may order a nonbanking institution to make payment. If the document is a *sight bill*, it must be paid on presentation. But payment may not be immediate. A bill of exchange written and signed on May 1 might, for instance, be marked as payable on August 1, thus representing an advance of short-term credit to the buyer of the goods involved in the transaction. If the recipient holds the bill until it comes due, then the recipient has extended short-term credit to the buyer. The cost of the credit would be covered by figuring it into the price or cost of the good when it was sold in the first place.

If the buyer signs the bill when it is drawn up, signifying that he or she does indeed owe the money, then the document becomes what is known as a *commercial acceptance*—the buyer "accepts" the debt. An acceptance is a valuable piece of paper, and the seller who holds such a *90-day bill* that is not immediately payable can sell it (called *discounting*) to a bank or other financial institution. The price received will be lower than the face value by the amount of the discount, which represents interest for 90 days and risk, if any. Here too credit has been extended to the buyer, but in this case the seller gets payment at once.*

For centuries the bill of exchange was the primary transfer mechanism for funds. London was the chief center for trading bills, since during the nineteenth century interest rates there were lower than anywhere else. Bills and acceptances, generally denominated in pounds, were the chief source of credit to importers and exporters alike. But the cablegram, telex, and the telephone have cut deeply into traditional practices. In 1920 the great market in bills maintained at London's Royal Exchange closed down; it had specialized in trading bills since the 1500s. Nowadays, only a small portion of international currency transfers use this mechanism, though it remains an important instrument for small importers and exporters.

International Bank Balances

Whatever the method Stillman chooses for making payment, the purchase of Scotch whisky by Stillman from Reekie is now complete. The buyer has fifty barrels; the seller has £10,000. But the effect of the transaction on the international exchange rate between the pound sterling and the dollar is still far from complete. We must now look behind the doors of the banks involved to see its further ramifications and how they influence the exchange rate.

As part of its normal operations, any bank that handles much international business must maintain balances in foreign currencies to make payments for customers and to receive payments made to customers. Stillman, for example, is at liberty to deposit any sterling receipts obtained during the course of business in the First National Bank of Boston, and can also ask that bank to pay its sterling debts. Now of course no bank wants to hold useless stacks of foreign banknotes, which take up space and bear no interest. So First National maintains its holdings of foreign currency in checking accounts at banks located abroad. (Such checking accounts ordinarily do bear interest in foreign countries, although not in the United States.) If First National maintains a sterling account with Barclay's in London, and at the same time Barclay's has a dollar account with First National, the two institutions are called *correspondent banks*. In some circumstances, the American bank will choose to deal with one of its own subsidiaries abroad. Several New York banks (Chase Manhattan and the First National Bank of New York in particu-

---

*There are further variations on acceptances that are still commonly used in international trade, but these are more appropriate for manuals on the practice of trade.

lar) have extensive networks of subsidiaries that engage in commercial banking abroad. Even some small banks now have European subsidiaries—for example, the Fidelity Bank of Philadelphia and the Wachovia, North Carolina, Bank and Trust Company.

A number of foreign banks have similar subsidiaries in the United States. Barclay's, for instance, has a chain of banks in California. Because of the need for separate incorporation in each state, there are over 120 foreign banks in the United States (the vast majority in New York and California), most of which are "full-service" banks. There are many more foreign banking offices and investment companies, which do not accept deposits, but wish to be in the United States in order to serve their foreign depositors, participate in bond issues, or solicit foreign business from American companies. These banks hold only a very small part of the bank deposits in the United States.

To trace the method by which the international banking system transfers funds, let us watch the progress of the dollar check that the Stillman Company sent to Barclay's Bank to replenish its sterling deposits following the whisky purchase. This particular check for $20,000 was drawn on the Stillman account at the First National Bank of Boston and sent to Barclay's main office in London to be deposited to Stillman's sterling account there. The stamps on the back of the check tell the following tale:

1. It was received by mail at Barclay's in London. If the ticker tape reads £1.00 = $2.0500 at the moment the clerk processes it, then Stillman's account is credited with £9,756.

2. It was deposited, again by mail, in Barclay's dollar checking account at the Chase Manhattan Bank in New York.

3. Chase Manhattan deposited the check in its account with the United States Federal Reserve System.

4. The Federal Reserve sent the check to the First National Bank of Boston.

Just as soon as Stillman's account in Boston is debited the $20,000 of the check, the transaction is complete from the banks' point of view.

Basic to understanding the exchange rate is realizing that while this one transfer of money will have little or no effect on the rate between the pound and the dollar, the multitude of transactions in any day or week most certainly will have an effect. Suppose, for instance, that most of the Americans with deposits in Barclay's Bank acted exactly as Stillman did within a short period—that is, they transferred dollars to their sterling accounts in London—and meanwhile few customers were seeking U.S. dollars. Barclay's deposits in the United States would rise sharply. Should it hold onto these balances, or find some way to be rid of them? The foreign exchange officers working for big banks commonly operate within a set of ground rules that help them to answer this question. Such rules will take into account the following factors:

1. Liquidity needs in the United States. If Barclay's expects to sell American dollars to a customer in the near future, it is foolish to convert its "excess" dollar holdings into pounds only to reconvert almost immediately thereafter. To meet such contingencies Barclay's will want to hold some minimum balance in American dollars.

2. Liquidity needs in Britain. United States dollar assets, even in the form of cash banknotes, cannot be counted as bank reserves under British law (nor could pound notes be counted as reserves under American law). They will not serve to meet a bank's legal reserve requirement. Should Barclay's in Britain be creating additional deposits that need reserve backing, at some point it will have to bring money back from its deposits in the United States to serve its domestic needs. That is to say, should the demand for lending be high in Britain, Barclay's will keep its U.S. deposits closely pared.

3. Speculation and risk. Having credited Stillman with £9,756, Barclay's will not want to see the value of its new $20,000 holding decline to less than this sum in pounds. There are various forms of insurance (discussed in Chapter 4) that can be used to avoid loss. However, there is also a chance for gain—$20,000 might in a few days be worth somewhat more than £9,756. Thus many banks allow a certain percentage of their foreign currency holdings to go "uninsured," speculating that the value of their foreign currency will rise. Naturally, the greater the expectation of such profitable rises, the more willing the bank will be to hold larger sums in foreign currency, and vice versa.

4. Interest rate differentials. Assume that the general structure of interest rates is higher in the United States than in Britain. Should this be so, Barclay's might choose to keep its dollars in U.S. Treasury bills or other securities even when these dollar holdings are beyond the immediate needs of customers. Indeed, most foreign banks do keep substantial amounts of U.S. dollar securities (mostly Treasury bills) in their asset portfolios. A higher level of interest rates in Britain would have the reverse result.

The Foreign Exchange Market

Having considered all these factors, suppose Barclay's decides to allow its deposits of U.S. dollars to rise by $10,000 and to convert the remaining $10,000 into pounds sterling. To accomplish this conversion, Barclay's will enter the foreign exchange market. This market is the most unified in the world. Connected by instant communication between major centers, it deals in "products" (dollars, pounds sterling, marks, and so on) that are perfectly uniform, since one dollar is like any other dollar.[1] It has little concern with transport costs because transactions are usually made via bank balances and not by shipping cash. Thus it comes nearer to the economist's model of perfect competition than anything else. The foreign exchange market is also the world's largest. In New York alone, as much as $50 billion worth of foreign currency is traded every day (compared to a paltry $2.4 billion in the New York Stock Exchange), and there are lesser centers at London, Frankfurt, Zurich, Amsterdam, Paris, Tokyo, and—until the civil war of 1976—Beirut.[2]

Assume Barclay's makes use of the New York facilities because the $20,000 check was sent there in the first place. Its most likely course would be to telephone one of the eight foreign exchange brokers in New York, requesting the price at that moment of the U.S. dollar in terms of the British pound.[3] The broker throughout the day has been in constant contact with other banks seeking to buy and sell both dollars and pounds, and will suggest a going price—indeed, the broker may already have a buyer at that price. The broker quotes the rate as a fraction, say "3/8 to 5/16." Everyone in the market knows the general region in which the rate lies, so it is unnecessary to say more. The customer has only a few seconds to react if it is a telephone inquiry, perhaps a minute or two if the conversation is by telex printer. Otherwise the transaction is terminated. Brokers guard jealously their good reputations; failure to come through on a quotation in some reasonably large amount would jeopardize their place in the market. The rate brokers quote will leave room for their small "commission"; their buying and selling rates will be a few hundredths of a cent apart. Often today the spread between buying and selling rates on small transactions is actually unprofitable for brokers, but the brokers go ahead with the transaction to keep the business of potentially large volume users. At times, also, banks avoid the brokers and deal directly with one another.

If Barclay's accepts the rate, a broker would within a few seconds or minutes have a buyer. Say, for example, that Irving Trust Company of New York is the confirmed purchaser of the $10,000 at the agreed rate. Irving Trust would transfer the pounds sterling for the purchase, by check, from whatever British bank account they were held in to Barclay's, and Barclay's would transfer its $10,000 from its Chase Manhattan deposit to the Irving Trust Company.

If, however, Barclay's does not like the price being offered in New York, and if it were early enough in the day so that in spite of the five-hour time difference the London money market was still open for business, it could then call a broker in London for a better price. Since Barclay's and all other major banks are in instant touch by telex between New York and London, and are constantly checking prices in the two markets, any difference in the exchange rate would be quite small. Even so, considering that a big international bank trades many billions of dollars worth of currency in just one week, a difference of a few hundredths of a cent on the rate will certainly cover a salary or two.

Determination of the Exchange Rate

When brokers quote a price for one currency in terms of another, they have in mind a rate that will fill the various buying and selling requests on their desk at that time. By typing a request into the console computer terminal at their desk, they can see instantly a video display of all unfilled buy-and-sell orders at that moment. If they find that there is an increased total of orders (demand) for one currency, they will tend to quote a higher rate for that, and if they succeed in getting the higher rate, they may quote a new rate that is marginally higher still. Obviously, brokers must have an almost instinctive "feel" for the market—no matter how much computer aid they may receive. Their main task is to recognize the existence of market forces and react to them.

The easiest way to visualize the process of market forces working through and upon the brokers is to use the demand and supply curves learned in first-year economics. The forces of supply and demand determine the price of currency just as they do the price of wheat or any other good. Figure 2.1 shows how the supply and demand for a currency can be illustrated diagrammatically. The vertical axis displays the dollar price of one pound. On the horizontal axis is shown the quantity of pounds traded in return for dollars. The supply curve shows the quantity of pounds being brought into the market at various different prices for these pounds. Note the shape: The broker gets many more offers to sell pounds when sellers get a high dollar price for their pounds. A price of four dollars per pound would be, for holders of pounds, an extraordinarily good bargain. But a price of one dollar per pound will call forth only a small offering, for then it is not a bargain for sellers of pounds.

The demand curve for pounds in Fig. 2.1 shows the quantity demanded at various dollar prices. If pounds are very cheap—that is, if a pound can be obtained for only one dollar—then the demand will be high. If pounds are expensive, so that perhaps four dollars are needed to purchase one, then the quantity demanded will be low.

At the point of intersection between the two curves we find the equilibrium rate of exchange. As with any other market price, only at the intersection will there be no pressure for the price to fall or rise. At a price of four dollars per pound, the quantity of pounds supplied far exceeds the quantity demanded. The broker's phone rings all day long with sell orders, but hardly a peep comes from prospective buyers. The forces of competition lead the broker to cut the price, and induce sellers glutted with holdings of pounds to accept the lower offer. Conversely, at one dollar per pound, the quantity demanded far exceeds the quantity supplied. Eager buyers of pounds swamp the broker with orders; shy sellers stay silent. Market forces push the price upward, and dissatisfied buyers are prepared to pay the higher price—for otherwise they go without. The forces acting to change the dollar/pound exchange rate disappear only when there is neither shortage nor surplus. On the diagram, there is only one possible exchange rate between the pound and the dollar that will "clear the market," leaving neither pounds nor dollars left over at the close of business. That rate is £1.00 = $2.05, labeled E for equilibrium.

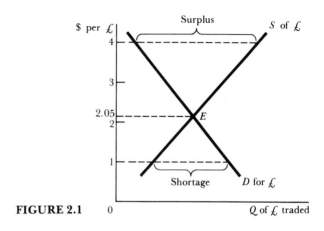

FIGURE 2.1

Brokers are dealing not just with two currencies, pounds and dollars, of course, but with many different ones being traded at the same time. A whole set of supply and demand curves underlies the market's simultaneous deter-mination of many exchange rates, as shown in Fig. 2.2. The cross rates be-tween currencies are one of the chief concerns of the brokers, as we shall see in the following section. In fact, in order to obtain equilibrium in the foreign exchange market as a whole, both rates and quantities traded must be in bal-ance. Thus if, on a given day, sellers want to change £100,000 into dollars when the rate is £1.00 = $2.05, then this rate can be an equilibrium rate only if buyers of pounds have $205,000 that they want to dispose of. There is only one structure of rates and quantities at any given time that will give an overall equilibrium. Figure 2.2 shows that one possible structure for such an equilib-rium would be:

£1.00 = $2.05   £1.00 = Fr 10.25
$1.00 = Fr 5.00   £1.00 = DM 7.79
$1.00 = DM 3.8   DM1.00 = Fr 1.316
$1.00 = £0.488

The reader may wonder how such a complicated movement toward over-all equilibrium, involving perhaps ten or a dozen major currencies and scores of cross rates, would ever occur. How is it possible that so many supply and demand curves for currency would, all at the same time, move toward posi-tions that simultaneously clear the market for them all? The answer lies in the meaning of a word of French extraction—*arbitrage* (pronounced to rhyme with garage), to which we now turn.

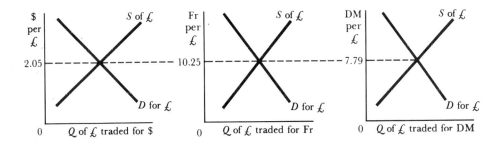

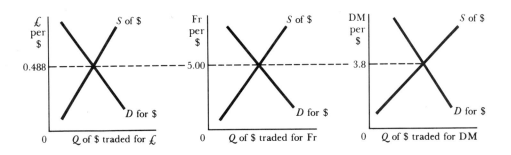

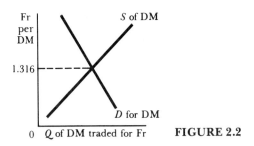

FIGURE 2.2

Arbitrage. The market for foreign exchange is a model of economic efficiency. Bank accounts are costless to store. Unlike commodities, they do not deteriorate or wear out. They require no insurance, and need no transport services when moved from bank to bank. Finally, no one can distinguish a dollar in one bank account from a dollar in any other account. There thus being no quality differences to worry about, there is no need to buy from one bank rather than from another. In such a situation, vast sums of money can change hands with only tiny margins being taken by banks and brokers. Such efficiency assures buyers or sellers of currency that they will get virtually the same exchange rate in any major financial center if they deal through a large bank, and also that when they buy currency there will be no greater advantage in going some indirect route—say spending dollars to buy francs to buy marks—than would be obtained by purchasing marks directly with dollars. The process that ensures the very close correspondence of all rates in all foreign exchange markets is called *arbitrage*.

Arbitrage is the buying and selling of anything simultaneously. A person who buys a carload of artichokes in California and sells it at the same time for a higher price to someone in Chicago is an *arbitrageur*, performing the function of lowering the artichoke price in Chicago and raising it in California. Arbitrage must be distinguished from *speculation*. When speculating, the artichoke middleman does not have an immediate buyer for the artichokes and thus runs a risk. When arbitraging, the middleman does have a buyer and runs no risk. (Needless to say, because of the risk element, the rewards for successful speculation are far greater than those for successful arbitrage.)

Since the facilities of the foreign exchange market are nearly perfect for arbitrage, there is much simultaneous buying and selling both between major currency centers (New York, London, Zurich) and between currencies (pounds, dollars, marks). Example 1 and Figs. 2.3(a) and (b) show where an arbitrage opportunity has opened between two portions of the international money market. In Example 2 and Figs. 2.4(a) and (b), an arbitrage opportunity has arisen because of *disorderly cross rates*, meaning that the indirect route to buying a currency carries a different price from the direct route. For the sake of clarity, both examples employ price differentials and currency volumes larger than those expected to occur in everyday currency operations, but they do illustrate dramatically the profits awaiting the successful arbitrageur.

Example 1
Two-Point Arbitrage

Situation:	Price of sterling in London: £1.00 = $2.0510
	Price of sterling in New York: £1.00 = $2.0575
Strategy:	Sell pounds in New York and buy pounds in London.
Example:	Take £10,000 and buy $20,575 in New York, simultaneously selling 20,510 of those dollars in London for £10,000.
Result:	Arbitrageur earns $65 minus the cost of a few minutes of time and a telex message. The demand for pounds rises slightly in London, as shown in Fig. 2.3(b), and the dollar becomes slightly cheaper there (the pound will

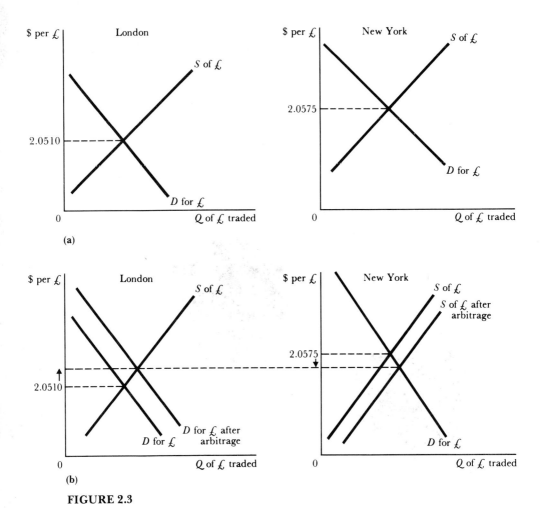

FIGURE 2.3

now buy somewhat more than $2.0510). In New York the supply of sterling rises slightly, as also shown in Fig. 2.3(b). There the dollar becomes slightly more expensive, a pound buying less than $2.0575. Arbitrage continues until the difference in the rates between New York and London is so small as to eliminate any significant gains to arbitrageurs.

Example 2
Cross-Rate Arbitrage

Situation: In New York £1.00 = $2.0500
$1.00 = DM3.65
£1.00 = DM7.35

Strategy: Buy deutsche marks with dollars, then use the marks to buy pounds, and then use the pounds to purchase dollars once again.

Example: Take $10,000 and purchase DM36,500. With the DM36,500 buy £4,966 (36,500 ÷ 7.35 = 4,966). With the £4,966 buy $10,180 (4,966 × 2.05 = 10,180)

Result: Arbitrageur earns $180 minus the cost of a few minutes of time. Buying marks with dollars raises the supply of dollars, as shown in the middle section of Fig. 2.4(b), with the mark/dollar rate falling somewhat. Buying pounds with marks raises the demand for pounds in the righthand section of Fig. 2.4(b); the mark/pound rate rising somewhat with $1.00 now buying slightly more than DM7.35. Buying dollars with pounds increases the supply of pounds in the lefthand portion of Fig. 2.4(b), the dollar/pound rate falling slightly with £1.00 now buying slightly fewer dollars and cents than before. Arbitrage continues until the cross rates are so close together that any significant possibility of gain is eliminated.

As Fig. 2.4 shows, the actions of arbitrageurs move the cross rates together. It is unlikely that the rates will always be exactly consistent. Arbitrageurs must attain some minimum level of earnings to make their activities worthwhile. For a long time it was believed that arbitrage would not take place unless a gross profit of 1/2 of 1 percent was to be expected. Nowadays, however, as faster and cheaper communications have become available in the foreign exchange market, margins of 1/16 or even 1/32 of 1 percent have been enough. In fact, some banks may engage in arbitrage even without direct profit, in order to enlarge their scale of operations and so attract other types of business.

Motives for Acquiring Foreign Currencies. We have seen that the foreign exchange market is a most efficient mechanism for establishing the price of currencies against one another. What is it, however, that determines the various amounts of currencies brought to the market in the first place? This question may be treated on several different levels, the more sophisticated of which are covered in later chapters. For now, let us once again return to the market for foreign exchange—this time, however, separating the sources of funds brought to the market according to motives.

The overall assumption of this simplified picture is that people and businesses who want either to buy or to sell foreign currencies will do so through their commercial banks, and that these banks will then bring the currencies into the foreign exchange market. The purposes for doing this are illustrated in Fig. 2.5, and are as follows:

1. *For trade.* In 1975 the United States imported annually some $98 billion worth of goods and used another $30 billion worth of services by firms that need payment in currencies other than the dollar. Firms and individuals

New York

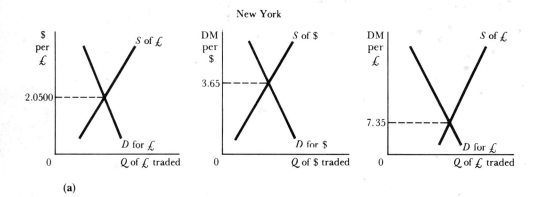

(a)

New York

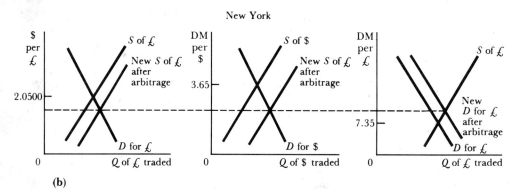

(b)

FIGURE 2.4

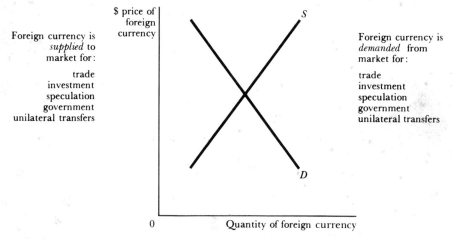

Foreign currency is *supplied* to market for:

trade
investment
speculation
government
unilateral transfers

Foreign currency is *demanded* from market for:

trade
investment
speculation
government
unilateral transfers

FIGURE 2.5

therefore had to purchase foreign currencies with dollars, a demand shown on the right side of Fig. 2.5. The United States also exported a somewhat larger amount of goods ($107 billion) and services ($41 billion) so that considerable supplies of foreign currencies were offered in the market by foreign buyers of American exports who were seeking to purchase dollars. (This supply is seen on the left side of Fig. 2.5.)

2. *For investment.* Another large source of money on the foreign exchange market is the block of funds destined for investment in another country. Such investment may be short term, including the financing of trade, the purchases or sales of the securities of foreign governments and corporations by banks, and the increases in working balances held by banks or firms in one nation or another. Most of these funds are lent, paid back, and re-lent several times a year. United States government statistics on short-term investment record only the net outflow from year to year, a figure recently (1975) on the order of $12 billion. Much of that money, however, may have flowed through the foreign exchange market many times in the course of a year.

Other funds will be destined for long-term investment, including the purchase of foreign stocks and long-term bonds (called portfolio investment), and the establishment of wholly or partially owned enterprises abroad (direct investment). In 1975, some US $15 billion were brought to the foreign exchange market for such purposes.

3. *For speculation and arbitrage.* It is important analytically to distinguish between speculation and arbitrage on currencies and investment, although it is impossible to do so from the statistics available. (All are lumped together in the official data as investment.) The sole motive of the speculator is to buy a currency in the belief that its value will rise, or sell it in the expectation that its value will fall. A speculator does not, as an investor does, purchase a currency to extend credit, or to gain interest or profit. Nonetheless, speculation is often rather intimately connected with investment, because the very banks that finance overseas investment transactions for their customers will commonly be speculating in a minor way. If one were to look at the origins of all the funds on the foreign exchange market between 10 A.M. and 11 A.M. next Wednesday, for instance, one would find a proportion being channeled into the market by banks speculating that they could buy a foreign currency a few hundredths of a cent cheaper at 9:30 instead of waiting until noon. Later on in the day or week, however, these same funds acquired on speculation may be sold to the private traders and investors for whom they were purchased in the first place.

In the three years before 1972, when speculation reached its all-time high during the currency crises of this period, the flows of speculative funds reached astounding proportions. Flows as high as $75 million an hour were reported in the 1969 revaluation of the German mark, and the dollar crisis of 1971 touched off a situation in which funds moved at more than $125 million an hour!

4. *For government grants and lending.* Government grants and loans between countries will also create a demand for and supply of foreign currencies on the foreign exchange market. Spending for foreign aid, diplomatic missions, and (most importantly for the United States, Russia, and a number of other countries) military shipments and operations are all included. The United States figure in 1975 was $3.8 billion.

5. *Private unilateral transfers.* "Unilateral transfer" is the economist's jargon for primarily gifts by immigrants to relatives abroad, and pensions paid to people who have retired overseas. The 1975 net figure was $1.7 billion.

All these items lumped together—trade, investment, speculation, and government and unilateral transfers—underlie the demand for and the supply of foreign currencies first illustrated in Fig. 2.1. They are the building blocks of the foreign exchange market. Whenever they change in magnitude, they automatically alter the exchange rate. An increase in demand for a currency is a shift of the demand curve to the right and upward. Under ordinary conditions this results in a rise in the price of that currency. An increase in supply means a shift in the supply curve to the right and down, resulting in a fall in the price of that currency.

Methods for Stabilizing the Value of a Currency. So far the emphasis has been on changes in exchange rates and the underlying flexibility of the exchange rate system; no consideration has been given to certain funds flowing into the foreign exchange market that are designed to have a stabilizing effect. These are the funds supplied directly by the monetary authorities, which are government agencies that issue money; namely, the Federal Reserve System and the Treasury in the United States, and the various foreign central banks such as the Bank of England, Banque du France, Banca d'Italia, Deutsche Bundesbank, and so forth. These institutions may in some circumstances try to keep the price of their own national currency fairly stable in terms of some other currency—particularly the dollar. After World War II and until December 1971, the monetary authorities of almost all countries attempted to hold rates within 1 percent on either side of some stated, fixed exchange rate. (A 2 percent overall movement was thus permissible.) After the reforms of December 1971, the permitted degree of fluctuation was raised to 4½ percent (2¼ percent on either side of par value), but ensuing economic difficulties made even this hard to maintain, as discussed in the next chapter. Nonetheless, monetary authorities still attempt to manipulate exchange rates, often on a daily basis. They do so by bringing to the market quantities of whatever currency is rising "too much" in value because it is in short supply. One could also view this as buying from the market supplies of whatever currency is weakest.

To illustrate how this is done, take as an example the supply of Canadian dollars and United States dollars in the foreign exchange market on a certain day (Fig. 2.6). Suppose that the Bank of Canada wants to ensure that the

Canadian dollar remains within 1 percent of 100 United States cents. Under the conditions of Fig. 2.6, demand and supply are such that without intervention the price will rise to C$1.00 = US$1.10. In the figure it can be seen that the Bank of Canada must put on the market C$10,000 (equal to the distance Q_1Q_2, which just fills the gap between demand and supply at the desired rate) in order to prevent this. Alternatively, the United States government could supply C$10,000 to the market to achieve the same end. This is also equal to the distance Q_1Q_2. In either case, or both if the two nations cooperate, the actions of the government to stabilize the market have taken the form of attempting to make up the difference between the excess demand and the insufficient supply at the chosen rate. The reader should note that this could have been illustrated by moving the whole supply curve. We have chosen not to do this because government intervention to maintain a rate is so unlike any of the other factors that go to make up a supply curve for foreign exchange. The government here is correctly seen as "filling a gap" between supply and demand.

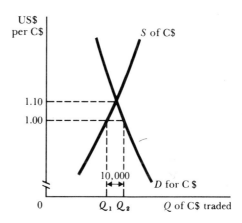

FIGURE 2.6 Intervention to keep the Canadian dollar from rising.

Should the problem have been the opposite one of keeping the Canadian dollar from falling, as in Fig. 2.7, then either government, or both, could have purchased Canadian currency, buying up the excess supply that would otherwise have caused a fall in the rate. The amount of intervention necessary to maintain the rate at US$1.00 = C$1.00 is shown here as the distance Q_3Q_4. The aim of the authorities is thus to intervene with just the right quantity of purchases or sales of currency so that the price of the Canadian dollar will neither rise nor fall against the United States dollar.

As an example of this sort of policy in operation, consider the market for the United States dollar in 1971. Monetary authorities around the world spent almost $11 billion worth of currencies other than the dollar to keep the dollar from falling in value. This was more than these authorities had purchased in all previous years put together. In similar circumstances during the first week of February 1973, the German central bank was spending nearly a billion dollars' worth of marks *per day* to prop up the dollar. By contrast, under the different economic conditions of 1975 the world's monetary authorities spent some billion dollars of United States currency to keep the *dollar* from rising in value.

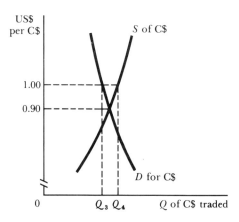

FIGURE 2.7 Intervention to support the Canadian dollar.

How the Monetary Authorities Intervene. Monetary authorities do not ordinarily wait for a crisis to develop before they enter the market. (If they do wait that long, they have not been performing their job very well!) Rather, the foreign exchange officers of a central bank are in constant close touch with the market. If they see the value of their own currency rising or falling too steeply, that is, outside a range they have set for themselves, they telephone a foreign exchange broker or bank and make a bid counter to the trend of the market.

Let us look at a typical transaction involving the chief foreign exchange officer at the New York Federal Reserve Bank (which handles the official foreign currency transactions of the United States). Suppose that officer at the New York Fed detects one morning that the dollar is weakening, and determines to support it by selling a foreign currency, in this case Canadian dollars. The foreign exchange officer's next step will be to contact a broker, and within minutes the Fed has agreed to purchase US$50,000 at a price of US$1.00 = C$0.99 from some Canadian commercial bank, say Toronto's Imperial Bank of Commerce. The Fed obtains the Canadian dollars it needs to make the purchase out of an account already established at the Bank of Canada (the Canadian central bank) in Ottawa. It replenishes this account from time to time by purchasing Canadian currency whenever the U.S. dollar is strong, by selling off any Canadian securities it possesses, or (in a method now obsolete but formerly important) by requesting the Treasury to sell gold to the Bank of Canada.

The process can be observed in operation by using a set of "T-accounts" of the sort commonly encountered in any first-year economics course. Figure 2.8 shows the numbered steps of the transaction (the steps are circled):

New York Federal Reserve Bank
United States $

Assets	Liabilities
① Account at Bank of Canada −50,000 (equals C$49,500)	Account in National City Bank −50,000 ⑤

National City Bank
United States $

Assets	Liabilities
⑤ Reserves −50,000	Account of the Imperial Bank of Commerce −50,000 ④

Imperial Bank of Commerce
Canadian $

Assets	Liabilities
② Reserves +49,500 ④ Account in National City Bank −49,500 (equals US$50,000)	± 0

Bank of Canada
Canadian $

Assets	Liabilities
± 0	Account of the New York Fed −49,500 ③ Account of the Imperial Bank of Commerce +49,500 ③

FIGURE 2.8

(1) The New York Federal Reserve Bank draws on its account at the Bank of Canada in order to (2) pay the Imperial Bank of Commerce. (3) The Bank of Canada debits the New York Federal Reserve and credits the Bank of Commerce. (4) The Bank of Commerce in turn would pay the Federal Reserve by drawing on a correspondent bank in the United States, here shown as the National City Bank in New York. (5) Finally, the Federal Reserve would debit the National City Bank, and the transaction is complete.

In the opposite case, with the U.S. dollar strengthening against Canadian currency, the foreign exchange officer at the New York Fed might intervene in the market by selling dollars in exchange for the foreign currency.

The long and short of it is that behind the relatively simple facade that we call foreign exchange rates lies a large and complicated structure involving banks, brokers, and extensive government intervention in the market. The first-year student who learns only that exchange rates are set by the impersonal forces of "supply and demand" thus learns only a half-truth, for supply and demand make themselves felt in foreign exchange in ways both interesting and unique.

Notes

1. A degree of nonuniformity arises with exchange control (see Chapter 3).
2. New York developed slowly as a foreign exchange market. For several decades into the nineteenth century, exchange was carried out by advertising holdings of excess currency in "for sale" notices in newspapers.
3. The number of brokers in New York has fallen substantially since the 1930s, when forty-five were operating. At most only a hundred or so U.S. banks deal with these brokers, some of these dealing in only two or three currencies.

3

A WORLD OF
UNCERTAIN FOREIGN
EXCHANGE RATES

The world's monetary authorities can and generally do intervene in the foreign exchange market, but there is no absolute requirement that they do so, nor any guarantee that their intervention will be consistent or successful in its aims. Essentially, then, businesspeople must operate under conditions of uncertainty—sometimes extreme uncertainty—whenever they buy and sell foreign currencies. The following two chapters explore, first, this world of uncertain foreign exchange rates, and second, the ways in which business firms may reduce the risks of operating in such a world.

Systems of Exchange

Monetary authorities differ enormously in their approach to maintaining the value of their own currency in the foreign exchange market. Some central banks intervene on a daily or even hourly basis in the manner described in the last chapter. With other central banks, intervention may be more sporadic. Still others (a distinct minority) may make no attempt to influence the price of their currency. At the other end of the spectrum, there are central banks that diligently attempt to keep their exchange rates at some announced parity value, even if that means heroic feats of borrowing or the actual rationing of foreign exchange to their citizens. These approaches toward exchange rate stability, several of which may be in operation at the same time, may be broadly characterized as follows:

I. *Fixed rates.* The government announces an exchange rate, frequently called a parity rate, and defends it. Fixed rates are ordinarily found in four different forms:

1. Permanently fixed rates.
2. Rates that are periodically adjusted (the adjustable peg).
3. Rates maintained through the rationing of foreign exchange (exchange control).
4. Rates fixed, but with a considerable amount of fluctuation allowed around these rates (wide bands).

II. *Floating (or flexible) rates.* The government does not announce a parity rate. Floating rates ordinarily are found in three different forms, as follow:

1. "Pure" floats, with no intervention by the monetary authorities.
2. Mixed, or "dirty" floats, with monetary intervention designed to smooth out fluctuations by reducing abnormal swings in value, or to maneuver the rate for other purposes.
3. Creeping rates, which are allowed to move upward or downward without limit, except for a restriction on the amount of movement permitted in any one year.

Fixed rates are similar to floating rates in that under fixed rates, a currency's value is still variable to some extent, if only within narrow limits around an announced, fixed currency parity. But the basic difference is clear. The fixed rate is a goal stated and defended by the government with whatever degree of intervention is thought necessary, whereas under floating rates such intervention will be smaller in scale and will presumably not be meant to defend a rate for any long period. (Warning: There have been countries that *say* their exchange rate is floating, but that act just as they would had their exchange rate been fixed. "Don't believe what they say, only what they do," to quote an American ex-statesman.) The development of these basic patterns and their operation in the late 1970s can best be appreciated through a brief historical survey.

History and Description of Exchange Rate Systems

Before the Gold Standard. In ancient and medieval times, national monies were exchanged by weight and not by individual counting, and for many centuries foreign exchange resembled today's trade in expensive metals. Weighing and testing for precious metal was an integral part of foreign exchange operations. Many of today's famous currency names date from the Middle Ages when it was still important to know the weight of metal contained in a coin.

Most obvious of these is the British pound, the pound referring to the amount of silver coined into money. The sterling in pound sterling is a technical term describing the fineness of the silver used. Similarly, the word lira means pound in Italian; the word peso—so common a currency in Hispanic countries—is Spanish for "weight"; drachma, the Greek monetary unit, is the word from which the English weight "dram" is derived; while the mark was also originally a unit of weight equal to about half a pound.

During the many centuries when foreign trade was immensely risky, a few monies stood out as trusted and secure, and were much used internationally. The Roman golden aureus and silver denarius were for decades an unimpeachable standard, accepted as far away as China. Although Roman currency was often debased from the time of Nero onward, full-value coins (picturing the emperor Tiberius) were minted on occasion as dictated by the requirements of foreign trade. Gold bezants of the Byzantine Empire at Constantinople commanded equal respect in a later age, especially the coins of Emperor Michael VII (1071-1078), which were minted for many years after his death. The denarius of Charlemagne, the florin of Florence, and the Venetian ducat were strong currencies in the Middle Ages, standing out in a dark sea of monetary deceit. The values of these currencies, before the era of the gold standard, tended to float against one another as determined by the forces of supply and demand. We will return to the subject of floating rates later in the chapter.

The Gold Standard. By the sixteenth century there was developing a creature that came to be known as the gold standard. It reached its prime in the period lasting roughly from 1870 until the start of World War I. Most countries in those days had circulating gold coins and paper money redeemable in gold at stated rates. In fact, the essence of the gold standard was the legal obligation of countries to buy and sell gold to all comers at some fixed price. Around 1900, the United States was doing this at approximately the same price that had been in use since long before the Civil War, namely $20.67 per ounce. (Take care: Dealing in gold is not so simple as it might seem. The gold ounce is not the normal avoirdupois weight, but instead is troy weight, with only 12 ounces to the pound. Complicating matters even further, these ounces are slightly different from the avoirdupois ounce.) Anyone visiting an office of the U.S. Treasury was able to sell gold to the Treasury in the form of coins, bars, or gold dust, collecting the fixed price of $20.67 per ounce minus only a service charge of ¼ of 1 percent. Anyone with dollars in hand could visit that same office or others like it and buy gold at the identical price, except that this time the service charge was added on.

Meanwhile, other countries through their own legislation guaranteed that they too would purchase and sell gold at some fixed price in terms of their own currency. In Britain, by an act of George III dated June 1816, the gold price was established at £4.2477 per ounce.[1] A little thought will show that the mutual agreements to buy and sell gold at fixed rates meant that the exchange rate of one currency in terms of another was fixed also. Consider what ensued if the dollar started to fall in value against the pound sterling in London, then the greatest of all the foreign exchange markets. A holder of dollars never needed to accept a highly unfavorable rate under the gold standard because the mechanism of that standard gave the holder a further option. The holder of dollars could take them to a bank or office of the Treasury in the United States, redeem them in gold, then ship the gold to Britain, selling it there for pounds sterling. Say that in 1900 the amount of a debt to be paid in London was £1,000. Americans would find that a gold bar weighing 123,274 grains would be worth exactly £1,000 if sold in London. By American law they could buy this size bar in the United States for exactly $4,866 including service charges. If they were to purchase one such bar and ship it by sea to London, additional costs of shipping and insuring might amount to $26, raising the total cost of getting gold to London to $4,892. As long as the price of pounds on the London foreign exchange market remained above £1.00 = $4.892, traders would benefit by using this mechanism for shipping gold.

Conversely, British buyers of dollars would ship gold to the United States any time their £1,000 sterling were to buy them less than $4,840. Notice, however, that since the purchase, insurance, and shipping charges for gold all involve real costs, no gold would in fact be shipped unless the dollar/pound exchange rate moved far enough from the gold equivalencies to cover these costs. In actual practice, therefore, the exchange rate under the gold standard was free to float within a short distance of the gold parities. In our example, the range of the float was between £1.00 = $4.840 and £1.00 = $4.892, or a little over 1 percent.

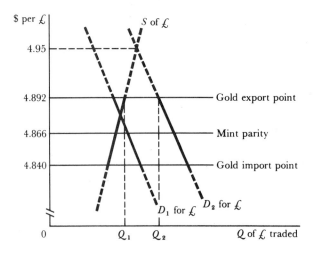

FIGURE 3.1

Illustrating the operation of the gold standard by means of a diagram is a simple matter. A demand for pounds sterling was generated by demands for imports from Britain, a desire to invest in that country, and the like. A supply of pounds was simultaneously generated by, for example, British purchases of American exports or investment by Britishers in the United States. These curves of demand and supply, shown in Fig. 3.1, are thus far identical to those met in the last chapter. The importance of the gold standard was its mechanism for keeping the exchange rate from varying. For example, if the demand for pounds rose (due perhaps to a desire by Americans to consume more British goods) from the old level D_1 to a new and higher position at D_2, then the equilibrium rate of exchange would be changed by the forces of the market. In the diagram, these market forces would apparently push the exchange rate as far as £1.00 = \$4.95. But the actions of the gold standard would keep such a rise from occurring. No American who knew the ropes would ever pay \$4.95 for a pound when a bar of gold could be bought for \$4,866 in the United States and sold in London to the Bank of England for exactly £1,000. Law fixed the two prices £4.2477 = 1 ounce and \$20.67 = 1 ounce, giving an implicit exchange rate of £1.00 = \$4.866, since 20.67/4.2477 = 4.866. This figure is called the *mint parity* of the pound and dollar. Recall, however, that there were transport and insurance costs to consider, equal to \$26 on a £1,000 gold bar, so that the real cost of moving gold to London was \$4,892. Only when the pound/dollar rate moved away from mint parity as far as £1.00 = \$4.892 would gold actually begin to flow to England. It is for this reason that there is a horizontal upper line drawn on Fig. 3.1 that represents the so-called gold export point. How much gold will be exported? It is possible to see the quantity exactly in the diagram. A gold flow equal in value to $Q_1 Q_2$ will just balance the demand and supply for pounds, thus keeping the rate at the gold export point. Reversing the logic, should the exchange rate ever drop below £1.00 = \$4.840, then it would be profitable to buy gold in London, ship it to the United States, and sell it here. The lowest horizontal line represents the "gold import point," the point at which gold starts to flow to the United States because British traders find it cheaper to ship it, including transport costs, than to receive anything less than \$4.84 for their pounds. In short, rates were fixed under the gold standard—but only outside certain limits. The supply and demand curves of Fig. 3.1 are shown as dotted lines outside these limits. Within the gold export and import points, exchange rates could and did differ from mint parity. A combination of relatively high supply and low demand could give a pound/dollar rate of £1.00 = \$4.85 today, while tomorrow a rising demand and a falling supply could give a rate of £1.00 = \$4.87.

The first known calculation of the gold export and import points was made by Sir Thomas Gresham (of the famous Gresham's Law—"bad money drives out good") in a letter to Queen Elizabeth dated 1558. Over the centuries the spread between the points narrowed dramatically. The steamship cut travel time from a month or more to as little as five days, and since gold bars stored in the hold of a ship obviously earned no interest, saving time also meant saving a great deal of money. Safer conditions at sea and a more organized market for insurance also cut costs. Whereas before the Napoleonic Wars the spread between mint parity and a gold export or import point was as much as 6 percent, even for short distances such as from London to Dublin or Paris to Amsterdam, by 1900 the spread was reduced to something on the order of ½ of 1 percent even for transatlantic voyages.

By the last quarter of the nineteenth century, it was seldom necessary for the typical trader or even bank actually to ship any gold. Instead, specialized bullion dealers acting in the role of arbitrageur would scrutinize closely the structure of rates. If this structure ever deviated beyond the gold export or import points, these dealers arranged for shipments of gold in bulk on their own account.

The true golden age of the world's money markets lasted from about 1870 to the outbreak of World War I in 1914. By then communications were vastly improved (the Atlantic cable was laid in 1865), making arbitrage rapid, inexpensive, and routine. There was during these years an almost universal belief in the stability, even indestructibility, of the system. The belief was naive, perhaps, and was not to survive the First World War, but while it lasted its implications were awesome. It was a time when private citizens of all occupations and nationalities could exchange major currencies without fear of a change in value, when in fact no major currency *did* change in value for several decades. It was a time of almost unbelievable convenience in the arena of foreign trade, with currencies exchanged against one another at fixed rates that were in part selected for ease of calculation. The traveler of today must regard with envy the exchange rates of 1914, shown below (remember that some small variation was possible and did occur):

German mark = almost exactly one British shilling.
U.S. dollar = almost exactly 50 British pence; thus one penny = US $0.02.
Japanese yen = almost exactly US $0.50.
Italian lira = 10 British pence = US $0.20 = one Austro-Hungarian krone.
Austro-Hungarian krone = 10 British pence = US $0.20 = 1 Italian lira.

(Note: as of 1979, the tourist or businessperson dealing with the part of the world in which the krone used to circulate now has to face the Czechoslovak koruna, the Hungarian forint, the Yugoslav dinar, the Austrian schilling, the Romanian leu, and the Polish zloty.)

Russian ruble = US $0.50.
Swedish krona = US $0.25.
Norwegian krone = Swedish krona = US $0.25.
Danish krone = Norwegian krone = Swedish krona = US $0.25.

The golden age was ended by war. The four years after 1914 brought the system crashing down. Even after a year of hostilities, however, in 1915, its legacy was still so strong that British prisoners of war in Baghdad were able to cash pound sterling checks in Turkish banks. The Turks were confident that, in spite of being at war with Britain, the checks would clear and the exchange rates would remain stable.

Adjustable Parities. Active central bank intervention in the foreign exchange market originated during World War I. To keep gold out of German hands, the British refused to sell it, even to neutral countries that held British Treasury securities guaranteed convertible to gold.[2] At the same time a severe inflation set in, which caused the money value of trade to rise both during and after the war. As the gold stock was largely fixed in quantity, a real scarcity of gold developed. Finally, New York evolved into a major financial center, and the increasing magnitude of financial flows, in particular between New York and London, necessitated more intervention in exchange markets.

To stretch the world's limited gold reserves further, a new system, sometimes called the *gold exchange standard*, was instituted. Under this new standard gold would ordinarily remain in government hands, traded between central banks when it was necessary to settle accounts between countries. Exchange rates among monies were kept stable not by the shipping of gold but by the intervention of the monetary authorities, who bought and sold foreign currencies when necessary to keep the rates from altering. Foreign currencies (convertible into gold) thus had to join gold as part of a country's stock of international reserves.

Even before 1914, some central banks had taken to holding foreign exchange along with gold. As early as 1885, the central banks of Norway, Sweden, and Denmark agreed to hold balances with each other and to count these balances as backing for the domestic money supply. From 1894 on, Russia maintained part of its reserves in the form of balances held abroad, especially in Berlin. By 1913, about 12 percent of the total reserves of European central banks was in the form of foreign exchange convertible into gold, and not in gold itself. The system grew rapidly, and by 1925-1930 the proportion of foreign exchange in the reserves of twenty-five major countries was in the area of 20-25 percent. In some years the figure reached 40 percent or more. Not only did this modification to the old system successfully economize on gold, but it also increased earnings. Gold bears no interest, but bank balances denominated in marks, pounds, or dollars do. Ministers of finance and secretaries of treasuries saw this as a straightforward advantage of the gold exchange standard.

A great setback to the new standard came with the Depression of the 1930s. Speculation against the pound sterling caused Great Britain to suspend payments in gold in 1931. The speculation was as much by governments as by private firms and individuals. For example, France had accumulated large stocks of foreign currency, and in 1931 began to demand gold for these, selling some £6 million in New York one Saturday morning. This was a major factor in Britain's decision to suspend gold payments. Thereupon the value of the pound dropped rapidly. Speculators then turned their attentions to the dollar, and under repeated attacks President Roosevelt was forced to suspend United States gold payments in April 1933. The value of the dollar dropped by 41 percent. Then the speculators attacked the major remaining nations still exchanging their currencies for gold—France, the Netherlands, Belgium, and Switzerland. These nations held out until 1935-1936, but after they succumbed the values of their currencies fell in the range of 20-30 percent. This cataclysm, the most thorough peacetime collapse of currencies since before the days of Adam Smith, extinguished a large proportion of the world's supply of reserves. The countries that rushed to exchange their foreign currency holdings for gold simply shifted the total gold stock among them, and ceased to count foreign exchange in their reserves.[3] Thus by 1932 only 8 percent of the reserves of twenty-four major countries comprised foreign exchange, and the figure fell further in the years that followed. These events were a major contributing cause of the length and severity of the Great Depression.

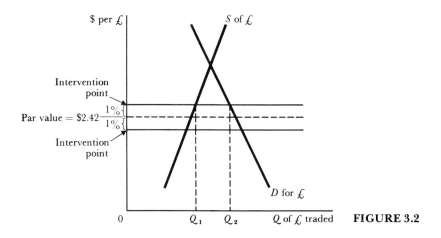

FIGURE 3.2

The international money market had no time to settle down before World War II was upon it, and it was not until seven years of war had passed that official attempts to restore the gold exchange standard succeeded. In 1947, when the International Monetary Fund (IMF) came into operation as a result of the Bretton Woods Conference three years earlier (see Chapter 9), the world's nations for the first time agreed in treaty form that they would state an exchange rate and maintain it.[4] They also agreed to rules on monetary intervention. (Previous to that time only custom, not international obligation, lay behind the announcement and defense of a stated exchange rate.)

By these rules, exchange rates were to be kept within 1 percent of their announced, or par, values. Par value was obtained just as under the old gold standard, with countries defining their currency in terms of a per ounce price for gold. Figure 3.2 diagrams the upper and lower intervention points designed to keep the exchange rate within 1 percent of par value. A most important aspect of the new system was that permanently fixed parities were abandoned, and were replaced by a system of parities that could be changed periodically. This capacity for changing rates is the reason the mechanism was given the name *adjustable peg*. Under the adjustable peg, nations pledged that they would maintain the gold value of their currency by intervening on the foreign exchange market. But in some situations the exchange rate could be officially changed, with the government now undertaking to defend a new parity. One such situation the IMF referred to as "fundamental disequilibrium," by which they meant mainly a long period of inflation in one country that raised its demand for foreign exchange (imports appear cheaper) and lowered the supply (exports appear more expensive to foreigners). Lowering the value of one currency relative to others, the most frequent type of change, was called *devaluation*. Raising the value was known as upward *revaluation*. Both devaluation and upward revaluation are demonstrated diagrammatically in Fig. 3.3. Indeed, changes of this sort, especially devaluations, were not new; many had been made before the Bretton Woods Conference during the period of serious trading difficulties caused by inflation, wartime devastation, and political disarray following the First World War. We have already noted how Britain was forced to abandon her old fixed parity in 1931, following years of stoutly maintaining the value of the pound sterling at prewar rates, and how the United States and many other countries were forced to follow suit shortly thereafter. (By contrast, no major currency was devalued or revalued in the entire forty-year period before World War I.) The novelty of the 1947 IMF agreement was to institutionalize the process of adjusting pegs and to require consultation before the making of major changes in rates (see Figs. 3.3 and 3.4).

In the twentieth century the United States has devalued the dollar three times. In 1934 the buying and selling price for gold was raised from $20.67 to $35.00 per ounce; in December 1971 the price was raised further to $38.00 per ounce; and finally, gold was officially priced at $42.22 per ounce in 1973. The much rarer act of upward revaluation has never been engaged in by the United States and Britain, but Germany, Switzerland, the Netherlands, and Japan have done so. Revaluation means lowering the price of gold, as when Germany announces that one ounce will now be bought and sold for DM105 instead of DM140. If other countries do not at the same time change *their* gold price, then it follows that the old par value has been altered.

Whether these actions are taken by one country, or by several at the same time, the economic effect is the same. Par value is changed, and the intervention points that the government is pledged to defend are dragged along with it. In Fig. 3.3, on the left-hand diagram, the United States is initially having to "spend" foreign exchange (represented as pounds) equal in quantity to the distance Q_1Q_2 in order to counter the shortage in pounds that is apparent in the foreign exchange market. The same process can be viewed in terms of dollar purchases in Fig. 3.4. The sale of Q_1Q_2 pounds in Fig. 3.3, translated into dollars at the prevailing exchange rate, is shown to be the equivalent of q_1q_2 dollars in Fig. 3.4. Thus £50 million (Q_1Q_2) sold at a rate of $2 a pound equals $100 million ($q_1q_2$). Such expenses cannot go on indefinitely. Here the clear solution is to devalue the dollar so that the supply and demand situation will no longer require government intervention to maintain some par value. Hence the price of the pound is seen to rise (Fig. 3.3) and that of the dollar falls (Fig.3.4). This may not be a palliative or a cure for the problem; if the underlying cause of the high supply of dollars and demand for pounds was due to inflation in the United States and that inflation continues unabated, the problem is bound to reoccur. (This problem is explored at length in later chapters.) Under the adjustable peg system, it is vitally important to take corrective action against inflation as well as to devalue if the drain on foreign exchange reserves is to be ended.

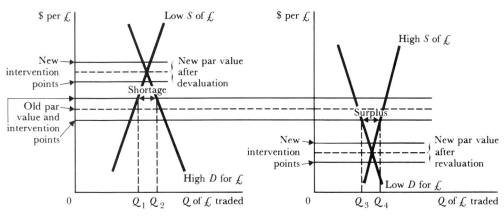

FIGURE 3.3

To examine the opposite case, on the right-hand side of Fig. 3.3 we see the United States in a position wherein there is a low demand for pounds and a high supply of them, leading to an accumulation of surplus pounds, and considerable expenditure of U.S. dollars. The United States must have accumulated a quantity of pounds equal to the distance Q_3Q_4 in Fig. 3.3 and be spending dollars equivalent to q_3q_4 of Fig. 3.4 in order to keep the rate within the original intervention points. There is no upper limit to the quantity of pounds the United States can accumulate, since it can create as many dollars as it needs through its banking system; normally, however, it will not want to go beyond some reasonable level predicated on future need.

To halt the accumulation of pounds, the United States could revalue upward so that supply and demand will equilibrate at or near the new par value. In the right-hand diagram, the new par requires no further government intervention to maintain the rate. It was these two aspects of Figs. 3.3 and 3.4, devaluation and upward revaluation, that gave the name "adjustable" to the adjustable peg system.

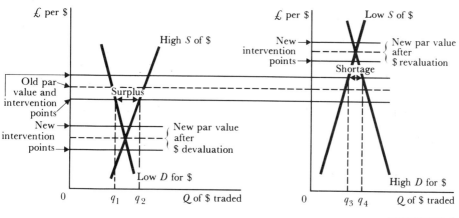

FIGURE 3.4

Exchange Control. In their attempts to maintain fixed parities, nations in the 1930s and 1940s began to rely less and less on monetary intervention, which after all was limited to the amount of foreign currency or gold a nation had accumulated or could borrow. In place of intervention, there came to be more reliance on the direct rationing of foreign exchange, called exchange control. The shift to such controls reflected the increasing role of the state in all aspects of economic life during the 1930s. Generally controls involved restrictions on the purchase of foreign currencies, often by requiring a foreign exchange license to accompany any transfer of funds abroad and by requiring recipients of foreign currencies to sell them to the government. National monies that cannot be freely bought and sold are described as *inconvertible*, and the main international monetary problem of the 1930s and 1940s was that of *convertibility*. Nazi Germany was one of the first to make its currency inconvertible, but inconvertibility was hardly restricted to any particular ideology. By the end of World War II, practically every nation but the United States had exchange control in one form or another. Even the United States, in the 1960s and 1970s, began to prohibit the unlimited transfer of funds abroad through restrictions on bank lending (1964) and later on corporate investment (1968), although these have since been dropped. These restrictions are explored more fully in Chapter 7.

Although many developed countries still retain some degree of control over capital movements, the great bulk of transactions among them are nowadays free of foreign exchange controls, and the licensing of money movements disappeared along with the other familiar manifestations of the 1940s, ration cards and price controls. Among the less developed countries, however, foreign exchange control is still in full flower, and remains more the rule than the exception. Some such systems are extremely complicated and involve vast amounts of red tape—India's, for example. Diagrammatically, exchange control involves supply and demand curves for foreign exchange, as shown in Fig. 3.5. Assume that the Republic of Sans Souci wants to keep the rate at 10 soucis per dollar, instead of allowing the market to depreciate the souci to 20 per dollar as would happen if supply and demand were allowed to operate. (The government of Sans Souci is thus attempting to maintain an overvalued souci, the rate on which would sink drastically in the absence of exchange control.) Exchange control is, as already noted, simply another form of rationing. The government must ration the available quantity of foreign exchange (here $0X$ at the controlled rate) among its citizens, who are seen to demand the greater total of $0Z$. Governments most often institute such controls when other efforts to maintain a fixed rate have failed due to exhaustion of their gold stock and foreign exchange reserves, and when further depreciation (or devaluation) of the currency is unpalatable on political grounds. $0X$ of foreign exchange is available in the normal course of trade at the controlled rate, and equilibrium is assured by simply limiting purchases of foreign currency to this amount. The problem is that $0X$ of foreign exchange is actually worth well more than 10 soucis per dollar. Following the demand curve in Fig. 3.5, we can see that there is enough demand even at a price of 30 soucis to sell all of $0X$. Exporters, however, are prohibited from selling on a free market and must sell to the government at the prescribed rate. (Indeed, if exporters could get 30 soucis a dollar, and the supply of foreign exchange were as Fig. 3.5 shows, there would be a surplus of foreign exchange.)

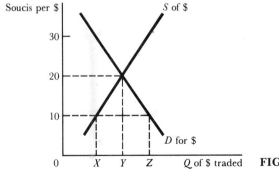

FIGURE 3.5

Because people want to buy 0Z of foreign exchange and only 0X is available, and because they can buy something worth 30 soucis for only 10, the government must decide on a system of priorities in the allocation of foreign exchange. The Peruvian case of 1945-1948 illustrates what happens when the rules are not set well. The government failed to establish detailed priorities and importers discovered that the more requests they sent in, the greater the chances were that they would receive a foreign exchange license. The administrators were drowned in a sea of applications, reapplications, and rereapplications. Worse, the officials promised more foreign exchange (equivalent to 0Y on Fig. 3.5) than was available. Importers, having ordered the goods with the assurance of getting a foreign exchange license, found that when their ships came in they lacked the means to take possession of the merchandise. The port of Callao became piled high with goods, cargoes could not be unloaded, and fuming captains cruised up and down the coast waiting for berths.

Very often, a country does not ration all of its foreign exchange earnings. It fixes a cheap (overvalued) rate, such as 10 soucis per dollar, for some transactions, and then allows all other transactions to take place at some free market equilibrium. Accordingly, two markets are created, one at the "official" rate and one at a "free" rate. The free market serves for all the buyers of foreign currency who cannot get permission to use the controlled rate and for all the sellers of foreign currency who manage to escape government control. (Indeed, in some cases the free market rate is merely a legitimization of an existing vigorous black market.) The price in that market is therefore determined by how much the buyers of foreign currency are willing to pay to the suppliers. This price is always above the official rate (if it were below, no importer would use the official rate). Because the supply of currency in the free market is usually low, the price is also generally above the hypothetical equilibrium rate. (When Peru tried to clear its ports after it had promised too many licenses, it just told the importers to use the free market rate.) The use of two or more exchange rates is known as a *multiple exchange rate system*, defined as a system wherein the buyer and seller of foreign exchange face different rates depending on the intended use of the currency or on how the foreign exchange was first earned.

Within the past ten years or so one could find multiple exchange rates in Afghanistan, Bolivia, Brazil, Taiwan, Indonesia, Paraguay, Uruguay, and Yugoslavia, to name a few. Under such a system, the government must channel all purchases and sales of foreign exchange through its own departments, usually buying from exporters and selling to importers. The normal policy is to assign an overvalued rate (10 soucis per dollar, for example, in Fig. 3.5) to any export considered a necessity by foreigners. Sans Souci's titanium exports will decline only a little with a price rise (inelastic demand), thus making them more expensive, with a dollar buying only 10 soucis worth instead of 20. This will generate substantially greater revenues for the republic. The government in effect has forced a higher price on the foreign buyer. The foreign exchange thus obtained can be sold by the authorities to importers at the controlled rate if desired. Thus any import considered vital to the nation—food and machinery, for instance—might be allowed at the overvalued 10 soucis per dollar rate, which represents a substantial subsidy since importers would otherwise have had to pay 20 soucis to obtain a dollar.

The government creates in essence two separate markets. The official market subsidizes favored imports and some capital transactions, while penalizing many exports. The free market penalizes some imports and some purchases of foreign capital and subsidizes a few favored exports, most capital transactions involving purchases of soucis, and often tourists' purchases as well.[5]

Systems of multiple exchange rates can be endlessly complicated by the establishment of dozens of separate rates, all representing some element of tax and subsidy, and all enforced by law. If Sans Souci has an export monopoly on some product, such as its kryptonite exports, it might force sellers of kryptonite to accept a hugely overvalued rate for their foreign exchange. Equally it can subsidize some exports, to develop the industry, by charging an undervalued rate on them. Imports can be subsidized (by an overvalued rate) or taxed (by an undervalued rate) as desired.

Below we take a look at one such system—that of Chile—as it appeared some years ago. The rates quoted are Chilean pesos per dollar. (Incidentally, this is not the most complicated structure the Chileans ever used. At one point they had twenty-three different exchange rates, and some transactions took place partly at one rate and partly at another!)

TABLE 3.1.

Buying Rate (from exporters and other buyers)		Selling Rate (to importers and other sellers)	
19.37	(nitrate rate). Exchange from sales of nitrate exports.		
		110.00	A few necessities, including food and some machinery.
		203.00	(banking rate). Sugar, kerosene, antibiotics, government imports.
300.00	(free banking rate). Most exports.	303.00	(free banking rate). Most imports.
519.00	(fluctuating free brokers' rate). Exports of fish, travel receipts, private capital receipts.	529.00	Travel expenses.
573.00	(special area fluctuating rate). Wine exports, iron ore exported from small companies.	583.00	(special area fluctuating rate). Imports of luxury goods.

If we assume that 300 per dollar was close to free-market equilibrium, then the rates in the 100s and 200s are overvalued, taxing exports and subsidizing imports, while those in the 500s are undervalued, taxing imports and subsidizing exports. Note the small spread between comparable rates: 300 to 303, 519 to 529, 573 to 583. This represents a commission being creamed off by the government, presumably to finance the costs of operating the system.

The imposition of exchange control involves a number of difficulties, just as does the rationing of any product. First there is the probability of inefficient allocation of resources. The big subsidy to food imports combined with a free market rate on any food exports had a depressing effect on Chilean farming for many years. The export taxes represented by an overvalued rate may stimulate a foreign search for substitutes (aluminum for copper in wires), while subsidizing exports through undervalued rates may not reflect true efficiency for the economy. (Farmers abandoned food crops for wine.) Second, and much more obvious in a country using exchange control, the government must extend its area of law enforcement considerably. It is all too easy to avoid paying an overvalued price for exchange. The postal authorities have to search the mail from time to time, because the exporter who earned a dollar for nitrate exports and stands to get in exchange 19.37 pesos from the government could get about 300 pesos by putting the dollar in an envelope and sending it to a New York bank for exchange at the free market rate. Strict controls also have to be imposed on the use of currency. There must be a bureaucracy with police powers to ensure that the buyer of dollars who said he or she was going to purchase machines with them does indeed do so, and does not rush out and buy perfume and Cadillacs. A new species of economic crime, and commonplace visits from the police, are typical end results. Thirdly, the authorities must guard against under- and over-billing. How simple a thing for a Chilean exporter to bill a $10,000 export at only $8,000, thus receiving the undervalued peso rate only on that portion of the real transaction. The remaining $2,000 could then be deposited by the conniving importer in some secret Swiss bank account with the two sharing the take (see Fig. 3.6). Or a foreign exporter may overbill on a shipment to Chile, sending only $8,000 in goods but billing for $10,000. The importer buys subsidized foreign exchange from the government at an overvalued rate, with the understanding that some of the dollars thus obtained will be credited to a foreign bank account (see Fig. 3.7).

Finally, the allocation of foreign exchange licenses car become an important source of corruption, as firms find that a small payment to an appropriate official in return for a license at a favorable exchange rate means large savings. One signature allowing the official (subsidized) rate to be used could cut the import bill in half. The temptation to bribe and/or extort often proves irresistible and foreign exchange operations become a principal source of corruption. The Peruvian, Philippine, and Sri Lankan governments have all cited corruption as one reason for ending exchange controls.

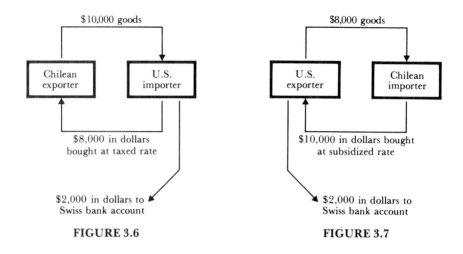

$10,000 goods

Chilean exporter   U.S. importer

$8,000 in dollars bought at taxed rate

$2,000 in dollars to Swiss bank account

FIGURE 3.6

$8,000 goods

U.S. exporter   Chilean importer

$10,000 in dollars bought at subsidized rate

$2,000 in dollars to Swiss bank account

FIGURE 3.7

Floating Rates. The history of floating rates, as we have already noted, is as old as the history of money itself. Copper, silver, gold, and other metals formed the basis of the coinage in the ancient world, and the relative values of these metals tended to fluctuate. Besides frequent debasements of the coinage, "clipping" could be tried. This involved shaving the edges of a large number of coins, thus accumulating a supply of metal that represented pure though illegal profit to the clipper. Money changers, ever alert to these variables, would seldom exchange the coins of two nations at a fixed rate because the condition of the coins themselves was likely to differ, as was the underlying value of the metal that constituted them. One could even claim with considerable justification that uncertainty of exchange rates was the normal condition for trade from ancient times right up to the nineteenth century.

For an example of wide fluctuation in currency values, take the U.S. dollar during the Civil War. During this period various dollar bills were redeemable either in gold or in silver, or not redeemable at all in any metal. (The latter bills were the first to be printed with the color green predominating, on the reverse side; hence the name "greenback.") What then of the value of the dollar? Was it worth its gold content, its silver content, or the paper on which it was printed? In truth, there was considerable variation in the rates at which these different dollars would exchange against foreign currency, with the greenback in particular fluctuating widely in value and consistently "discounted" in the world's money markets. Although the United States cleared up these problems by making its currency redeemable only in gold in 1870, many nations continued to issue silver-backed money or unsupported paper money until the turn of the century, and China remained on a silver standard until 1934. Thus even during the heyday of the gold standard, there were always some exceptions where currency values would fluctuate.

For many years following the widespread adoption of the gold standard, however, floating rates were not well thought of. Earlier in this century their main use was as a temporary measure during periods of considerable instability, for example, Germany in 1923 and again in 1929-1933. The usual reason for floating during this era was that the monetary authorities simply had no gold or foreign exchange left for the purposes of stabilizing the exchange rate, and were unable or unwilling to employ exchange control. Until the 1970s, floating rates were in only a very few instances used as a permanent policy. Canada was the main example; the Canadian dollar was allowed to float between 1950 and 1962 even though there was no emergency and plenty of foreign exchange was available to the government. The Bank of Canada did intervene from time to time, but only to iron out occasional fluctuations it suspected were abnormal. Peru in the years 1932-1945 and 1950-1954 also experimented with a long-term floating rate, as did Thailand, Ecuador, and Mexico in the years following World War II. All in all, floating rates as an intentional policy were rare for almost a century.

Then a period of intense crisis in foreign exchange markets changed the situation remarkably. The crises included the failure of British attempts to maintain the old value of the pound sterling in 1966, then the similar French failure with the franc in 1969, the weakness of the dollar in the late 1960s and early 1970s, and the great oil crisis of 1973. All proved highly disruptive to the foreign exchange markets. Speculative movements of currencies between nations were far too large to be controlled by monetary intervention. As a result, virtually all countries allowed the value of their currencies to float. Several attempts were soon made to reestablish fixed parities (for example, the Smithsonian Agreement of December 1971), but these proved unworkable.

The present system of exchange rates might be described as *controlled floating*. No fixed values are stated, but monetary authorities from time to time intervene in the market to protect or alter the value of their currency. Sometimes this is done simply to smooth out seasonal or unexpected fluctuations. At other times governments intervene to hold down the value of their currency in order to stimulate exports and discourage imports. This so-called dirty floating annoys other nations also trying to limit their own imports and is potentially disruptive to international trade. Daigrammatically, a dirty float appears identical to the defense of a currency shown in Fig. 3.2, with the exception that there is no announced par value.

To control the disruptive tendencies of dirty floating, central bankers by 1976 had developed a variation that can be called *negotiated floating*. Central bankers from industrial nations meet frequently to discuss what value exchange rates should have and the kinds of intervention needed to support them. The system appears to be more flexible than the old adjustable peg, but apparently attempts to maintain a considerable degree of formal control over the movement of exchange rates, thus inhibiting dirty floating.

One of the central issues behind the question of negotiated floats is the insistence of several members of the European Common Market, West Germany and France in particular, that the currencies of the Common Market eventually be unified. The dream of currency unification led in 1972 to the birth of a most unusual creature called the *EMU snake*. The names EMU and snake, both more appropriate for a zoology text than for an economics book, stand for European Monetary Union and the appearance of the EMU negotiated float on a diagram respectively. As seen in Fig. 3.8, the snake is a flexible band within which the nations of the Common Market (those participating in the scheme, that is) attempt to keep their exchange rates. The initial agreement, drawn up at Basle, Switzerland, in April 1972, provided that the participating countries would keep their exchange rates from varying more than 2.25 percent against a central average rate. Initially the Common Market currencies were also to be fixed against the dollar within wider margins of 4.5 percent (hence the original term, "snake in the tunnel"), but the dollar "tunnel" was abandoned during the currency crisis of March 1973, less than a year after its inception. Nowadays the EMU snake floats jointly against the dollar and other major currencies, leading some to use the term "snake in the lake"[6] (Fig. 3.8).

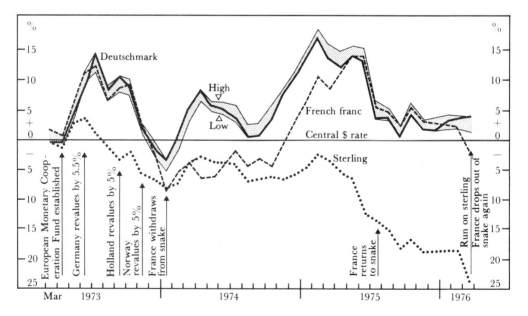

FIGURE 3.8.   The EEC snake. Born in April 1972, technically the snake aims to keep common market currencies from varying more than 2.25 percent against some central average rate.

The snake has had a fairly unhappy life. Great Britain and Italy opted out very early in the game (Britain after only seven weeks), although two other countries, Norway and Sweden, which are not EEC members, have joined the snake. France has had a rough time with its snake membership, dropping out in 1973, in again in 1975, and out once more in March 1976. Sweden dropped out in August 1977. The intent of the EMU snake seems clearly more political than economic, aiming for closer integration of the EEC's financial markets and thereby encouraging further political unification. Maintaining this form of fixed rate in a world of floating rates has proved to be expensive: In two days of March 1976, the Bank of France bought a billion dollars' worth of francs to keep the franc from falling through the bottom of the snake, with the Germans helping out to the tune of another billion in that week, an effort which failed two days later (March 15) when the French government abandoned the snake. About the only gain from all this activity is the constant personal contact between European central bankers and the coordinated policies in foreign exchange management, which were very rare in the days before the birth of the snake. The creature will no doubt continue to exist in spite of its costs as long as it remains a shibboleth for the great aim of European economic, monetary, and political union. [In 1979, the EEC adopted a new enlarged version called the European Monetary System.] It is in support of these aims of unity that European central bankers have engaged frequently in discussion of their goals and strategies with representatives of the U.S. government and other industrial nations.

Wider Bands and Creeping Pegs.   Two final mechanisms for controlling foreign exchange rates have had a brief place in the sun, and have actually seen some use from time to time. The two ideas of wider bands and creeping pegs both attempt to combine fixed and floating rates. At the Smithsonian Conference in Washington in December 1971, the large industrial countries agreed on a proposal for *wider bands*. Instead of pegging exchange rates within 1 percent on either side of parity, as under the old system, the proposal was to allow much greater swings in rates on either side of some stated figure, while still promising intervention at some point. Although up-and-down ranges as high as 5 percent were mentioned, the proposal actually adopted in 1971 was on the conservative side, permitting bands of 2¼ percent in each direction from parity. However, in spite of President Nixon's comment that the Smithsonian Agreement was the most important of all time in international economics, it broke down within a few months in a climate of general currency crisis and was abandoned.

The *creeping peg* is an interesting idea, in use for some years in Brazil, whereby the central bank intervenes frequently to control the exchange rate, but instead of defending it at some fixed level, allows it to float upward or downward by some stated percentage per year. Thus the Brazilian cruzeiro might be permitted to fall in value by only 2 percent over any one year, the parity rate being gradually changed during that time. Many believe that the Brazilian experiment ought to be applied widely, because changes in rates of 10 to 12 percent over ten years would have accomplished most of the adjustments that eventually had to be made under crisis conditions in the early 1970s. Thus it is not surprising that the idea of a creeping peg has attracted a good deal of favorable attention outside Brazil. (It has been used also by Colombia, Israel, and Chile.)

Both wide bands and creeping pegs introduce some measure of certainty to exchange rates at the cost of some loss of flexibility. The major difference between them is that the wide band gives considerable short-run flexibility around some fixed parity, but no long-run flexibility since the rate is not free to fluctuate outside the band; while the creeping peg gives considerable long-run flexibility but none in the short run, since the exchange rate cannot be moved far in any one year.

Summary

The world's systems of exchange may be divided basically into fixed rates and floating rate systems. We have attempted to describe their operation, sketch their historical origins, and see them in use today. We delay until Chapter 9 the consideration of a fundamental question: What are the advantages and disadvantages, the benefits and costs, of these very different ways of managing exchange rates? This question has both a theoretical and a practical side. We need to understand both more about international money and banking and more about economic theory before attempting such an answer. The ensuing two chapters examine the former, the following three the latter.

Notes

1. Once again there is a further complication. The British definition of gold was "standard gold," that is, 11/12 pure and 1/12 alloy. The United States used a different definition, namely 9/10 pure and 1/10 alloy. Before calculating the exchange rate, this discrepancy had to be resolved—and of course this was done by clerks using longhand arithmetic, who doubtless would have sold their inheritance for an electronic calculator.
2. Neutrals in World War I suffered through a number of indignities in the area of international economics. Several centuries of legal developments guaranteeing the rights of neutrals to trade with combatants in everything except a short list of "contraband" items—mainly arms and munitions—were swept away. Before the war's end, practically everything was declared contraband. The British mined the sea approaches to Germany; the Germans declared unrestricted submarine warfare on any ship, including neutrals, sailing in prohibited zones around the British Isles. The word convoy, which in its nineteenth-century legal sense meant a group of neutral ships sailing under the protection of a neutral warship, soon acquired its

modern meaning of a belligerent's navy protecting its own ships and those of allies. As a result, life was hard in some neutrals. The neutral Netherlands found itself virtually under British blockade, its trade destroyed, ships sunk, and food supplies cut to levels that required rationing.

3. This move was from a parochial point of view understandable. The risk that a country whose foreign exchange was held as part of international reserves would suspend gold payments meant that the risk of falling currency values outweighed the gain from earning interest on balances in that country.

4. The IMF had been a major result of the Bretton Woods Conference of 1944, held at the resort hotel of that name on the south side of New Hampshire's Mount Washington. Bretton Woods, with its bright orange roof, is a familiar sight to the skiers of New England, but to economists it conjures up the memory of John Maynard Keynes, who played a leading role in this, his last major international conference. Some writers use the term "Bretton Woods system" to describe the framework of adjustable parities in use after World War II.

5. In countries where the government makes tourists buy at the official rate, there are generally friendly people in alleyways and hotel lobbies willing to offer better terms. Even in the Soviet Union, which has an unfavorable rate for tourists, roving currency exchangers are not unknown, but one is advised to steer clear because the secret police sometimes tempt the unwary. One party found the same friendly exchanger in both Moscow and Leningrad!

6. Within the body of the snake, there was a further scheme for fixing rates against one another. The Dutch guilder and the Belgian and Luxemburg francs were allowed to fluctuate in the narrower range of only 1.5 percent. This was called "the worm in the snake." In March 1976, the Belgian franc weakened to the point where the Belgian government refused to support it within the narrow 1.5 percent range against the Dutch guilder, and thus the worm died.

4

OPERATING
IN A WORLD OF
UNCERTAIN
EXCHANGE
RATES

Whether fixed rates, floating rates, or some halfway system is adopted, businesspeople nowadays have to accommodate themselves to a world of uncertain exchange rates. Under a fixed system (the adjustable peg), changes occur infrequently but are large in amount. Under a floating rate, changes are likely to be small but take place on a continuing basis.

The response of businesspeople, be it voluntary or involuntary, is either to speculate in foreign currency or to hedge. This chapter studies both responses in detail because an understanding of such behavior is essential to an understanding of international economic policy.

Speculation

Speculation is a normal part of every firm's operations. It is as commonplace as ordering solid-color instead of striped pants, starting the "post-Christmas sale" on December 22, purchasing property for possible future expansion, or buying a load of raw materials early in the expectation of a price rise. Any firm doing business abroad must by the very nature of the foreign exchange market engage in speculation.

Speculation in foreign exchange is on the whole less risky per dollar spent than are most other forms of this practice. Under the fixed rate system, if governments were successful in defending the parity, the most one could lose was 2 percent. Even when parities were adjusted downward or upward, changes in a major currency of more than 15 percent were very rare. Under floating rates, changes in any given year are almost always much smaller than this figure. The risk of speculation in commodities, or real estate, or clothing is usually much higher than it is in the foreign exchange market.

Speculation is eminently functional. It serves to ration goods in times of plenty or low demand, and to provide them in times of scarcity or high demand. The person who buys apples in October, holds them until March, and then sells them off helps to bid up October prices and hold down March prices. As shown in line *A* of Fig. 4.1, without speculation the price of apples shoots up and down. The actions of the speculator smooth out the lumps as in line *B*. This smoothing out of both supplies and prices increases buyer satisfaction. The apple despised by the kid on Halloween ("Not another apple!") is a real treat by April.

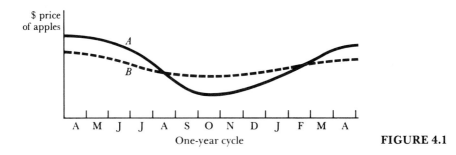

One-year cycle   **FIGURE 4.1**

Foreign exchange speculation performs the same function as apple speculation. It smooths out changes in foreign exchange rates. Assume, for instance, that there was a general opinion in the mid 1970s that New Zealand's exports would decline over the years because Great Britain has joined the Common Market, which in turn would cause a decline in the value of the New Zealand dollar. Assume further that the most serious problems are not expected until about 1980. In the absence of speculation, the price of the New Zealand dollar would be determined only by trade, government intervention, and investment factors. Since the real effects are not expected to be felt for several years, the New Zealand dollar would not fall right away, as shown on the curve labeled *A* in Fig. 4.2. However, speculators who suspect the impending decline will begin unloading New Zealand dollars onto the market early in the game, as along the curve labeled *B*, thus bringing the New Zealand dollar down gradually. The result is that the decline occurs earlier and less steeply, giving exporters a more immediate stimulus to export (more New Zealand dollars for their foreign currency earnings) and helping to protect domestic producers from a sharp drop. Rather than having to adapt suddenly to a new situation in 1979-1980, New Zealand has a much longer period in which to adjust.

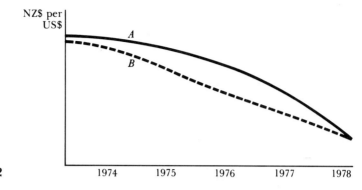

FIGURE 4.2

It may be a bit surprising to the reader to learn that speculation usually tends to be "correct"—that is, rightly anticipates future price movements. In a kind of Darwinian survival of the fittest, unsuccessful speculators cease to be speculators so that only the better ones are left. In fact, if most businesspeople were not largely correct most of the time the economy could hardly function. A few spectacular examples of speculative failure dominate the public imagination—the great stock market crash of 1929, the South Sea Bubble of the eighteenth century, the Florida Land Boom of the 1920s, and the colossal losses suffered in 1974 by some foreign exchange speculators. But these cases are no more typical of the process of speculation than is cancer of the process of cell division.

Foreign exchange speculation is not likely ever to take on the character of stock or land speculation. The latter depend on large changes in the values of whatever is purchased. Shares of stock do double or triple in value, and they also fall as far. Land value around Lake Hoocheekoochee may even quadruple (or halve). Moreover, the underlying causes of such changes are often difficult to assess. Currency values, on the contrary, cannot double or triple or halve or quarter in value, with the rare exception (in a major country) of galloping inflation where prices are doubling or tripling—but this phenomenon is readily identified. If there are rumors that the Belgian franc is going to rise in value, one might buy in anticipation of a 10 percent increase over the existing rate, but not a 30 percent or 100 percent increase. The currency could not possibly change that much in value in any reasonably short length of time.

Speculation is often decried as somehow immoral or unfair. The shop owner whose post-Christmas sale starts before Christmas may be cordially detested by competitors, and the "hoarder" of canned goods who buys the day before the flood waters peak is generally despised. Even the general condemnation, though, does not mean that the shopkeeper and hoarder were speculating incorrectly or that they failed to maximize their own personal interest.

Foreign exchange speculation, too, has had something of a bad press—so much so that companies who regularly engage in aggressive speculating play down or even hide this aspect of their operations. Foreign exchange speculation has in the past proven such a spectacular event largely because of the way in which the world's monetary authorities managed the adjustable peg system up to 1971. The problem facing the authorities under that system was that they had to maintain the exchange rate until the very moment they changed it. Consider the case of Great Britain in 1967. Up to the very day on which the pound sterling was devalued, the Bank of England was buying enormous quantities of pounds in a last-ditch attempt to maintain the rate at its floor level of £1.00 = $2.785. By doing so, the Bank of England (and other monetary authorities who pitched in to help defend the pound) set up a situation whereby speculators might win but could not lose.

This "one-way option," as it has been called, can be shown by a brief example. Imagine yourself the treasurer of Transatlantic Electric, a London-based subsidiary of an American company that in 1967 is holding some £50,000 in cash in its vault and demand deposits at its local bank. These assets, of course, are highly liquid. If you suspect that the British pound is in serious difficulty, and that it might be devalued sharply because the Bank of England can no longer afford to defend the old rate, your course of action is crystal-clear. You will convert all your pounds into dollars at today's rate of £1.00 = $2.785, receiving $139,250. If there is no devaluation after all, you can always buy back pounds with your dollars, and if the rate is the same your $139,250 will purchase £50,000. Of course there will be a small differential in the buying and selling price, representing the commission of the foreign exchange dealer, but this will be small and cost your company little. Even if the pound strengthens a bit in the interim, the rise is not likely to be more than a few tenths of a percent, and this added cost would be quite small also. Against these tiny risks, consider what you and Transatlantic Electric stand to gain if the pound *is* devalued. Had it been the weekend of October 27, 1967, you would have awakened to find the pound down to £1.00 = $2.40. On Monday morning, you could then repurchase your £50,000 for $0.385 less on every pound, representing a gain to your company of $19,250, or in sterling, £8,021.

There was no possibility of your incurring any serious loss, but a good possibility of your making a very large gain in a very short time (16 percent in a two-day weekend is 2,920 percent on an annual basis). This is the reason why the flows of liquid funds out of a suspect currency (often called "hot money" flows) can reach the flood-tide proportions already mentioned in Chapter 2.

Under the old adjustable peg, it was fully understandable that governments were unhappy with speculation since it made defense of a fixed exchange rate much more difficult. It forced governments fighting devaluation to buy millions, and sometimes hundreds of millions, in dollars' worth of their own currencies. Speculation under these circumstances of easy-to-win, hard-to-lose became something of a self-fulfilling prophecy. The growing suspicion that a government could not defend its fixed rate led to speculation, which in turn made the defense more difficult and perhaps impossible.

In no other area of government economic policy making has there been more dishonesty than in the realm of defending an exchange rate. To avoid massive speculation, governments operating with fixed rates give the appearance of never intending to move the peg. Finance ministers or treasury undersecretaries never speak about devaluation except in the most condemning terms. If on a Monday the ministers meet to decide whether to devalue on the following Friday, no minister emerges from the meeting to give an inkling of what has transpired. No comment is made beyond the firm assurance that "the government is prepared to defend the existing parity at all costs." If that were *not* said, the speculation would be so large as to force devaluation within the next day or two. For this reason a government defending a fixed rate will continue to issue reassuring statements, often wholly untrue, right up to the very hour of the devaluation. As long ago as 1551 we find this behavior: In that year the value of the pound sterling was changed shortly after the Duke of Northumberland, in charge of English finances, denied firmly that it would ever happen. Over 400 years later, on May 9, 1969, the German government announced officially that the existing par value of the mark was "valid for eternity." "Eternity" lasted almost five months; the mark's par value was altered on September 24. Such behavior can be more than a joke. In one of the great betrayals of economic history, the British gave their firm commitment to the Dutch government in September 1931 that they would not devalue the pound. The Dutch continued to hold sterling and were the losers thereby.[1]

In justification of these actions by the monetary authorities under the system of adjustable pegs, it should be noted that in many and perhaps most cases intervention helps to stabilize expectations. The willingness of a government to intervene in the foreign exchange market may be seen as a sign that it intends to take corrective action or that it judges the problem to be temporary. In accord with this, speculators may cease betting that the currency will change in value. The converse is almost certainly true too. If the monetary authorities do not intervene, it will be taken as a sign of intent to change the parity and speculation will be heavy. Even an eventual devaluation or revaluation may not stop the speculators once they have tasted blood. In 1961, intense speculation against the German mark continued even after a parity change, the belief obviously being that if they changed the rate once they might well do it again.

It is now (as of 1979) only six years since the last great outbreak of speculation against fixed rates. There is no better way to acquire a feeling for the speculator in action, nor to understand the crucial impact of "hot money" on the old adjustable peg, than to review briefly the tumultuous events of 1973 on the world money markets. These events brought an end to the last full-scale attempt to maintain fixed exchange rates on a general basis, and were the immediate cause of the move to floating rates, which we live with at the present time. The story shows how speculators pay close attention to several distinct factors in determining their course of action: first, the difference in rates of inflation between countries; second, which currencies appear to be "overvalued" and which "undervalued" at any given time; and third, how outside events may spur speculators to action.[2]

The twin peaks of the crisis, which in money terms was the worst ever, occurred in February and March of 1973. Observers of financial markets had been uneasy over American economic policy for some weeks. The Vietnam War had suddenly heated up in the previous December with renewed bombings of Hanoi. Indications pointed to a fatter (inflationary) budget deficit as a result. Simultaneously, in January, the strict Phase II price and wage controls were superseded by the much weaker guidelines of Phase III. The money supply expansion in 1972 had been the highest in recent years. All signs pointed to a resumption of inflation in the United States. An initial reaction was a slump in the New York stock market. Holders of foreign exchange watched nervously.

Events in other countries contributed to the eventual crisis. Italy's lira appeared to be overvalued at its Smithsonian Agreement rate set in 1971. After repeated attacks by speculators, the Italian central bank adopted a dual exchange rate allowing the lira to float for banknotes and other capital transactions while maintaining its fixed rate for ordinary trade. Within two days of the establishment of this "two-tier" market, the floating lira slumped about 7 percent. Italian banks tried to compensate by buying Swiss francs, in part to ease their problem of paying off debts in now-depreciated liras. The Swiss franc thus was strengthened, not only against the lira, but also against the dollar, which was the currency by which many of the francs were being purchased. The Swiss National Bank had to intervene by buying dollars and selling francs to keep the franc from appreciating beyond its Smithsonian upper limit. The Swiss intervention was hardly large by the standards of the month to come, but the government decided that it had had enough and floated the franc on January 23. The move was announced as temporary, but a wave of uncertainty passed through the foreign exchange markets. Obviously the Smithsonian Agreement was not very stable if the Swiss were going to abandon it with so little provocation. Who would be the next to tire of buying dollars? Germany? Japan? A week passed quietly, but on Monday, January 29, the dollar weakened in the major markets in spite of central bank support. That week, multinational companies began to switch out of dollars and speculation began to build as speculators tested the willingness of central banks to defend the old parities. On Friday, February 2, central banks in Europe and Japan bought a billion dollars on top of the billion already purchased earlier that week. Monday February 5 passed without incident, but on the next day a tidal wave of speculation arose. Perhaps $3-3.5 billion were purchased from speculators by the Deutsche Bundesbank on Thursday and Friday, making $6-7 billion in the last seven days. This was the highest rate of speculative attack ever recorded for a short period; only $2.2 billion had been purchased in the seven days around the peak of the 1971 crisis. The support of the New York Fed was much smaller in scale, involving purchases of only some one-third of a billion dollars.

The sheer massiveness of the assault portended the demise of the Smithsonian Agreement. It seemed inconceivable that an attack of these proportions could be sustained. And in fact on Saturday February 10 the Japanese closed the Tokyo market (one of the few to open for business on Saturdays). At once the major governments involved announced that their markets would stay closed on the following Monday. That day U.S. Treasury Secretary George Schultz announced a 10 percent devaluation of the dollar. Japan floated, and Italy floated the other tier of its lira. Most countries kept their old parities against gold, thus allowing the dollar to be devalued against them.

For about ten days the dollar seemed strong at its new parity. The U. S. trade position appeared sound, and the speculative attack eased off. But the speculators were merely catching their wind. The mark and the yen had seemed undervalued, and the dollar overvalued, for so long that sheer instinct seemed to dictate further attacks against the latter. Germany put a 10 percent negative interest rate on nonresident deposits (the Swiss had similar punitive rates), and the speculators wondered why the Germans felt they needed to do this. The dollar had been devalued once, why not yet again? Holders of dollars continued to be nervous. Secretary Schultz on television did not give the usual resounding "no" to a question about further devaluation, and Helmut Schmidt, the German Finance Minister, indiscreetly mentioned the possibility of a floating mark. The honesty was commendable, but it broke a cardinal rule in the era of fixed rates. Suddenly the pressure was on again. On Friday, February 23, the dollar fell to its new low-side intervention point against the mark, the Dutch guilder, and the French and Belgian francs. After two days of relative calm, the dollar sank back again, and Thursday, March 1, set new records in a year that already held the record for speculation. Before noon on that day the Bundesbank bought $2 billion, $2.5 billion for the whole day, an all-time high. Other central banks in Europe supported the dollar to the tune of $1 billion in purchases. Again it was a tidal wave; again the massive support of the dollar by central banks did not suffice; again, on Friday, March 2, the exchanges were closed. This time they remained closed for two weeks. On March 11, 1973, the great decision was announced. From that time the world's major currencies were now floating against the dollar, and most were floating against each other. The only important exception was the EEC snake discussed earlier. March 11 marked the end of a long era of fixed rates, and the beginning of the new age of generalized floating.

The sense of urgency, of crisis, and of international excitement so apparent in the preceding events is very much a result of fixed rates wherein speculators are presented with an excellent chance of winning on any bet they choose to make—the "one-way option," to use the term employed earlier. Speculation under floating exchange rates is, however, a much more prosaic proposition, lacking the sense of emergency we have just seen. This is because floating rates largely avoid the problem of immense "hot money" flows. The incentive to speculate is not nearly so great, because there is no longer a one-way option. Sharp devaluations are no longer to be expected, and there is no guarantee that the rate will not move back in the other direction. You, as the treasurer of Transatlantic Electric, might believe the pound will fall tomorrow and thus buy dollars with pounds at £1.00 = $2.00. But you are not assured of being able to move back into pounds at that rate. You might have to do so at, say, £1.00 = $2.06 or worse. The risks of speculation are thus much higher under floating rates, and the chance for gain substantially reduced.

Controlled or "dirty" floating reestablishes the one-way option. Whenever governments intervene to protect their exchange rate, perhaps for some political purpose, then speculators may well judge that there are not sufficient reserves to maintain that rate—just as was true under the old adjustable parity system before 1973. The outstanding recent example of this was the attack by speculators on the floating British pound during 1976. The pound was in the neighborhood of £1.00 = $2.00 in March 1976. Worry over rapid British inflation, on average about twice as great as the inflation occurring in the United States and West Germany, led the pound into decline. The British government supported sterling, first from its own reserves, then through a $5.3 billion loan obtained from other central banks around the world. By the end of June 1976, $1.1 billion of this had been spent in a vain effort to keep the pound above $1.77. Speculators had their one-way option back again, and they rushed to make use of it. For a time, the Bank of England halted its support, but in October the British applied for an additional $3.9 billion from the International Monetary Fund to prop up the pound. The stage was set for renewed speculation, and the lesson was clear enough—"floating" the exchange rate is not enough to deter speculative attack. A dirty float may be as tempting a target as was the old adjustable peg.

Hedging

If speculation is a normal part of business operations, so is hedging. Someone who is forced or persuaded to take a large risk may frequently cut the size of that risk by making counter-investments that pay off only if the main investment fails. The office gambler, having wagered $50 that the Blackhawks will defeat the Bruins, but unable to sustain a possible loss of that magnitude, hedges the bet by wagering $25 on the Bruins. A hardware store may build a new facility outside what it thinks is a dying downtown area, but hedge by keeping the downtown facility for several years. A merchant may invest heavily in solid-color trousers, but just for safety, order some stripes too.

Hedging, it should be noted, is different from covering, wherein all risk is eliminated. A person hedges a $50 bet by wagering $25 on the opposite outcome; he or she covers by wagering $50 on the opposite outcome.

In their international operations, firms frequently have to hedge because it is virtually impossible to avoid overcommitting the firm to one currency or another. Quotations must be given, contracts entered into, foreign sales financed, or foreign facilities expanded, all of which involve the firm in an increase of assets in other currencies. If the foreign currency is expected to go up in value, then the firm has few worries. If, however, there is even a small chance of it declining in value, the firm may seek to hedge.

Hedging does cost money. The gambler may find that counterwagers must be made at less favorable odds. Stocking extra pants means larger inventories. Keeping two stores where one would suffice is even more of an expense. And so it is with hedging in foreign exchange markets.

The simplest way to hedge is to borrow money in a foreign currency and convert it immediately to the home currency. The cost is the interest rate that must be paid on the borrowed money. Any firm deciding on whether to hedge a foreign exchange risk will base its decision on (1) the cost of hedging; (2) the potential loss to the firm if the risk goes unhedged; (3) the likelihood of that loss occurring; and (4) the attitude of the company toward taking risks.

These points may be illustrated by a day in the operations of Turner & Turner Lathes. This small producer of technologically advanced lathes located in Waltham, Massachusetts, is negotiating a contract with a French firm to sell it some $500,000 worth of equipment to be delivered after one year and paid for after two years. T & T originally wanted the contract in dollars, but it now appears there will be no sale unless the payment is in francs.

You are T & T's treasurer. Your problem is that during a two-year period the dollar/franc rate may change, causing you losses. Do you go ahead with the deal or not?

Your first step is to determine the cost of hedging the contract. T & T's bank, the First National Bank of Boston, has an office in Paris and can arrange through a French bank a loan in francs. T & T could then take the francs and buy dollars at the current exchange rate, then pay back the French bank when the French buyer of lathes settles its bill. Depending on the size of the franc loan, T & T could hedge a part of its risk, or cover it entirely.

The difficulty for T & T is that the interest rate it would pay in France is higher than what it would be charged in the United States, both because T & T is not well known there and because the structure of interest rates in France is as a whole higher than in the United States. T & T figures that in France it will have to pay at least 2 percent more than in the United States for any money it borrows in francs. The cost of fully covering the $500,000 transaction would thus be 2 percent of the amount borrowed, amounting to $10,000 per year or $20,000 in all for the two-year period.

Say that you as T & T treasurer are advised by your bank that your highest potential loss if the franc declines would be about 10 percent, but that the likelihood that the franc will slip against the dollar is rather small. Here is a dilemma. What will you do? A loss of $50,000 to a firm of T & T's size would be a considerable blow, and most likely the blow would be even more serious for you the treasurer. Moreover, the firm is not accustomed to many foreign operations. The choices open to you are to bear the entire risk of a fluctuation in the franc, cover the whole transaction to eliminate all risk by paying out the $20,000 in interest to avoid a possible $50,000 loss, or to hedge only part of the risk by borrowing, for instance, only half the amount needed for full cover. Note that very large firms might not undertake hedging at all. The more able a firm is to absorb losses of these dimensions, the more willing it will be to speculate in francs. Underlying the whole question of hedging against changes in the exchange rate is the firm's attitude toward risk taking.

Although borrowing francs from a French bank might seem the simplest way to hedge, similar protection may be sought by various other means. Here are several different options:

1. T & T could borrow the francs from a non-French bank (many foreign banks keep accounts in Paris out of which they lend francs).

2. If T & T were already holding francs in France, it could reduce these holdings by up to $500,000, converting them to dollars.

3. It might even borrow in a currency other than the franc, if it were fairly certain that this other currency would move in tandem with it. One candidate might be the Belgian franc.

4. It might try to get out from under the problem by renewed attempts to invoice the sale in dollars. This is not likely to be a successful move, but sometimes it is worth a try.

5. It might write in an adjustment clause that would require the French buyer of lathes to increase the amount of francs paid if the franc fell in value by some pre-agreed amount against the dollar. Such clauses do exist, but if the French firm would agree to this, then why wouldn't it agree to invoicing in dollars?[3]

6. Finally, and by far the most important, T & T could enter the *forward market*. Here is a whole new world of exchange rates, much less well known than the rates we have spoken of thus far, and amounting to an organized system of insurance for firms and individuals wishing to avoid exchange risks.

Forward Contracts

The standard means for hedging all short-term (thirty- to ninety-day) foreign currency debts is the *forward contract*. Though complicated, forward contracts have a very long history; the first known example dates from the thirteenth century. A businessperson can arrange such a contract with any large bank that has international connections. Take, for example, an American exporter who expects to receive £10,000 sterling some three months hence, in exchange for $20,000 worth of goods sold. Should the pound plunge to $1.98 by the time payment is due, the exporter will receive only $19,800 for the goods when the pounds are exchanged for dollars. This $200 loss, though only 1 percent of the full value of the transaction, will of course be a much higher proportion of the expected profit.

To hedge against this risk, the exporter can utilize the forward exchange market. He or she will contract with the bank to make a future sale of £10,000, the actual transfer to take place in ninety days' time, at a rate agreed on today (the forward rate). The exporter will thus know exactly what the £10,000 will bring in dollars, and the uncertainty concerning future fluctuations in the exchange rate is removed.

On the other side of the Atlantic, British importers will also be worrying about exchange risks. Their problem is that rates may move in the opposite direction. The British importer who pays £10,000 now for American goods worth $20,000 will stand to lose if the dollar/pound rate moves to £1.00 = $2.02, for then competitors will be able to buy the $20,000 worth of American imports for less than the £10,000 the importer paid in the first place. The importer too may want to insure against exchange rate changes, and can do so by agreeing with the bank to buy pounds at today's forward rate. Then, if in three months' time the pounds have risen in value, the importer has covered the risk. (You can figure out for yourself that an American *importer* and a British *exporter* dealing in dollars rather than pounds, and also wishing to protect themselves against exchange rate fluctuations, can also enter the forward market.)

In a typical day's business, a large bank may write many hundreds of such forward contracts calling for both the future sale and the future delivery of sterling, the time period being as short as 15 days and as long as 180 days, and sometimes even one year.

Generally, the contracts a bank writes to receive and deliver a particular currency on a certain day do not match. The Chase Manhattan Bank in New York, for instance, may find that it has made agreements to deliver more sterling than it will receive three months hence. To redress this imbalance, the foreign exchange officer of the bank may phone a foreign exchange broker in New York, who will in a matter of seconds arrange for Chase Manhattan to purchase sterling for delivery in ninety days from some other bank that will need dollars then. It is the price set between banks for this sort of exchange that is usually quoted in the newspapers as the forward rate. The businessperson cannot expect to receive exactly that figure in any forward contract, because the bank will discount the rate slightly to cover its costs including a small margin for profit.

The forward exchange rate quoted either bank-to-bank or bank-to-customer is almost never the same as the exchange rate prevailing in the market on that day for immediate transfers of currency. The latter rate is known to bankers as the *spot rate*. On July 19, 1978, spot sterling was selling for $1.895 while sterling that was to be delivered on October 19, 1978, was selling at $1.882, a discount of 0.7 percent. Other currencies, such as the German mark, were at a premium on July 19, 1978, with the forward rate higher than the spot rate (see Table 4.1).

TABLE 4.1. SPOT AND FORWARD RATES (July 19, 1978)

Currency	Spot	Forward	Premium or
	(units per dollar)		discount*
British pound	0.5277	0.5314	D 0.0037
French franc	4.4570	4.4586	D 0.0016
German mark	2.0595	2.0350	P 0.0245
Swiss franc	1.8120	1.7823	P 0.0297
Japanese yen	201.57	198.75	P 2.82

*Note that discount means that more foreign currency units can be purchased for a dollar on the forward market.

The sizes of these discounts and premiums on the forward market are highly important. For one thing, they indicate the cost of hedging. If sterling is at a discount, sellers of sterling in the forward market will receive less than what they could get at the spot rate. For another thing, changes in the size of such discounts or premiums often indicate that changes in the spot exchange rate are expected.

Under conditions in which there is little speculation, the relation between a currency's forward rate and its spot rate is highly predictable. This relation can best be seen by looking once more at the Chase Manhattan Bank, which when last seen had agreed to buy £10,000 in ninety days from an American exporter. Now the bank too is subject to the risk that exchange rates will move during the period specified. One certain way for the bank to cover its risk is to sell spot pounds for dollars today at the known exchange rate. Then it could hold the dollars for ninety days, using them to complete the deal when the forward contract comes due. The bank does have the option to leave itself uncovered, thus gambling that the spot rate will move in its favor. Such uncovered operations in foreign exchange, proving unlucky, caused the serious 1974 losses to the I.D. Herstatt Bank in Germany (£83 million), Lloyd's Bank in London (£33 million), the Franklin National Bank of New York (£20 million), the Union Bank of Switzerland (£65 million), and the Westdeutsche Landesbank (£45 million).[4]

Assuming the bank does protect itself by holding spot dollars in New York for ninety days, it may have incurred a cost. The cost would occur if interest rates in Great Britain are higher than in the United States. Pounds held in London and earning British interest rates would have earned more for the bank than the equivalent amount of dollars held in New York earning United States interest rates. The bank thus stands to lose a little because of the interest rate differential.

Adding some arithmetic to the example may be helpful. Say the dollar/pound spot rate is £1.00 = $2.00, and the bank has sold £10,000 spot. Meanwhile interest rates are 10 percent in London and 8 percent in New York (the difference being due to unlike rates of inflation, differing monetary and fiscal policies, and so on). There is thus a 2 percent interest rate advantage for London. In a ninety-day period, that amounts to ½ of 1 percent, which multiplied by £10,000, amounts to £50. As a result the bank would, in making a forward purchase of pounds from the American exporter, offer a price lower than the $20,000 it expected to pay in ninety days for the British pounds. How much lower? £50 lower, which at £1.00 = $2.00 is $100 or $19,900 in all. So if £10,000 exchanges for $19,900, then £1.00 = $1.9900 is the forward rate. The pound is at a forward discount, which is to be expected because interest rates are higher in Britain. Note that the amount of the forward discount, .01/2.00, is equal to ½ of 1 percent, which in turn is exactly equal to the interest rate differential.[5]

Had the interest rate differential been even higher between New York and London, say 4 percent or 5 percent, then of course the bank would offer even less for the pound in the forward market, discounting it further. And naturally, the longer is the time period of the forward contract, the more the discount, and vice versa.

What will happen when a strong demand for forward pounds raises the price to, say, £1.00 = $1.9950 at a time when the interest rate differential is still the same? Here is an opportunity for arbitrageurs to profit from entering into contracts. Arbitrageurs can sell spot dollars from their holdings and buy spot pounds in exchange. They now have in hand the pounds with which they can contract to sell forward in ninety days at only ¼ of 1 percent less than they could obtain by selling spot. Meanwhile they can invest the pounds in London in ninety-day securities, earning ½ of 1 percent more there than in New York. Their $50 gain is easy and riskless.[6]

Note the further ramifications. The arbitrageurs' action of selling pounds forward (an increase in supply) will *lower* the price of forward pounds back toward $1.9900, the rate to be expected from the interest rate differential.

Now consider the case where a weak demand for forward pounds has lowered the forward price to a point beyond the interest rate differential, say £1.00 = $1.9850. Arbitrageurs will now attempt to profit from the situation by buying spot dollars and selling spot sterling. They will then have acquired the dollars with which to enter into forward contracts to buy forward pounds. It is true that the dollars have to be held for ninety days in New York at interest rates that will earn ½ of 1 percent less than could have been earned in London, but after ninety days pounds are acquired for only $1.9850, an advantage of ¾ of 1 percent over the spot rate. Again, the arbitrageurs stand to gain $50 with little effort and virtually no risk.

The ease and safety with which such transactions can be made mean that the pressures of the marketplace to keep the forward rate approximately equal to the interest rate differential are strong. As might be expected, however, the forward rate will seldom be exactly what is predicted by the interest rate differential, because arbitrageurs will not be interested in doing the work for very small yields of, say, less than ¼ of 1 percent. Depending on the point at which artibrageurs go into action, the forward rate will ordinarily vary from the spot rate by an amount slightly greater or slightly less than the interest rate differential.

The only time when large disparities from this predicted result will develop is when the belief is widespread that a currency's spot rate is certain to decline (or increase). Speculative pressures may then become so strong that even the arbitrageurs enter the market to gamble on the movement taking place, turning down an assured small profit from arbitrage in the expectation of a much larger profit if a change in currency values actually occurs. Obviously, this situation was more familiar under the system of adjustable pegs, with its occasional large alterations in rates, than under the floating rate system with its frequent small changes. It follows that significant forward discounts or premiums beyond the interest rate differential are a strong indication of speculative activity.

Compared to the days of the gold standard, or even in comparison with the period between the world wars, there has been an immense increase in the amount of hedging of all types. Whereas hedging was once fairly rare, it is now the rarity to find a large exchange operation that is not hedged, at least in part. Note the economic effect of this. Whenever a currency appears to be threatened for whatever cause, the amount of hedging will certainly rise. As we have already seen, this almost always involves sale of the threatened currency—either by a company, as when Turner & Turner Lathes converted its franc loan into dollars, or by a bank such as Chase Manhattan covering a forward purchase of pounds with dollars by buying spot dollars with pounds now. Thus pressure is put on the threatened currency that would not have been there short decades ago. The great attacks on the pound, the dollar, the lira, and the franc that were so familiar in the ten years before 1976 are only in part speculative attacks. In large measure they are the net result of thousands of firms engaging in the innocent and thoroughly understandable act of hedging their risks.

Leads and Lags: Or, Moving What Can Be Moved

The question of leads and lags concerns, not hedging, but reducing the commitment to pay or receive a certain currency. Returning to our betting analogy, it means making a $25 bet instead of one for $50. (Hedging, you recall, would mean counterbalancing the $50 bet by a wager on the opposite result.) In essence, leads and lags refer to the processes by which money ordinarily moves between one currency and another. When these processes are speeded up (these are the leads) we expect a movement from a weak currency to a strong one. When they are slowed down (the lags) the expectation is for a movement from a strong currency to a weak one. Utilizing the lessons of leads and lags, it is often possible to move a very significant proportion of a firm's liquid assets out of weak currencies and into strong ones.

Table 4.2 shows the typical leads and lags that might face a German firm such as Baden-Wurst, an exporter and importer of meat products. The table

TABLE 4.2. THE USE OF LEADS AND LAGS TO PROTECT AGAINST LARGE CHANGES IN THE EXCHANGE RATE (example of a German firm)

Procedure for imports	Normal	Lead (mark may depreciate)	Lag (mark may appreciate)
1. Order import	When need is clear	Immediately	As late as possible
2. Purchase forward cover	When good is shipped	Immediately	Skip it
3. Collect from German distributor	60 days	As quickly as possible	Take your time
4. Pay for import	90 days	As quickly as possible	Take your time

Procedure for exports	Normal	Lead (mark may appreciate)	Lag (mark may depreciate)
1. Ship export	Within 7 days of order	Speed shipment	Delay shipment
2. Purchase forward cover	On shipment	Immediately	Skip it
3. Collect export proceeds	60 days	As soon as possible	Take your time
4. Dispose of export proceeds	30 days	As soon as possible	Keep abroad until absolutely needed

assumes that (1) under normal circumstances this firm has ordered its imports under some procedure designed to secure an optimal inventory; (2) it has usually waited a week or so to buy forward cover in order to cut costs; (3) when it distributes the imports to retailers in Germany, it normally takes about sixty days before cash is received for them; and (4) when it does not finance the imports itself, it normally waits about ninety days before paying its foreign suppliers.

If the German mark is expected to fall in value, it behooves the firm to pay for imports while foreign currency is still inexpensive. Consequently, it leads by speeding up the outflow of money under the categories shown in the table. With exports, however, the firm lags in order to keep its expected receipts abroad as long as possible—after all, if there is a significant decline in the mark, Baden-Wurst will be able to buy more marks with its foreign currency earnings. In consequence it is slow to make shipment, slow to collect the money for shipments it makes, and slow to exchange these receipts for marks.

Like hedging, leads and lags can be expensive because they involve abnormal changes in inventory, unusual patterns in bill-collecting efforts (with perhaps the loss of a customer or two), or the keeping of too much cash in some geographical areas in which the firm operates and too little in others. Nonetheless, if the stakes are high enough, this is the way the firm will operate. In fact, shifts in leads and lags have been called the main cause of the pound's 1967 devaluation. Studies undertaken at that time showed that a shift of just one week in the scheduling of payments for imports and exports would have caused a loss in Britain's foreign exchange reserves of £200 million—and a shift involving only a few weeks more could easily have chewed up the entirety of that country's reserve holdings.

Notes

1. The episode was especially shocking in that Dr. Vissering, head of the Netherlands Bank, telephoned in person to the Bank of England to ask if the Dutch sterling reserves were safe. He was given a "yes" answer even though devaluation had almost certainly already been decided upon. Trusting in the British promise the Dutch did not convert their pounds into gold, as they had plenty of time to do. It was many years before this nastiness was forgotten.
2. The description of the 1973 crisis here and in following pages draws on the more comprehensive discussion in Leland B. Yeager, *International Monetary Relations: Theory, History, and Policy* (New York: Harper & Row, 2d ed., 1976). See especially pp. 595-604.
3. One of the authors recalls an agent for a Japanese firm telling with relish how he had bargained a currency-adjustment clause into a United States government contract to buy Japanese goods shortly before the United States devaluation of 1971. "I just put it in as a bargaining point," he said, "but they took it without much question, and we saved thousands of dollars on the contract."

4. Banks were not the only ones to lose. Some corporations took large exposed positions in the forward market, speculating by selling forward currencies they didn't have. In 1974, the International Telephone and Telegraph Corporation (ITT) sold forward a huge sum in currencies it thought would weaken against the dollar. They strengthened instead, and ITT lost $48 million. See *Newsweek* (August 16, 1976), p. 60.

5. The value of forward currencies can also be viewed in terms of the present value of future assets. Since the present values of British assets are lower (reflecting the higher interest rates) than United States present values, the value of pounds to be delivered in the future is also lower.

6. Very often central banks bid in the forward market, rather than the spot, to drive up the price of their own currency. Hence Britain could buy forward pounds, opening up an arbitrage opportunity and causing the arbitrageurs to buy spot sterling. Hence even without having foreign exchange, the Bank of England can support sterling. Of course, when those forward contracts come due some months hence, the Bank of England had better have the foreign exchange it needs to fulfill its contracts to buy pounds.

INTERNATIONAL CAPITAL MARKETS

This chapter examines the mobilization of international savings for international investments. As has already been shown, it is normal procedure for investors in one nation to buy bonds or stocks in another, to extend commercial credit to foreign importers, or to purchase physical assets in another nation. None of these presents any particular international problems beyond the needs to exchange currency and hedge foreign currency positions, which have already been discussed. The reader may already suspect, however, that international finance is never that simple and that there are particular instruments available for international lending and borrowing, and specialized capital markets.

National Capital Markets

National capital markets—with the exception of the American market—are limited in the quantity of lending or borrowing they can do (relative to the needs of the typical large borrowers) and in the degree of financial specialization they can provide. As a consequence, large international firms make only limited use of strictly national banking facilities. An American firm operating in France, for instance, would use the French banks for holding deposits in local currencies, for making international transactions, for helping to finance buyer credits, and for providing small loans and working capital. Yet there are only a few cities with facilities for raising money for multimillion dollar investments—New York, London, Zurich, and Frankfurt in particular. And among those, only New York would try to raise the great bulk of the loan or bond issue domestically. It would therefore be unusual for firms to attempt to raise very large sums through banks in smaller markets. For example, if Chrysler's Simca wants to raise $30 million to tide it over some short-term difficulties, it probably would not go to Paris. Neither, for that matter, would Renault or Citroën. What is wrong with Paris?

Paris is a difficult market in which to raise large sums of money. Even if Simca did attempt to do so with a Paris bank, that bank would probably turn for assistance to other banks in New York or London. The capital market in French francs is a thin market; certainly there are French government bills and bonds, commercial paper, and other short-term assets, but their value is tiny compared to the amount of similar assets traded in London or New York. Secondary markets, where bills and bonds purchased directly from the government or corporations can be sold before maturity, are not well developed. In such circumstances, a few requests for 30 million francs would cause banks to sell off franc-denominated securities at considerable discounts, given the scarcity of ready buyers. Hence their interest rates on very large loans are likely to be surprisingly high.

The thinness of the market in French franc bills and bonds also means that the banks and investment houses in Paris cannot offer the variety of financial instruments—different terms on deposits, certificates of deposit (CDs), and the like—that are tailored to fit different customers' needs. It also means fewer banks and less competition. As a result, French banks supplement their franc holdings with marketable assets denominated in dollars, pounds, Swiss francs, German marks, and the like. And they establish foreign branches and subsidiaries in New York and London so that they can offer their customers more services. The result of this is that not only banks, but private citizens and corporations with spare cash, end up channeling money into United States Treasury bills, sterling note securities, and the like. This can be done directly or indirectly through banks. Since the same pattern exists in virtually every other nation, the capital markets in New York and London are swollen with foreign savings, which in turn strengthen the markets and make them even better places to do business. The huge earnings of the OPEC oil exporters since 1973 have meant even greater funneling of new savings into these major markets as the oil nations have not found their own banking systems sufficiently developed to handle such funds.

Background of the Euromarkets

The weakness of national capital markets has been known for years, but it was only in the 1950s that bankers began to search for some international means to provide financing. Borrowers in Europe knew that the money was there, particularly as Europe recovered from the war. If only they could raise a few million in France, a few in Germany, and a few elsewhere, they could then borrow the amount needed without putting any undue strain on any single national capital market. The cost of arranging separate loans or bonds, however, was prohibitive.[1] It was much cheaper to go to New York or London, where all the savings were being deposited anyway. This, of course, threw all the really big international business to the American and British banks (and, as the pound weakened, only the American). Further, the system depended on the willingness of these two governments to allow their capital markets to be used as centers of world finance. When in the 1950s and 1960s the United States and Britain sought to close off their capital markets, the European bankers came up with a unique solution to the problems created—the Eurodollar. This is best understood in historical perspective.

The first part of the Eurodollar saga goes all the way back to the financial chaos that succeeded the First World War. For more than a century London had been the major international banking center. There was, in fact, no other city with the strength and depth of capital market to attract significant amounts of foreign funds. As a result, most international investments and a great deal of world trade were financed through London. Since the financing was in sterling, it is hardly surprising that most firms wanted to invoice in sterling. The result was that most of the world's trade was in fact conducted in terms of the British pound—despite the inconvenience of the pound-shilling-pence system. (To the average foreigner who was less than a titan of arithmetic, the system could be almost incomprehensible. First exposure to a bill for, say, "ten pounds seventeen shillings threepence ha'penny farthing" was an experience to be remembered. There were twenty shillings to the pound, twelve pence to the shilling, and four farthings to the penny, until the pound was decimalized in 1971.)

In the 1920s New York began to rise in importance as a capital market, and a rivalry grew up between London and New York as centers of international trade and finance. The world monetary crisis of the early 1930s, however, prompted the British to suspend the convertibility of the pound into gold before the Americans did, causing many firms and governments to switch their business to New York. The nations of the British Commonwealth (excepting Canada) continued to use London as the major market for many years, however. Such countries were considered to be part of the "sterling area."

With the economic recovery following the end of World War II, New York came to dominate world finance, leaving London a distant second. New York had become the center for vast holdings of foreign deposits, and it was the major source of funds for innumerable international firms and foreign national, provincial, and municipal governments.

It was in the mid-1950s that the momentum began to build in Europe for a new type of capital market. The impetus came from a number of government decisions that, by hindsight, seem unwise as far as their impact on the New York and London capital markets is concerned. First, in 1957 the British government responded to one of the recurrent crises of the pound by placing tight controls on the borrowing of sterling by nonresidents through British banks. This cut British bankers out of international lending, which was, so to speak, the *coup de grâce* for the London market after nearly forty years of struggle. Or so it appeared. Then, in the early 1960s the United States began to feel uncomfortable in its role as world banker: American officials began to express concern about the problems of all those short-term debts and long-term loans to foreigners. With American gold stocks dwindling, these investments posed a danger of possible massive capital outflows. (This problem will be examined in detail in later chapters.) As a result, Congress passed the *interest equalization tax* in 1963. This taxed any United States resident buying a foreign debenture 1-1½ percent of its value per year—in other words, on a $10,000 note the tax might be $150 per year, meaning the foreign firm would have to discount the note before even offering it in New York. (On the flotation of foreign stocks, the tax was 15 percent.) The tax was sufficiently severe to cut off most foreign bonds issued in New York that did not come under the list of "exceptions" in the law. (Exceptions to the tax were listed in some fifty pages of the seventy-five-page act, and included most of the less developed countries and Canada.)

Soon after the interest equalization tax went into effect, American banks found that those foreign firms unable to float bonds came to them for loans, and their level of foreign lending rose. Concern then mounted about these large outflows of dollars, and President Lyndon Johnson instituted in 1965 a voluntary program of direct controls over lending by American banks and other financial institutions to foreigners—the so-called Voluntary Foreign Credit Restraint (VFCR) Guidelines. These guidelines were strengthened year by year, and in 1968, for all practical purposes, they were made mandatory. At the same time, new controls over U. S. direct investment abroad limited the use of U.S. bank credit to finance new capital formation in foreign countries. Again, New York's position as an international capital market was weakened. Indeed, had there been any alternative anywhere near as strong as New York or London, many funds would certainly have moved to it. But there was no close competitor, and what happened was even more interesting.

The Eurodollar Market

We have seen that London banks could not lend sterling freely, and investors were in any case nervous about holding their funds in sterling. At the same time, New York could not lend out dollars freely. The international capital markets responded to this challenge by creating the Eurodollar. The idea came from a tiny embryo that, rather remarkably, involved the Soviet Union. In the 1950s a number of Soviet-bloc countries had stocks of American dollars that they wanted kept on deposit for use in financing trade. They were very concerned, however, that under the political conditions of the time—Senator

McCarthy's anticommunist crusade, The House Un-American Activities Committee, the execution of the Rosenbergs—these dollars might be subject to confiscation if they were held in American banks. Hence the Soviets deposited a quantity of dollars with their banking agent in France, the Banque Commerciale pour l'Europe du Nord. The bank's cable and telex address was EUROBANK, and brokers began to refer to the dollars deposited there as Eurodollars. Dollars deposited abroad have received this name ever since.

Soon it was seen that such dollars might be very useful. There was no law in France or in Great Britain (which almost at once took over leadership in the market) that said French or English people (or banks in these countries) could not lend dollars to borrowers at home or abroad. Nor did American law restrict overseas operations of this type. By the late 1950s, the same London banks that were less able to lend sterling to foreigners were beginning to offer their customers *dollar financing*. If a customer wanted to borrow $50,000 from Barclays in London, Barclays would give the customer a $50,000 check drawn on its correspondent bank in New York. (In the same manner, when a homeowner borrows from a savings and loan institution, the check is drawn on that institution's account at a commercial bank; or when Paul borrows from Peter the check is drawn on Peter's account in a commercial bank.)

How, then, did the London banks get the dollars they lent? They could not just go out and buy them with sterling because the Bank of England would not have approved the sterling outflow—that would be the same as lending sterling. The problem could be solved by attracting more dollar deposits of the sort the Soviets and East Europeans had been making. The mechanism was already there. As a service to their customers British banks had for years been accepting just this sort of dollar deposit in return for which they would give the depositor a dollar account.[2] (Note that this would be illegal in the United States. Banks in most foreign countries, however, are completely free to take deposits denominated in a foreign currency.) It was, and is, a simple matter to establish such an account. In his first week of graduate studies in London, one of the authors simply walked into the Midland Bank and thirty minutes later had an "external" dollar account complete with handsome book of checks. Similarly, a British firm doing business with American firms and wanting a dollar account did not have to go to an American bank to get one. Such accounts were available at British banks. All London had to do was to turn a minor service into a major investment medium.

Most investors were not interested in putting dollars into London simply for current account use. Rather, they wished to make short-term deposits for periods of a few weeks to a few months. While the British did pay some interest on the regular "external" checking accounts, investors sought higher returns and London was ready with a variety of means for attracting them, offering successively higher interest rates on dollars deposited "on call" and for thirty, sixty, and ninety days. After the Americans invented the certificate of deposit (CD)—a negotiable certificate indicating a fixed sum has been deposited in a savings account—in 1961, London was soon to follow with its own dollar CD called the London CD.

The popularity of Eurodollars grew rapidly. They were convenient. European borrowers of dollars did not need to develop contacts with American banks, and could instead deal with their own banks. American banks and corporations with dollars to lend found it much easier to lend these dollars to European banks than to try to place the dollars themselves in Europe. They thus avoided the problems of risk and lack of knowledge concerning local markets and conditions. The aggravating difference in business hours between Europe and America (five hours between London and New York) could be avoided by Europeans who dealt in dollars with European banks. Finally, there was also a crucial competitive factor. British banks found that dollar-denominated deposits were an excellent way to attract additional deposits, and they could pay higher interest rates than New York.

A principal reason for this interest rate difference concerned the government regulation of banking. Under the Federal Reserve's Regulation Q, American banks were subject to reserve requirements while British banks were not. This meant that American banks had to keep 5 percent of all savings deposits or CDs while London banks could lend virtually the whole amount.[3] More important was the fact that American banks could not pay interest on CDs of less than ninety days and faced time limitations on savings deposits as well. British banks could pay on money deposited for one day. Regulation Q set a ceiling on the interest American banks could pay. British banks had lower overheads than American banks and so had less of a spread between rates paid on deposits and those charged on loans. The combination of higher returns on shorter-term deposits plus larger profits for banks proved a great stimulus to the growth of the Eurodollar market.

In the late 1960s it became apparent that the Eurodollar market was an effective way for United States banks to avoid the Fed's Regulation Q. In 1969 the Fed tightened money as part of its anti-inflationary strategy. Regulation Q kept commercial banks from raising their interest rates on savings accounts and on the CDs so popular with large corporations. As a result, funds flowed out of United States commercial banks and into assets bearing higher interest rates. At this point U.S. banks found they could borrow Eurodollars, relend them in the United States, and maintain the scale of their business. Of course the Eurodollar market was flush with funds because depositors (the very ones who might have been putting their money in U.S. banks) found their earnings considerably higher on Eurodollar deposits.

American commercial banks rushed to establish subsidiaries abroad. In 1965 there were 459. In two years, 1967 to 1969, the assets of foreign branches of American banks nearly tripled ($15.7 billion to $41.1 billion). The rate of growth was spectacular and largely unexpected. Finally, the Fed put restrictions on Eurodollar borrowing. Soon afterward (in 1970-1971), the Fed eased its monetary policy and relaxed Regulation Q on large CDs. By this time, the market was firmly established and businesspeople had become used to the convenience of Eurodollars.[4] Plenty of borrowers were found all over Europe, even as American banks ceased to borrow Eurodollars as a way to beat Regulation Q.

Soon trade in Eurodollars appeared in other market centers outside Europe, as did overseas deposits of other currencies such as the mark and Swiss franc. Slowly the name Eurodollar became less and less appropriate. Nowadays there are important centers of "Eurodollar" trade in Singapore, the Bahamas, and Panama, for example, and West German banks have established a large "Euromark" banking business in Luxembourg.[5] Between 1969 and 1973, for example, the nondollar share in Euromarkets grew from 17 percent to 28 percent. The most important nondollar Eurocurrencies are the German mark and the Swiss franc.

Nowadays London is still the main center for Euromarket trade. A total of 256 banks there are currently authorized to deal in Eurocurrencies. The share of U.S. banks in the London market peaked in about 1969 at approximately 54 percent of total business, but at the present time that figure has fallen back to something less than 40 percent. The share of banks with home offices in neither the United States nor the United Kingdom has grown rapidly, and by the beginning of 1975 exceeded the 30 percent mark. Measuring the total size of the market is difficult because official statistics are seriously deficient. Estimates for 1975 range from a low of some $200 billion to a high of about $400 billion. The Eurodollar market has grown prodigiously; it contained only about $7 billion in 1963, and in 1967 there were still only some $18 billion in the market. In fact, the size of the markets has contracted only once—in late 1974 following the abolition of U.S. controls on lending and other capital movements several months before. This combined with the great oil crisis of that year led to a case of jitters that brought a good many dollars (some 5 percent of the market) home or led to their being exchanged for foreign currency. But steady growth was resumed toward the end of 1974, and still continues. The Eurodollar market has established itself as a key feature in international exchange, and is arguably the major innovation in the world's currency and capital markets during the twentieth century. Without an enormous expansion of the Eurodollar market during the oil crisis of the 1970s, it is hard to see how the system of exchange rates could have survived the pressures of billions in new oil revenues surging through the currency markets.

Monetary Analysis of Eurodollars

The Eurodollar market has a number of unusual features. First, it is a "wholesale" market in which the size of individual transactions tends to be very large, governments and large corporations being the major borrowers. Second, it is a highly competitive market free for the most part from controls and from central bank regulation. Certainly there is no central authority making the rules for Eurodollars the way a central bank does for national currencies. Third, the market is very much an interbank one. Similar to the foreign exchange market itself, banks can telephone brokers and arrange to lend to each other any idle U.S. dollar deposits they have no present use for. Finally, it is basically a market for short-term (under three years) lending and borrowing. Longer-term loans are handled in the Eurobond and Eurocredit markets.

Any institution so large and so quick in its growth must create a certain amount of controversy among businesspeople, academicians, and government officials. This is certainly true of the Euromarkets. Among the principal concerns are (1) where Eurodollars go once they are lent by banks, (2) whether there is a multiple expansion of Eurodollar deposits, and (3) whether by their actions European central banks have had a hand in creating new Eurodollars. The best way to answer these questions is to examine some typical Eurodollar transactions and analyze their effect.

Here is how $50,000 might enter the Eurodollar market. Pechiney, the French metals company, finds it has $50,000 more than it has immediate use for in its checking account at the Chase Manhattan Bank in New York. (Alternatively, it might have had excess francs with which it decided to buy an additional $50,000.) In either case it ends up with $50,000 in its New York account. Instead of taking out a CD or buying a U.S. Treasury bill, it might send a check drawn on its Chase Manhattan account to Barclays in London as a Eurodollar deposit, as shown in Fig. 5.1, step 1. (Alternatively, the deposit might have originated from an American business transferring dollar deposits to foreign banks, from foreign exporters to the United States who are paid in dollars and deposit them in foreign banks, or from holders of foreign currency such as francs, marks, or pounds, who choose to exchange these for dollars and keep the dollars in foreign banks.) Pechiney probably views its new deposit as a substitute for a U.S. CD, a U.S. Treasury bill, or some other short-term asset. The deposit is thus unlikely to be a checking account; not money (M_1) but near-money. The next step in the transaction (Fig. 5.1, step 2) is for Barclays to credit Pechiney with $50,000 and then send the check to its correspondent bank in the United States, in this case the Irving Trust Company. Irving Trust credits Barclays' account (step 3), thereby providing the backing for Barclays' new Eurodollar deposit (step 4). Irving sends the check to the Federal Reserve Bank of New York, which credits it with $50,000 (step 5) and debits Chase (step 6). Chase then debits the Pechiney account already recorded (see step 1), and the transaction is completed. Note that, unlike a movement in the foreign exchange market, there is no foreign exchange risk in establishing a Eurodollar deposit because all assets and liabilities in the transaction are in dollars.

Chase Manhattan (New York)

	Assets	Liabilities	
⑥	Reserves −$50,000	Checking account of Pechiney −$50,000	①

Barclays (London)

	Assets	Liabilities	
④	Deposit in Irving Trust +$50,000	Eurodollar deposit for Pechiney +$50,000	②

Irving Trust (New York)

	Assets	Liabilities	
⑤	Reserves +$50,000	Checking account of Barclays +$50,000	③

FIGURE 5.1 Creating a Eurodollar Deposit

Note that the $50,000 does not leave the U.S. banking system. A checking account changes ownership and bank—$50,000 that was Pechiney's in Chase Manhattan becomes Barclays' deposit in Irving Trust—and with the change in checking accounts goes a change in reserves from Chase to Irving. With total reserves thus unaffected, there is no overall effect on the U.S. money supply. Any loans that Chase cannot renew because its reserves have declined can now be made by Irving, whose reserves are higher by an equal amount.

What does leave the borders of the United States is the ability to lend out Pechiney's new $50,000 Eurodollar deposit. This is shown simply in Fig. 5.2, which pictures the combined T-account for all U.S. banks in regard to Pechiney's $50,000 before the Eurodollar transaction. (Assume a legal reserve requirement of 20 percent and no excess reserves.)

All Banks

Assets	Liabilities
Reserves $50,000	Pechiney's demand deposit $50,000
Loans $200,000	Other deposits $200,000

FIGURE 5.2

In the banking system as a whole, with a 20 percent reserve requirement, $50,000 in reserves are backing $250,000 in total deposits. However, when Pechiney puts its money into Eurodollars, it is Barclays Bank in London that is now able to loan the $50,000 deposit. True, the "other deposits" category in

Fig. 5.2 rises to match the elimination of Pechiney's U.S. deposit, but this leaves the situation unchanged for American banks. What Eurodollars do is to transfer the ability to lend Pechiney's deposit from New York to London, along with the interest to be earned on the loan. This, of course, is annoying to American banks who would like to earn this themselves—especially in a Eurodollar market at least $200 billion in size—and certainly helps to explain why so many American banks have foreign branches and subsidiaries.

Basically, there are three different sorts of Eurodollar loans: interbank lending; loans whose proceeds are spent in the United States; and loans whose proceeds are spent outside the United States. The differing implications of these loans are examined below.

Interbank Lending. Because of the efficiency of the Eurodollar system, Barclays would probably lend the Eurodollars almost immediately. If it could find no borrower itself, it would lend them in the interbank market. There will ordinarily be other banks with customers aplenty, and some banks may borrow even when they have no need for funds if they expect interest rates to be a bit higher later that day or week—they might then relend just to make a small fraction of a percent on their money. This results in chains of banks handling dollars originating from some Eurodollar deposit. No such interbank activity is going to be profitable, however, unless there are firms and governments on the "retail" end wishing to borrow Eurodollars. It is these "retail" customers who make the interbank market a viable one.

A Loan Whose Proceeds Are Spent in the United States. Say the Irish toolmaking firm, Toolan-Digh, wishes to import an automatic lathe from the Massachusetts firm of Turner & Turner. Toolan-Digh's treasurer might negotiate a loan in dollars through an office of Barclays Bank in Dublin. Toolan-Digh pays off Turner & Turner with the proceeds of the loan, and Turner & Turner in turn deposits the dollars in its Boston bank. As the checks clear, the dollars Barclays held would end up in Turner & Turner's account in Boston, and that would end the American banking system's involvement. But Eurodollars still remain in existence as a chain of debt in Europe. Toolan-Digh still owes Barclays, and Barclays still owes Pechiney. Both Pechiney's original deposit and the loan to Toolan-Digh are outstanding, one a liability and the other an asset of Barclays Bank, and the size of the Eurodollar market is swelled accordingly.

A Loan Whose Proceeds Are Spent outside the United States. Assume now that Barclays has not lent directly to a commercial borrower, but has lent instead to the Banque National de Paris in the interbank market, which in turn lent the money to the final borrower, the French cosmetic firm of Moulin Rouge. Assume further for simplicity that both the Bank of Paris and Barclays have accounts at the Irving Trust in New York, so that the actual transfer of dollars is just an accounting transaction at Irving. Now, however, Moulin Rouge wants to spend the dollars in France, so it asks the Bank of Paris to convert the dollar loan to francs. That bank will then have a T-account like that shown in Fig. 5.3.

Banque National de Paris

Assets	Liabilities
Deposit in Irving Trust Co. US$50,000	Demand deposit of Moulin Rouge Fr 250,000 (after conversion at Fr 5 = US$1)

FIGURE 5.3

What the Bank of Paris actually did was to loan dollars to Moulin Rouge, and then for that firm's convenience, buy the dollars back in exchange for a new franc deposit. Since the bank's reserve is in dollars against a franc loan, it now must consider the problem of exchange risk already discussed at length in Chapter 4. Presumably the Bank of Paris will turn its dollars into francs, other things being equal, because it must have been short on francs or it would not have borrowed from Barclays in the first place. So to cover its position when Moulin Rouge withdraws the francs from its new deposit (an event that will occur very soon, since Moulin Rouge is paying interest on the loan), it will turn its dollar reserve into francs.

Once the dollars are sold on the foreign exchange market by the Bank of Paris, they lose their identity as Eurodollars. Other banks will buy them for the same reason they buy any other dollars—to satisfy their customers' needs for that currency. The bulk of the dollars will go to people who wish to pay for something purchased in the United States, whether it be a good, service, or financial asset. Some small amount of these dollars is also likely to find its way back into the Eurodollar market as banks and firms choose to invest some money there.

Is There a Multiple Expansion of Eurodollars? The process outlined above poses a question: Is there a multiple expansion of Eurodollars akin to the expansion of the domestic money supply? The answer is that multiple expansion is certainly possible, but that it is likely to be limited by great leakages from the Eurodollar system. The following example demonstrates how multiple expansion *can* take place.[6] Say that higher interest rates on dollar deposits in London compared to New York cause a holder of United States dollars to shift $1,000 from an account in New York's Morgan Guaranty Trust Company to London's Midland Bank, by writing a check (see Fig. 5.4).

The Midland Bank will keep the $1,000 on deposit in its correspondent New York bank. This is a Midland asset. But Midland knows full well that it

Morgan Guaranty Trust Co.
(New York)

Assets	Liabilities
	Demand deposit of American firm −US$1,000

Midland Bank
(London)

Assets	Liabilities	
Demand deposit in United States +US$1,000	Demand deposit of American firm +US$1,000	**FIGURE 5.4**

can meet all potential dollar withdrawals by holding only about 10 percent of its dollar demand deposits as a reserve. It is thus possible for Midland to loan $900 to some British importer, thus crediting the importer's deposit with that amount (Fig. 5.5, step 1). Obviously the British importer wishes to use this $900 to pay for imports from some other firm and country, say from a German exporter who agrees to (and perhaps demands) payment in dollars (step 2). The German firm, having received payment by a check drawn on the Midland Bank, now deposits the check at its Frankfurt bank, one of the many offices of that country's famous Commerzbank, and receives credit for $900 in its demand deposit there. Commerzbank then adds the 900 new dollars it holds to its account in its correspondent New York bank, assumed here for simplicity again to be Morgan Guaranty (step 3). Commerzbank thus has a new $900 demand deposit (liability) belonging to the German exporter, and a new $900 asset of its own deposited in New York. Meanwhile, in New York, $900 shifts from the demand deposit of Barclays Bank to the demand deposit of Commerzbank (step 4).

Notice in particular that claims on New York remain the same at $1,000, equal to the remaining $100 belonging to Midland plus the $900 that has now shifted into Commerzbank's dollar deposits. *But the amount of Eurodollars has been increased.* There is still the original $1,000 deposit of the American firm in London, plus the new $900 on deposit in Frankfurt. There has been a multiple expansion of Eurodollars, which in theory is measured just as is a domestic multiple expansion of the money supply, by a formula that shows the change in demand deposits as equal to the original new deposit times 1 over the percentage of dollars kept as a reserve plus any leakages of dollars out of the banking system, or:

$$\Delta DD = \text{original new deposit} \times \frac{1}{\text{reserve requirement} + \text{leakages}}$$

Step 1
Midland Bank, London

Assets	Liabilities
Loan to British importer +$900	Demand deposit of same British importer +$900

Step 2
Midland Bank, London

Assets	Liabilities
Demand deposit in Morgan Guaranty, New York −$900	Demand deposit of British importer −$900

Loan is spent by British importer

Payment is made to German exporter

Step 3
Commerzbank, Frankfurt

Assets	Liabilities
Demand deposit in Morgan Guaranty, New York +$900	Demand deposit of German exporter +$900

Step 4
Morgan Guaranty, New York

Assets	Liabilities
No change	Demand deposit of Midland Bank, London −$900
	Demand deposit of Commerzbank, Frankfurt +$900

FIGURE 5.5

In actual practice, however, the multiple expansion of Eurodollars is likely to be rather low, certainly much lower than for domestic dollars in the United States banking system. The reason is clear enough: There are many competing uses for funds in the Eurodollar market. Even though banks taking Eurodollar deposits commonly carry much smaller reserve requirements (indeed, they are usually self-imposed rather than set by any supervising agency), the leakages out of Eurodollars will be very great. Unlike the ordinary demand deposit in an American bank, the Eurodollar does not circulate as currency. The dollar loaned domestically is likely in large part to flow back into the banking system after the loan is spent. A Eurodollar loan, however, is likely not to be redeposited in the Eurodollar market. Both Eurodollar loans used to pay for American goods and those converted into a local currency will disappear into ordinary American demand deposits, unless the eventual recipients take the explicit decision to acquire a Eurodollar deposit all over again. This *can* happen, but only when the recipients have spare cash (and certainly only a small proportion would ever be spare), and when Eurodollar deposits are preferred to a variety of other short-term assets. The best analogy is to near-monies in the domestic market. One might imagine the builder of new homes being paid from homeowners' loans made by a savings and loan institution, but it would be unusual to find the builder redepositing all receipts back in a savings and loan institution. Some might go there, but not very much.

More generally, the supply of new Eurodollars (as any near-money) is related not so much to the number of Eurodollars loaned, but instead to overall liquidity, and alternative opportunities for saving and investment. A recent study by the IMF indicates that in the period 1968-1972, the factor of Eurodollar multiple expansion was only ab ɪt one, meaning little or no multiple expansion was taking place.[7] The overall economic impact on the world money supply (and hence on the rate of inflation) caused by the growth of Eurodollars has thus been far smaller than might otherwise have been expected. The IMF has accordingly concluded that Eurodollars by themselves have not been the source of much inflationary pressure.

There was an interesting interlude in the late 1960s when Eurodollars *were* being created in an unusual and unexpected way. European central banks, which had been buying up huge quantities of dollars as part of their effort to peg exchange rates, found that they could earn interest on these dollars by depositing them in the Eurodollar market. But as a result, interest rates were depressed on the Eurodollar market and European businesspeople thus increased their borrowing there, in turn exchanging these cheap dollars for their domestic currency. The large new deposits of Eurodollars, turned into loans and then converted back to local currency, meant new streams of dollars coming back into the hands of these same central banks. Thence back into the Eurodollar market they would go. In essence, the central banks were manufacturing Eurodollars through their own operations, all the while complaining about the great dollar glut. Finally, at a meeting in Basel, Switzerland, in May 1971, the European central banks agreed to stop feeding this money machine, and decreased substantially their deposits of dollars in the Eurodollar market.[8]

Eurobonds

Eurodollars are essentially *short-term* loans and deposits used for the financing of inventories and commercial (both domestic and foreign) sales. No firm makes long-term investments like plant expansion out of short-term loans; that is too chancy for both firm and bank. Rather, companies try to finance their long-term needs with *bonds*. The decline of London as a capital market and the imposition of the interest equalization tax in the United States had serious effects on the international markets for bonds. In 1963, for instance, over $380 million worth of foreign bonds were sold in New York. In 1964 that figure was down to $191 million—and none of those were European bonds.[9] Where could big borrowers go to get money? European bankers had been developing the solution—the Eurobond.

Since 1957 the European bankers had been trying to devise a means of floating bonds on a continental scale. Their efforts had met with some success, and by the end of 1963 they had managed to place some $423 million worth of such issues. Hence they were prepared for the rush of borrowers who came in 1964, when some $739 million worth of bonds were sold. Over the next twelve years well over $30 billion worth of Eurobonds were to be placed.[10]

What, then, precisely is a Eurobond? The Eurobond is essentially a bond issued and sold outside the country in whose currency it is denominated, and sold by an international group of banks and investment houses. Most of these are and have been in dollars (Eurodollar bonds). This would be a bond denominated in United States dollars, issued outside the United States, and sold outside the United States. In all likelihood the receipts from the sales of bonds would be collected in dollars (and deposited in United States checking accounts either directly or through Eurodollar deposits). Interest and repayment of principal would also be in dollars. What is interesting is that the lenders do not start with dollars but purchase them only to buy the bond, and the borrowers do not necessarily want dollars but will convert the dollars into whatever currency they happen to need. The dollar, in essence, becomes only a unit of account.

There are other varieties of Eurobonds besides straight Eurodollar bonds.

1. Bonds in other currencies, particularly the deutsche mark, and often the Canadian dollar. These developed as doubts about the dollar grew. Bonds issued in 1974 and 1975 by currency are shown in Table 5.1.

TABLE 5.1. EUROBONDS 1971-1975 BY CURRENCY OF ISSUE (in millions of dollars)

Currency	1971	1972	1973	1974	1975	Total In US$	In %
US$	$2,113	$2,993	$1,883	$857	$2,692	$10,538	56.0%
DM	805	1,177	958	221	1,596	4,758	25.3
C$	—	—	—	58	515	573	3.1
F Fr	47	466	152	—	239	904	4.8
Others	50	329	159	49	209	796	4.2
Currency cocktails	251	30	158	237	563	1,240	6.6

Source: Federation Bancaire. Taken from Hambersin, "The multinationals come to the cocktail party," p. 40.

2. Bonds in more than one currency. These "currency cocktail" bonds come in a variety of types. Some allow the bondholder to prescribe one of two currencies for payment of interest and repayment of principal—for example, sterling or German marks. Others work off averages of currency values. A few are even stated in terms of units of account no longer in existence (such as the 1971 Swiss franc), a practice common enough in the Renaissance, but rare since.

3. Convertible bonds. Used by American companies in the late 1960s, convertible bonds allowed bondholders to convert their holdings to common stock. These were supposedly a hedge against inflation and were popular for a while, but as the values of corporate shares failed to rise with inflation, enthusiasm for them waned.

The market has been a vigorous one. Table 5.2 shows the year-by-year sales of Eurobonds issued. Note how the market jumped in 1964, after the

TABLE 5.2. EUROBONDS—BY TOTAL VALUE (in millions of dollars)

Year	Total	Year	Total
1957	$ 25	1967	$2002
1958	49	1968	3518
1959	57	1969	3224
1960	15	1970	2770
1961	73	1971	3600
1962	26	1972	5495
1963	178	1973	3310
1964	739	1974	1423
1965	1064	1975	5814
1966	1139		

Sources: 1957-1972, Park, *The Euro-bond Market*, p. 12.
1973-1975, Michel Hambersin, "The multinationals come to the cocktail party," p. 40, in turn based on Federation Bancaire figures. There are slight discrepancies between the Park and Hambersin figures, but they are of little consequence.

interest equalization tax, and then sagged in 1974 with the removal of that tax. Nonetheless, the vigor of the market returned and as of 1979 it was extremely strong.

The Eurobond market is rather different from the American bond market. From the borrower's point of view it is not as good a market as New York. Interest rates are higher, as are the commissions charged by the underwriters (2.5 percent compared to 1.7 percent in New York).[11] The market is not regulated by any government and tends to be somewhat more wild and woolly than the American. Secondary (resale) markets, though much better developed today than in the 1960s, are thinner and much less efficient. Bonds are harder to resell than in the United States. Why, then, is the market used at all?

The Eurobond market has advantages as well as disadvantages. Not every borrower can borrow in New York at the prevailing New York rates. The borrower may not be well known; his or her credit rating may differ (European bankers look at a different set of criteria in assessing creditworthiness). The borrower may want to borrow more than could be placed by a single company in the New York market—for instance, in the financing of the trans-Alaska pipeline. In addition, the higher interest rates in the Eurobond market must be contrasted to the even higher interest rates and placement costs in national markets other than New York.

Beyond those reasons for avoiding New York are two more of importance to some buyers. The first is that American law requires borrowers to reveal far more information about their companies than many European companies like to reveal. Securities and Exchange Commission and state "blue sky" disclosure laws (as they are dubbed) are meant to protect the investor from the kinds of fraud that were perpetrated in the 1920s. Secondly, some nations that borrow on the Eurobond market are not on friendly terms with the United States.

Looking over the "tombstone advertisements" (see accompanying illustration), which announce the placement of bonds after they have been sold, one can pick out three major classes of borrowers: (1) governments (national, city, and provincial); (2) quasi governmental or semiautonomous governmental institutions like development banks, state-owned oil companies, and port authorities; and (3) private corporations, whether subsidiaries of American firms or foreign firms. Back in the early 1960s, the market was almost exclusively for the first two types of borrowers, but after United States balance of payments restrictions tightened, American subsidiaries began to enter the market, establishing it as viable for private corporations. Now there are many types of borrowers. The November 1976 issue of *Euromoney*, for example, contained announcements for Eurobonds of all types. Among many others were US$0.5 billion for Sohio/BP Trans Alaska Pipeline Capital, Inc., $200 million for a Czech government bank, $35 million for the Newfoundland Municipal Development Corporation, and $300 million for the Commonwealth of Australia. Although U.S. dollar issues predominated, there were a number of deutsche mark issues and one Canadian dollar issue.

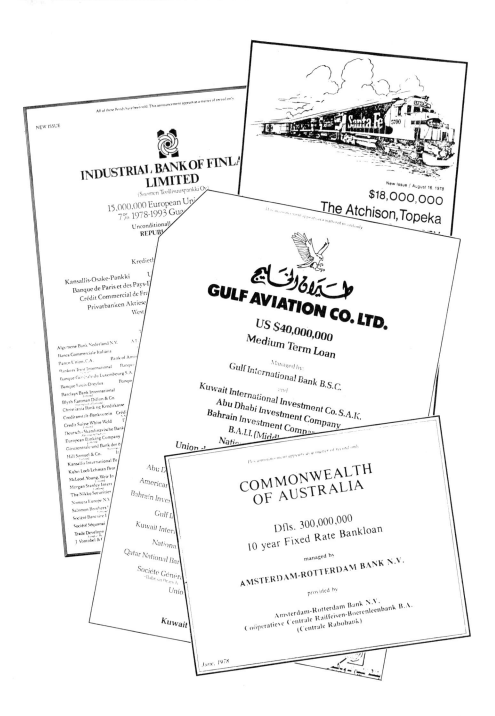

Buyers of Eurobonds are a more difficult group to track down. Formal announcements indicate only what banks or investment houses managed the issue and what institutions bought the bonds; these financial institutions then resell the bonds to private investors. The identity of the buyer may sometimes be deduced by looking at the advantages of the Eurobonds over bonds bought in the United States. Such advantages include the following: (1) Interest rates are higher (perhaps appropriately higher, given the greater risk and lower liquidity of the bonds). (2) The bonds allow investors to diversify their portfolios. (3) Payment on Eurobonds is to the "bearer," not to an identified and registered owner, as it is in the United States and Canada. (4) There is no withholding tax on interest paid to owners of Eurobonds. The attractions of higher interest rates and the ability to diversify portfolios are obvious. The "payment to bearer" feature is in line with European patterns and familiar to the typical European investor.

There is more to the purchase of Eurobonds, however. Both the "bearer" feature and the "no withholding tax" feature are very attractive to individuals who are either evading taxes or have some special tax considerations. They serve much the same purpose as a Swiss bank account—and they pay interest, while in recent years the Swiss have *charged* interest on foreign deposits. The bonds are held anonymously. All one need do is clip a coupon off and present it for payment, or direct one's banker to do so. Besides, if one is keeping money anonymously, it becomes very difficult to get back any withholding tax without sacrificing the anonymity—and more.

To illustrate this, take the hypothetical case of one Carlos Saco-Escondido, a wealthy Venezuelan with $10,000 interest from U. S. bonds. In Venezuela, he pays moderate taxes and is faced with the question of whether to declare the $10,000 U. S. income. If he so declares it, he figures his Venezuelan tax will rise by $3,500 (35 percent of the $10,000). Under international convention he can take off the U. S. tax as a credit to his Venezuelan taxes. Thus:

Venezuelan taxes on the newly declared $10,000	$3,500
Less: Credit for United States taxes paid	1,500
Additional taxes owed Venezuela	$2,000

Saco-Escondido decides that he will not mention the U.S. income, so he in essence "loses" the $1,500. Now if he had a Eurobond instead of a U.S. bond, he would not have to pay even the $1,500 tax. Hence the withholding tax is especially important if one intends to evade taxes, but of less significance if one plays it straight. Even then, there are circumstances where foreign withholding taxes cannot be claimed as tax credit—if an American uses the standard deduction method for figuring income taxes, for instance.[12]

Note that Eurobonds fall between national governmental restrictions. London does not care if Caracas gets its taxes from Sr. Saco-Escondido. Nor, since relatively few British residents will buy the bonds, will the interest accrue to British subjects—hence, London is not interested in withholding taxes. Besides, if it taxed Eurobond interest, then it would lose the Eurobond business. Neither Britain nor Venezuela cares if Saco is properly informed, so there are no disclosure rules. Lastly, the United States, whose currency is being used, has no say whatsoever in the matter, since everything is happening outside its territory. Hence, while it might be in the interest of all nations collectively to regulate and disclose information on Eurobonds, it is not in the interest of any one nation to act singly.

Medium-Term Facilities

The Euromarkets in their beginnings lacked good medium-term (three to seven years) credit facilities. Today, such facilities may be their strongest point.

Eurodollar loans were fine for short-term uses and bonds fine for the long term, but there was a tremendous demand for medium-term loans. The bankers solved this in two ways: (1) by developing a market for three- to seven-year notes, and (2) by organizing banking syndicates to spread the risk of any one large medium-term loan or line of credit. In October of 1976, for instance, in a typical operation, forty-one banks participated in a seven-year loan of $125 million to the Puerto Rican Development Bank. Such medium-term arrangements have become very important in recent years as sources of finance for governments with balance of payments difficulties.[13] During one month in 1976, as an example, various less developed countries were able to borrow well over $150 billion in medium-term facilities.[14]

The three market levels—short, medium, and long term—are interrelated. The tremendous pool of Eurodollars helps sales of both the long- and medium-term issues because lenders who lack the ready cash to purchase the long-term issues can themselves borrow short term in the Eurodollar market while they mobilize their funds. Indeed, the continued popularity of dollar bond issues can be at least partially explained by the ease of access to Eurodollars (whereas it would be more difficult to borrow Euromarks) to help finance a bond purchase or medium-term loan. There is also, of course, mediation among the three markets as investors shift from short to medium or long term and vice-versa.[15]

Significance of the Euromarkets

The Euromarkets serve the valuable function of uniting many small capital markets into one large one. They enable large amounts of capital to be mobilized quickly at reasonable rates, while providing savers of dollars with safety, liquidity, and a substantial return on their money. They provide a variety of lending and borrowing instruments ranging in maturities from money on demand to twenty-five-year bonds. Choice of markets is wide. For convenience in dealing with American banks and businesses, the Bahamas have rapidly developed as a center and there is a healthy "Asiadollar" market in Singapore. Those preferring to deal in nondollar currencies can search out the Euromark and Euro-Swiss-franc.

All this is a tribute to the substantial skill shown by businesspeople and bankers who succeeded in creating a wholly new set of institutions unknown to academic theory at the time of their creation. They thus avoided to a considerable degree the foreign exchange controls designed by government, managed to maintain a viable international capital market, and revitalized London as a center of international banking.[16] In the great oil crisis of 1973-1974, and in the years since, with the price of crude oil at least four times as high as it had been before the OPEC cartel, the Eurodollar markets were an enormous positive force in averting breakdown of the world's money markets. With dollars flooding into OPEC countries (the dollar being the chief means of payment for oil imports), there was the unprecedented danger of a deflationary impact unless these same dollars could be quickly recycled into the normal conduits of trade and investment. In actual fact many of the new oil earnings found their way into the Eurodollar market for both short- and long-term investment. Not very surprisingly, such funds were called "petrodollars." Without the ease and security of the Eurodollar, the story of the last three or four years would surely have been much more gloomy.

True, there are some inherent dangers. Eurodollars are subject to little central bank control. The vast sea of Eurodollar liquidity in banks abroad is a perfect medium for immense speculation if holders of Eurodollars ever decide to shift to another currency. Eurodollars are extremely sensitive to changes in interest rates. There is no lender of last resort in the market, no regulatory agency. Nor is there any central information source—banks are more in the dark about what other banks are doing than in a domestic money market, and there is the distinct possibility of becoming overcommitted to one country, or one borrower. If ever coordination and monitoring of the market comes about, it will surely have to come via international agreement and cooperation. The days when any one country could have exerted control over the market are now gone.

In conclusion, it is no longer possible to understand national monetary or balance of payments policy without a knowledge of Euromarkets. As Chapter 9 shows, the International Monetary Fund (IMF) was developed to provide international liquidity and for nearly two decades was the principal and often sole source of foreign exchange to nations seeking to defend their exchange rates. Today, however, the Euromarket can provide funds in amounts that dwarf anything the IMF itself can provide. And, not so incidentally, it can also provide funds for a run on a currency that can swamp any nation's foreign exchange reserves.

Notes

1. Before Euromarkets were developed, there were a few issues of "parallel bonds"—that is, bonds issued by one organization and sold simultaneously in several nations. These proved rather difficult to manage, and have not been issued in recent years.
2. This practice had been in suspension for a number of years after World War II, but it was restored by law in 1958 in Britain and several other European countries.
3. Note that the Eurodollar deposit is an alternative to a savings or a CD deposit and not an ordinary banking account. Writers have often spoken of a contrast between a United States reserve requirement of near 20 percent and the lack of any such requirement in Britain as being the source of the foreign advantage. That is erroneous as subsequent analysis shows.
4. The chronological developments were as follows:

   a) At the end of 1969 the Fed imposed new reserve requirements on Eurodollar borrowings by American banks. These were originally 10 percent of all borrowings (meaning that only 90 percent of what was borrowed could be lent), and later a marginal rate of 20 percent was put on borrowings over a base figure.

   b) In the middle of 1970, the Fed suspended Regulation Q as it applied to thirty- or ninety-day certificates of deposit of over $100,000.

   It is interesting to note that in explaining the reserve requirements, the Fed made the essentially erroneous comparison of Eurodollar deposits with demand, rather than time deposits mentioned in footnote 3.
5. Beirut was another new center until the Lebanese Civil War broke out in 1975.
6. The example is taken from the June 1969 issue of the *Business Review* of the Federal Reserve Bank of Chicago.
7. See John Hewson and Eisuke Sakakibara, "Eurodollar Deposit Multiplier: a portfolio approach." *IMF Staff Papers,* July 1975.
8. Leland Yeager quotes Dr. Stopper, president of the Swiss National Bank, as saying as early as March 1967 that "central banks ought to stay away from the Euromarket." Central banks "can hamper one another in their fight against inflation if they lend the dollars they have received to banks of other countries in the Euromarket." See Yeager's *International Monetary Relations* (New York: Harper & Row, 1976), p. 437. Incidentally, the Swiss Bank has been a leader in the campaign to stop dollars from flowing into Europe.
9. Yoon S. Park, *The Euro-bond Market* (New York: Praeger Publishers, 1974), p. 9.
10. Park, *The Euro-bond Market,* p. 12 (figures to 1972). Michel Hambersin, "The multinationals come to the cocktail party," *Euromoney* (July 1976), p. 40. Figures for 1972-76, "Dollars remain in favor," *Euromoney* (August 1976), p. 101, indicate that sales in the first half of 1976 were over $6.5 billion.

11. Park indicates the following costs:

Costs of Raising Capital for Corporate Bonds
(in percentage of face value of issue)

Country	Underwriting cost	Additional charges*
United States	1.7%	0.65%
United Kingdom	2.7	0.94
Germany	2.5	0.20
France	5.0	0.50
Switzerland	2.5	0.66
Netherlands	2.1	0.48
Eurobond market	2.5	0.02

*Subject to negotiation and depending on type of issue.

Source: OECD Committee for Invisible Transactions, *Capital Market Study, General Report* (Paris: Organization for Economic Cooperation and Development, 1967), p. 175. Taken from Park, *The Euro-bond Market,* p. 41.

12. One of the author's regrettable experiences.
13. Park, *The Euro-bond Market,* pp. 104-110 has a general discussion of the medium-term markets.
14. "Gloom just makes them lend faster," *Euromoney* (July 1976), pp. 108-110.
15. Clear lines between short, medium, and long are hard to define. A three-year loan backed by two or three banks borders on a regular Eurodollar, while a seven- or eight-year note borders on the Eurobond.
16. London has been buffeted, however, by the decline in the value of the pound sterling starting in 1975. Foreign banks based in London suffered serious capital losses in that year because their assets had to be written down in terms of the home currency. Accordingly, there was a sudden loss of enthusiasm for opening new branches in London, and more banks closed their British operations in 1975 than new ones opened. Meanwhile, the Eurodollar business of new centers such as Nassau in the Bahamas, the Cayman Islands in the Caribbean, and Singapore doubled approximately between 1973 and 1975. American banks in particular are opting for the convenience of the Bahamas and Grand Cayman. Whereas the overseas branches of U.S. banks held 66 percent of their assets in London in 1969, by the beginning of 1976 that figure was down to 43 percent and appears to be still falling. Many of these assets were deposited in the Bahamas and Grand Cayman, where overseas branches of U.S. banks held 26 percent of their assets at the start of 1976, a figure that has more recently climbed to over 30 percent.

PART II

MONETARY, FISCAL, AND EXCHANGE RATE POLICY

6

THE
BALANCE OF
PAYMENTS

Perhaps no area of international economics is more in the news or subject to more misunderstanding than what is called the balance of payments. The balance of payments statement is the principal statistical tool for assessing a country's international economic position. It is especially significant for countries employing fixed exchange rates or engaging in a substantial degree of dirty floating, because it allows governments to evaluate the impact of their economic policies and to change these policies if the evaluation proves displeasing. Given an attempt to maintain fixed rates, a balance of payments showing substantial money outflows will often lead governments to one or another of the numerous adjustments that might be made (these will be discussed in full in the next chapter). These adjustments may go beyond exchange rates and convertibility, extending to the management of domestic economic activity. So it is not only foreign exchange operations, but internal economic activity that is intimately related to interpretations of the balance of payments.

The Balance of Payments as a Record of Receipts and Expenditures

In many ways the balance of payments statements compiled by most countries are poor presentations of information. They are frequently faulty and controversial in design. Many countries have different ways of reporting the information, even though the IMF suggests a standard format. The United States in particular used a most baffling balance of payments account in the publications of the Department of Commerce and in the widely circulated *Federal Reserve Bulletin* until 1977, when it altered radically the presentation of its balance of payments material. The balance of payments account used in this chapter is constructed from the new reformed version, which is far simpler and more straightforward than the ones used in the past.[1]

The concept of a balance sheet that records the sum total of transactions between residents of a country and foreigners during the course of a year is an ancient one. As early as 1381, Englishman Richard Aylesbury had actually gone beyond the collection of such statistics and was advancing several points of analysis as to why the accounts behaved as they did. Basically, a balance of payments records or estimates in money terms (1) the sources of foreign exchange (that is, the manner in which purchasing power over foreign goods, services, and assets, is acquired); and (2) how this foreign exchange is disposed of through being spent, invested, or given away. The principles of the balance of payments accounts can perhaps be seen better in the accounting practices of a careful individual, a certain John Dough.

TABLE 6.1. PERSONAL ACCOUNT OF JOHN DOUGH (after taxes)

Item	Receipt	Payment
Salary	$10,000	
Dividends	350	
Interest	150	
Loan for car	500	
Cash from sale of bonds	1,000	
Personal consumption (not including car)		$7,500
New car (after trade-in)		2,500
Home improvement		1,000
Deposits into savings account		300
Gifts (Christmas, charities, etc.)		500
Net increase in checking account over last year		100
Net increase in cash carried in wallet over last year		50
Error		50
Totals	$12,000	$12,000

Table 6.1 above shows how John Dough draws up his annual balance sheet. As receipts, Dough lists all the sources of funds at his disposal during the year. This includes earnings for that year (salary, interest, dividends), the amount used from his savings accumulated in previous years, and any gifts or loans he received. (We will soon see that a nation similarly totals its receipts of foreign exchange by counting its earnings from exports of goods and services,

any loans made to it, any gifts, and the extent to which the monetary authorities have had to dig into past accumulations of gold, foreign exchange, etc., to finance an excess of spending over receipts.)

Mr. Dough knows that the payment column is there to explain what he did with the money he received. He attempts to explain the disposal of his income as consumption expenditures, gifts, long-term investments such as his savings account, and cash on hand. When the figures do not match up exactly with his income, he has to assume that there is an error somewhere and lists it as such.

A nation calculates its payments and receipts on exactly the same principles. It explains the disposal of income, indicating as best it can what money was spent on imported goods and services, what was used for gifts, and what was set aside for possible future use in the form of long- and short-term investments. The receipts must match the payments, since the payments only reflect the disposal of the receipts; thus if the collected statistics show receipts higher than payments or vice versa, then a term for error is added to the opposite column to make the figures come out even.

The concept of receipts and payments is closely related to the simple diagram of supply and demand for foreign exchange we first met in Chapter 2. "Receipts" in the balance of payments represent the dollar value of foreign exchange coming on the market to purchase dollars. The foreign exchange is supplied because foreigners want to purchase American exports, to invest in the United States, to speculate, and so on. Whatever the motive, the total foreign exchange brought to the market at various exchange rates was, in Chapter 2 and thereafter, shown as a supply curve (see Fig. 6.1). Similarly, "payments" in the balance of payments are the dollars brought to the market with which to purchase foreign currencies. Americans demand foreign exchange because they want to import, invest abroad, speculate, give foreign aid, and so on. Whatever the motive, the total foreign exchange demanded at various exchange rates can be shown as a demand curve (see Fig. 6.1).

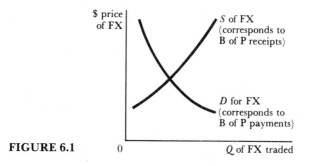

FIGURE 6.1

Actually, the information contained in an annual balance of payments account and that found on the quantity axis of Fig. 6.1 will not be identical. The balance of payments on many items represents *net* flows during the year, while the diagram conceptually seeks to measure all flows. For example, much of the money coming into the foreign exchange market is not counted in the balance of payments, in the sense that a good proportion of it involves loans that are repaid before the end of the year. What the balance of payments counts on many items is the *net* movement of capital in various categories, for example, the net value of portfolio investment made by Americans (new purchases of stock minus those sold off) or the net short-term credits for trade left at the end of the year. There is a second reason why the balance of payments is not identical to the supply and demand for foreign exchange. This involves several items that go into the payments balance but do not actually involve a cash flow. For example, just as John Dough's $500 car loan did not involve the turning over of cash to him, yet was considered a receipt, so are credits advanced for imports not yet paid for also considered receipts. Other items traditionally counted in the balance of payments but not involving actual cash flows are (1) exports shipped with no payment yet received (the export itself goes in as a receipt, while the credit extended to the buyer is considered a capital outflow, or payment); (2) foreign aid given in kind, for example, grain sent to India (the grain itself goes in as an export or receipt, while the value of the grain is counted as a gift, or payment); (3) barter deals, where both exports and imports result but no cash changes hands; and (4) defaults on payments.

The balance of payments is divided into several subaccounts, reflecting both the government's interest and the availability of statistics. The subaccounts deal principally with four areas: (1) trade in goods and services, (2) gifts, called unilateral transfers, (3) capital movements such as bank deposits and stocks and bonds, and (4) the monetary activities of central banks. Table 6.2 is constructed from the United States international accounts for 1975, following the methods suggested in the 1976 report of the president's advisory panel on the balance of payments. Each line is numbered separately and explained.

1. Exports of goods and services. This item includes not only *visibles*, or merchandise exports (1a), but also *invisible* exports, as they are called (1b). Invisibles include receipts for the rendering of business services such as transportation, communication and consultation, insurance, the royalties on films, books, or inventions, and the interest earned on money lent abroad. The expenditures by tourists visiting the United States are also considered an invisible export.

2. Imports of goods and services, including both visibles and invisibles (2a and 2b).

3. Merchandise trade balance (lines 1a + 2a). This figure is obtained by subtracting the dollar value of visible imports from the dollar value of visible exports. The merchandise trade figures are usually the first to be made available.

4. Balance on goods and services, or simply, "the balance of trade" (lines 1a + 1b + 2a + 2b). This figure is constantly in the news. Between 1893 and 1976 it has almost always shown a surplus in the American experience, with 1971 and 1972 the only exceptions, until recently.

The 1975 figure was the largest surplus in U.S. history, but by 1977-1978 deficits were appearing here. Note that exports and imports are only a subaccount of the overall balance of payments. They need not be equal, and hence one can properly speak of a balance of trade surplus or deficit. A trade imbalance is often confused with a balance of payments surplus or deficit. The latter, defined below, is a very different and more controversial concept.

5. Unilateral transfers (net). This figure includes pensions paid to people who have retired overseas, gifts by Americans to relatives or charities abroad, and any other private transfer to foreigners (all totaling −$1.7 billion in 1975), plus U.S. government foreign aid (−$2.9 billion in 1975).[2] The figures have been netted against the small flow of gifts and pensions paid from foreign countries to residents of the United States.

6. Balance on current account (lines 1a + 1b + 2a + 2b + 5). Here the transfers of line 5 are lumped in with the trade account to give the current account. In the current account, a nation's gifts to foreigners are subtracted from its balance of trade surplus or deficit. Frequently, the United States makes grants large enough to turn a balance of trade surplus into a current account deficit, although the trade surplus in 1975 was so very large that this did not happen.

The current account figure can be a particularly significant one. Consider John Dough: Perhaps he spends more than he earns, but he also inherits (a unilateral transfer) a goodly sum so that his "current account" balance is positive; he can still increase his investments (that is, his claims on others) despite the fact that he did not earn what he spent. Similarly, a developing nation that has a goods and services deficit, but a larger inflow of aid grants, may increase its claims on the rest of the world (or reduce its net indebtedness) despite the trade deficit. In the opposite situation, a nation with a surplus trade balance may give away so much through aid that it must increase its net indebtedness. Many of the Arab oil producers in the late 1970s purposely increased aid to keep their current account balances from rising even more than they did.

7. Private capital payments.[3] As seen in the table, this item is a large one covering several different types of transactions. An outflow of funds to foreign countries is generated by purchases of foreign stock, private or government bonds (portfolio investment, line 7a), and the direct acquisition of companies or property abroad (direct investment, line 7b). Or outflows can result when American banks loan to foreigners, when businesses make credit advances abroad to finance U.S. exports, or when dollar accounts in U.S. banks are converted by their holders into foreign currency accounts in foreign banks (line 7c). When the credit advance or maturity of the deposit in line 7c is for one year or longer, the movement is called long-term; less than that is a short-term movement. It is in this area of private capital payments that outflows of hot money used to be detected when there was a danger of dollar devaluation under fixed exchange rates. Such movements are also sensitive to interest rate differences between countries. All other things being equal, higher interest rates in one country than in another will attract funds from the latter to the former.

8. Private capital receipts. This is the counterpart of American investment abroad. It represents foreign purchases of American stocks and bonds (line 8a), foreign direct investment in the United States (8b), and loans from foreign banks to Americans, business credits made to Americans, and increases in bank deposits held by foreigners in the United States (8c). The United States has never attempted to control inflows of this type, but the actions taken by Switzerland, the Netherlands, West Germany, and Japan to lower inflows into those countries have been stringent (see Chapter 7).

9. Changes in official United States government reserve assets. Official reserve assets are defined as gold (now, we recall, called a "secondary asset"), SDRs (a new form of reserve allocated by the IMF and discussed at length in Chapter 9), the U. S. reserve position in the IMF, and U. S. holdings of foreign exchange reserves. Any one of these could be utilized by the U.S. government when confronted with dollars held by foreign central banks in excess of their requirements, or added to when foreigners wish to acquire additional dollars. Gold (9a) is now almost never used, and the U.S. gold stock of $11.6 billion has been unchanged since August 1975, except for an obscure outpayment of $1 million in April 1976. The U.S. gold stock in 1976 was less than 25 percent of the estimated world total held by other governments, which was then $49.5 billion. (The United States used to hold far more than one-half of the world's official gold—its stocks reached a high of $24 billion in the early 1950s and were still at $22.9 billion in 1957. But the various gold crises depleted the stock through the 1960s.) The world's second largest holder of gold is West Germany, with nearly $5 billion worth. Incidentally, much of the gold belonging to other countries (approximately $16.5 billion in 1976) is actually held in New York City, in the basement of the Federal Reserve Bank of New York, with the bank acting as custodian for the foreign governments. Such "earmarked gold" did not have to be transported abroad when the United States paid it out in exchange for surplus dollars. There was thus a substantial saving in transport costs.

TABLE 6.2. U.S. BALANCE OF PAYMENTS, 1975 (in billions of dollars)[*]

	Transaction	Receipt	(+)	Payment	(−)
1. a)	Merchandise exports		$107.1		
b)	Invisible exports		40.9		
2. a)	Merchandise imports				$98.1
b)	Invisible imports				33.6
3.	Merchandise trade balance				
	(1a + 2a)		9.0		
4.	Balance on goods and services				
	(1a + 1b + 2a + 2b)		16.3		
5.	Unilateral transfers, net				4.6
6.	Balance on current account				
	(1a + 1b + 2a + 2b + 5)		11.7		
7.	Private capital payments				29.3
	a) Portfolio investment			$ 6.2	
	b) Direct investment			6.3	
	c) Bank and non-bank claims			16.7	
8.	Private capital receipts		8.4		
	a) Portfolio investment	$5.2			
	b) Direct investment	2.4			
	c) Bank and non-bank claims	0.8			
† 9.	Changes in official U.S.				
	government reserve assets				0.6
	a) Gold			0	
	b) SDRs			0.1	
	c) Reserve position in IMF			0.5	
	d) Foreign currencies			0.1	
†10.	Changes in foreign official				
	assets in the U.S.		5.2		
	a) U.S. treasury securities	4.3			
	b) Other U.S. government				
	bonds and obligations	3.0			
	c) Bank deposits	−2.2			
11.	Discrepancy (errors, omissions)		4.6		

BALANCE OF PAYMENTS = 0
(6 + 7 + 8 + 9 + 10 + 11)

*In some cases totals and subtotals do not tally exactly due to rounding.
†These are the balancing items in the official settlements version of the balance of payments (see Table 6.3).

The next item, SDRs (9b), may also be paid out in exchange for surplus dollars presented by foreign governments. The IMF allocated to the United States $867 million on January 1, 1970, $717 million the next year, and $710 million on January 1, 1972, making $2.3 billion out of a total world issuance of $9.4 billion. Loans from the IMF can similarly be used in exchange for surplus dollars, and item 9c represents changes in the U.S. reserve position in the IMF. Finally (9d), we have changes in U.S. holdings of convertible foreign currencies. Such holdings usually comprise a quantity of German marks, Swiss francs, Canadian dollars, and the like, often employed on a small scale in day-to-day efforts to iron out what the government believes to be erratic fluctuations in an otherwise floating rate.

Since the advent of floating rates, the active use of U.S. government official reserves has declined enormously. Instead of using its reserves to defend a rate, as, say, in 1970 ($3.3 billion) or 1971 ($2.3 billion), the predilection now is simply to let the rate fall (or rise) in a floating market without intervention. Thus in the first year of floating rates, 1973, losses of official reserves were very small, only $209 million, and there have been no outflows since, with the United States actually gaining a small amount of official reserves in 1974, 1975, 1976, and 1977.

10. Changes in foreign official assets in the United States. These are dollars held by foreign central banks and other official agencies. Foreign citizens (exporters to the United States, recipients of U.S. dividend income, hotel-keepers, and the like) who find themselves holding more dollars than they want to keep in a given year will exchange these dollars for other currencies. A foreign central bank might decide simply to let the dollar depreciate against its own currency as a result of these sales. But in a world of fixed rates or dirty floating, these banks might step in to buy dollars with their own currency. This may well succeed in keeping the exchange rate in some desired range, but it also means that the country involved must add to its holdings of dollars. These dollars may be held as U.S. Treasury securities (10a), as other U.S. government bonds and obligations (10b), or in the form of bank deposits in the United States (10c).

The size of item 10—it was over $37 billion in 1977, for example—mirrors a great many concerns. Countries have been willing to accumulate dollars for a mixture of reasons, including the acquisition of reserves to support dirty floating or fixed rates mentioned above. Germany keeps most of its large quantity of reserves in dollars, for example. Oil-exporting nations have been willing to accumulate large holdings also. Smaller countries often fix their rate against the dollar and defend the rate with their dollar reserves. Thus it is that the quantity of dollars held as a reserve currency by other countries was less than $10 billion in 1949, was still under $20 billion in 1962, but was over $100 billion by 1974. Some countries, particularly France, have resented the fact that foreigners have been willing to hold dollars as part of their foreign exchange reserves, thus allowing the United States to buy more abroad than it sells. Historically, only Great Britain's pound has also served as a major reserve, although at the start of 1977, official holdings of the pound sterling were below £3 billion.[4] Nowadays small amounts of German marks, Swiss francs, Japanese yen, and a few others are commonly held as reserves by numerous countries alongside the much larger quantity of dollars.

The placement of items 9 (changes in official U.S. government reserve assets) and 10 (changes in foreign official assets in the United States) in the plus or minus columns sometimes confuses people. For example, in item 9, when the United States sopped up excess dollars by (1) dipping into its gold reserves, (2) spending some of its SDRs, (3) drawing on its account with the IMF, or (4) spending some of its accumulated holdings of foreign exchange, in every case these are recorded as receipts (+) in the balance of payments. Some people are baffled by the thought that when America's gold stock goes down, or when it takes out a loan, these are considered a receipt. However, it is quite logical. Remember that when John Dough got cash by selling bonds, or took out a loan for a new car, he considered these as receipts in his personal account. Similarly in the balance of payments. You might think of it as an export of gold, SDRs, or foreign banknotes. As for item 10, that too is logical enough. Just think of it as an American export of dollar bills (or dollar checking accounts) that for some reason foreigners are willing to retain. An export of merchandise is a plus in the balance; so is an export of paper money.

   11. Discrepancy (also called errors and omissions). After completing the 1975 balance of payments, the statisticians discovered that they had calculated U.S. payments (−) to be $4.6 billion more than receipts (+). Since disposal of receipts (payments) has to equal the receipts themselves, the statisticians had to assume that somehow the United States had received another $4.6 billion that they could not locate, and they put in an error term of $4.6 billion.

Concepts of Balance of Payments Surpluses and Deficits

The balance of payments by its very nature must show receipts equaling payments. Why, then, is there so much discussion of balance of payments surpluses and deficits? The question is more than rhetorical because the rather elusive concepts used in the past have complicated the presentation of payments statistics and have led to considerable confusion.

   A surplus or deficit is a statistical creation. It is created by removing one or more items from the receipts or payments side and then calculating the balance from there. The items removed are then added to or subtracted from the payments *after* the surplus or deficit has been figured. John Dough, for instance, could create for himself a personal balance of payments deficit by removing from his receipts the amount he obtained from digging into his bondholdings. He might represent his situation, taken from Table 6.1, as follows in Table 6.3.

   Such an account shows clearly the amount by which Mr. Dough dipped into his bondholdings. The clarity is achieved by dividing the account into a "regular" section and balancing section—often called "above the line" and "below the line." Actually that could have been found in the old account (Table 6.1) without resorting to any separate statistic, and in fact the whole idea of a balance of payments surplus or deficit suffers from just this problem of obscuring what might otherwise be just as clear.

TABLE 6.3. JOHN DOUGH'S DEFICIT I

Item	Receipt	Payment
Salary	$10,000	
Other receipts	1,000	
Personal consumption		$7,500
Other payments		4,500
Totals	$11,000	$12,000
DEFICIT	−$1,000	
	Balancing Items	
Cash from sale of bonds	+$1,000	

Suppose, however, that Mr. Dough has a more complicated task in mind. He may want to determine exactly by how much he went into debt or reduced his savings during the year. His account might then appear as in Table 6.4, which gives him the news that his savings/borrowing situation was $50 worse during the year.

Actually, John Dough can juggle his account almost any way he desires, emphasizing some item or group of items by putting them below the line. In short, Dough's deficit is anything he makes it out to be.

A nation's balance of payments accounting is similar to John Dough's. The balance of payments is equal to zero, except that a surplus or deficit can be created by removing certain items from the regular account and treating them as balancing items. It shows what the statisticians make it show. As in the case of Mr. Dough, it often makes quite a lot more sense to leave all the items in the regular account ("above the line") and make the comparisons there, but there is a long tradition of seeking to define deficits and surpluses, and whether we like it or not, the government and the press refer to deficits and surpluses quite often.

The Balance of Payments on Official Reserve Transactions and the Liquidity Balance. In the old days, a balance of payments deficit meant a loss of gold, and a surplus meant an increase in gold holdings, so gold was entered as the "balancing item." Then, as monetary authorities came to hold foreign currency assets and to have accounts at the IMF, there had to be a way to handle these new assets. Consequently not only gold, but other holdings of the monetary authorities, were moved into the balancing section. There was still not complete satisfaction, however, because many foreign central banks accumulated substantial dollar and sterling holdings that they did not turn in for gold. (Indeed, the usual situation was that they *could* not turn them in because there was not enough gold available to make the exchange.) Calculating that dollars and pounds were held abroad at least to some extent as a substitute for turning them in to the United States or Great Britain for gold, the statisticians decided to consider all of these holdings as balancing items. When all such

TABLE 6.4. BALANCING ITEMS

Item	Receipt	Payment
Cash from sale of bonds	$1,000	
Loan for car	500	
Home improvement		$1,000
Net increase in checking account		100
Net increase in cash		50
Deposits in savings account		300
Totals	$1,500	$1,450
NET BALANCING ITEMS		+50

items involving monetary authorities are removed from the regular account, one creates a "balance of payments on an official reserves basis." The reader can see the result in the 1975 balance of payments (Table 6.2) by removing the items marked with an asterisk and putting them below the line. The official settlements deficit in that year was $4.6 billion, and it was "settled" by foreign governments holding 5.2 billion more dollars than before at the same time that the United States accumulated $0.6 billion in reserve assets.

For a decade following the publication in April 1965 of the Bernstein report, named for Professor E. M. Bernstein, the official settlements version was the standard one used by the U.S. Department of Commerce, which compiles the statistics. Another version, however, called the balance of payments on a liquidity basis (or liquidity balance for short), was always published side by side with it, and indeed was published regularly *before* 1965. In the liquidity balance, all highly liquid capital inflows to the United States (short-term notes, currency holdings, bank deposits, and so on) were removed from the regular account and put below the line along with changes in official reserves. This reflected the idea, or really the fear, that such inflows are temporary, likely to be reversed, and potentially a threat to the dollar in that foreign holders of these new claims might transfer them out of the country again. (For example, $8.8 billion in short-term capital flowed into the United States in 1969 when interest rates were high, and $6.2 billion flowed out again when interest rates went down the next year.)[5] Consequently, the highly liquid investments in the United States by foreigners were removed and put below the line along with the monetary items that received similar treatment under the official reserves basis.

Note that these two concepts of deficit and surplus were quite different and were designed to emphasize different aspects. For example, in 1969 the official reserves account was in strong surplus (+$2.7 billion) while the liquidity balance showed a large deficit (−$7 billion). The reason was that there was a heavy inflow of liquid foreign assets into the United States. The United States bought foreign currencies with dollars, which ended up being held by foreign central banks and swelled the official settlements surplus. But that selfsame inflow of liquid short-term capital was pulled out of the regular accounts and counted below the line in the liquidity balance version, creating a large deficit. Similarly, in 1974 the official settlements deficit was a large −$8.4 billion, but still less than half the huge liquidity deficit of −$18.9 billion. The cause was identical—short-term capital inflows had purposefully been put below the line as a balancing item, and as they were large in that year, the deficit was correspondingly large.

The liquidity version of the balance of payments was always subject to much criticism. Some writers played down the issue by pointing out that the liquidity problem was largely an inherent one. Any nation having a large and liquid capital market will tend to garner short-term deposits and lend long; this, after all, is a major function of any banking center. Europeans, Japanese, OPEC countries with large oil revenues, all lacking a capital market of sufficient size, naturally invest in the United States (or Britain to some extent) and come there for borrowing, whether directly or through the Eurodollar markets. By such analysis, the United States can almost always expect to have a liquidity balance of payments deficit, and its main problem then is to avoid a "run on the bank." Indeed, banks face the same problem, but it is seldom a very serious one. For hundreds of years banks have realized that they can normally borrow short (from their depositors) and lend long to their customers, keeping only a fraction of the deposits in cash or reserves. They do this safely because it is most unlikely that all claims on the bank will ever be cashed in all at once. The same thing is true for the United States.

A further objection to the liquidity balance idea is that the real concern ought to be for "hot money"—money that could move out of the United States in, say, seven days or less. By no means are all short-term deposits "hot" under such a definition. Some will stay in the United States because their owners, though foreign, need them there or are slow in getting them out. More critical by far is that much "hot money" is not owned by foreigners at all—for example, General Motors can get its dollars exchanged into foreign currency and transferred out of this country faster than can many foreign companies. If the American position were ever so weak that foreigners were shifting their deposits out of the country wholesale, Americans would be right in there with them. Thus the changes in the level of *foreign* short-term claims seem to have no especially important meaning.

Finally, a last objection to the liquidity deficit—and indeed to any concept of deficit in the balance of payments—is that it compares objects that are not the same. Losses of gold or U.S. government expenditures of foreign currency may closely resemble each other, but they are not really equivalent to a liquid inflow of capital or even to a purchase of a U.S. Treasury bill by a foreign central bank that may just want the interest on it. A single deficit figure can thus tend to obscure rather than highlight some possibly very important distinctions. Calling apples and oranges "fruit" when detail is desired may be no help at all.

The 1976 Reform of the Balance of Payments.[6]   After eleven years of publishing the liquidity balance and the official settlements balance side by side, the U.S. Department of Commerce in May 1976 accepted a presidential advisory panel's recommendation that it drastically alter the presentation of this country's international accounts.[7] It seems only yesterday that news of a worsening deficit was a headline that caught the attention of the whole world. Now, however, the new version of the U. S. balance of payments does not show any overall deficit or surplus at all. As in Table 6.2, all the entries are above the line. It is still proper to discuss deficits and surpluses, but only in the subaccounts such as the balance of trade, or the balance on current account. Floating rates will not necessarily make these subaccounts equal, and attention will continue to be directed to them.

The main reason for the 1976 reform, beyond ending the confusion already mentioned, was that the very concept of a balance of payments surplus or deficit has been altered by the move to floating rates. From 1973 the dollar was free to rise or fall against other currencies. The balance of payments (official settlements version) can still be in temporary surplus or deficit, of course, because capital still follows high interest rates, rates of inflation differ, and tastes for imported goods change, among other factors. But now, under floating rates, rather than spending reserves to maintain the old rate and finding that these are equal to the balance of payments deficit, the floating rates make the adjustment, rising or falling as required until the supply and demand for foreign exchange approach equality. As floating rates work to eliminate surpluses or deficits, they thereby work to reduce the usefulness of the traditional measures.[8] Both the liquidity balance and the official reserves (especially the latter, which did so explicitly) measured the degree of government intervention to maintain the exchange rate. Now that this is not done (or is done only from time to time, as in the case of dirty floating), there seems no reason to publish a relatively meaningless figure for surplus or deficit. The wonder is not that reform was undertaken, but that the old measures continued to be put forward for nearly three years after their *raison d'être* was lost. For the United States at any rate, the reform makes life far easier for students and professors of international economics, and within a few years only the economic historians will have to deal with the ins and outs of the old balance of payments concepts. And high time too!

For the country that still fixes its rates to the American dollar, such as Guatemala or the Bahamas, or engages heavily in dirty floating, such as the members of the EMU snake, the old concepts of surplus and deficit have some lingering usefulness. These countries may still want to know at a glance what proportion of their central bank's reserves have been committed during the last few weeks or months in defense of a fixed rate. With all the confusion that surrounds this topic, however, the authors have a simple suggestion. Even for countries that are fixing their rates it seems simpler, less confusing, and eminently more sensible to follow the new trend of publishing a balance of payments that puts everything above the line as in Table 6.2 and allows the reader to search out and identify the items of consequence for the moment.

How Accurate Are Balance of Payments Figures?

As the reader may suspect, the balance of payments is not a highly accurate set of numbers. Many figures are by their very nature estimates. The expenditures of tourists are a case in point. The U. S. government cannot go around following all American tourists abroad and all foreign tourists in the United States to see what they spend. Half the time even the tourists themselves would not know. Even trade figures, which are generally among the most reliable, are often overstated or understated by importers or exporters. A firm may, for instance, seek to avoid high tariffs or seek to depress profits in a subsidiary and raise them in the parent for tax purposes. Smuggling, both in and out, can be a major problem for the statistics of some nations. Burma, for instance, whose high tariffs, export taxes, and price controls, combined with a border leaky as a sieve and in considerable part controlled by rebel armies, cannot have much of an idea at all about some of its main exports (opium and gems in particular) and its imports of consumer goods. More routine trade problems involve also the problem of commodities sold on consignment, where the goods have been exported but the price not decided upon by year's end. The beginner may be a little shocked to find that even with good bureaucracies, there are problems. For a pertinent example, note that American figures for "exports to Britain" often do not match very closely the British figures for "imports from the United States."

When one comes to capital flows, where misreporting is common and evasion easy, the problems are even greater. The U.S. balance of payments discrepancy figure, for instance, behaves very much like the short-term capital figure, shrinking dramatically when short-term capital is flowing in and swelling when the capital flows out. The large positive error in the U.S. account in 1975 was probably caused by money transferred into the United States in violation of various foreign governments' exchange control, plus amounts that simply were not caught in the statistics. When there is a "hot money" flow out of the United States, some of it will appear in the short-term capital account, but much also appears in the discrepancy account as well.

Other Nations' Balances of Payments

Most nations other than the United States keep payments accounts generally similar to the revised American ones. To give the reader further perspective and to demonstrate the use of payments figures, we examine briefly two rather different balance of payments situations: one in Canada and another in a developing nation, Thailand.

The Canadian Account. In the three years shown in Table 6.5 we see some patterns that are consistent with Canada's experience in the last decade.

1. The Canadian balance of payments account for the years 1973 through 1975 shows a typical Canadian pattern of a consistently negative balance on "nonmerchandise trade" (reflecting principally Canadian foreign travel and payments on capital and technology brought from abroad), and a more volatile merchandise trade. If the merchandise trade can generate enough of a surplus to cover the nonmerchandise deficit, as it did in 1973, the overall balance on goods and services is positive. In 1974 and 1975, however, that balance was negative.

TABLE 6.5. THE CANADIAN BALANCE OF PAYMENTS, 1973-1975 (in millions of Canadian dollars)

	1973	1974	1975
Merchandise Trade Balance	$ 2,735	$ 1,698	$ −639
Merchandise Exports	(25,461)	(32,591)	(33,347)
Merchandise Imports	(22,726)	(30,893)	(33,986)
Balance on Nonmerchandise Trade	−2,639	−3,190	−4,326
Balance on Goods and Services (with United States)	96 (−831)	−1,492 (−1,516)	−4,965 (−4,667)
Balance on capital movements (Net short term) (Net long term)	−563 (−948) (385)	1,516 (414) (1,102)	4,561 (639) (3,922)
Overall balance	−467	24	−404
Monetary movements (change in Canadian government reserve assets)	467	−24	404

2. Canada as a whole is a net importer of long-term capital—and payments for that capital were reflected in the negative nonmerchandise trade account. Short-term capital, however, can move either way. In 1973 it left Canada; in 1974 and 1975 it flowed back in.

3. In 1973 the balance on goods and services was positive, but the capital account deficit, reflecting the outflow of short-term funds, overwhelmed that surplus. As a result the Bank of Canada spent some $467 million to make up the difference. In 1974, the capital inflow was positive, just overcoming the deficit on goods and services. This allowed the Bank of Canada to recover some $24 million of its 1973 expenditures. In 1975, however, the capital account surplus could not cover the large current trade account deficit and the Bank of Canada again made up the difference.[9]

4. Canada also has had an interest in its special problems with the United States, so it keeps separate track of that particular balance.

5. Last, note that Canada is not interested in stating a figure for a balance of payments deficit. The information is there, should the reader care to compute one. Canada is also not a nation whose currency is used as a reserve by other nations so it has no cause to keep track of foreign official holdings of Canadian dollars.

The Thai Balance of Payments. Thailand's balance of payments shown in abbreviated form in Table 6.6 shows a pattern of consistent borrowing of long-term funds to finance trade deficits. Or, to put this process in a more favorable light, it shows a pattern of using the proceeds of its borrowing to bring additional goods and services into the country.

TABLE 6.6. THAILAND'S BALANCE OF PAYMENTS, 1975-1976 (in millions of baht)

Balance on merchandise trade	−20,161.2	−12,990.0
Merchandise exports	(44,364.5)	(58,250.0)
Merchandise imports	(−64,525.7)	(−71,240.0)
Balance on nonmerchandise trade	6,160.8	2,511.4
Balance on goods and services	−14,000.4	−10,478.6
Unilateral transfers	1,362.1	516.8
Balance on current account	−12,368.3	−9,961.8
Balance on capital movements	7,754.7	9,792.6
Net short term	—	(5,529.3)
Net long term	—	(4,533.3)
Errors and omissions	1,755.6	86.4
Overall balance	−2,858.0	82.5
Monetary movements (change in Thai government reserve assets)	2,858.0	82.5

The Thai payments show the method of covering a trade deficit—how much came through gifts, and through long-term and short-term borrowing. In the two years shown in Table 6.6, we see several patterns that are consistent with Thailand's experience in preceding years also.

1. The deficit on merchandise trade is reduced considerably by a surplus on nonmerchandise trade. Thus when politicians or newspapers complain of the "trade deficit," it is quite important to know if they are referring to the balance on merchandise trade or the balance on goods and services. (Behind the scenes, one finds the principal items of invisible trade to be foreign travel in Thailand, investment income from abroad, and military services provided for other governments.)

2. The deficit was further overcome by gifts from abroad, such that the amounts of deficit that had to be financed were considerably less than the balance on goods and services. Hence the importance of the balance on current account concept.

3. The remaining fairly substantial deficit was covered largely by long-term capital inflows. (More detailed statistics showed these to be substantial loans to the government from private parties, many secured in the Eurocurrency markets; some lending to private corporations; and direct investment.)

4. In common with many other nations, many money flows were untraceable, leading to substantial errors and omissions. In Thailand's case, the errors almost always serve to improve that balance of payments situation. The large amount of untraceable inflows are at least in part due to illegal exports of opium and heroin.

5. The final balance was settled by monetary authorities, who were forced to spend some 2,858 million baht in 1975 and 82.5 million baht in 1976. Hence, what seemed at first glance to be a massive trade deficit on the merchandise goods account eventually made rather modest demands on Thailand's central bank.

Conclusion

Balance of payments concepts, while not particularly difficult in themselves, require precision in their use—a precision frequently ignored in the media and in the political forum. Headlines reading "Trade Deficit Highest in History," or fifteen-second radio notices that "the nation sustained a payments deficit for the third successive quarter" are virtually meaningless. Is it a deficit on merchandise trade? Merchandise and nonmerchandise trade? The current account? As both the U.S. and Thai balance of payments show clearly, these are very different figures. Besides, the important thing with a trade deficit is to know how it is financed—long-term borrowings, short-term borrowings, or monetary expenditures. As we saw, too, from the U. S. account, it is possible to have a large surplus on goods and services and still have to rely on expenditures of monetary authorities to balance the account.

As we shall see in the ensuing two chapters, governments must assess carefully their balance of payments figures to determine if there is a problem: too high a trade surplus (which, as we shall see can be a very serious problem); or too great a trade deficit; too risky a form of financing deficits or of financing foreign investments; and a number of other problems. Once having made this assessment, governments can decide on appropriate policies. What those policies may be and their possible effects will be discussed in the following two chapters.

Notes

1. A good description drawn on in this chapter is Norman S. Fieleke, *What Is the Balance of Payments?* Federal Reserve Bank of Boston Research Department Special Study, July 1976.
2. The figure for U.S. government foreign aid excludes military transactions. These are included as regular exports and imports in lines 1 and 2.
3. Small amounts of U.S. government capital payments not involving the "official reserve assets" described below are included in this item. In 1975 the amount involved was $1.7 billion.
4. In 1968, pounds sterling made up 17 percent of total world reserves. Today (1977) the figure is just 2½ percent. Official holdings of pounds declined from £5 billion in March 1975 to £2.8 billion in January 1977.
5. The massive inflows of short-term capital in 1969 largely represented Eurodollar borrowing by U.S. banks from their foreign branches. Such borrowing showed up below the line, as a short-term capital receipt from foreigners, in the liquidity version of the balance of payments. Thus the huge deficit. But, as private capital movements and not official changes in reserves, they were above the line in the official settlements version and contributed to the large balance of payments surplus in that form of accounting. The chief result was confusion, largely unjustifiable in the authors' opinion.
6. See the summary article by Janice M. Westerfield, "A Lower Profile for the U.S. Balance of Payments," *Business Review* (November/December 1976), pp. 11-17.
7. "Report of the Advisory Committee on the Presentation of Balance of Payments Statistics," *Statistical Reporter*, 76 (1976), pp. 221-238.
8. Westerfield, "A Lower Profile for the U.S. Balance of Payments," p. 14.
9. The Canadian dollar was floating in this period. The effect of the government's intervention was to moderate its movements, but not to keep it within predetermined boundaries.

7

MONETARY AND FISCAL POLICY IN AN INTERNATIONAL SETTING

The examination of international aspects of monetary and fiscal policy requires some elaboration of models developed in the principles texts, which frequently ignore international repercussions in their discussion. In the United States, imports account for less than 10 percent of American expenditure, and exports for less than 10 percent of earnings, so the omission is perhaps understandable. In other nations it is difficult to be quite so cavalier about trade. Some small industrial nations spend half of their national income on imports and earn half of it from exports, as shown in Table 7.1.[1] This means that trade has a much greater impact on the national economy. A 10 percent change in U.S. export earnings, for instance, amounts to about 1 percent of U. S. national income, while for the Netherlands this figure would be 5 percent, having far more serious consequences for earnings and expenditures.

Although the United States is unusual among industrial nations for the rather small percentage of its national income involved in trade, that figure alone is quite large in relation to world trade. U.S. trade amounts to 13 percent of the world total, so small changes in American trade may have larger effects abroad. Prime Minister Pierre Trudeau of Canada has compared his country's dependence on the U.S. economy to sleeping with an elephant— every cough, every slight movement, inconsequential as it may be to the behemoth, has major effects on its bedfellow.

In the monetary area, too, the United States is not strongly affected by the inflows and outflows of funds involved with foreign transactions. With a money supply of well over $300 billion and over $19 billion in reserves, in-flows and outflows of a few billion dollars are rarely any problem for Ameri-can monetary authorities. With most other countries, however, international currency flows form a much larger proportion of their total bank reserves, and the difficulties of handling the ebb and flow of international currency movements are much greater. It is to this monetary topic that we first turn.

TABLE 7.1.

Country	Percentage of national income spent on imports
Belgium	50%
Norway	50
Denmark	43
Sweden	37
South Africa	35
Italy	33
Great Britain	30
West Germany	29
Canada	29
Venezuela	29
Philippines	29
France	28
Thailand	26
Japan	20
Peru	16
Brazil	10
United States	9
India	4

Source: *International Financial Statistics*, November 1976.

Monetary Effects of Trade and Foreign Investment

Chapter 2 left the monetary authorities in a position to buy or sell foreign currency. Under fixed or controlled rates, these purchases or sales of foreign exchange can have important monetary effects. Consider the case where there is an inflow of foreign funds due either to foreign investment or to a surplus of exports over imports. The upward pressure on the nation's cur-rency causes the monetary authorities to intervene and purchase foreign cur-rency, as in Chapter 2. This has the effect of increasing reserves; in turn, it ordinarily also increases the money supply.

To see how the inflow of funds increases the money supply it is necessary to observe a typical transaction such as the one in Chapter 2, where the Fed-eral Reserve Bank of New York is buying sterling (and selling dollars) in an attempt to keep the dollar from appreciating against the pound. A side effect of this action is that the Fed has created new reserves for the U.S. banking system. Assuming an exchange rate of £1 = $2, step 1 in Fig. 7.1 shows the New York Fed buying £10,000 from the Chase Manhattan Bank, Chase Manhattan having held the pounds in its London branch. The New York Fed pays for the £10,000 in step 2 by crediting $20,000 to the reserve account of the Chase Manhattan Bank.

The upshot is that a private bank exchanges pounds sterling, on which it can make no loans in the United States, for dollar reserves on which it *can* lend money. Moreover, following the logic of multiple expansion—the manner in which the banking system creates new money—these additional reserves can support perhaps five to seven times their original value. According to standard economic analysis, an increase in bank reserves will indeed ordinarily lead to increased lending by banks. Interest rates will tend to decline and banks will permit loans they previously had denied. Economists recognize that in depressed periods, businesspeople and consumers may be unwilling to borrow and banks may be unwilling to loan, with the result that new reserves will not increase the money supply. Normally, however, such expansion does take place following the inflow of foreign funds. When the money supply expands, economic theory predicts a resulting rise in investment and consumption (an upward shift in the schedules for investment and consumption), with this new spending made more significant by the multiplier effect.

New York Federal Reserve

Assets	Liabilities
① Account at Bank of England +$20,000 (= £10,000)	Reserve account of ② Chase Manhattan +$20,000

Chase Manhattan Bank

Assets	Liabilities
② Reserves at New York Fed +$20,000	± 0
① Account at London branch −$20,000 (= £10,000)	

FIGURE 7.1

Unless a monetary expansion is desired, the United States normally copes with these effects by selling an equivalent amount of U.S. Treasury bills on the open market. Such open market operations have the effect of removing from the banks the new reserves just created. The process is shown in Fig. 7.2.

where $20,000 worth of reserves is destroyed. It is assumed here that Chase Manhattan itself buys the bills but in actuality it is only necessary for some bank or depositor to buy them for the excess reserves to be extinguished.

New York Federal Reserve

Assets	Liabilities
U.S. Treasury bills −$20,000	Reserve account of Chase Manhattan −$20,000

Chase Manhattan Bank

Assets	Liabilities
Reserves at New York Fed −$20,000	± 0

FIGURE 7.2

The United States can successfully control the monetary inflows or outflows through the Treasury bill market, but American conditions are quite special because inflows of foreign exchange into the United States are small when compared to the amount of Treasury bills traded every day or week. With other countries (Great Britain is a partial exception), the problem of neutralizing, or, to use the proper word, *sterilizing* the inflow of foreign funds is difficult because the government bill markets are relatively thin. There are, of course, other monetary tools, but the impact of large inflows of foreign exchange is serious, and pressure from this source was an enormous problem in the late 1960s and early 1970s. The fixed exchange rates of the Bretton Woods system were not originally meant to be transmitters of inflation, but that is the way it turned out. The main role was played by the American dollar. As dollars became the principal item in the foreign exchange reserves of most countries, those countries became willing to hold more and more of them. When the Fed expanded the American money supply, this raised U.S. national income and led to higher inflows into the United States. The foreign central banks that ended up with the dollars could have exchanged them for gold or demanded some other hard currency from the Fed—but the dollar was *the* standard reserve currency and bore interest where gold did not. As a result (just as in Fig. 7.1, except that it affected foreign countries), the acquisition of a foreign currency stimulated an expansion of the domestic money supply. Even when open market selling or raised reserve requirements were used to sterilize the inflow, trouble followed because the resulting higher interest rates attracted liquid capital from abroad. Meanwhile, the Fed in the United States did not allow the outflow of dollars to constrict the American money supply. Rather than suffer the deflationary effects of such constriction, the Fed successfully neutralized the outflow through the creation of new money.

For the world as a whole, bank reserves were expanding in many countries due to the inflow of dollars, but were not contracting in the United States. The net effect was inflationary. The situation might have been held under control for many years, except that the U.S. authorities eventually lost control of it. Massive budget deficits and rapid monetary expansion during the height of the Vietnam conflict fueled American inflation. Foreign central banks tried to cope, often with unusually stringent controls on the inflow of dollars. Switzerland in 1971 banned interest on nonresident Swiss franc deposits, and in 1972 established an 8 percent commission (essentially negative interest) on increases in such deposits. Combined with a possible reserve requirement of 90 percent, these Swiss Bank regulations administered by the bank's appropriately named Dr. Stopper were the world's toughest. Japan put a 50 percent reserve requirement on nonresident yen deposits above their 1972 level, and prohibited branches of foreign banks from accepting new nonresident yen accounts. Germany banned interest on nonresident deposits from 1971, and established 30-40 percent reserve requirements on them. The Netherlands and Belgium both stopped interest payments on similar deposits, and banned foreigners altogether from holding guilder and Belgian franc time deposits during 1971-1972. Most of these countries also put strict controls on foreign investment and the purchase of stocks and bonds, and Japan attempted to hit the "leads and lags" problem by prohibiting advance payment for exports valued at over $5,000. But it was very difficult to enforce these regulations, it being so easy to circumvent them. When central banks resorted to standard monetary policy to stop the flows, with easy money to promote imports and stifle exports, the results were inflationary. When monetary policy was tightened to hold the domestic inflation, interest rates rose and foreign funds were attracted at an even more rapid rate, again fueling the inflation. The problem appeared insoluble.

These inflationary pressures from the inflows of foreign currency (mainly the dollar) were a major cause of upward revaluations in the Bretton Woods system, and finally, of free floats. By stopping the purchase of foreign exchange, countries like Canada (in 1950 and 1970) and Germany (in 1969, 1971, and 1973) were able to put a stop to a truly extraordinary creation of domestic reserves. The cleaner the float, the greater the degree of control regained over monetary policy. Thus, in 1973, after floating, Germany was able to cut its money growth rate to less than 6 percent compared to 14 percent the year before; and Switzerland, where growth in the money stock had been 18 percent in 1971 and 13 percent in 1972, cut this growth to a negative 0.3 percent after floating in 1973.

The long and the short of it is that floating rates, when the float was clean, freed economic policy makers from the responsibility of adjusting the exchange rates, which were henceforth left to market forces. Monetary policy was thereafter "liberated" for use against inflation or deflation. There are, as we shall see, some objections to floating rates, and the topic is more fully explored elsewhere in the book, but it is well to note this advantage in the present context.

National Income Approaches

The analysis of the impact of flows of money on the national economy leads us only so far. It serves to relate interest rates, hence investment and consumption expenditures, to international factors. Hence we see that an inflow of funds from abroad could lower interest rates and in turn stimulate consumption and investment, which in their turn would expand expenditure and income. But that is only the indirect effect of trade and income. It has a very direct effect as well. For example, exports not only provide additional money, but also provide income. Imports not only cause the money supply to fall, but also remove expenditure from the economy. Hence we can further analyze the linkage between each country and the rest of the world by adapting for international purposes the national income models of first-year economics.

Export and Import Schedules. As a rule, increases in exports generate more income for the residents of a country. Some of this income will be spent and respent, so that the total increase in national income derived from the initial increase in exports is usually considerably larger than the increase in exports itself.

Exports provide income. Their proceeds swell wages and salaries, interest, rent, and profits. As with other spending in the economy, such as investment or government expenditure, the income from exports is subject to the multiplier effect familiar to first-year economics students. Figure 7.3 shows a standard diagram of income determination with consumption plus investment plus government spending $(C + I + G)$, which in the absence of any foreign trade would result in an equilibrium level of national income equal to "E". Dollars of spending are shown on the vertical axis; dollars of income on the horizontal. Where $C + I + G$ crosses the 45° line, total spending is exactly equal to total income and hence output. No level of income other than E could long maintain itself. To the right of E spending would be less than output, inventories would accumulate, and businesspeople would cut back on their production decisions. To the left of E spending is greater than output, inventories decline, and businesspeople compensate by increasing their orders for output. Only at E do such pressures to raise or lower the national income disappear. In the simple algebra of a first-year course, total spending $C + I + G$ is equal to total output and hence income. Income itself can be expressed in terms of how it is disposed of—as consumption (C), as savings (S), or in payment of government taxes (G_t). Thus at equilibrium, $C + I + G = C + S + G_t$ (Fig. 7.3).

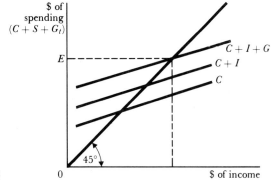

FIGURE 7.3

Exports are a form of spending (from abroad) just as are consumption, investment, or government expenditure. As with these other forms of spending, exports can be added onto the diagram by simply raising $C + I + G$ by the dollar amount of exports at any level of national income. For simplicity, Fig. 7.4, which shows this, assumes that exports are a constant at every level of national income.

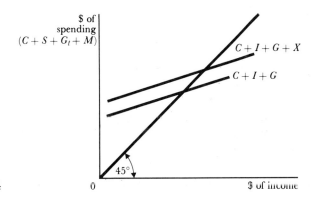

FIGURE 7.4

Imports, however, do *not* represent additional spending within the home country. Consequently they resemble savings—a net leakage from a country's income stream. The equilibrium condition for national income remains unaltered in that total spending must equal income and output. When the foreign sector is added, expenditures giving rise to income must include exports $(C + I + G + X)$ and this must equal income, *including* the income used for importing $(C + S + G + M)$, with X and M here the symbols used to identify exports and imports respectively. Only when $C + I + G + X = C + S + G_t + M$ will spending on the nation's output be equal to the amount of that output, resulting in neither an accumulation of excess inventories nor an unintended decline in those inventories.

The full scope of the relationship among exports, imports, and the national income can be shown more clearly if we use a variation of the model used in Figs. 7.3 and 7.4. We can concentrate directly on the foreign sector by clearing away everything but exports and imports. To do so we choose an alternative model, a variant of the injections equals leakages ($S = I$) presented in many, but not all, principles books. The model notes that, algebraically, if $C + I = C + S$, then $S = I$, and draws only the investment (injection) and the savings (leakage) curves to determine equilibrium as in Fig. 7.8.

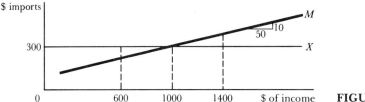

FIGURE 7.5

Figure 7.5 shows a possible relationship between exports and national income. The horizontal line X (for exports) reflects an assumption that exports are not dependent on the level of income. This assumption is not far off the mark for many countries that consume little of what they ship abroad. Malaysia's exports of rubber and copper, or Saudi Arabia's exports of oil, have little to do with domestic levels of national income and are almost wholly dependent on foreign demand. But the assumption is only a simplifying one and is not vital to the theory. In some other countries, exports *do* correlate closely with national income. As that income rises, the country consumes a greater amount of what it had been exporting; as income falls, exports rise, because firms push foreign sales more energetically. Such a situation resembles the actual one in countries such as Japan or West Germany. To reflect this, the line for X in Fig. 7.5 would slope gradually downward instead of staying horizontal.

Imports, on the other hand, are in all cases very much related to changes in national income. Because a portion of all incomes earned goes to imports, as income rises so do imports, and as income falls, imports fall. This is reflected by the upward slope of the line M in Fig. 7.5.[2]

The sketching of the import schedule, M, suggests three useful relationships. The first of these is what percentage of income is spent for imports, algebraically M/Y. (The letter Y traditionally stands for national income.) This relation is called the average propensity to import, or APM. In Fig. 7.5, a national income level of 1,000 is seen to be associated with imports of 300, and thus $M/Y = 300/1000 = 30$ percent. The percentages given in Table 7.1 earlier in this chapter are in fact average propensities to import for the countries involved.

The second relationship is between *changes* in the level of national income and *changes* in the level of imports. In Fig. 7.5, the small triangle drawn on M shows that a \$50 rise in income is associated with a rise in imports of 10. Algebraically, this is $\Delta M/\Delta Y$, called the marginal propensity to import, or MPM. In this case the MPM = 10/50, or 20 percent. The little triangle in Fig. 7.5 is in effect a measurement of the slope of M, and the slope of M is the marginal propensity to import. The MPM will be high if consumers switch into imports with rising income—buying foreign-made luxuries or small foreign cars as their second vehicle—or low if luxuries are manufactured at home and necessities are imported. In the United States, the MPM was about 16 percent in the period 1972-1975, but much of this was due to petroleum imports. In more "normal" times, say 1969-1971, the MPM had been only about 10 percent, and earlier in the 1960s the MPM had been on the order of only 7 percent.

The third relationship is an elasticity measure called the income elasticity of imports. First-year economics courses discuss how quantity demanded responds to income changes (the income elasticity of demand), and how a good can be classified as normal or inferior depending on whether more or less of it is purchased as income increases. It is possible to do exactly the same thing with imports, measuring the percentage change in imports associated with any given percentage change in income. The actual formula is $(\Delta M/M)/(\Delta Y/Y)$. If the resulting answer is less than 1, then a 1 percent rise in income leads to a rise in imports of less than 1 percent.[3]

We can now look at the diagram as a whole. For the sake of ease in identifying the exact roles of exports and imports in income determination, let us assume for the moment that investment and savings are both zero, and that there is neither government spending nor taxation to worry about. In such simple conditions, equilibrium income is determined by $C + X = C + M$ (instead of the more complicated $C + I + G + X = C + S + Gt + M$). Since $C = C$ on both sides of the equation, equilibrium will occur where $X = M$. Only there, at 1,000, where the schedules for X and M intersect, will aggregate demand exactly equal the aggregate supply. Consider what would occur if income, instead of being at 1,000, was at a level as high as 1,400 (Fig. 7.5). At 1,400, imports obviously would exceed exports. The aggregate supply of goods (consumption goods and services plus imports, or $C + M$) exceeds the aggregate demand (generated by income derived from sales of consumption goods and services plus exports, or $C + X$). With aggregate demand lower than aggregate supply, inventories accumulate in stockrooms, businesspeople reduce their orders for new goods, and the output and income decline toward 1,000. Conversely, at 600, exports exceed imports. Aggregate demand for goods is greater than aggregate supply, or $C + X > C + M$. Inventories decline, businesses place more orders for new goods, and output and income increase toward 1,000. Only at 1,000 do the forces generating aggregate demand exactly equal those creating aggregate supply, and equilibrium is reached.

The multiplier effect characteristic of national income models also occurs with trade. Whenever the schedules for exports or imports rise or fall, that change is multiplied. Suppose exports rise because of a greater foreign demand. Since this change is not dependent on the level of income (it is autonomous), the change in exports would be seen in Fig. 7.6 as a rise in the export schedule from X_1 to X_2. The *injection* of new export spending causes national income to rise toward a new equilibrium (E'), with the resulting level of income Y_2, up from Y_1, when the process is complete. Notice that the geometry of the diagram allows us to calculate the multiplier exactly. Both the change in exports (ΔX) and the change in income (ΔY) are seen at a glance. Euclid tells us that dividing the distance along the vertical leg of a right-angle triangle by the length of the horizontal leg (here $\Delta X/\Delta Y$) gives the slope of that triangle's hypotenuse. In Fig. 7.6, the hypotenuse is in fact the import schedule, and we already know from our earlier discussion that the slope of the import schedule is the marginal propensity to import, MPM. Hence $\Delta X/\Delta Y$ = slope of M = MPM. By simple rearrangement, $\Delta Y = \Delta X \times 1/\text{MPM}$. In short, any initial change in X will be multiplied to give a larger resulting change in national income. Note on Fig. 7.6 that the higher level of exports does indeed generate a higher level of income. Note further that the higher level of income results in a rising quantity of imports along the upward-sloping import schedule, and that at the new equilibrium E' we find M once again equal to X.

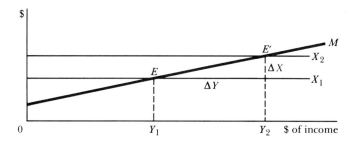

FIGURE 7.6

An autonomous change in the level of imports, caused by supply difficulties at home due to strikes, for example, has a similar multiplier effect, as seen in Fig. 7.7. A rise in imports from M_1 to M_2 acts as a leakage and reduces income; a fall in imports from M_1 to M_3 cuts back on leakages and raises income. There is a multiplier effect, with the change Y_1 to Y_2, and also Y_1 to Y_3, much greater than the initial change in M. The exact calculation is the same as that given for a change in exports in the last paragraph. Note that the changes in income caused by initial changes in the desire to import have the effect of altering imports still further. If at Y_1 people desire to import more, so that the import schedule rises to M_2, then the resulting fall in income will inevitably dampen this desire to import until X once again equals M back at Y_2. And conversely in our simple model, an initial decrease in the desire to import will so raise income that importing is stimulated to the point where $X = M$. So long as the only injection to income is exports, imports will always be equal to exports (Fig. 7.7).

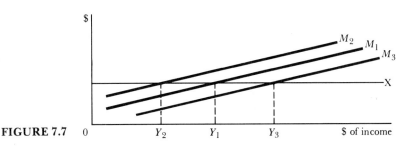

FIGURE 7.7

The general lessons to be learned from all this are that an autonomous rise in exports acts to raise national income; a fall in exports lowers national income; a rise in imports reduces income; and a fall in imports raises income. This effect was not discovered until the 1920s, when Professor Frank Taussig and some of his graduate students at Harvard noticed that in some unexplained fashion, changes in exports and imports were influencing the level of national income.[4] Ever since this important discovery, which was "Keynesian" in what was still a pre-Keynesian age, the relationship between foreign trade and income has been seen as fundamental.

The Model with Savings and Investment Schedules. It is now possible to expand the analysis to make it more complete and more realistic. Let us reintroduce savings and investment, S and I. We know from earlier in this chapter that the equilibrium condition for national income will be total output (and hence income earned), or $C + S + M$, must equal total spending, or $C + I + X$. Because $C = C$, equilibrium may be stated as $S + M = I + X$. The two leakages, S and M, and the two injections, I and X, can be conveniently added together on the same diagram, showing the equilibrium level of income. The technique is as follows: Take the upward-sloping savings schedule of Fig. 7.8 and add to it the upward-sloping import schedule of Fig. 7.9. Since both schedules rise with income, it follows that the slope of the two together rises even more steeply, as shown in Fig. 7.9. The distances *ab* and *cd* at incomes *a* and *c* are added to the import schedule of Fig. 7.9. Then one can add to investment, also shown in Fig. 7.8, the level of exports at any income (as shown in Fig. 7.5) to get a combined schedule for $I + X$. The addition of I and X is a vertical one, as shown along the dashed line *ef* in Fig. 7.10. Now note the lesson: Any autonomous change in either exports or imports, or in savings or investment, will have a multiplier effect. Thus in Fig. 7.10, a rise in investment, or exports, or both, from $I + X$ to $I' + X'$ raises national income from Y_1 to Y_2, a change in income that exceeds (because it is multiplied) the initial change in $I + X$. Following the algebra used earlier in the chapter, the slope of $S + M$, which is the sum of MPS + MPM, must equal the change in X or I divided by the change in Y, or MPS + MPM = ΔX or $\Delta I/\Delta Y$. By rearrangement, the multiplier formula can then be written as $\Delta Y = \Delta X$ or $\Delta I \times 1/(\text{MPS} + \text{MPM})$. Note that in Fig. 7.10 the actual multiplier effect is likely to be less than when just one leakage, S or M, is considered. The double leakage to savings and imports, which gives the steep slope to $S + M$ in the diagram, is responsible for the low multiplier. Note too that imports do not have to equal exports so long as investment does not equal savings. And, logically, any excess of exports over imports must be matched by an excess of savings over investment—an idea we will return to in Chapter 8.

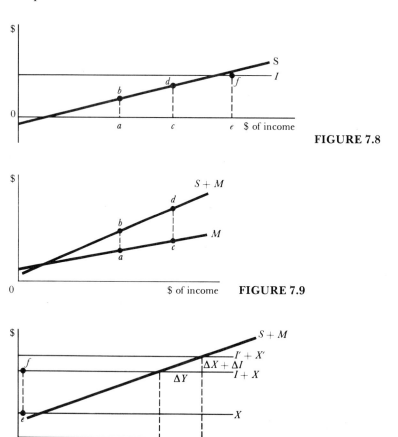

FIGURE 7.8

FIGURE 7.9

FIGURE 7.10

In actual practice, this income multiplier is not nearly so simple as it has just appeared. Expenditures on imports increase income in foreign countries, whose imports then increase. This is sometimes called the "foreign repercussion effect." An example follows.

Suppose investment rises in Germany, as shown in Fig. 7.11. Income will rise as a result, by a multiple, from Y_{g1} to Y_{g2}. Germany's imports will thus rise also, along the upward-sloping schedule $S + M$. *But*: If imports are up in Germany, then some other country's *exports* must be up also. Let us say that the foreign repercussion affects mainly France, as in Fig. 7.12. The rising exports of France are not independent of income, as we already know. They are seen to cause a rise in French national income from Y_{f1} to Y_{f2}. This in turn generates new imports into France, with French $S + M$ higher than before. This income effect in France will in turn rebound in Germany, because French imports are German exports. To some extent exports will rise in Germany; this is shown by $I' + X'$ in Fig. 7.11, leading to higher German income (Y_{g2} to Y_{g3}) and more German imports. Round and round continues the process, starting from some initial stimulus that leads to higher income and higher imports in one country; higher exports and thus income and imports in another country; and thus higher exports, income, and imports once more in the first country, until finally the effect dies away. The full impact of this foreign trade multiplier, with foreign repercussions included, is complicated algebraically and is more appropriate for graduate-level texts. The full formula is given in the footnote.[5]

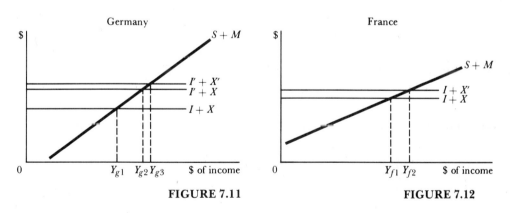

FIGURE 7.11   **FIGURE 7.12**

It must never be thought that the foreign trade multiplier is only a theoretical issue, useful mainly for constructing tough examination questions. It is all an immensely practical matter. In 1974, at the height of the energy crisis, there were predictions of imminent doom for many western economies when the multiplied contractionary impact of a $40 billion rise in oil imports was felt. If the full foreign trade multiplier is no lower than two and perhaps as high as four to five on average (estimates given in *The Economist,* October 12, 1974), then the weight of the new oil imports as a depressing effect on national income would have been enormous. That the weight was eventually shouldered, and the deflationary impact not as bad as predicted, was largely due to a rapid increase in imports by oil-producing nations (*exports* of oil importers, of course) and to investment of surplus funds in the Eurodollar market. All this is examined in greater detail in Chapter 17.

Figure 7.13 gives a schematic portrayal of the effect of the oil price increase on a representative country. $S + M_1$ represents the high multiplier assumption, while $S + M_2$ represents the low. The increase in the price of oil is shown as an autonomous rise in $S + M$, reflecting the fact that at any level of national income people will be forced to pay a higher percentage of their income on imports; this creates the curve $S + M_1'$ and $S + M_2'$. The conclusion is that under the optimistic "low multiplier" assumption, income would fall from Y_3 to Y_2, and under the high multiplier assumption, income would fall to Y_1. Fortunately, however, the increase in spending by the oil countries raised $I + X$ (not shown) to moderate the fall.

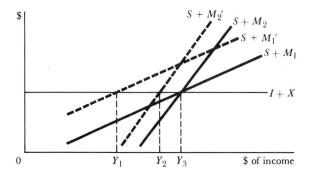

FIGURE 7.13

Factors Underlying the Import Schedule. The reader should not be misled into thinking that the curves for X and M are in fact precise statistical statements that one can go to the library and look up. One will not find the MPM published in a book of statistics (any more than the MPC). Indeed, some economists argue against its use at all on these very grounds. But, like demand or supply curves, the import function is not meant as a statistical model, but rather as a "mechanical" model—a statement of a general and logical relationship of imports to national income. With this warning in mind, we may examine some of the factors that influence the slope of the import function.

The best clue to the import function's slope is in the composition of imports themselves, particularly if it is viewed in conjunction with the domestic economy's ability to provide import substitutes. Clues to the response of imports to income changes may be seen by examining a nation's imports for the following five classes of goods.

1. Income-Sensitive Consumer Goods. Imports often tend to be goods that are more in demand when people's incomes rise—that is, they are "income-elastic." Typical American imports of this kind are electronic goods (radios, TV sets) or medium-priced automobiles. Similarly, many nations are likely to find that meat consumption rises sharply as income rises, and if a nation lacks a wide agricultural base, imports of meat soar. Imports of luxury goods, such as fine wines, exotic jewelry, and the like, also rise with increasing wealth.

Conversely, if a nation's consumer imports tend to be largely staple foods (particularly grains), or if they are generally considered inferior to domestically produced goods (for example, Americans prefer domestic men's shirts or suits), then people are not going to spend a great deal of their newer income on imports. Such a reason has been suggested for the rather weak response of American imports to income changes in the mid-1950s. In those years, Europe and Japan could not produce the kinds of goods Americans wanted to buy with their higher incomes. The situation today, however, has changed dramatically, as the strong domestic markets and technological sophistication of the European countries and Japan allow them to produce many goods that Americans desire.

2. Fuels and Raw Materials. Some imports are essential to "fuel" the economy. American imports of petroleum, for instance, vary directly with the use of energy, and the use of energy in turn increases whenever the economy heats up. Since petroleum already represents a major part of United States imports (some 20 percent in 1976), and domestic stocks do not respond quickly to changes in demand, virtually all of the increase in oil consumption must be provided through imports. Similarly, but in not so marked a fashion, imports of minerals and metals used in manufacturing rise and fall in response to the level of economic activity.

The following three categories are likely to affect the import function's slope mainly in the later stages of an economic boom. They are closely allied with the "accelerator" effect discussed in introductory economics.

3. Industrial Goods in Short Supply. Often as domestic plants reach capacity, they are forced to quote longer periods of delay before filling orders. In response, buyers abandon their regular domestic supplies in favor of foreign suppliers who promise a quicker—even if sometimes more costly—delivery. This is very common in the steel, aluminum, and chemical industries.

4. Inventories. In periods when there is a sharp recovery from a recession, there is often a sudden increase in demand for inventories of raw or semifinished materials. The inventory problem is particularly serious for Japan and Great Britain, which rely heavily on imported materials to feed their factories. The sudden increase in inventories of raw materials, although generally short in duration, can send the import figures skyrocketing and put a lot of pressure on the home currency in the foreign exchange market. Often a ticklish situation then develops in which the government must balance the speed of the economic recovery against the threat to the currency.

5. *Capital Goods.* If imports include many capital goods, then in the later stages of an economic recovery, when firms seek to expand their capital equipment, there will be heavy imports.

Discussion so far has dealt with the slope of the import curve. What about the "autonomous changes"? (They may be autonomous to income levels, but they are certainly dependent on something.) Basically, these are three:

1. Changes in tastes. American imports of foreign cars and radial tires represent a change in taste toward things unavailable domestically. This raises the American import schedule. Abroad, it moves the foreign export schedules up.
2. Changes in supply conditions. Nations exhaust resources (the United States was an oil exporter from the 1860s through the 1950s). Other nations find or develop new resources. In the short run there are sometimes supply interruptions caused by such things as strikes, transportation difficulties, and weather; the North American winter of 1976-1977 caused important domestic supply interruptions, causing buyers to turn to imported goods where possible.
3. Finally, price levels may change, making imports cheaper relative to domestic price levels, a subject discussed in the next chapter.

National Income Policies and the Balance of Payments

We are now able to determine how national income policies are related to the balance of payments. We can see from Fig. 7.10 how an autonomous rise in investment causes imports to rise; in turn this could lead to a balance of payments deficit. Unfortunately, our diagram does not show this as clearly as it might. There is, however, a way to rearrange the M, X, I, and S curves to clarify this. To do so, take the original equilibrium conditions, $S + M = I + X$, and transpose it so that $X - M = S - I$. Of course, this shows equilibrium just as surely as did the prior formulation. Graphically, this appears as in Fig. 7.14, where I, a constant, has been subtracted from an upward-rising S, so that $S - I$ still rises; while M, an upward-riser, has been subtracted from the constant X, so that $X - M$ slopes downward.

This is a useful diagram, because at zero along the vertical axis $X - M = 0$. Whenever $X - M$ is above the base line, then exports exceed imports by the vertical distance up to that line. Whenever $X - M$ is below the base line, then imports exceed exports, and once again it is the vertical distance from the base line down to $X - M$ which shows the dollar amount.

For example, in Fig. 7.15, $X - M = S - I$ at a national income level of Y_1. At that income level, the vertical distance aY_1 equals $X - M$, the excess of exports over imports. And in Fig. 7.16, with $X - M = S - I$ at Y_2, the distance bY_2 is the excess of imports over exports. The relevance of this is that the country in Fig. 7.15 is running a balance of payments surplus, and in a world of fixed exchange rates or controlled floating is acquiring new foreign exchange reserves in the amount aY_1; while the country in Fig. 7.16 is suffering a balance of payments deficit that must be financed by outpayments from foreign exchange reserves equal to bY_2.

Note that any upward movement in the schedule $X - M$, due to a rise in exports or a fall in imports, or any downward movement in the schedule $S - I$, due to a fall in savings or a rise in investment, will enlarge the equilibrium level of national income, moving it to the right on our diagrams. Note also, however, that the resulting outflows or inflows of foreign exchange are not so large as the initial change. This can be seen in Fig. 7.17, where an initial rise in exports of Y_1w has moved $X - M$ upward to $X' - M$, but has also caused

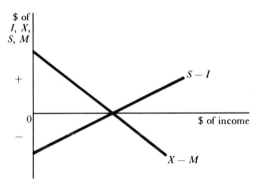

FIGURE 7.14

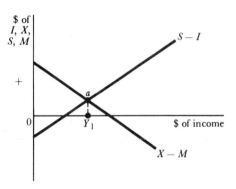

FIGURE 7.15

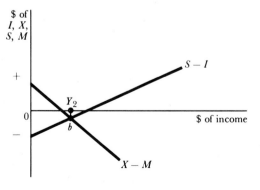

FIGURE 7.16

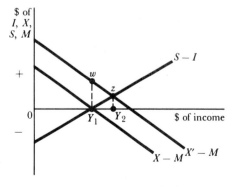

FIGURE 7.17

income to rise from Y_1 to Y_2, in turn stimulating imports to some extent and thus reducing the eventual net inflow of foreign exchange from Y_1w to Y_2z.

Readers can check their understanding by imagining a diagram such as Fig. 7.17, with X initially equal to M, and then tracing through the following: (1) higher imports, which lower $X - M$, lower national income, and cause an outflow of foreign exchange; (2) higher savings, which raises $S - I$, lowers national income, and causes an inflow of foreign exchange; and (3) higher investment, which lowers $S - I$, raises national income, and causes an outflow of foreign exchange. When reversed, each of these examples has the opposite outcome also.

It should be noted that the diagrams used here can easily handle the case where exports are not autonomous, but are instead related to the level of income. Such a relationship would, as mentioned earlier, be a negative one, with exports falling as income increases. As new domestic orders flow to firms, management tends to pay less attention to export markets; and when domestic sales are dwindling, the search for foreign sales intensifies. This phenomenon is particularly marked with capital-intensive goods where a high and steady volume of production is necessary; for example, petrochemicals and steel. Where this is the case the schedule for X has a downward slope as income increases, and so $X - M$ must decline more sharply than otherwise. The result is that any change (higher I, lower X, and so on) will have a greater effect on the inflow or outflow of foreign exchange, and a lesser effect on national income, than shown in our "standard" diagrams.

The policy implications stemming from the theory outlined here are important. *Outflows and inflows of foreign exchange can be adjusted by deliberate changes in the national income.* Assume, as in Fig. 7.16, that the United States has a balance of payments deficit and hence an outflow of reserves equal to Y_2b. The United States has several policy alternatives involving income with which it can attempt a cure for the situation. First, as shown in Fig. 7.18, it might raise the level of savings, S. (Presumably this would be government savings, obtained through running a budget surplus or lowering the deficit.) If the level

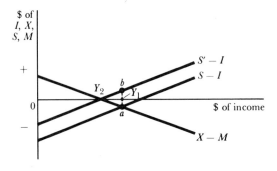

FIGURE 7.18

of savings is raised in an amount just equal to the vertical distance between $S - I$ and a new schedule of $S' - I$, shown by ab in the diagram, payments are brought back into balance. Alternately, investment I might be lowered an equal amount (presumably through the use of restrictive monetary policy).

The chief problem involved in this sort of adjustment is readily apparent in Fig. 7.18. See how the initial rise in S or fall in I ($= ab$) must be greater than the actual outflow of reserves Y_1a, and how the result is a deflationary fall in national income back to Y_3. (So long as there is any saving at all, a decrease in national income will cause a decrease in savings and imports.) Hence, a $10 million decrease in national income with a ¼ MPM and a ¼ MPS produces decreased savings of $2.5 million and decreased imports of $2.5 million. This multiplier of 2 [$= 1/(¼ + ¼)$] means we need a $20 million change in national income—caused by a $10 million change in the savings schedule, in the investment schedule, or both—to achieve the desired result.

As the diagram shows, deflation as a policy can work to cure international imbalances. Unfortunately, however, the fall in national income will be politically most unwelcome except in periods of high inflation, and so this policy is ordinarily used only when the national income level Y_1 is inflationary. Note in particular that countries with a low marginal propensity to import (MPM), and hence a relatively flat schedule for $X - M$ (one such country is the United States) would have to reduce national income quite a bit to get rid of any given balance of payments deficit, while the Netherlands with a high MPM could achieve adjustment with a much smaller change in income. The converse is also true. The United States with its low MPM can stimulate the economy within broad limits and not suffer very significant balance of payments deficits and outflows of reserves. In the Netherlands, by contrast, any fiscal or monetary policy that raises I or reduces S would have a very high leakage into imports, and this is one reason why that country and countries like it have difficulty in stimulating a lagging economy without serious balance of payments problems.

The reverse case is also true, and has been one of the sources of several foreign exchange crises. As income falls, the surplus of exports over imports tends to increase. When Germany went into a recession in 1968 and again in 1973-1974, the $S - I$ curve moved upward. As a consequence imports fell and the balance of trade grew. (To see this on a diagram, simply carry further the movement shown in Fig. 7.18.) The size of the trade surplus and the inflow of foreign funds gave rise to expectations that the mark would be revalued, causing a further inflow of foreign funds. Again, in 1977 and 1978 it was just this problem that caused tension between President Carter and German Chancellor Schmidt. The expansionary U.S. domestic economic policies were causing a severe trade deficit, helping to give other nations export-led growth, as in Figs. 7.11 and 7.12. Germany, however, was following rather conservative economic policies such that its economy was not expanding; U.S. exports to

Germany and to third-country markets accordingly lagged. This was the major economic problem addressed at the Bonn summit meeting of 1978.

Investments made from abroad have the same effect on a country as any made domestically: When rising they have an expansionary effect on national income, and when falling, a contractionary effect. Foreign investment in this sense is included within the export schedule and needs no separate treatment.

Conflicts between Payments and Income Goals

Countries that have used their monetary and fiscal tools to adjust the balance of payments by altering income have often run into political difficulties. Usually, in fact, the shoe is on the other foot, with national income having the highest priority and balance of payments troubles farther down on the list. Governments aiming to eliminate unemployment and reduce inflation often see payments problems as an interference with their domestic plans. If, for example, the French government is trying to induce a recovery from a recession and finds the country suffering simultaneously from a payments deficit, it is not only unlikely but probably politically suicidal for the government to create another recession just to eliminate the deficit. Nor would Germany abandon a successful effort to hold down the rate of inflation just for the purpose of eliminating an unwanted trade surplus. What one actually finds in the policy arena is not so much a manipulation of income levels to achieve desired trade effects, but more a modification of plans—a slowing of a recovery or a relaxation of policies holding down a boom.

The experience of Great Britain since World War II provides an example of substantial policy modification due to serious international complications. Whenever Britain's economy has expanded, imports have risen. This is particularly true in the early stages of recovery as inventories are built up. In essence, general economic recovery leads to increased imports; the increased imports cause a weakening of the pound; and to defend the pound the government has to stifle the economic recovery. The result has led to the coining of a new term—"Stop-Go," the British call it—to describe their dilemma wherein booms never really get going and economic growth is accordingly low.

Unemployment, low incomes, and related poor rates of growth are costly ways of achieving a trade balance. Similarly, inflation, while it might indeed eliminate a trade surplus, is also a rather costly way of doing so—especially since the major reason for wanting to avoid the surplus in the first place may be to avoid a monetary inflation! Adding to the difficulty, as noted earlier, the relation between changes in imports and changes in income (the marginal propensity to import) must be fairly strong for initial changes in income to have a pronounced effect on the balance of trade. Although in some countries this relationship may be 1:4, 1:3, or even more (meaning a three- or four-billion change in national income could cause a billion change in imports), in many countries the relation is much more tenuous. In the case of the United States, for example, to get a billion-dollar change in imports might require a $10 billion change in national income. No government could base its income and employment policies on the supposition that it would engineer a $10 billion cut in income just for a billion-dollar change in the balance of trade. Even where the relation is more powerful, as 1:4 or 1:3, the cost of balancing the trade accounts through income changes may be politically far too high.

About the only time one could really expect a government to follow "appropriate" policy with respect to income would be when it was doing so anyway because of domestic needs. A trade surplus during a recession should call for an expansion of national income. A trade deficit during an inflation should remind the government to contract the level of spending—which, of course, the government should be doing anyway to counteract the inflation.

The various conflicts in using fiscal and monetary policies to adjust national income and the balance of payments at the same time can be neatly shown on a diagram first worked out by two professors of international economics, Trevor Swan and Robert Mundell. It is shown here somewhat modified as Figs. 7.19(a)-(c). Fiscal policy is shown along the vertical axis, with the government's budget shown running upward from deficit to a balanced budget to surplus. A budget deficit is presumed to be expansionary for the economy as well as for imports, a balanced budget neutral, and a surplus contractionary for the economy and for imports. On the horizontal axis is shown the interest rate as an indicator of monetary policy. Low rates of interest are presumed to be expansionary for the economy, and thus for imports, and at the same time are expected to discourage inflows of short-term capital, thus worsening the balance of payments. High rates will do the opposite.

In Fig. 7.19(a), the curve labeled external balance shows all the various combinations of fiscal and monetary policy that at a given exchange rate would require no government intervention to support that rate (in short, no deficit or surplus in the official settlements version of the balance of payments). The logic behind the curve can be seen as follows: Starting with balance of payments equilibrium at A on the curve, assume that the budget goes into deficit. The result would be an expanded economy, higher imports, and a payments deficit. To achieve payments equilibrium with the budget in deficit, interest rates would have to be higher, as at B. The higher rates act to cool the economy and discourage imports, and at the same time they promote an inflow of short-term capital. Both effects tend to bring the balance of payments back to equilibrium. The steep slope of the curve implies that this double-barreled impact of monetary policy on both trade and capital movements is relatively strong, and that fiscal policy is relatively weaker where external balance is concerned.

Now consider the curve for internal balance in Fig. 7.19(b). This shows the various combinations of fiscal and monetary policy that could bring about the best attainable level of low inflation and low unemployment. For example, starting at W, say the government budget goes into deficit. This will expand the economy and be inflationary unless interest rates rise, leaving us at X. The higher rates will have a cooling effect and will restore internal balance.

In these diagrams, exchange rates are assumed to be fixed. If they were altered, then both curves would shift. For instance, a dollar depreciation would stimulate exports and discourage imports, thus improving the balance of payments. For any given government budget, external balance would thus require lower interest rates, which would stimulate the economy and raise imports plus restrain the inflow of short-term capital. The leftward shift in the curve—to the dashed line in Fig. 7.19(a)—would be relatively large because of the effect on both trade and capital movements. Meanwhile, depreciation will shift the curve for internal balance upward and to the right, to the dashed line in Fig. 7.19(b). There would be more spending on our exports and

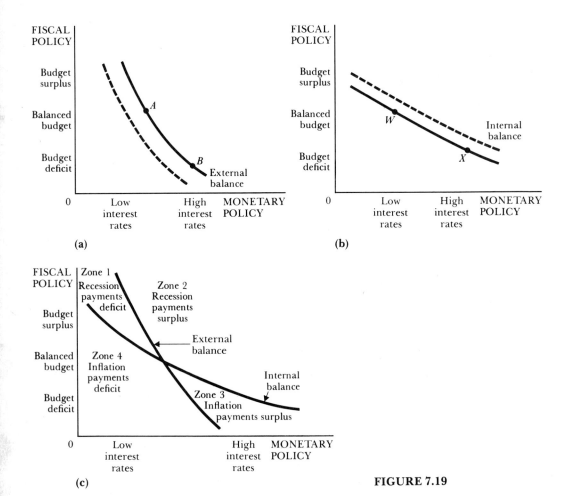

FIGURE 7.19

switches away from our imports to domestically produced substitutes. For noninflationary internal balance, a greater budget surplus or smaller deficit would be required at any given rate.

The diagrams can be conveniently divided into zones that show at a glance what the policy alternatives are and what their ramifications might be. Use the solid lines as dividers. Figure 7.19(a) pictures the curve for external balance. It has a zone below and to the left of the curve where any combination of fiscal and monetary policy would result in a balance of payments deficit. Upward and to the right of the curve is a zone where the policy combinations would bring about a payments surplus. The same technique of division into zones is employed in Fig. 7.19(b) with internal balance. Here an area below and to the left of the curve indicates where policy combinations are inflationary, while above and to the right of the curve is a zone where policy is deflationary.

All that now remains is to juxtapose the curves for external and internal balance on the same diagram. This is done in Fig. 7.19(c). There are now four distinct zones, each with a different mix of problems. In zone 1, fiscal and monetary policy produces recession and a balance of payments deficit. In zone 2, there is recession but a payments surplus. Zone 3 shows inflation and a payments surplus, while zone 4 has a simultaneous inflation and payments deficit. The most interesting element of this diagram is that proper policy is easy to determine in zones 2 and 4, but involves direct conflicts in zones 1 and 3. Take first zone 2. The economy should be stimulated both to counter the recession, and to reduce the balance of payments surplus. Both fiscal and monetary policy can be expansionary. Consider now zone 4. Contractionary fiscal and monetary policy is just what the Keynesian doctor should order to cool the inflation and reduce the payments deficit. So far no problem for the policy maker. But alas, zone 1 calls for expansionary policy to cure the reces- sion, but contraction to counter the payments deficit, while the opposite holds in zone 3, where contraction is called for to counter the inflation and expan- sion for the payments surplus. In selecting the proper policy in these two cases of conflict (zones 1 and 3), the managers of the economy will take note of the fact that the external balance curve is steeper than that for internal balance. It looks as if monetary policy has the more powerful effect on external balance, and fiscal policy on internal balance. The managers will thus presumably pre- fer tight money and expansionary fiscal policy in zone 1, and easy money plus a budget deficit in zone 3. But a solution is not simple, and the country located in either zone 2 or 4 has a much easier time deciding on its policy options.

Selective Monetary and Fiscal Policies

The last method for correcting surpluses and deficits in the balance of pay- ments is by concentrating on changing the price or availability of goods di- rectly involved in trade—without trying to alter income or price levels. There is a whole range of policies that governments use to make changes in the level of imports or exports, thus dispensing (or seemingly so) with the need to make more basic economic changes. The policies may be as direct as levying a tariff or imposing a quota, or they may be as indirect as subsidizing the advertising of exports or inducing firms to invest in export-producing activities.

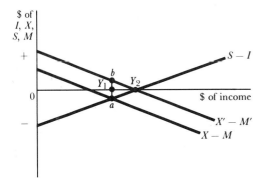

FIGURE 7.20

Nations frequently change tariffs to help their payments balance. A country in deficit might add a surcharge to its tariffs, require importers to put up a cash advance against imports, or impose a strict quota limit on imports. As in Fig. 7.20, this can certainly reduce imports and eliminate the payments deficit, which was originally Y_1a in the diagram. There are very serious drawbacks to this sort of action, however. A much more detailed discussion of the effects of tariffs and quotas is provided in Chapter 12 of this book, so for now let it suffice to mention the following: (1) Such policies might well be inflationary. If the national income level Y_1 in Fig. 7.20 is at or very near full employment, then the reduction of imports shown in the diagram will be inflationary as income moves up to Y_2—made worse by the fact that tariffs and quotas have their own direct effect on the prices of imports and import substitutes. The decline in imports, just as a decline in savings, results in increased expenditures on domestic goods, in turn driving up their prices. The inflationary problem can be countered by macroeconomic policy, but the inflationary pressure is a serious problem nonetheless. Moreover, given full employment and a switch to import substitutes, the resources for the manufacture of the import substitutes have to come from somewhere. One of these places is from exports. Suppose, for example, that a cotton-exporting nation cuts down on grain imports through tariffs. Some land that was previously used for exported cotton will undoubtedly be shifted to grain, decreasing exports. (2) Any use of tariffs or quotas to adjust the balance of payments must have a greater effect on imports than on the balance of payments deficit this action is designed to solve. Thus in Fig. 7.20 the distance ab is greater than the distance Y_1a. This is because the rise in income Y_1Y_2 itself generates some imports in addition to what would have occurred otherwise. (3) Other nations may retaliate, increasing their tariffs against the country that initiated the tariff hike and causing a resulting decline in the latter's exports. Time and again, as will be seen in later chapters, countries either threaten to retaliate against proposed tariff increases, or actually do retaliate when put to the test. (4) Finally, the inefficiencies involved in such economic distortions (familiar to students from first-year economics discussions of comparative advantage and explored at length in Chapters 10 and 12 here) reduce the potential real income. The nation cannot produce as much because it cannot specialize as much. This moves the full employment point to the left, possibly intensifying inflationary pressures.

It is also possible to correct payments imbalances by means of export subsidies—say, a 10 percent bonus for every dollar's worth of foreign currency earned. The effect is to raise the export schedule, giving a picture identical to that of Fig. 7.20. As with import tariffs and quotas, problems are encountered. (1) Unless there is significant unemployment, such a policy is likely to be inflationary. (2) The amount by which exports must be increased to correct a payments deficit is greater than the deficit itself. And (3) foreign nations may simply retaliate against the bonus by raising their own tariffs—10 percent in this case would do the trick on all imports of subsidized goods.

One special case is a much more acceptable means of adjustment: eliminating a payments *surplus* by cutting import duties. There will be no foreign retaliation, of course, and the move will be acclaimed internationally. However, such action will undoubtedly create some unpopularity among protected industries at home. So great, in fact, is the opposition from the beneficiaries of protection that in the annals of economic history one finds very few cases of voluntary, unilateral tariff cuts made for the purpose of eliminating a payments surplus. The Labour government in Australia cut tariffs 25 percent in a burst of economic logic for just this purpose; it did, however, lose the next election.

Analytically related to tariff and quota restrictions on imports are a number of other measures. Tightening exchange control can be attempted, with the authorities refusing to allow importers to buy foreign exchange. The supply of imports will fall, their prices rise, and people will attempt to buy more import substitutes. The net result, as with a tariff increase, is inflationary pressure and the likelihood that foreign countries will retaliate. Similar are various "buy domestic" requirements; for example, that all government expenditures be made on locally manufactured goods (the Buy American Act discussed in Chapter 12 is an example) or that all foreign aid proceeds must be spent on goods from the donor country, regardless of price. Such regulations are inflationary. They increase the cost of government operations (and perhaps a budget deficit) and run up the prices of domestic goods. The inflationary effect is moderated to some undetermined extent as private corporations and individuals, faced with rising prices and no requirement for *them* to buy domestically, buy from abroad. There is also little chance that such regulations will be retaliated against.

Finally, nations have developed numerous devices for controlling capital movements to eliminate a deficit. The list of such individual policies is very long, and we note here only some examples. One sort of action is designed to work through the overall level of interest rates. As with any policy intended to change the level of income, interest rate policy is awkward to use for the correction of the balance of payments. Nonetheless, it can and has worked, particularly in the cases where there have been plentiful interest-sensitive funds available in the short term. Great Britain in the era of the gold standard was able to attract funds back to London whenever the pound weakened through the simple act of tightening monetary policy and raising interest rates. The United States sought for years to keep foreign funds in this country through the manipulation of interest rates. The authorities have actually tried to push short-term interest rates higher than they would normally have been in relation to long-term rates. This so-called Operation Twist twisted the structure of interest rates and (supposedly) encouraged U.S. corporations to borrow long term at low rates while simultaneously encouraging foreigners to keep their funds in the United States through high short-term rates on liquid assets. However, it is clear that few nations want to have their interest rate policies determined by foreign considerations. In the early 1970s, for example, the United States lost considerable amounts of short-term deposits that it could have kept had it allowed rates to rise. The money managers declined to permit rises, however, because they knew high rates would have seriously interfered with attempts to stimulate a lagging economy.

Earlier experiments at holding onto capital through selective instruments had failed. During the 1960s, the capital outflows from the United States were so large that Congress passed the Interest Equalization Tax, already discussed in Chapter 5, in effect lowering the earnings received by U.S. buyers of foreign bonds by an average of about 1¼ percent (¾ of 1 percent after 1968). The tax applied to stock purchases as well, and came to a little more than 11 percent of the original purchase price. In 1965 the program was extended to U.S. bank loans made to foreigners. Also in 1965 the Voluntary Credit Restraint Program (VCRP) was established, with nearly 1,000 large firms asked to alter their own contribution to the balance of payments by 5 percent. In 1968 the program was made mandatory, with legal controls imposed. Firms could invest abroad only $200,000 a year without restriction.[6] Above that figure, 65 percent of the past year's investment could be invested in Japan, Canada, Australia, and Great Britain, and more than that in most underdeveloped countries. The Office of Foreign Direct Investment was set up to police the controls. Incidentally, a proposal made during this period to tax

Americans who traveled abroad was fiercely criticized, and the idea was dropped. (For many years, Britain had a £50 ceiling on the currency that tourists could take abroad with them.) All the American restrictions were phased out beginning January 1, 1974, and they are now gone. The attempts by Germany, Switzerland, and others to reduce earnings on deposits held by foreigners are further examples of selective capital controls designed to alter a balance of payments surplus or deficit.[7]

Conclusion

The use of fiscal and monetary policy on either a general or a selective basis to maintain the exchange rate has obvious limitations. The general measures often interfere with highly desirable internal goals of high employment and little inflation, while the selective measures create economic inefficiencies that inhibit sound growth. Ultimately, the nation must consider the advisability of altering the exchange rate itself. As we have suggested, this has become more and more of an accepted policy, but as we shall see in the next chapter, that solution also has its own problems.

Notes

1. Little Luxembourg's import bill is about 90 percent of its national income.
2. Note that this schedule for imports M looks like the savings schedule S shown on similar diagrams in first-year texts. However, M does not dip below the base line the way S does. One can tap past savings, but one cannot send back imports made previously and already consumed.
3. Note that by rearrangement of the formula $(\Delta M/\Delta Y)/(M/Y)$, we know that $\Delta M/\Delta Y$ is the marginal propensity to import, and we also know that M/Y is the average propensity to import. Thus MPM/APM = the income elasticity of imports. This is common sense. If a rise in income leads to a rise in imports exactly in proportion to what is already imported, say 10%/10%, then MPM/APM = 1 and also the income elasticity of imports = 1.
4. Taussig's discovery is noted in Yeager, *International Monetary Relations*, 2d ed. (New York: Harper & Row, 1976).
5. The multiplier for Country A when repercussions in Country B are considered is:
   (1) For an autonomous change in exports

   $$\Delta Y = \Delta X \times \frac{1}{\text{MPSa} + \text{MPSb} + \text{MPMb}(\text{MPSa/MPSb})}$$

   (2) For an autonomous change in investment

   $$\Delta Y = \Delta I \times \frac{1 + (\text{MPMb/MPSb})}{\text{MPSa} + \text{MPMa} + \text{MPMb}(\text{MPSa/MPSb})}$$

6. In 1969, the permitted figure for uncontrolled investment was raised to $1 million per firm.
7. In the mid-1970s, some countries were moving away from capital controls while others were adopting them. The following quotation is from page 5 of Weir M. Brown, *World Afloat: National Policies Ruling the Waves*, Princeton University Essay in International Finance No. 116, May 1976.

> Although the Federal Republic of Germany withdrew in 1974 most of the special capital-import limitations it had introduced in 1971-73 and the United States chose the beginning of 1974 to dismantle the disincentives and limits on capital export that had existed since 1963, several other countries moved in the opposite direction. France strengthened and extended its controls on outward capital movements, the United Kingdom tightened up on capital export and re-imposed drastic limits on tourist expenditures abroad, and Japan and Italy increased controls to differing degrees on capital outflow. Switzerland experienced a strong inflow of funds for investment or security reasons that contributed to the upward pressure on the Swiss franc and was not discouraged by the prolonged appreciation of the franc. The Swiss authorities re-imposed controls and disincentives, some of them at severe penalty levels, against many types of financial inflow.

8

EXCHANGE RATE
POLICY

Monetary and fiscal policies are only two of three macroeconomic tools available to governments: The third is exchange rate policy. Changing an exchange rate may eliminate a trade deficit just as surely as will restraining aggregate demand. Revaluing a currency may have the same effect as stimulating the domestic economy. Moreover, as our conclusions to the last chapter suggested, exchange rate policy may achieve these objectives with fewer serious side effects. Nonetheless, changing the exchange rate also has its own side effects, and it is not always the most effective policy. There are situations in which monetary and fiscal policies are preferable. More commonly, as we shall see at the end of this chapter, what is needed is a mix of all three macroeconomic tools. A careful examination is in order.

Exchange Rates and Purchasing Power

We start by examining the subtle relationship between exchange rates and the purchasing powers of the currencies exchanged. In the simplest of propositions, we could suggest that the Thai baht, worth five cents in the foreign exchange market, buys five cents' worth of goods in Thailand. Such a proposition suggests a direct relationship between domestic purchasing power and foreign exchange value.

Every traveler, however, knows that this is very much oversimplified. A thousand baht buys far more in Thailand, for example, than does $50.00 in the United States. Outside Bangkok, a pineapple costs $0.20; lunch is $0.15 (and in the nicer hotels $1.50-2.50); a private room in a hospital, air conditioned, is $15.00 a day; a jitney ride of four miles is $0.10; a year's private schooling can be had for $50.00-100.00; rent in a spacious house is $150.00 a month, and a servant costs $50.00 a month or less. Foreign exchange rates, determined to a large extent by the balance of trade, are dependent on *traded* or *tradable* goods and services—yet a great part of people's spending is on goods and services not easily traded.[1]

This problem takes on particular significance when it becomes necessary to compare incomes internationally. The administrators of the Marshall Plan to aid European recovery from World War II faced just such a problem, as they were required to disperse aid "fairly" in Europe. To do so, they wanted to make a valid comparison of per capita income. The two economists chosen to do the job, Milton Gilbert and Irving Kravis, devised a plan in which they took a typical "market basket" of goods used in the cost of living index figures and then priced this basket both in the various countries of Europe and in the United States. They discovered that in 1950 a Britisher earning £357 (or $1,000) a year could actually purchase a basket of goods and services worth US$1,625. Gilbert and Kravis recognized another problem: European and American tastes differ and the market baskets differ; why not price an American basket in Europe? They did this too, and the Britisher still came out ahead—the American basket would be worth $1,417 in Europe. This amounts to saying that in Europe any given salary would go farther for a person living as a European than for one living as an American, but that in either case, the translation of income per capita at the exchange rate seriously understated the actual living standard. The two economists made still another interesting discovery: Italy, the poorest of the countries surveyed in 1950, showed the most discrepancy between income per capita based on exchange rates and income based on comparing market baskets. Italy thus showed the largest "Gilbert and Kravis effect." This has led to the general conclusion that the poorer the nation, the larger the "G and K effect."

While one cannot compute exchange rates by comparing the purchasing powers of currencies, we need not throw out the baby with the bathwater and discard purchasing power entirely. There is some evidence that one can compute *changes* in exchange rates from changes in purchasing power. In the short run, at least, the G and K effect is probably rather constant—tradable goods and tastes change more slowly than do price levels. And one can choose a price index involving more tradable goods—such as the wholesale price index rather than the cost of living index—to reduce the G and K discrepancy. We then have a new proposition. The percentage change in the price level of one nation compared with the percentage change in the price level of another determines the alteration in the relative values of their currencies. As an example, if France had an inflation that doubled its wholesale price index and the United States had none, then the French franc would fall from its current value of US$0.20 to US$0.10. Usually, however, all nations are inflating at the same time, though some at a more rapid rate than others. The calculation cannot be done so easily in the head, so we need a formula:

$$\frac{PP_a}{PP_b} \times \frac{Ca_0}{Cb_0} = \frac{Ca_1}{Cb_1},$$

where PP_a = change in purchasing power of currency a;
PP_b = change in purchasing power of currency b;
Ca_0 and Cb_0 = value of currencies a and b in original period; and
Ca_1 and Cb_1 = value of currencies a and b in new period.

As an example, suppose the United States had an inflation of 100 percent over a given period of time and France had one of only 50 percent. In the initial period the exchange rate was Fr5 = US$1. Then

$$\frac{150}{200} \times \frac{5}{1} = \frac{750}{200} = \frac{3.75}{1}$$

The French franc would tend toward a value of 3.75 to the dollar.

The purchasing power parity theory was initially expounded after the First World War. As noted in Chapter 3, the war had unleashed inflation, but the rate varied from nation to nation. The above solution was devised to straighten things out again. It was never in fact used for that purpose. Indeed, it may not have worked because the war and reparations may have fundamentally altered the G and K discrepancy. The theory, however, is in fairly common use among bankers and exchange analysts as an important indicator of the direction and extent of foreign exchange movements. Predictions of future relationships between the Canadian and United States dollars, for instance, are regularly made with the aid of purchasing power parity theory. Indeed, the "track record" of purchasing power parity in predicting the degree of exchange rate change is rather good.

The purchasing power parity model is useful because it highlights two important aspects of the price level problem. First, it emphasizes the idea that price level increases are relative to prices in other nations. Often a country with a trade deficit needs only to keep its inflation less than its trading partners' to restore purchasing power parity. Like a steady tennis player who just returns all shots and waits for the opponent to err, this nation holds back inflation while its trading partners let theirs plunge on. To a considerable extent, this was true of the United States in the mid-1970s as its trading partners "outinflated" it, and this led to a strengthening of the dollar. Often, however, the causes of inflation are so political and so deep-seated that the inflation-prone and the stability-prone remain just that way. Germany, with its deeply rooted fear of inflation, has constantly had smaller price increases than its less austere trading partners, leading to steady upward pressure on the German mark. Second, purchasing power parity also highlights the policy open to a government—to change the purchasing power of the currency with respect to domestic goods and services or to change the value of its currency with respect to foreign currency. Purchasing power parity's limitation, however, is in its explanatory power. It gives us a useful statistical model, but it does not explain the forces at work. Our alternative, to which we now turn, can explain the effect of devaluations better, though it is hardly a handy statistical tool.

Elasticities and Devaluation

Import Demand and Export Supply Curves. Our concern at this point, then, is to develop the analytical tools showing how imports and exports will react to devaluation. To do so, we must move into some microeconomic approaches. We begin our approach by examining the demand and supply conditions concerning a specific (but very abstract) good, the widget. The domestic demand and supply for widgets is shown in Fig. 8.1(a). If the widget-producing country is isolated from the world economy, the equilibrium price for widgets would be where supply crosses demand at $0P_e$ with a quantity of $0Q_e$. Suppose, however, that its economy becomes integrated with the world economy and the world price for widgets is $0P_a$. (Our country, being relatively small, is presumed to have no effect on the world price of widgets.) At $0P_a$ domestic producers are discouraged and production would drop to point $0Q_a$. Consumers are delighted, however, and increase consumption to $0Q_b$. Hence a consumer demand for $0Q_b$ widgets is supplied partially from domestic producers ($0Q_a$) and partially from imports (Q_aQ_b).

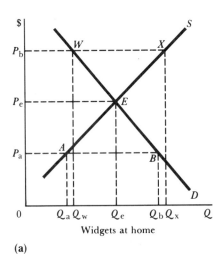

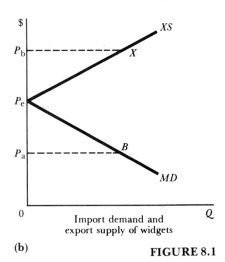

(a) Widgets at home

(b) Import demand and export supply of widgets

FIGURE 8.1

Figure 8.1(b) shows the import demand (sometimes called "excess" demand) for widgets. The first point on this curve we know—that at $0P_a$ the imports are Q_aQ_b, so the distance Q_aQ_b (Fig. 8.1(a)) becomes the same distance on Fig. 8.1(b). We also know that at $0P_e$ there are no imports, so we have two points; and we are dealing with a straight line so we can sketch out the *import demand* curve. Note that the right triangle P_aP_eB is equal in area to the triangle AEB in Fig. 8.1(a). Technically, the slope of the import demand curve is figured by adding together the slopes of demand and supply (changing the sign of the S curve to a negative).

Suppose, however, world price had been $0P_b$—above the domestic equilibrium price. Producers would jump to manufacture (or perhaps grow or breed) more widgets and produce $0Q_x$, while consumers would cut widget consumption at that high price down to $0Q_w$. Domestic production of $0Q_x$ *less* the domestic consumption of $0Q_w$ equals the amount available for export, Q_wQ_x. Thus, as the world price rises above $0P_e$, our country becomes an exporter and an *export supply* curve emerges (this time with a positive slope), shown in Fig. 8.1(b).

In the extreme cases where there is no domestic supply (for example, Canadian bananas) or where domestic consumption is a tiny part of demand (Guatemalan consumption of bananas), the slope of the import and export curves will be the same as the domestic. Otherwise the slopes of the import demand and export supply curves are less steep and their elasticities therefore greater than their domestic equivalents.

Individual demand and supply curves can be connected to the total response of all imports and exports only with some care. A simple summation of individual demand and supply elasticities would be very misleading because of the complicated cross-elasticities of demand and supply. Take the examples of corn and soybeans. The crops compete for the same land; individual farmers in the corn belt can and regularly do grow both crops. An increase in the price of either would call forth a considerably larger quantity as one crop replaced the other. An increase in the price of both crops, however, calls forth only a marginal response. Thus the sum of the two elasticities tells little about the response of both crops together.

A better approach is to consider a single schedule as *representative* of the response of all imports to price changes, and to do the same for exports. One can try to get some idea of the actual historical responses of exports and imports to price changes through econometric studies. Or one can look at some of the basic components of imports and exports to get some idea of their possible responses, much as we did when looking for the income elasticities of imports. The United States, for instance, exports agricultural goods and capital goods, both of which are known to have inelastic demands (and have few cross-elasticities to worry about), suggesting that U.S. exports are probably not very price elastic as a whole. U.S. imports, on the other hand, are far more mixed: Many consumer goods are probably rather price elastic, while fuels are markedly less so.

The next step in gauging the effect of a change in currency value is to estimate a number of things. In order just to talk about the effect of the fall in the value of the U.S. dollar, for instance, we would like to know the following:

1. The elasticity of demand for U.S. imports. This would help us to know how effectively an increase in their price would reduce the quantity demanded.

2. The elasticity of demand abroad for American exports. This would tell us how effective American price cuts would be.

3. The elasticity of supply of American exports. If American supplies are limited, exporters might raise their dollar prices (not cut their prices much, as expressed in foreign currency), so exports will not increase greatly.

4. The elasticity of supply of foreign exports to the United States. A highly inelastic foreign supply might cause foreign firms to lower their prices such that Americans would still purchase a large quantity of imports.

To keep the discussion from becoming too hard to follow, we shall examine all problems in the context of a U.S. dollar devaluation, and shall consider the American trading partner as Germany. The understanding gained in this way should allow the reader to generalize and to reverse the process. We begin by examining the elasticities of demand.

Elasticity of Demand and Devaluation

Effect of devaluation on the value of U.S. exports. In examining a devaluation of the dollar for its impact on U.S. exports, we come up with a curious problem—the devaluation itself changes nothing in the export supply conditions in the United States. The supply curve for exports does not move because neither the cost of making the good nor the demand preferences within the United States are affected. Nor does the import demand abroad change—foreigners like the goods as much or as little as before. Again using the German mark as symbolic of all foreign currency, we can set up a model. A German import demand curve, expressed in terms of marks, and a dollar supply curve cannot be drawn on a diagram with dollar prices, nor can they both be put on one with mark prices. One has to "translate," so to speak, the marks into dollars, or the dollars into marks. And what devaluation *does* is to change the translation. Naturally, only one curve gets translated; the other is already in the currency desired. Observe how this works in the case of the dollar devaluation.

Our first concern is to see what happens to the *dollar* value of U.S. exports after devaluation. To discover this, we bring the German import demand curve onto the U.S. export supply curve. That means translating the German curve into dollars. Figure 8.2 shows a hypothetical U.S. export supply. D_1 represents the German demand, translated at the old rate. After devaluation, each mark purchases more dollars of exports, so the demand is translated anew, shifting upwards. To American eyes, the German demand appears to have altered. Because the devaluation is in percentage terms, the curves are farther apart where they are high than where they are low, so the curves are not parallel. We can see a devaluation of 33 percent, noting that what was once priced at $1.00 now brings $1.33. At that price, of course, more Americans would export than the market could bear, so the prevailing price would be a lower $0P_2$.

No matter what the supply conditions (discussed later), we can draw some general conclusions about devaluation and dollar receipts. In the most unfavorable case, German demand for U.S. exports would be completely inelastic. (Such a case might arise if the Germans had a quota limit on U.S. goods.) Then the second demand curve would sit right over the first, as in Fig. 8.3. Even then, though, dollar receipts do not decrease. Hence we can say as a rule that devaluation must increase or (in extreme cases) leave unchanged the quantity of home currency earned.

More important than dollar receipts are the foreign exchange receipts. After all, a devaluation is supposed to help bring in foreign exchange. To arrive at their value we must construct a diagram in marks. Taking the import demand curve of the Germans, already in marks, we can translate the dollar export supply curve into marks. Again we have two translations. Figure 8.4 shows the mark demand curve crossed by S_1, the U.S. supply for exports translated at predevaluation terms, and S_2, the postdevaluation translation. To the German buyers, U.S. supply apparently has shifted. American suppliers, who formerly needed 30 marks to supply $0Q_1$, will now supply the same amount for 20 marks—the dollar receipts at 20 marks are as large as they had been at 30 marks.

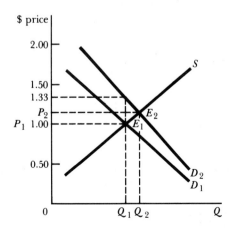

FIGURE 8.2

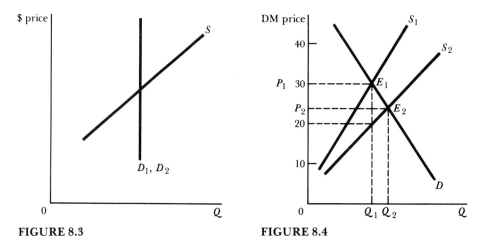

FIGURE 8.3   **FIGURE 8.4**

The conclusion about whether the mark receipts will rise or not with the devaluation is not so clear cut as with dollar receipts. The dollar receipts were based on an upward shift of the demand curve on a *fixed* supply. Since supply curves have positive slopes, this means that the area under the supply curve (total costs) always increases as prices rise. Mark receipts, however, are based on a lowering of price along a *fixed* demand curve. If demand should prove elastic (that is, the percentage change in quantity is greater than the percentage change in price), then receipts measured in marks will rise. If, however, demand is inelastic, total DM receipts will fall.

Figure 8.5 demonstrates these two possible results of a devaluation. Using the idea that demand curves have both elastic and inelastic portions, the figure contrasts the effect of devaluation in the upper (*elastic*) portion of this curve and in the lower (*inelastic*) portion. Thus a devaluation of one-third from S_1 to S_2 brings an increase in quantity from $0Q_1$ to $0Q_2$ (roughly a doubling), and DM receipts rise from the rectangle of $0P_1E_1Q_1$ to the rectangle $0P_2E_2Q_2$. The same 33 percent devaluation in the inelastic portion of the demand curve, however, brings forth a percentage change in quantity considerably lower than the 33 percent devaluation, such that total receipts fall from $0P_3E_3Q_3$ to $0P_4E_4Q_4$. Theoretically, then, it is uncertain whether a devaluation will increase the *foreign exchange* receipts from exports, though it is virtually certain it will increase the *dollar* value of those exports.

Effect of devaluation on U.S. imports. The reaction of U.S. imports to devaluation is as important as that of exports. To see that reaction we need no additional analytical tools and have only to change our point of view. The government hopes to stem the amount of dollars being spent on imports. (1) In *dollar* terms, the U.S. demand for imports does not have to be translated, while the German export supply does. This is shown in Fig. 8.6, with S shifting on a fixed demand curve. The devaluation shifts the S curve from S_1 to S_2, indicating the higher costs of imports. (2) The U.S. demand for imports measured in marks is shown in Fig. 8.7; this time the export supply curve is in marks (not translated) and the import demand curve is translated from dollars into marks. Because U.S. buyers are less able to buy marks and therefore German goods, the demand curve appears to the Germans to move from D_1 to D_2. The outside limiting case is perfectly inelastic demand. Here the already vertical demand curve is not shifted, and thus the mark value of U.S. imports is unchanged (as in Fig. 8.3) with the DM price on the vertical axis. The conclusion of this exercise is that with a dollar devaluation, the mark value of U.S. imports will ordinarily decrease (*D* moving on a fixed *S*). However, the dollar value may go either way (*S* moving on a fixed *D*).

Our conclusions so far are summarized in Table 8.1.

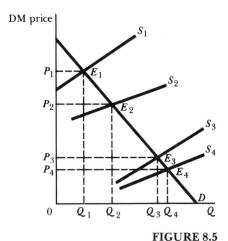

FIGURE 8.5

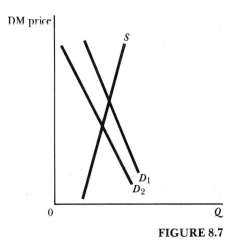

FIGURE 8.6   **FIGURE 8.7**

TABLE 8.1. EFFECT OF DOLLAR DEVALUATION ON FOREIGN EXCHANGE MARKETS

Effect on	Demand elasticity	Change in dollars offered	Change in foreign exchange offered
U.S. exports	0	0	−
	> 0 < 1	+	−
	> 1	+	+
U.S. imports	0	+	0
	> 0 < 1	+	−
	> 1	−	−

Elasticity of Supply and Devaluation.   The elasticity of demand for imports in both trading partners indicates whether or not a devaluation will be effective. It also indicates how much of a price change of exports and imports will be needed. It does not, however, indicate the relationship of the amount of the devaluation to a price change—for example, if the dollar falls by 10 percent, will prices also fall by 10 percent? In Fig. 8.2, for instance, the devaluation was by one-third but the price change was much less. This is important because sometimes large changes in currency value may induce only small changes in the price of traded goods, as can be seen by example.

Figure 8.8 shows an import demand of the home country, this time in Thai baht with two perfectly elastic supply curves. Perfectly elastic supply curves could occur where the importing nation was small in relation to the rest of the world; thus only a tiny portion of world production goes to that nation. The foreign producers, unaffected by the drop in demand, do not lower their prices in dollar terms. Since dollars now cost more baht, however, the import supply curve shifts upward by the full devaluation—in other words, since the supply curve is horizontal, prices rise the full amount of the devaluation. A devaluation of 10 percent, therefore, causes a 10 percent increase in the baht price.

If, however, supply is highly inelastic, producers will tend to lower their prices, canceling some of the effects of the devaluation. Guatemala's banana exports could serve as an example. Since the bananas are planted and the trees are producing anyway, producers will export so long as the proportionally small harvesting and transportation costs are covered, yielding a highly inelastic supply curve over a fairly large range. This is represented in Fig. 8.9(a) by a completely inelastic supply curve. Suppose, now, the U.S. dollar is devalued. U.S. demand in terms of Guatemalan quetzals appears to fall. Yet producers have to sell $0B$ of bananas, and the fact that the United States is now willing to buy only $0A$ at that price leads to price cutting in terms of the quetzal; price falls to where the quantity demanded is the same as before. The only price that will hold is where the price of bananas in quetzals falls the full amount of the devaluation. Figure 8.9(b) shows the same situation in terms of dollars—the supply curve of bananas shifts upward in dollar terms, but since it is a vertical line, it does not move; hence the dollar price remains the same. The result—the same dollars, fewer quetzals.

The Marshall-Lerner Condition. Policy makers have been haunted for some years by a fear that devaluation might make the balance of payments worse. It is important, then, to define not just the abstract possibility, but the underlying conditions necessary for the balance of payments to worsen, and then to assess them. In essence, we need not know the supply conditions (unless supply is completely inelastic) because even if there must be a large change in the exchange rate, the price effect will still be in the right direction. Hence we focus on the two demand curves—the import demand in foreign nations and the import demand at home. The "rule," known as the Marshall-Lerner condition after the economists involved in its establishment, is that *the sum of the two elasticities of demand must be equal to or greater than one* for devaluation to improve the balance of payments.

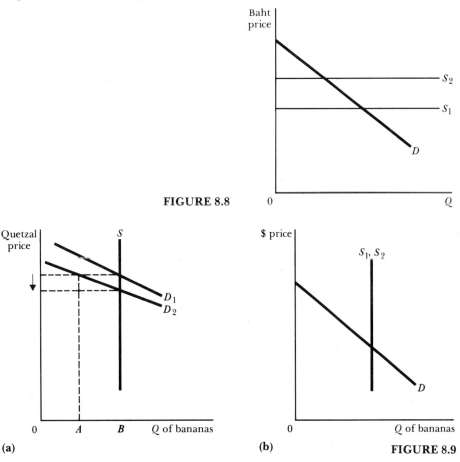

FIGURE 8.8

(a)

(b)

FIGURE 8.9

Two examples will show this.

1. If the elasticity of demand for U.S. imports is zero, as our analysis has already shown, devaluation will not decrease the foreign currency value of our imports; it will remain the same. If, however, there is a foreign elasticity of demand of one or greater, foreign currency earnings will increase. In short, no change in our foreign currency outpayments for imports and an increase in our receipts from exports bring a net reduction in the balance of payments deficit.

2. Now say that the elasticity of demand for our *exports* is zero. In that case, depreciation will decrease the foreign currency value of our exports by the amount of the decline in price. Meanwhile, if the demand for U.S. *imports* has an elasticity greater than one, then the decline in U.S. imports will be greater than the increase in price. Only if the elasticity of demand for our imports had been unitary would total spending on imports have fallen by just the percentage of the price increase. In that case, there would have been no improvement in the balance of payments.

Elasticities in Practice–An Assessment. Most economists agree that nearly always there exist the minimum elasticities required to avoid the Marshall-Lerner bind. Studies by A. C. Harberger have shown that the short-run elasticities of demand for imports into a typical country are at least as high as 0.5 or 1, while the elasticity of demand for the same typical country's exports is at least 2 and usually higher. The result is that the stability (or Marshall-Lerner) conditions are almost always satisfied, and that we can confidently predict that devaluation will work as intended. This would also help explain why the less analytical purchasing power parity figures work so often.[2]

One very practical aspect of this whole problem is time. Some of the shifts discussed above occur faster than others. It is only over time that market forces cause consumers to cut their consumption of imported goods and thus reduce outpayments of foreign exchange. On the other hand, *earnings* of foreign exchange from the sale of exports fall immediately. A $4,000 Chevrolet can now be bought by a German for fewer marks than before the depreciation and at once fewer marks are available. The British call this the "J-curve effect," the shape of the J corresponding to an initial worsening of the balance of payments deficit (even when the elasticities are right), preceding the improvement that follows. The theory of the J-curve implies that the country using devaluation as a policy against a deficit must be ready to see a temporary setback before an improvement.[3]

Even assuming that Marshall-Lerner frustrations are unlikely, policy makers still worry about the possibilities of rather low elasticities, hence large and embarrassing devaluations. Some observations on elasticities are in order. Not only should these ease the policy makers' worries, but they should help justify the shape we gave to our currency curves in Chapter 2.

For one thing, import demand and export supply curves are *excess* demand and supply curves, and therefore are always as elastic as, and generally more elastic than, the domestic demand and supply curves.

Second, as a general rule, the freeing of world trade has led to increasing opportunities for substitution, and thence to high demand elasticities. Several examples show the rule in operation. The demand for Peru's sugar and coffee is very elastic, there being many producers and an easy substitution among them. (Demand for Peru's fishmeal, however, is far less elastic because there are considerably fewer producers. Similarly, Eastern European nations are often obligated to purchase Russian goods, even when better opportunities appear in the West.) Historically, demand elasticity has also been furthered by the standardization of industrial products, which makes substitution easier, although this trend is in part offset by firms that concentrate on product differentiation.

Third, supply elasticities may vary greatly. In general, the more developed countries have greater abilities to switch production from one good to another—whether in manufacturing or in agriculture—and will be quicker to drop or start production of products in accordance with changes in world prices. The United States, for instance, can cease or begin producing vacuum cleaners much more easily than can Brazil, which lacks comparable industrial flexibility.

The Effect of Imperfect Competition. Imperfect competition can alter the expected results of devaluation. The models so far have been based on assumptions of perfect competition, but policy makers must face a world of imperfections. The underlying assumption about competition is that if exporters of $10 widgets suddenly find their exports worth $12, other widget firms will begin exporting and drive the price of widgets down. Since each producer sees a small part of the total demand curve, each faces an elastic demand even if the industry does not. While producers may realize that more industry-wide sales are no help, like wheat farmers in a period of glut, they still continue to sell.

Imperfect competitors, however, not only face a sloped demand curve that they recognize, but can to some extent control the degree to which they are forced by competition to lower price. They will not lower price if the demand appears to be inelastic. The producer of a jet airplane, facing an inelastic demand, will not cut prices unless forced by competitors. The competitors, however, are unlikely to engage in a dangerous price war. As a result, the prices of American exports do not fall. This has two implications. If the demand for U.S. exports is indeed inelastic, foreign exchange rates will not fall, making it easier for the United States to avoid the Marshall-Lerner bind. The United States could have its cake and eat it too, getting a decline in imports as a result of the devaluation but no decline in foreign exchange receipts. If, however, demand is elastic, yet the imperfect competitors do not cut prices, the devaluation will be made less effective. In practice, however, the problem of imperfect competition is even more subtle because we must examine *nonprice* competition as well.

Students of business behavior know that price is only one of a number of variables that can be used to sell more goods. Since a great many exports are differentiated goods, there is considerable opportunity to use nonprice competition—particularly product and service improvement, better distribution systems, and additional promotion. These, along with price changes, are known as "the marketing mix." In the firm's judgment, it may be more effective to increase distribution centers by 10 percent, double the sales force, or sell a better quality product than to decrease price. U.S. exporters of many capital goods, for instance, felt after the 1972 devaluation that it would be silly to cut price, given the apparent inelastic demands. A 10 percent discount on a computer or a jet plane will not sell 10 percent more. But if the firm takes its additional earnings and visits more trade shows and gets more salespeople to visit more plants, it may indeed sell 10 percent more. Hence, effort in the sales of capital goods is usually put into showing potential customers the products' benefits and how to use them. These factors ultimately may be worth more to the customer than any 10 percent saving. The results of such changes, incidentally, come more slowly than the results of price changes, but they do serve to show how a devaluation could increase exports with no apparent price cuts. (For theoretical correctness, it should be noted that improvements in information, delivery, or service improve the quality of the product and thus are an implicit price reduction. Statistically and analytically, however, this point is generally missed.)

Deriving Demand and Supply Curves for Foreign Currency

The more adventurous may wish to see the relationship of the curves for imports and exports to the curves in the foreign exchange market. In Chapter 2 we showed the supply and demand curves for foreign exchange like normal *S* and *D* curves. Now we can ask some questions about their relation to import demand and export supply curves. We assume for simplicity that the entire supply and demand curves for foreign currency derive from trade. Readers may later wish to make their own modifications to fit a particular situation.

The supply curve of foreign currency is dependent on two things—the elasticity of the demand abroad for U.S. exports, and the supply of those exports in the United States. Consider what we know already: As indicated in Table 8.1 and Fig. 8.5, the foreign exchange receipts can either increase or decrease, depending on the elasticity of foreign demand. If we consider a wide range of prices, we would find that the import demand curve had both elastic and inelastic portions.

From this information we can construct a (slightly unusual) total revenue curve from the demand for U.S. imports in Germany. Figure 8.10(a) shows the demand curve. By taking several total revenue "readings" (*PQ*) from Fig.

8.10(a), we can sketch out on Fig. 8.10(b) a total revenue curve. Total revenue in this case is shown on the horizontal axis and price on the vertical.

The supply curve of marks should have the same general shape as the total revenue curve in Fig. 8.10(b). A devaluation of the dollar may create more demand at low mark (and high dollar) prices, but as the mark gets more valuable, the point of unitary elasticity is reached. (More dollars per mark, recall, means moving upward on the vertical axis.) This produces the maximum mark receipts in all three parts of Fig. 8.10.

Figure 8.10(c) changes the vertical scale from price in marks to dollars per mark. This creates an additional problem. A devaluation of 20 percent may in fact reduce mark *prices* only 10 percent. Accordingly, the supply of marks on the foreign exchange market responds to dollar price changes at only half the rate of its response to mark price changes. Only when the supply of exports is completely elastic will the price in marks fall exactly as much as the devaluation. In such a situation, the supply curve for foreign currency would look just like the total revenue curve of Fig. 8.10(b). There, a 20 percent change in the exchange rate yields a 20 percent change in price: This is shown by curve S_1 in Fig. 8.10(c). If, however, supply were less elastic—such that a 20 percent change in the exchange rate yielded a 10 percent change in price, the supply curve would form a larger arc, as in S_2 of Fig. 8.10(c). (If supply were completely inelastic, the supply curve would be a vertical line.)

The demand curve for foreign currency derives from the U. S. demand for imports. As Table 8.1 indicates, a decrease in the value of a dollar will always result in the same or less foreign exchange being demanded. Therefore the demand curve for foreign currency can never bend the "wrong" way; at worst—zero elasticity for imports—it would be vertical. Hence we show a demand curve for foreign exchange sloped downward. Combining demand and supply we end up with Fig. 8.11.

We can see in Fig. 8.11 our Marshall-Lerner effect and other devaluation considerations. From P_1 to P_2, devaluation will improve the balance of payments as in our Chapter 2 diagrams. Improvement continues from P_2 to P_3, the demand for foreign exchange continuing to decline and its supply increasing. After P_3 the supply of foreign exchange begins to fall. The balance of payments, however, still meets the Marshall-Lerner conditions. While supply is falling, demand is falling further. At P_4, however, the slopes of demand and supply are the same—savings in the demand for foreign currency exactly match the declining export receipts. From that point on, the Marshall-Lerner bind occurs. As we have argued above, we feel that the chances of a nation being near P_4 are not great.

Macroeconomic Effects of Devaluation

The microeconomics of devaluation lead us to the macroeconomic effects. If we assume that devaluation is successful in reducing the trade deficit through changing imports and exports, we must assume as in Fig. 8.12, that $X - M_1$ is

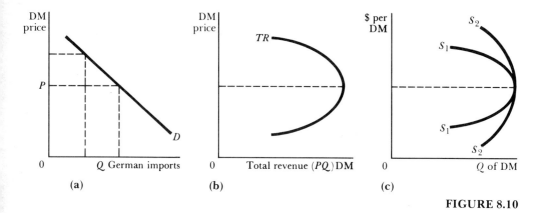

FIGURE 8.10

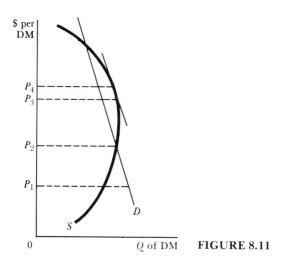

0   Q of DM   **FIGURE 8.11**

shifted to the right. Assume that $X - M_1$ shifts to the dotted $X - M_2$, moving equilibrium income from E_1 to E_2. Consider now the effect.

1. If E_1 were a full employment point, then E_2 is clearly inflationary. Government policy should accordingly be to shift $S - I_1$ to the left by cutting investment or increasing savings. The income effect, however, of returning to E_1 would produce a balance of trade surplus.

   If the government correctly recognized the situation, it would, as in Fig. 8.12, use a smaller devaluation and more moderate deflation to achieve the balance.

2. If E_1 were a point rather less than full employment and E_2 full employment, then the expansion of income would not necessarily have inflationary consequences. This shows the kind of policy that was common in the 1920s and 1930s devaluations to encourage employment. As each nation

tried to "export" its unemployment by encouraging exports and discouraging imports, there grew up a rash of "competitive devaluations."
"Beggar thy neighbor" policies these were also called. It was to avoid just
such a situation that rules were drawn up on devaluations in the post
World War II period (see Chapter 9).

We cannot yet take leave of the discussion, however. Our next proposition
is simple. Even if the nation manages to devalue and adjust income in such a

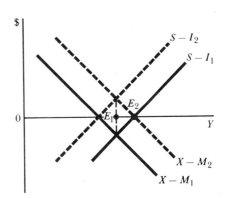

FIGURE 8.12

way as to come out at an income of E_1 with no deficit, our fully employed
nation would still be experiencing inflation. The reason is that the full-
employment level would already have shifted, back along the axis to the left of
E_1.

The situation could be compared to that of an individual such as Chapter
6's John Dough. Dough could consume beyond what he earned by financing
his personal trade deficit through savings, borrowings, or gifts. When he decides or is forced to end his deficit, however, he must take one or more of the
following actions: (1) work more so that he earns more in order to consume
the same amount of goods: (2) work more at providing his own services, such
as cooking his own meals instead of dining out; or (3) cut his rate of consumption. Indeed, on this last point he could also cut any illiquid investments, such
as renovating his house. Whatever he does, it is clear that Dough is either
working harder or consuming less than before. If he were already "fully employed" to begin with, alternative 1 would be out of the question and, if he
were very busy, perhaps number 2 is out also. In either case, he is clearly
worse off than before.

A nation can have problems similar to John Dough's. The trade deficit is
an indication that it is consuming or investing domestically more than it is
producing. This is clear because imports exceed exports, meaning there are
more goods coming in than going out. It is also evidenced in the trade deficit,

which must be financed out of past savings, borrowing, or unilateral transfers. When the devaluation occurs, the nation no longer has to use these savings or borrowings to buy the extra goods. Imports fall, reducing the stock of goods and services available. Like Dough, the nation can make for itself what it would otherwise import. If fully employed, however, it must sacrifice the manufacture of something else to make those import substitutes. It will increase exports, presumably, but again resources have to be diverted to the exports, further decreasing the stock of goods and services available for domestic uses. Hence if national income is maintained at E_1, aggregate demand will exceed aggregate supply and prices will rise.

If there is substantial unemployment already, so that unemployed resources are drawn into the manufacture of exports and import substitutes, the nation may not experience inflation. Suppose, for instance, that E_2 were the full employment level (after devaluation); then the nation would not undergo inflation. Before thinking that this may be a good way to stimulate growth, however, note that the nation is merely working harder to get the same real amount of goods for domestic uses—it is only replacing what was previously imported. There may be social and political benefits from more employment—just as John Dough may feel happier fully employed—and the nation is no longer digging into savings, but total goods available are unchanged.

Reconciling Exchange Rate Changes with Income Changes in Adjusting the Balance of Payments and National Income

We have now seen that depreciation (devaluation) and appreciation (revaluing upward) can be used to eliminate balance of payments deficits and surpluses. We have also seen that the same ends can be attained through fiscal and monetary policy and their impact on the national income. At any given moment, the world's countries may face a bewildering variety of macroeconomic problems. Some will be facing inflation; others, depression. Some will be mired in a balance of payments deficit; others will have a surplus. The "right" macroeconomic medicine will have to face several tests. Will it cure internal problems but perhaps worsen the balance of payments? Will it do all that is required for our country, but be unfavorable for our trading partners abroad? In answer, we can put together three matrices of policy options that show all the various possibilities at once. The tables below are taken from the work of Professor James Meade of Cambridge University in England.[4]

The first matrix (Table 8.2) shows the effects of monetary and fiscal policy (income adjustment) on both the domestic economic situation (internal balance) and the balance of payments (external balance) in two countries, one with a payments surplus, the other with a payments deficit. Our particular aim is to identify potential conflicts of economic policy between the countries, and between the attainment of internal and external balance. The policy op-

TABLE 8.2. INCOME ADJUSTMENT VIA FISCAL AND MONETARY POLICY

National income in surplus country is such as to give:	National income in deficit country is such as to give:	External balance	Policy options to obtain:		
			Internal balance in surplus country	Internal balance in deficit country	
	Recession	$S+$	$S+$	$S+$
		$D-$	$D+$	$D+$
Recession				
	Inflation	$S+$	$S+$	$S-$
		$D-$	$D+$	$D-$
	Recession	$S+$	$S-$	$S+$
		$D-$	$D-$	$D+$
Inflation				
	Inflation	$S+$	$S-$	$S-$
		$D-$	$D-$	$D-$

tions are for the surplus country to inflate its economy ($S+$) or deflate it ($S-$); and for the deficit country to inflate ($D+$) or deflate ($D-$).

The matrix appears a bit complicated, but it is really not. Take the first two lines at the top of the table, $S+, S+, S+, D-, D+, D+$. The matrix shows the policy problem at a glance. There is a recession in the country with a payments surplus, and also a recession in the country with a deficit. What should the surplus country (S) do? For its balance of payments problem, the course is clear: Inflate ($S+$). In so doing it will raise its level of imports relative to exports, tending to bring payments back into balance. What about its own recession? Equally clear: Inflate the domestic economy ($S+$). And what about the recession in the other country? We can help most by inflating at home ($S+$), for this will raise our imports, which are the other country's exports. An increase in its exports will raise its national income. Now what about the policies open to the deficit country (D)? For its balance of payments, it should clearly deflate ($D-$) to lower imports relative to exports. However, in order to stimulate income in its neighbor it should inflate ($D+$) because this will *raise* its imports, and thus the other country's exports and income. For its own income problems it should also inflate ($D+$) its economy. Every other line in the table follows similar logic.

The upshot is that at every point in the table, some conflict of policy appears. In no case is it possible to achieve all aims at the same time. Adjustment via income is sure to give problems somewhere.

Now take the other method for adjusting national income and the balance of payments: Devalue ($c-$, with the c standing for currency) or revalue ($c+$). Here too the impact of a change in currency values has a double-barreled effect. It alters the balance of payments at home and abroad, and also alters national income here and abroad. The question is the same as before. What policies should be followed? And can these policies ever cure both balance of payments problems (external imbalance) and national income problems (internal imbalance) at the same time?

Once again a matrix (Table 8.3) is used to show one country with a pay-

TABLE 8.3. CURRENCY ADJUSTMENT VIA APPRECIATION AND DEPRECIATION

National income in surplus country is such as to give:	National income in deficit country is such as to give:	Policy options to obtain:		
		External balance	Internal balance in surplus country	Internal balance in deficit country
Recession	Recession	$Sc+$	$Sc-$	$Sc+$
		$Dc-$	$Dc+$	$Dc-$
	Inflation	$Sc+$	$Sc-$	$Sc-$
		$Dc-$	$Dc+$	$Dc+$
Inflation	Recession	$Sc+$	$Sc+$	$Sc+$
		$Dc-$	$Dc-$	$Dc-$
	Inflation	$Sc+$	$Sc+$	$Sc-$
		$Dc-$	$Dc-$	$Dc+$

ments surplus (S) and another with a deficit (D). The policy options are for the surplus country to appreciate its currency ($Sc+$) or depreciate it ($Sc-$); and for the deficit country to appreciate ($Dc+$) or depreciate ($Dc-$).

Here too the policy decisions follow the logic developed earlier in the chapter. Take the first two lines in the table, $Sc+$, $Sc-$, $Sc+$, $Dc-$, $Dc+$, and $Dc-$. Again the matrix shows the policy problems. There is a recession in the country with a payments surplus, and also a recession in the country with a deficit. What should the surplus country (S) do? For its balance of payments problem it will clearly want to appreciate ($Sc+$), as this will lower exports and raise imports. For its own recession it should depreciate ($Sc-$), as this will raise exports and thus national income. And for the recession in the other country it should appreciate ($Sc+$), which would raise imports, thus stimulating the other country's exports and income. Meanwhile, what about the deficit country (D)? For its balance of payments it should depreciate $(Dc-)$ to raise exports and lower imports. To stimulate income in its neighbor it should appreciate $(Dc+)$, for this would increase imports and thus the neighbor's exports and income. Finally, to counter its own recession it should depreciate $(Dc-)$, thus raising its own exports and income. Every other line in the table follows identical logic.

Only row 3 shows no conflict in policy. An inflation in the surplus country and recession in the deficit country can successfully be attacked by adjustments in exchange rates alone. But all other rows in the table show policy conflicts. In fact, row 1 shows a competitive depreciation (devaluation), with both countries believing that depreciation will propel them out of the recession. This explains in a nutshell many events in the economic policy of the early 1930s, and was a significant fear in the period 1973-1978, when unemployment was high in most Western countries.

Although we have shown that policy conflicts will occur almost uniformly when countries seek external and internal balance at the same time, it is possible to select a combination of exchange rate and income changes that will successfully do the job. *If* countries consult carefully; if they select the correct policy mix without retaliation or hesitation because of debts fixed in dollars, gold, and SDRs, then adjustment of national income problems and balance of payments problems can be achieved at the same time.

Table 8.4 shows how such a mix might be arrived at.

TABLE 8.4. COMBINATION OF INCOME ADJUSTMENT AND CURRENCY ADJUSTMENT TO GET EXTERNAL AND INTERNAL BALANCE

National income in surplus country is such as to give:	National income in deficit country is such as to give:	External balance	Policy options to obtain: Internal balance in surplus country	Internal balance in deficit country
	Recession	$S+$	$S+$	
		$Dc-$		$Dc-$
Recession	Inflation	$S+$	$S+$	
		$D-$		$D-$
	Recession	$Sc+$	$Sc+$	
		$Dc-$		$Dc-$
Inflation	Inflation	$Sc+$	$Sc+$	
		$D-$		$D-$

Here, for example, as in line one, a surplus country in recession and a deficit country similarly in recession can combine to cure their woes. A policy of inflating in the surplus country and currency depreciation in the deficit country is without adverse side effects. In short, the tools are there. Getting governments to coordinate their use, however, is a much more difficult proposition.[5]

Notes

1. Both authors admit that they often take advantage of less expensive and sometimes better medical care abroad and always depart from developing areas with shoes shined and hair freshly cut. Nonetheless, they do not go abroad in order to have their hair cut.

2. See A. C. Harberger, "Some Evidence on the International Price Mechanism," *Journal of Political Economy*, 65: 506-521, and conveniently available in R. N. Cooper, ed. *International Finance* (London: Penguin Books, 1969). Harberger calculates the demand elasticities for a number of countries in this paper.

3. The very short-term effects of devaluation can be related to the currency of invoice. U.S. imports and exports are as a whole **invoiced** in dollars. This means with devaluation that exporters automatically get less foreign currency; on the other hand, importers do not have to pay out more foreign currency since their creditors have already agreed to accept dollars. The result: A decrease in foreign currency receipts to the extent of the devaluation and no change in dollar offering, clearly affecting the balance of payments negatively. This is logical because the very short-term demand schedules are highly inelastic. For small countries that invoice in dollars and devalue, the result is still negative, but it comes about in an opposite way. Imports become more expensive immediately, but the importers have ordered the goods and must pay the increased price of the dollar. Exports, however, do not change the foreign currency earned. The result: no change in foreign currency, but an increase in home currency offered and a negative effect on the balance of payments.

4. The matrix analysis of simultaneous adjustments of external and internal balance was first developed by Professor Meade, and the versions used in the text are a modified form of those found in Meade's *The Balance of Payments* (London: Oxford University Press, 1951), pp. 117, 154, and 156.

5. Admittedly, some policy conflicts still remain at a secondary level. For example, in row 1 the deficit country's depreciation ($Dc-$) will serve to lower imports—and thus exports—from the surplus country. It would have been advantageous to the surplus country to have its exports *increased*. But that simply means that the expansionary monetary and fiscal policies in the surplus country will have to be pushed further than otherwise would have been necessary.

APPENDIX:

INTERNATIONAL INVESTMENT FLOWS
AND THE REAL
TRANSFER PROBLEM

One more macroeconomic problem, frequently misunderstood by policy makers, remains to be examined: the real transfer problem. In the process of international investment we may distinguish two types of transfers: a *money* transfer, say $100,000 going from the United States to Canada; and a *real* transfer, say $100,000 worth of goods and services going from the United States to Canada. The two are linked but are not the same, so we must examine them more closely.

To begin, let us examine the formula that describes national income in equilibrium: $X - M = S - I$. Investment, as we know from introductory economics, is something put aside this year to be available in a later year—capital equipment, goods in inventories, or in some definitions new knowledge. A balance of trade surplus $(X - M)$ is no such thing; it is spent on the accumulation of claims on foreigners. Now note two points: (1) From the point of view of the nation, the investment in foreign paper assets is *real* in that saving out of present production has indeed been set aside for use in a future period. Resources taken out today can be brought back in a period of adversity, and the nation need not produce them at that time. (2) From a global point of view, no investment has occurred, since on redemption of the foreign assets, other nations must produce the desired goods.

An analogy may help. If Peter lends money to Paul, it is Peter's investment, just as real to Peter as a shelf full of canned goods to be used next year. Paul may use that money for investment (he may add a room to his house), in which case it is *Paul's* investment, not Peter's. (We don't want to count it twice.) Or Paul may consume it on a round-the-world trip. If so, when Peter demands his loan, Paul must work or save extra hard to provide Peter with the resources—that is, the amount of the loan must come out of another year's production. Hence, whether Paul invests or consumes Peter's loan, it is never Peter's investment in a real sense. Now if Peter and Paul live in different *countries*, then these arguments apply to their countries as well. It is Peter's country that has made an investment, from a national point of view, but it still is no investment from a global point of view. Hence when we look at things from a national level we can regard the investment made from balance of trade surpluses as real investment, but we must always recognize that from a world viewpoint they are income transfers only.

A related concept is that of *absorption*. We know that as Germany develops a balance of trade surplus with France, it is lending France resources. We do not know just what France will do—invest them, consume them, have the government spend them, or some combination thereof. Hence this whole "*C* + *I* + *G*" is more easily handled by calling it absorption. Paul, sponge that he was, *absorbed* the proceeds of Peter's loan, although we do not know exactly how he disposed of them. We can use these concepts in a hypothetical situation.

Germany, we will suppose, has a balance of trade surplus with its only trading partner, France. We shall represent this in a formula, substituting for $X - M$ the letter F, to stand for foreign investment. Using simple numbers we suggest this:

Germany (millions of dollars)	France (millions of dollars)
$F = S - I$	$F = S - I$
$5 = 100 - 95$	$-5 = 90 - 95$

Germany's absorption was 5 million less than its production, while France's was 5 million more. Germany's total investment was 100, including the accumulation of foreign assets. France's investment was only 90, if we subtract its disinvestment in foreign assets. Whether we total up investment either in each country ($I + I$) or made by each country ($I + F + I + F$), our answer comes out the same for total real investment.

The "real transfer" refers to the value of the German trade surplus. In real terms, Germany shipped to France 5 million dollars' worth of goods and services more than it bought from France. In money terms, Germany lent 5 million to France. This, however, is an *ex post facto*—after the fact—argument. The investments might have been trade credits for goods France ordered. Suppose, however, we make an *ex ante* (before the fact) assumption, and assume that Germany just gathered together 5 million and invested it in France. Our result may not be the same.

Suppose German interests lend a French corporation 5 million for construction of a power station. There is no particular reason to believe at this point that the construction of a power station has any abnormal requirement for German goods. So we assume that imports deriving from expenditures made in building it will be close to the French MPM of, say, ¼. Initially, then, we could expect only ¼, or 1.25 million, to be spent in Germany. We must remember, however, that the 5 million will be respent. If the MPS were 0, an unlikely case, then the multiplier would be 1/¼, or 4. Four times 5 equals 20, and a quarter of that as imports gives a real transfer of 5—equal to the money transfer (Formula 1). But if the MPS is anything over 0, imports will be less than the initial transfer. As an example, with an MPS of ⅛, the multiplier is 8/3, giving an income of 13.3 and imports of only 3.3 (Formula 2).

Formula: $\Delta M = \text{MPM} \times \Delta Y \quad \Delta Y = \Delta I \times \dfrac{1}{\text{MPM} + \text{MPS}}$

$$\Delta M = \text{MPM} \times \Delta I \times \dfrac{1}{\text{MPM} + \text{MPS}}$$

(1) $\Delta M = \frac{1}{4} \times 5 \times \dfrac{1}{\frac{1}{4}}$
    $\Delta M = 5$

(2) $\Delta M = \frac{1}{4} \times 5 \times \dfrac{1}{2/8 + 1/8}$

$\frac{1}{4} \times 5 \times 8/3$
$\frac{1}{4} \times 13.3$
$\Delta M = 3.3$

This simple model suggests, then, that borrowing abroad actually brings foreign exchange it does not need. The reason this is so, clearly, is that the added income produces additional domestic savings, such that not all the foreign savings that are borrowed are used.

If this is all perhaps a bit mind-boggling, it is well to remember that this is a rather restrictive example. Some of the assumptions could be changed.

1. We assumed that the MPM for the proceeds of the loan was the same as for the nation as a whole. Often foreign loans are made where all the money is expected to be spent abroad—for example, trade credits or development loans where the lender lends the "foreign exchange" component of a project's cost.

2. The model has assumed that the foreign investment was *net* new investment. In fact, the foreign investment may to some degree "crowd out" or discourage domestic investors by picking the best opportunities such that net new investment (I) may be lower than the new foreign investment. In such a situation, the income effect of the foreign investment would be lower and the induced imports lower yet. Plugging in 4 million instead of 5 million for the change in investment in Formula 2 yields only 2.6 million in imports.

3. If real savings are to occur, the economy cannot be at full employment. At full employment, foreign investment that did not crowd out existing investment would have an inflationary result, bringing both income and price effects. It is generally observed that the MPM rises steeply as full employment nears. Of course, if both Germany and France were at full employment, there would be price effects on both sides.

4. The model ignores monetary or foreign exchange rate effects of foreign investment. Both tend to increase imports and decrease exports, bringing the real transfer closer to the money transfer. Under fixed rates, the new investment will expand the money supply, and hence investment, income,

and imports. Near the full employment level, there would also be price effects. Under floating rates, the value of the franc would rise relative to the mark, for example, encouraging more imports and fewer exports.

The floating rate situation often occurs between the United States and Canada. The Canadians may borrow heavily in New York, then complain because the upward drift of the Canadian dollar hurts Canadian exports and encourages imports. The complainers fail to realize that this appreciation of the Canadian dollar in fact helps to bring the real transfer closer to the money transfer. Why go abroad to borrow it if it is not to effect a real transfer—that is, to allow absorption to exceed production?

Our policy conclusions are rather cautious. We do not know enough theoretically to predict easily the impact of large inflows of capital. Real transfer theory suggests that often these inflows do not yield an equivalent change in the balance of trade and therefore do not result in a real transfer of goods and services equivalent to the money transfer. In a situation of potential inflation, it will behoove governments to try to expedite as large a real transfer as possible (assuming, of course, the financing is safe). This, in fact, is the "lesson" in the Thai balance of payments figures—long-term financing for a deliberate balance of trade deficit. Attempts to have both long-term capital inflows and balance of trade surpluses miss the point of borrowing abroad in the first place. If there were potential savings available domestically, domestic economic measures should have been able to create them.

The real transfer issue is connected to one of the most important historical economic problems—the European war debts of the 1920s. During World War I the United States developed large trade surpluses with Britain and France. In order to achieve such surpluses, the United States had to produce more than it used for domestic absorption. The British and French, meanwhile, were involved in that most profligate consumer of resources, total war. Their absorption exceeded their production by far. Hence the situation was akin to that described in the example of France and Germany shown in Formulas 1 and 2, with the United States making a real transfer of goods to France and Britain in return for paper assets and monetary gold.

When the war ended and Europe began to recover, it was time for the real transfer to reverse itself. The sacrifices the United States made during the war—meatless Thursdays and other forms of restricted consumption—could have been extracted from the British and French in the form of British and French trade surpluses. The United States could have absorbed more than it produced.

The Americans viewed potential trade deficits (at least deficits with Britain and France) as a threat to profits and jobs and imposed a high tariff on imports. When Europeans pointed out that they could not repay the money they borrowed without developing trade surpluses, the United States was unsympathetic. Asked about the problem of repayment, President Coolidge's laconic answer was, "They borrowed the money, didn't they?" But the United States could not both have its cake (repayment) and eat it too (not have imports).

The problem was historically more complicated. The French and the British had placed reparations damages on the Germans and were planning to use that money to repay the Americans; hence it would be the Germans who developed a balance of trade surplus that would in turn be passed on to the Americans. So it would be Germany's savings—well in excess of its domestic investment—that would eventually be passed on to the United States. In a monetary sense, the Germans would "give away" their trade surplus through a unilateral transfer to cover reparation, and Britain and France would use that money to repay the United States. But with whom was Germany to develop *its* surplus? Not the United States, it appeared.

The "solution" was in fact no solution at all. Germans borrowed money in the bond market in New York, used the money for domestic projects involving low MPMs (marginal propensities to import), and paid Britain and France with the leftover dollars. These projects generated little demand for imports. Most of that money could thus be used to pay off reparations to the French and British, who could then repay the Americans with their own money.

This "house of cards" was not destined to last. Debts were rescheduled several times in the 1920s, as economic troubles continued to plague Europe. Then the stock market crash of 1929 and the demoralization of the investment climate effectively closed the U.S. bond market to Europeans. This led directly to the series of European bank failures that heralded the Depression. The private lenders in the United States saw the various German holders default, and in the ensuing fifteen years of chaos, the Americans were never repaid. The result was, ultimately, a unilateral transfer (by default) to Europe to cover the First World War real transfers. All the sacrifices in consumption, the underinvestments, and the limited government services that lowered American absorption during the war were never recouped because the United States was unable or unwilling to allow a real transfer to take place

9

RESERVES
AND REFORM
OF THE SYSTEM

We have seen that on the monetary side of international economics, it is the quantity of reserves in the possession of governments that, under fixed rates or dirty floating, determines the extent to which a given exchange rate can be defended. In this chapter we examine what kinds of reserves exist, and how reform of the international monetary system has tended to create more reserves. We then conclude with an analysis of how floating, when clean, dispenses with the need for reserves, and of the merits and disadvantages of floating in comparison with fixed rates.

Kinds of Reserves

Monetary reserves are the owned, liquid assets of a nation's treasury or central bank. They include gold, foreign exchange, and two items to be explored in detail later in the chapter: Special drawing rights (SDRs) and loans from the International Monetary Fund (IMF). Table 9.1 shows the composition of reserves in three recent years.

How Many Reserves Are Enough?

The question of sufficient reserves, like that of sufficient armaments, is exceedingly difficult and open to considerable controversy. Since under fixed rates or controlled floating, funds can flow out of a country at rates in excess

TABLE 9.1. COMPOSITION OF WORLD RESERVES IN SELECTED YEARS (in millions of dollars)

Kinds of reserves	1968	1971	1975
Gold	38,940	35,912	35,503
Foreign exchange	31,900	75,097	137,357
SDRs	- - -	5,900	8,800
IMF reserve position	6,488	6,351	12,624
Total	77,328	123,260	194,284

of $100 million an hour or $1 billion a day, it is difficult to conceive of ever achieving reserves large enough to stand off a heavy speculative onslaught. The real question then is not one of *absolute* security, but rather one of *relative* security, where the comfort of reserves is balanced against the costs of maintaining reserves.

The costs of holding reserves may be considerable. They are similar to those incurred by a firm that keeps large amounts of money in its checking account or in low-interest treasury bills. Profits may be considerably higher if it would instead plow this money back into the firm; indeed, if it cannot find investments that return more than 4 or 5 percent on the capital invested, it is not a very clever firm and might just as well pay the money out in dividends. A nation faces a similar situation: The accumulation of $10 billion worth of foreign treasury bills and gold means that it forfeits $10 billion worth of goods and services that it could add to its own economy. Managed correctly, most of that could go into increased investment to make the economy grow or to improve its trading position. Or it could be invested in higher yielding but less liquid foreign assets. Another cost of reserves is the possible inflationary consequences that follow from the purchase of foreign exchange by governments.

If reserves were merely a costly nuisance, there would be little demand for them. The fact that they are in demand indicates that there must be considerable perceived benefits. As with business firms, nations have a need for a certain degree of liquidity, though the need varies from nation to nation. Central bankers often gauge the adequacy of their reserves in relation to the amount of *transactions* they normally do, or that normally take place in the foreign exchange market. If, for instance, the Bank of France discovers that it frequently has had to spend $100 million in a month to even out the demand and supply of francs in normal times, it would like to have at least that much on hand every month. If transactions double, it would want to double the amount. A rule of thumb sometimes used is that a nation should have enough reserves to cover all imports for three months, or six months, or some such figure. (The United States, for instance, ordinarily has enough reserves to cover imports for three or four months.) This rule of thumb bases reserves on the transactions that take place in trade only.

Central bankers are, however, a bit like generals. There is never enough in the arsenal to defend against the onslaughts that are all too easily envisaged. They seek to hold reserves as a precaution against sudden changes in trading patterns or speculative attack. This precautionary motive becomes particularly important when there are large inflows of hot money. No nation, knowing that the inflow is likely to be temporary, is going to want to spend the reserves it has built up because the money will likely flow out again. A precautionary rule of thumb used by some central bankers is to have enough reserves to cover all liquid liabilities to foreigners. But for nations like the United States or Great Britain, with their large volume of short-term deposits by foreigners, this figure may be well-nigh unobtainable.

The last reason to hold reserves is for speculation. Not many central bankers aggressively buy and sell foreign currencies or gold to make money. They will, however, protect themselves as much as they can against holding currencies that are to be devalued. Consequently they may move money from one currency into another, demand devaluation insurance from a nation in whose currency they have reserves (such as Britain asked from the United States just before the crisis of August 1971), or move from currencies into gold on the London market.

Borrowing Ability

Owned reserves are nice to have, but nations also value the ability to borrow funds, and this ability also influences the behavior of governments and the level of exchange rates. There are two places from which to borrow—the Eurocurrency market and other governments. As noted in Chapter 5, there has been a sharp rise in the use of medium-term Eurodollar borrowings, which will ultimately be used to strengthen a nation's currency. Borrowing from governments is rather a different matter.

The ability to borrow depends as much on politics as on economics. Since only ten or a dozen nations possess reserves of any size that they are willing to lend, borrowing is not an open-market, price-determined process. It is, to use a homely analogy, less like borrowing from a bank and more like borrowing from a relative. A normal way of reducing the politics that surround any decision is to institutionalize a procedure, to make it more policy than politics and more dependent on objective criteria. There are two institutionalized forms of borrowing: That done from the International Monetary Fund and that done through the "swaps." Both will be examined in detail later in this chapter. There remain, however, numerous forms of *ad hoc*, essentially political, arrangements. These *ad hoc* arrangements are varied: They may involve the turning in of short-term bills for longer-term ones; loans from private banks, backed by government guarantees (used for less developed countries); or emergency extensions of loans. The businessperson and economist should be aware of the varied possibilities of such arrangements, which may be discussed in the financial papers, or may be rumored. Fortunately for the student, however, the institutionalized arrangements are not only more amenable to study, but they are also more important.

The Trade-Off between Adjustment and the Need for Reserves

The more easily a country can adjust the supply and demand for foreign exchange to achieve a given rate, or the less concerned it is about fixing a rate in the first place, the fewer reserves and the less borrowing ability it needs. One of the greatest difficulties with the adjustable peg system was that it seemed to require enormous quantities of reserves. This was because speculation was great, and adjustments in demand and supply were difficult to make and slow to take effect. If the world had truly been on a system of rigidly fixed exchange rates, with domestic prices rising and falling according to the flows of trade and investment, then prices alone would have made all necessary adjustments and little in the way of international reserves would have been required. As will be seen, however, that was not a plausible alternative. On the other end of the spectrum, a system of pure or clean floating rates would require no reserves because the exchange rate would make all the proper adjustments. Indeed, by the very definition of pure floating, a central bank *cannot* intervene to prop the exchange rate, and thus needs no reserves. Controlled floating, on the other hand, does require reserves, because it does imply intervention to support rates.

The total amount of reserves in the world is an important concern for businesses and governments alike. Too few may lead to difficulties in financing, restrictions on capital outflows and trade, and perhaps contractionary economic policies. Too many reserves, if they are spent to support an exchange rate, may well have an inflationary impact. The quantity of international reserves, in other words, is something like a domestic money supply: Too little brings restrictions, and too much brings inflation.

Unlike the money supply, however, international reserves are not completely under control. The amount of gold depends on what is mined. Foreign exchange reserves, held mostly in dollars, depend basically on the outflow of dollars from the United States. When the United States spends more abroad for imports and investment than it receives, then foreign governments are able to add to their reserves. When and if the United States should cease doing this, then foreign governments would be unable to accumulate any net additions to their dollar reserves even if they should desire to do so. Then central bankers would have to find substitute currencies other than the dollar, and no other nation has the capital market to provide them with the safety, convenience, and liquidity of the U.S. treasury bill market. Only SDRs and the amount available in loans from the IMF are under control as to quantity, and even here alterations are difficult to make (in any case, they make up a small proportion of world reserves). In short, the creation of reserves in the modern world of international economics is still largely an old-fashioned, un-controlled, and unplanned process. The real questions about the amount and kind of reserves have not been settled, and will continue to be a major concern for decades to come.

The Place of Gold

The gold standard in its pristine form is long gone, its demise dating from 1914. Yet a few economists, many of them followers of the French economist Jacques Rueff, and probably a larger segment of the public than is generally realized, would welcome a return to some sort of gold standard. The great appeal of gold lay in its potential for automatic self-correction of exchange problems. The theory underlying this self-correction was enunciated as long ago as 1752 by the British economist David Hume, and is called the *Hume price-specie flow mechanism*. As long as countries abided by the Hume rules, exchange rates would indeed approach total stability over long periods.

The mechanism was supposed to work through the money supply. Take any two countries in the pre-1914 period, say Ruritania and Transylvania. Both countries presumably have a money supply consisting of gold coins and paper notes backed either wholly or fractionally by gold reserves. Now should Ruritania be importing more goods and services in value terms from Transylvania than it is exporting to that country (due perhaps to a Ruritanian taste for imports), then we already know (from Chapter 2) that the Ruritanian currency will depreciate to the gold export point, leading to a gold flow from Ruritania to Transylvania. Consider, however, that this gold flow is intimately connected to the money supply of both countries. Gold either is the money supply (as coin) or backs it. Thus a reduction in gold holdings must automatically reduce the Ruritanian money stock. Recall the quantity theory of money taught in first-year courses. The money stock M times the annual turnover, or velocity, of that stock V must represent the total value of all transactions. The value of these transactions can also be represented as the average price P at which all transactions take place times the number of such transactions T. Hence $MV = PT$. In times of reasonably full employment, T is fixed because no further growth of real output can be obtained in the short run. And if velocity V is relatively constant over time, then changes in the money supply M have their immediate and direct impact on prices P. A drop in the money stock M thus means a reduction in the general price level P.

As a result, a gold flow out of Ruritania, which thus lowers the money stock, reduces prices there. Meanwhile the inflow of gold to Transylvania raises both its money stock and its general price level. Ruritania, with its prices now reduced, finds its exports of goods and services stimulated, its tourism booming, and the attractiveness of its stocks and bonds increased—all because people now find Ruritania a cheaper place in which to buy. But Transylvania is now an inflated market, its exports more costly, its tourism expensive, its investments less attractive. Thus, in Fig. 9.1, we can picture a gold export Q_1Q_2 taking place from Ruritania because of an especially high demand for foreign exchange to purchase imports from Transylvania. But this gold export will contract M in the country losing gold and raise M in the country gaining gold. The resulting lower prices in the gold-loser should raise the supply of foreign exchange, from S_1 to S_2, as foreigners increase their purchases there. Simultaneously, the higher prices in the gold-gainer will discourage imports from that country, and result in a smaller demand for foreign exchange in Ruritania (D_1 shifts leftward to D_2). The exchange rate is pulled back inside the gold export point, and the gold flow comes to an end.

It was also expected that the decline in the money supply in the gold-loser would cause interest rates to rise there, while the increase in M in the gold-gainer would cause a fall in interest rates in that country. As a result, liquid short-term capital was expected to move away from the lower and toward the higher interest rates. This too would give an equilibrating effect, with the gold-loser finding an increased supply of foreign exchange being brought to the market so as to take advantage of its high interest rates, and the gold-gainer discovering its bank accounts and bonds less attractive to foreigners, and hence a lower demand for its currency. The role of interest rates is thus to intensify the movement from S_1 to S_2 and from D_1 to D_2 in Fig. 9.1, helping to halt the gold flow.

Unfortunately for the proponents of gold as a great self-adjusting stabilizer, this price-specie flow mechanism was subject to several failures in operation. The main problem is a political one. The government and the central bank in the gold-losing country may abhor the deflationary effects of the gold loss. As twentieth century experience has showed so clearly, contraction in the money supply is unlikely to affect prices alone, especially when there are rigidities in both wage and price structures. In the example we have been using, if Ruritania (the gold-loser) follows the Hume price-specie flow rules, it is asked to undergo a domestic deflation. How long will its government stay in office if it continually pays more attention to the state of the exchange rate than it does to the level of unemployment? Similarly, Transylvania the gold-gainer, by following the rules, condemns itself to domestic inflation. Here too voters are almost certain to object. In short, both governments are rather likely to upset Hume's applecart by carrying on offsetting monetary policies—expansionary in Ruritania to counter developing deflation, and contractionary in Transylvania to counter the onset of domestic inflation. Domestic economic conditions will take precedence over the exchange rate.

Finally, there is a more complicated problem. Basically, this concerns the difficulty a country has in increasing its exports or cutting off its imports when it faces devaluation. The less sensitive trade is to price changes, the more difficult it is for the price-specie system to work. And there is suspicion

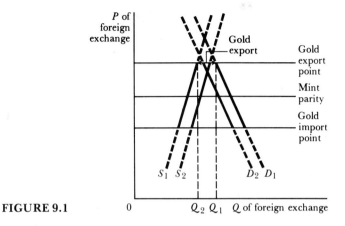

FIGURE 9.1

in some quarters that, in the short run anyway, the inelasticities of demand and supply may be so great as to make the price-specie mechanism useless.

Price-specie mechanism aside, gold still played an important role in nations' reserves for many years. Interestingly (and understandably), it was the less important and less well managed economies that had to maintain the larger gold stock, for these countries were the suspect ones whose currency defenses had to be perceived as strong. For example, before World War I Great Britain maintained a gold stock less than half the size of Russia's, and only one-fifth to one-fourth that of France. The United States had eight times more gold; even Argentina had more than 50 percent more. The preeminence of the pound and its stability meant that a large gold reserve was simply not necessary.

As noted in Chapter 3, an overall shortage of gold just after the conclusion of World War I led to the use of foreign exchange reserves as a supplement to gold, with these reserves (largely dollars and pounds) soon overtaking gold in value terms. Still, the position of gold as a national reserve remained secure, as it did during the first fifteen years of the Bretton Woods Agreement. Any sign that gold might be the center of enormous controversy was long delayed. The troubles began in 1960 in the London gold market, which was then as now the major center for trade in that commodity. The London market was the arena in which government and private buyers and sellers could meet on a day-to-day basis. It was a clearing house where new production was sold, where the Soviet Union could buy Western currencies for gold, where industrial users could buy, and where (this came to be of crucial importance) speculators could buy and sell unhampered by governmental restrictions. The onset of World War II caused the closing of the market in 1939, but it reopened in 1954. Par values all over the world were expressed in gold (US$35 per ounce; other countries similarly expressing a per-ounce price in their own currencies). There was great calm in the market for six years, with prices always within a few pennies of the Bretton Woods par values. But late in 1960, trouble arose on the London gold market. A number of foreign central banks took to buying gold there with dollars, instead of converting these dollars to gold via the U. S. Treasury. Some speculators were also beginning to foresee the wave of currency devaluations that was to occur later in that decade, and noted that if currency should shrink in value, gold would be a lucrative hedge. Within a few days during October of 1960, gold purchases in London sent the price up to $40 and demonstrated once and for all that the $35 official price was no real barrier. Only central banks, and not private arbitrageurs, could redeem their dollars for gold at the U. S. Treasury, and the United States would never have allowed central banks to act as arbitrageurs by selling for a higher price gold obtained at $35 per ounce in London. The high price of $41 hit in 1960 was convincing evidence that the gold price might in time end up far above the official Bretton Woods price.

In 1961 the central banks of seven European countries plus the United States attempted to regulate the London market by organizing a so-called Gold Pool, which would sell official gold on the market to keep the price down near the $35 figure and buy whenever the gold price weakened. The Pool seemed to work effectively for several years, helped by Russian gold sales to finance wheat imports from the United States and Canada and a high level of South African production. The U.S. share in the Pool's dealings was 50 percent; and the manager of the scheme was the Bank of England. The devaluation of the pound sterling in November 1967, however, began the breakup of the Pool. With the pound devalued, speculators turned on the dollar and the franc, and the Pool was forced to put a steady supply of gold on the London market to keep the price from rising drastically. When it became known that France had stopped supplying gold to the Pool, speculation increased. Nearly $3 billion worth of gold were sold by the Pool in a six-month period, and when this became known the speculation intensified. Finally, in March 1968, the member central banks gave up the fight and announced the end of the Pool arrangement. Henceforth, the London market price was to be allowed to float free from the official price of $35 per ounce in a two-tier situation, and by the end of the year the price had reached a new record of nearly $42. Another period of calm ensued as South Africa took advantage of the high price by selling more newly mined gold, but by 1972 the gold price had taken off again. It passed $60 in the spring of that year, hit $90 early in 1973, was over $100 through most of that year, then went into a spectacular climb in 1974 as speculators sought a hedge against inflation and against the dangers to the currency system posed by the OPEC oil cartel. In fact London proved to be the primary means for speculating against all currencies at the same time. No use buying marks with dollars at a time when even the mark might weaken because of huge payments for oil. Far better to buy gold, which might rise in price against all currencies. Gold buying reached unprecedented levels in

1973-1974, with thousands of new buyers joining the old speculators. French peasants, European businesspeople, college professors with some small inkling of economics, wealthy South Americans, Indians, and Arab oil sheiks were all buying, many trying to protect their savings, many looking for a profit. Buying gold on margin became common, as did borrowing Eurodollars in order to buy. In the United States, where it was illegal to own gold itself, close substitutes rose rapidly.[1] Shares of stock in gold-mining companies sprang ahead; silver, platinum, and palladium prices climbed sometimes 8 percent or even 10 percent in a week; prices of gemstones such as diamonds, emeralds, rubies, and sapphires reflected the panic.

The upshot was that gold reached an unprecedented high of $197.50 per ounce on December 30, 1974. The price reached a peak like this neither because supplies had fallen, nor because industrial demand had increased. It was a sheer case of bootstrap psychology, whereby individuals (and corporations) bought gold because they thought it a haven against inflation.

Alas for them, that boom did not last. New developments brought the price crashing down, to as low as $104 in September 1976. The underlying reason was an official policy change on the part of the International Monetary Fund (examined in detail later in this chapter), which owns a large amount of gold. The IMF at its meeting in Kingston, Jamaica, in January 1976, decided to sell one-sixth of its total gold holdings (25 million ounces) over the following four years, using the profits to finance loans for developing countries.[2] In some thirty auctions, the IMF is thus selling what amounts to about 60 percent of one year's new production. During the same four-year period the IMF is returning another 25 million ounces to its member countries (in accordance with the size of their IMF quotas), which also poses a threat of further sales and price reductions on the London market. Finally, the U.S. Treasury has begun to hold occasional auction sales (the latest in May 1978) from the U. S. gold stock. The amounts involved have been small, only 1.2 million ounces or less than 5 percent of the IMF's proposed sales, but the effect was to speed the decline of gold in 1974-1976. Speculators are a hardy breed, however, and gold retains an almost mystical appeal to people who would otherwise be hedging against inflation by buying houses, land, old masters, antiques, and the like. In spite of the proven volatility of the market and the certainty that official gold sales will continue, its price on the London market broke through the $200 per ounce figure in July 1978 and reached the $240 mark in February 1979.

Another decision of the January 1976 IMF conference in Jamaica was to abolish the official price of gold. This price, having been raised from $35 to $38 in 1971 and again to $42.22 in 1973, had become irrelevant because no central bank wanted to give up any gold at all as long as its free market price was so much higher. Even France, the greatest believer in gold, was hardly likely to give up metal that was worth more than five times as much on the free market as it was valued officially. As a result, gold has been demoted and almost wholly immobilized as a reserve. It is now commonly classified as a "secondary reserve asset" by the central banks that continue to hold stocks of it.

The Place of Foreign Exchange Reserves

As experience was gained with the Bretton Woods system, it became apparent that there was no adequate mechanism for raising the world's total of reserves to keep pace with the growth of world trade. Official gold reserves grew slowly, and even fell back when the Gold Pool was selling on the London market in an unsuccessful attempt to keep the price from rising (see Table 9.2, column 1). Foreign currency reserves grew much more rapidly (column 2), but not so fast as the total value of world trade (column 3).

As a result, reserves as a percentage of world trade sank from 33 percent in 1954-1955 to 18 percent in 1972-1973. As long as currencies were not under attack, this was of little consequence; and indeed, from the end of World War II until as late as 1961, the U. S. government stayed scrupulously out of the business of intervening in the markets for foreign exchange. The United States maintained a passive attitude, leaving it up to the other governments (82 in 1961 were defending their rates with dollars) to sell dollars when their own currencies depreciated, or buy dollars when they appreciated. But when the first real speculation against the dollar since the Great Depression broke out late in 1960, it culminated in a 5 percent revaluation of the German mark and Dutch guilder in March of 1961. This was the first blow in a decade to the system of fixed currency parities, and opened a fifteen-year era of speculation that, as we saw in Chapter 4, has never fully died down.

The response of the world's central banks was to negotiate a series of reciprocal credit agreements that increased massively the availability of foreign exchange for defending exchange rates. These agreements are called *swaps*. They survived the end of the adjustable peg, and are still in force as a method of providing reserves to countries undertaking dirty floats. In general, a swap agreement is a facility under which one central bank agrees with a number of others to exchange on request its own currency for the currency of another central bank at the existing rate. The swap lasts for a limited period only, say three to six months. The actual funds may be spent to maintain the rate, or may simply be made available for potential use. The latter case is called a standby arrangement.

Should a swap be drawn upon, it would work as follows in the case of Germany and the United States. Suppose in a period of crisis the United States wishes to obtain $100 million worth of marks (= DM300 million at the current exchange rate) at once. The terminology used is to "activate a swap line," which is jargon for the verb "to borrow." The Federal Reserve System, which administers the U.S. swaps, would credit the dollar account of the Deutsche Bundesbank with $100 million (step 1 in the T-accounts of Fig.

9.2). Simultaneously the Fed would obtain a credit (new deposit) of DM300 million (at a rate of $1 = DM 3) in the Deutsche Bundesbank (step 2 in the T-accounts). Naturally, neither the Bundesbank nor the Fed can simply issue

TABLE 9.2. WORLD TOTALS OF OFFICIAL RESERVES AND TRADE (in billions of dollars)

Year	Gold reserves	Foreign exchange reserves (largely dollars)	World trade (combined total of exports and imports)
1954-1955	35.4	16.0	157
1968	38.9	31.0	438
1972-1973	35.7	98.7	755

new liabilities without backing them with assets. In this case the backing is the foreign credit they are in the process of receiving. Hence the Bundesbank can credit the Fed with DM300 million because it has just received $100 million from the Fed, and the Fed can credit Germany with $100 million because it has the DM300 million (see steps 3 and 4). It is, in short, a kind of "monetary incest" whereby central banks can indefinitely create more money by lending to each other.

Deutsche Bundesbank

Assets	Liabilities
③ Bundesbank account at Fed +DM300 million (= $100 million)	Deutsche mark deposits ② of US Fed +DM300 million

Federal Reserve System

Assets	Liabilities
④ Fed account in Deutsche Bundesbank +$100 million (=DM300 million)	Dollar deposits of ① Deutsche Bundesbank +$100 million

FIGURE 9.2

To this point the swap line looks like a double loan, and the reader may be wondering how the United States is to get any benefit. The benefit comes when the Fed spends the marks in support of the dollar, but Germany does not spend the dollars. As the Fed buys up excess dollars from private banks, say on the Frankfurt foreign exchange market, the marks are transferred from the Fed's account at the Bundesbank to those of the private German banks, as in Fig. 9.3. In the United States, however, the $100 million stays put in the Bundesbank's account at the Fed, and hence there can be no further credit repercussions in the United States.

Deutsche Bundesbank

Assets	Liabilities
Bundesbank account at US Fed ± 0	Deutsche mark deposits of US Fed $-$DM300 million
	Reserve accounts of German private banks $+$DM300 million

FIGURE 9.3

As part of the agreement, the two central banks would pledge to reverse the transaction three months later at the identical rate of exchange, thus removing any fear of loss of value. Should the swapped currency not be used immediately, it would be placed in interest-bearing time deposits or treasury bills. Following consultation between the central banks, each is free to draw on the swapped foreign currency to conduct stabilizing operations in the foreign exchange market. It is possible to renew the swap if both parties agree.

Since the participating central banks are required to furnish only *their own* currency, the swap is not limited by the outstanding stock of foreign exchange reserves, and swapped currency at least for a short time becomes a net addition to world reserves. Table 9.3 shows how the swaps developed through the summer of 1962, and their twentyfold growth since that time. The grand total grew from some $900 million at the close of 1962 to $22 billion sixteen years later.

Typically, swaps are used by the Fed in the United States to absorb dollars from foreign central banks that are in excess of what these banks would usually hold, and would otherwise exchange in the market, thus depreciating the dollar. In effect the excess dollars are bought with the proceeds of the swap. True, in three months when the swap expires the Fed will have to possess enough foreign exchange to reverse the transaction.[3] The swap is thus by no means a cure for foreign exchange problems. But it does buy time—for making other arrangements, for management of the problem in other ways, and for cooling down speculative activity and hot money flows. In this limited role, it has effectively given a substantial boost to world reserves. U.S. swap lines have been much used—the Fed engaging in some 280 drawings and repayments, 1962-1976; and foreign governments in 190 such acts in the same period.

Defense of a currency's exchange rate has some resemblance to a battlefield of the First World War. Normal intervention to buy or sell foreign exchange from a country's own reserves is akin to the first line of fire. Behind it lie the swap agreements, the trench lines expected to delay the enemy (speculators) and give time to prepare a more thorough defense. Still further to the rear is the second line of trenches, which for the United States is a

TABLE 9.3. SWAP AGREEMENTS OF THE UNITED STATES OF AMERICA

	Original amount (in millions of dollars)	1978 amount (in millions of dollars)	Date of original agreement	Term of agreement (in months)
Bank of France	50	2,000	March 1962	3
Bank of England	50	3,000	May 1962	3
Netherlands Bank	50	500	June 1962	3
National Bank of Belgium	50	1,000	June 1962	6
Bank of Canada	250	2,000	June 1962	3
Bank for International Settlements	100	1,850	July 1962	3
Swiss National Bank	100	1,400	July 1962	3
German Federal Bank	50	4,000	August 1962	3
Bank of Italy	150	3,000	October 1962	3
Austrian National Bank	50	250	October 1962	3
Bank of Sweden	50	300	January 1963	3

In later years, four more swap agreements were added, to wit:

National Bank of Denmark	250
Bank of Japan	2,000
Bank of Mexico	360
Bank of Norway	250

political defense. It may be possible, with some exertion of political muscle, to somehow persuade foreign central banks with large excess holdings of dollars not to convert these dollars into foreign exchange (or, before 1971, into gold) but instead to hold them for a long period of time. Where the political leverage is adequate, the foreigner might be persuaded to put the dollars into special U.S. Treasury bonds and notes. Bearing interest but nonmarketable, these are called *Roosa bonds* after their inventor, Robert Roosa, Undersecretary of the Treasury in the Kennedy administration. Where the leverage is less, the foreigner may have to be persuaded to hold such bonds by a promise of no cut in value through dollar devaluation. This is achieved by denominating the bonds in a foreign currency such as the German mark or Swiss franc. The Germans might thus buy a Roosa bond with $1,000, but the bond would be payable in DM2,500, removing any fear that dollar decline would rob the bond of part of its value. At the height of the speculative crisis of 1973, over $14 billion had been placed in dollar-denominated Roosa bonds by foreign governments ($11 billion by Germany alone), and another $1.5 billion was held in Roosa bonds denominated in a foreign currency ($1.2 billion by Switzerland).

Alternatively, a whole range of political action might be employed to persuade foreign governments to spend their excess dollars rather than to exchange them in the market. Early repayment of loans made by the United States to foreign countries might be negotiated, agreements to buy more U.S. military equipment might be entered into, and attempts can be made to get foreign governments to pay a larger share of the cost of U.S. troops stationed abroad.

There is one last defense, the "last ditch" emergency line where a final effort can be made to stop the speculators. The so-called Basel Agreements, named after the town in Switzerland, were concluded from 1961 on among the most important central banks as a system for emergency aid. These banks are organized as the "Group of 10," consisting of the banks of the United States, Great Britain, Germany, France, Japan, Canada, the Netherlands, Belgium, Italy, and Sweden. Together, representatives of these banks confer on a monthly basis at the prestigious (and a little mysterious) Bank for International Settlements at Basel. This bankers' bank, with its high-powered little staff of economists and its doorkeepers who are said to be found daily reading the *London Financial Times*, is the medium through which *ad hoc* rescue operations can be mobilized. Among the lines of credit advanced by the Group of 10 were a three-year, $2 billion aid package to Great Britain in 1968 (the small amount of Group of 10 aid to Britain in 1967, only $250 million, had contributed to the devaluation of the pound in that year), a $2 billion line of credit to France in its 1969 struggle, large-scale aid to Italy in 1975, and the $5.3 billion aid package advanced to Britain in the spring of 1976. No country has a legal right to this aid, and the whole arrangement remains rather informal. It resembles a swap in that the participating central banks make available their own currency (often, however, the main currency is dollars supplied out of exchange reserves), and in the fact that the loan must be repaid at some future date. Thus if the problem is not solved by the time of repayment, that alone might worsen the crisis. In late 1976, exchange markets were clearly jittery at the approaching December repayment date for Britain's large loan from the Group of 10.

The Role of the IMF

The world's major institution designed (among other things) for the express creation of new reserves is the International Monetary Fund (IMF). Housed in a large building in Washington, D.C., and staffed by an international group of economists, the IMF is a complicated institution with a major role in establishing international economic policy and in making new reserves available to governments.

Many of our current international institutions were designed to prevent a rerun of the 1930s. The United Nations was intended to keep any new Hitler from power; the IMF was designed to prevent new exchange crises, devaluations, and exchange controls such as the thirties had seen. Plans for the postwar economic order were hammered out at the New Hampshire resort of Bretton Woods in 1944. The outcome was a set of rules that included:

1. Exchange rate stability. The result was the adjustable peg system discussed in Chapter 3, with the IMF providing loaned funds so that countries could fight off speculators by defending their exchange rate. The IMF would also provide some international supervision of exchange rates and related monetary and fiscal policies.

2. Convertibility, or the elimination of exchange control. The United States was particularly emphatic on this point, since it felt that exchange control had been used to block American exports and because it hoped for a postwar world with far fewer restrictions on trade.

In essence, the IMF was a fund or pool of monetary reserves, originally gold and currency. The British, led by Lord Keynes, had envisaged a powerful organism that could create new international reserves in the same way as a central bank can expand the domestic money supply of a country. Countries wishing to settle debts could make overdrafts (borrow) from a so-called clearing union. The overdrafts could be used like bank checks to pay bills, and the recipient government would deposit the check back in the clearing union, receiving a credit there. These credits could also be used as monetary reserves. On a T-account, the clearing union could expand world reserves as needed by the stroke of a pen.

	Assets	Liabilities
	Overdrafts of Central Banks	Deposits of Central Banks
FIGURE 9.4	+1,000	+1,000

The United States pushed through a much more conservative proposal. Each member nation of the IMF was assigned a quota that bore some general relation to the value of its wealth and trade. The quota was expressed as a certain amount of gold and *its own currency*. This became the property of the Fund. The Fund could in turn lend these reserves to countries having difficulty defending their exchange rates. Not only would this increase the stability of exchange markets, but it would give the Fund some degree of control over its members. If members violated a rule of the Fund—one such was not to devalue by more than 10 percent without "prior consultation"—then the Fund could deny loans to that country. The IMF soon organized a secretariat and technical staff to help make studies and offer advice. The power to send or withdraw a technical mission gave additional control over member nations. Finally, the IMF was given a very special weapon (never actually used) called the *scarce currency clause*. This entailed the power to declare the currency of a country "scarce" if that country were seen to be acquiring ever-increasing quantities of reserves, and showed no sign of adjusting, through upward revaluation, for example. In such circumstances all other countries could apply discriminatory exchange controls against the offender.

Such power, although certainly not enabling the IMF to dictate policy, was considerable, and the Fund's designers were not careless about its control. They were not about to adopt a one-country, one-vote rule, such as is employed in the United Nations General Assembly. Nor did the idea of an absolute veto by a single country (as in the League of Nations) or by a single key member (as in the United Nations Security Council) appeal to them. Instead, voting in the IMF was apportioned according to the quotas, the vote being directly proportional to quota size. Early in the Fund's existence, this did mean that the United States, with 24.3 percent of the votes, and Great Britain, with 11.5 percent could control the Fund. In the late 1960s, however, the quotas were altered to reflect the growing importance of the Common Market countries and Japan. As of 1976, the countries controlling the most votes were as shown in Table 9.4.

TABLE 9.4.

Country	Number of votes
United States of America	6,700
Great Britain	2,800
West Germany	1,600
France	1,500
Japan	1,200
Canada	1,100
Italy	1,000

Total number of countries: 130   Total votes: 29,213
Each vote is equal in value to one million SDRs, each in turn equal to about $1.15 in 1976.

Source: *International Financial Statistics,* November 1976. The smallest numbers of votes held by individual countries are: Grenada, 2; Western Samoa, 2; Comoros Islands, 1.9; Maldive Islands, 0.7.

Lending Operations of the IMF. The most important thing the Fund does is to lend money to nations that are having difficulty defending their exchange rate. This has served to stave off many a devaluation, to give time for adjustment, and to allow a more even battle with speculators. By 1976, a quarter-century after the Fund's inception, it had lent about $41 billion (nearly 90 percent of this since 1959) to 103 nations of a membership that then totaled 130, and had made loans to virtually every major country. As noted earlier, the resources of the Fund come from the quota subscriptions of member nations. These were for many years paid one-quarter in gold and three-quarters in the individual country's own currency. Portugal, for example, paid $18.8 million worth of gold and $56.2 million worth of escudos for its membership. The quotas, originally set in 1947, were increased in 1959 (by 50 percent), again in 1966 (by 25 percent), and once more in 1970 (by 30 percent). Another 33 percent increase was agreed on at the Jamaica meeting of the IMF in 1976. Special quota increases have also been made for Japan and the Common Market countries. Total assets of the Fund in 1978 were $48 billion, up from the $29 billion shown in Table 9.4. The U.S. quota was just under 20 percent of the new total.

This seems an enormous sum, enough surely to deal with almost any conceivable exchange crisis. However, probably more than half of this sum is actually useless, for the three following reasons:

1. Many currencies are "soft," that is, so hedged about by exchange restrictions that they are of little or no use in making international payments. Others are "hard" enough, but so unimportant that no one wants them anyway. The list runs literally from A (Afghanistan's afghani) to Z (the Zambian kwacha), with in-between currencies like the Laotian kip and the Paraguayan guarani. As of 1976, the Fund has never lent more than 38 of its 130 currencies, and several of these have been soft. IMF loans made in Argentine pesos and the Brazilian cruzeiro, for example, were useful only to Uruguay and Paraguay, whose foreign trade is overwhelmingly dominated by these two countries. The grand total of soft currencies that the Fund has never lent, and is very unlikely ever to do so, comes to about one-quarter of its assets.

2. Roughly another one-quarter of the Fund's assets are likely to be already lent out at any given time. As repayment is scheduled over a period of three to five years, this portion of the IMF's funds is effectively immobilized. True, some interest is being earned. There is a ¾ of 1 percent service charge, and a sliding scale of interest rates from ½ of 1 percent for small-scale borrowing over one year to 4 percent for large outstanding borrowings in the fifth year, and penalty rates thereafter. But the interest earnings are small compared to the total of loans.

3. Finally, some of the Fund's currency holdings are unusable because these are the currencies temporarily under attack. The pound sterling, the French franc, the Canadian dollar, and the Australian dollar, for example, are all usually hard currencies that have been lent by the IMF on many occasions. Yet at other times, each of these has had to be supported against speculative attack by borrowings from the Fund. It would be absurd for the IMF to loan Britain foreign exchange to support the pound, and then turn around and loan pounds to some other country. The increased supply of pounds would put downward pressure on the pound and undo the effect of the loan to Britain. Frequently, currencies under attack have amounted to nearly a quarter of the Fund's assets (this figure overlaps with the estimate of soft currencies given in reason 1 above).

What this means is that the IMF works well enough for small countries, but it generally does not have the funds to cope with a major crisis. The repeated quota increases have been one response. Another has been the formation of a small "lender's club" that has attempted to make additional resources available to the Fund outside its usual structure. The Group of 10 countries agreed at Vienna in 1961, under the so-called General Arrangements to Borrow, to make $6 billion available for lending in crisis situations. The money can be used only among the ten countries themselves, and outsiders wanting to join must pay a minimum $100 million into the GAB. The GAB gives three- to five-year loans, which must be approved both by the Group of 10 and the IMF and are protected against depreciation or devaluation by a gold-equivalent clause. A GAB member can refuse to participate by claiming its own currency is under attack. The $6 billion figure is not as large as it seems, of course, because some of the currencies in the GAB will be under pressure. For example, the U.S. share of $2 billion, the British share of $1 billion, and the French and Italian at $550 million each have been less useful than the German $1 billion. Just as with normal IMF operations, the GAB cannot very well defend a currency and lend it out at the same time.

On an emergency basis in the two years 1974 and 1975, additional funds were made available by the IMF to cope with the oil crisis. Its "special oil facility" was a scheme to attract funds from oil-producing states, mostly Arab, and to channel them to poor countries damaged by the need to find additional reserves to pay for oil. The scheme fell far short of expectations. Originally conceived of as mobilizing $30 billion, it actually provided less than $8 billion, of which over $2 billion came from Saudi Arabia, $1.7 billion from the richer European countries like Germany and Switzerland, and $1 billion from Iran. The big borrowers from the special oil facility were Italy, Great Britain, Spain, and India in that order. The funds available for lending within the oil facility are now exhausted, but plans were announced in August 1977 to make available new loans amounting to about $10 billion. Called the "Witteveen facility" after Johannes Witteveen, managing director of the IMF at the time, the new arrangement will permit selected countries to borrow about double the amount they would be able to borrow if dependent on the normal quotas alone. Saudi Arabia contributed the largest share to the Witteveen facility, about $2.5 billion (the United States share was about $1.7 billion). In the complicated bargaining leading to the new arrangement, the path was cleared for Saudi Arabia to assume a seat on the IMF's Board of Directors.

The Fund's system for lending works like this: Each nation is allowed to borrow what amounts to 125 percent of its quota. Denmark, with a quota of $301.6 million worth of gold and Danish kroner, can borrow $377 million worth of foreign currencies. Such a "borrowing" or "drawing" is actually a straightforward exchange. If Denmark were the borrower, it would "buy" the foreign currency with its own kroner. The borrowing privilege is divided into five equal parts or *tranches* (the French word for slice), with the understanding that the IMF's holdings of any member's currency will not increase by more than 25 percent of that country's quota in any one year. The only exceptions are when some other country has borrowed the currency in question recently, so that the IMF's holdings of it are below the quota level, or if the Fund waives the limitation, which is regularly done.

All this limits a member's purchases of foreign exchange from the Fund to 125 percent of its quota, spread over five years. Since the original IMF holding of the borrower's quota was 75 percent of that quota, with the rest in gold, the permitted 125 percent borrowing means that the IMF can hold no more than 200 percent of quota in any member's currency. However, since 1963 this does occasionally happen.

The first 25 percent tranche, equal to $75.4 million in the case of Denmark, is exactly equal to that nation's original contribution of gold and dollars. This can be taken back (repurchased with Danish currency) more or less automatically. If by chance other countries in the past have borrowed Danish currency, leaving the IMF with less than 75 percent of Denmark's quota in kroner, the automatic borrowing right will also allow the IMF to build back IMF holdings of its currency to 75 percent (called the super-tranche). Thus a country's gold subscription, plus any amount of that country's currency loaned by the IMF to others, can actually be considered a real part of that country's foreign exchange reserves. This amount is called the *gold tranche*, and its existence adds about $7 billion to world reserves (see Table 9.1).

The borrowing of the other four 25 percent installments, called the *credit tranches*, must have the permission of the Fund's Board of Governors and involve an ever-greater degree of IMF investigation. The second tranche will involve some substantial consultation with the Fund, and perhaps a visit from an IMF financial team—good examples are the pressure to reduce government spending put on Great Britain in late 1976 by the Fund's experts; the Fund's earlier exaction of a promise by Britain to cut its money supply expansion by two-thirds in return for a loan in 1969; and the 1977 money and spending ceilings put on Italy. The third, fourth, and fifth tranches become even harder to borrow. Normally, any loans made by the Fund must be paid back in three to five years, and the repayment must be in hard currency.

To facilitate these arrangements, the Fund began in about 1952 to allow and encourage so-called standby credit arrangements, whereby a member could apply for IMF loans, have the application approved, and have the foreign exchange immediately available before any anticipated problems with the exchange rate are actually encountered. Even if the credits are not used, the IMF has provided security since its support can be counted on immediately. As with other operations of the Fund, a standby credit involves a small service charge.

Special Drawing Rights. For many years, since the Keynes Plan for the IMF
had been turned down at the Bretton Woods Conference in 1944, many
academics and financial experts had advocated new powers for the Fund actually to create new reserves. Two plans advanced in the 1960s attracted wide
attention. The Triffin Plan, named for its inventor, Robert Triffin of Yale
University, saw the IMF's own newly created reserves as replacing foreign
exchange reserves on a worldwide basis. This aggressive creation of new reserves would be quite simple in operation. An *expanded* IMF, which we shall
call the XIMF, would henceforth keep as a deposit liability the monetary reserves of member countries. Individual holdings of key currencies like the
dollar, mark, or pound would henceforth be abolished. To create new reserves, the XIMF would simply purchase securities (government treasury bills
and the like) in the open market, paying by check, just as when a single country undertakes open-market operations within its own boundaries. The seller
of the securities would deposit the XIMF check with its commercial bank,
whence it would be cleared through that country's central bank and then deposited with the XIMF. The increased balances shown in Fig. 9.5 represent
new reserves.

XIMF

Assets	Liabilities
Securities purchased in open market +100	Deposits of central banks +100

FIGURE 9.5

This process of reserve creation could be pursued at any time when
reserves are short, or it could be reversed to counter a glut of reserves. Note
the special advantages: It dispenses with key currencies, and hence the
problem of attacks by those who hold the currency as part of their official
reserves (for example, British pounds held in 1976 by oil-producing states). It
also ties reserve creation to need, and not to the accidental effects of new gold
discoveries or the ability of countries like the United States and Great Britain
to supply their currencies to others as reserves.

An interesting and much-discussed variation of the Triffin Plan was the
Stamp Plan, named after the British economist Maxwell Stamp. This plan
envisaged an XIMF issuing certificates that would be accepted by members in
the same way as foreign exchange and would form part of the world's monetary reserves. The big difference from the Triffin Plan was that these transferable certificates would be distributed through some international
agency—perhaps the XIMF, perhaps the World Bank—as loans to less developed countries, the loans to be paid back many years hence on easy terms.
Countries receiving the certificates could purchase imports with them, and
the exporting country receiving the certificates would add them to its mone-

tary reserves. Given its posture of aid to the poverty-stricken, the Stamp Plan generated less enthusiasm than might have been expected. Many economists opposed it on the ground that the optimal quantity of world reserves needed for successful operation of the international monetary mechanism may have little or no relation to the optimal quantity of foreign aid.

XIMF

Assets	Liabilities
Debts of less developed countries	Certificates (reserves of central banks)
+100	+100

FIGURE 9.6

When reform finally did come, it was considerably different from either the Triffin or the Stamp Plan. A momentous meeting of the IMF Board of Governors took place at Rio de Janeiro, Brazil, in September 1967. The plan considered there was the result of four years of study by the technical staffs of the Group of 10. Over the next six months, and accompanied by an enormous amount of discussion, the details of the reform were hammered out as an amendment to the articles of the IMF. The details were as follows:

1. A new category of reserves called *special drawing rights* (SDRs) was established separate from the general accounts of the IMF but still part of the Fund's operations.

2. Any IMF member was eligible to participate, and any member could opt out. (The two great opponents of the SDR, France and South Africa, at long last decided to participate in the scheme.)

3. The initial allocation of SDRs, made on January 1, 1970, was $9.4 billion. Of this, $3.4 billion was made available at once, $3 billion in 1971, and the last $3 billion installment in 1972. It was expected that decisions on the further creation of new SDRs would be made every five years. However, only token opposition will suffice to stop new creation, since an 85 percent positive vote of the IMF must approve. The formula used to allocate the new reserves was based on voting strength in the Fund; hence, unlike the idea of the Stamp Plan, rich countries benefited far more than poor.

4. Holders of SDRs (which must be central banks) can exchange them for foreign currency directly with another country. As this resembles the way gold used to be employed as a reserve, the SDRs were not surprisingly nicknamed "paper gold." Initially, the SDRs were even defined in terms of gold, with the dollar designation being understood to mean the dollar at $35 per ounce of gold. More recently, in June 1974, the IMF decided to express the value of SDRs as a moving average worth of sixteen major currencies.[4] Either way, they are little affected by currency devaluations.

They hold a substantial advantage over gold in that interest (60% of the weighted average of short-term interest rates in America, Japan, West Germany, and Britain, over 5% since 1974) is paid to any country that holds SDRs in excess of its initial allocation, that interest rate in effect being paid by the countries having used the SDRs and thus holding less than their quota.[5] This seems to make a great deal more sense than the use of gold, which not only bears no interest, but takes up storage space, must be guarded, and has many industrial uses.

The transfer of SDRs occurs on the accounts of the IMF. The paying country is debited and the recipient country is credited. Thus there are no pieces of paper called SDRs, just numbers in account books and entries in computer memory banks. There is no requirement for corrective action or IMF supervision, as with the Fund's credit tranches. However, even though the IMF need not approve a transaction involving SDRs, the recipient country must agree, and does have the right to refuse acceptance. There is one exception. When a country is "designated" by the IMF—ordinarily this would be a country with a very large and growing stock of reserves—then it *must* accept SDRs in exchange for its own or some other convertible currency. The obligation ends when the designated country has acquired SDRs up to three times its own allocation. For example, a country allocated $100 in SDRs after designation would be obligated to accept $200 worth of additional SDRs from other countries.[6] (Under present levels of allocation, the EEC could swallow all U.S. SDRs if designated, and the United States could swallow the entire stock of the EEC.) After the required maximum figure is reached, the designated country can continue to accept the SDRs of others if it wishes, but there is no requirement to do so.

Perhaps the most hotly debated of all the topics concerning the SDR was "reconstitution." After using SDRs, must you eventually be required to return to your original position? Some countries advocated repayment as if an SDR were a temporary loan. Others wanted no reconstitution at all, as if holdings of gold or foreign exchange were involved. The result was a compromise. All SDRs may be used, but the average daily holdings by a country over a five-year period must be no less than 30 percent of its average daily allocations of SDRs. So—the country that never uses more than 70 percent of its allocation has no problems. If it uses 80 percent for six months, then it must reconstitute (buy back) enough SDRs to reach 40 percent of its allocation in some subsequent six-month period. How is reconstitution achieved? By exchanging holdings of foreign currency for the SDRs of some other country.

The SDR has loomed large in recent years. There is talk that the huge quantities of dollars now held by foreign central banks will eventually be converted into these new assets, with the IMF exchanging SDRs for dollars and then investing the dollars in some kind of U.S. long-term securities. Certainly they pass the important test of costing less than other reserves. They earn interest, unlike gold, and they are little subject to loss of value because of currency depreciation, unlike some individual currency such as the dollar. In some ways, however, the SDR idea has weaknesses. Conceivably the "three times" rule might bring the system to a halt if most countries are trying to spend their SDRs with two or three other countries whose exports are much in demand—oil states, perhaps. New creation of SDRs is difficult since near-unanimity is required in voting, major reserve currencies such as the dollar are buttressed but not replaced, and the problem of possible speculative attack on currencies is not rectified. Actually the whole scheme is a little less innovative than it appears, in that the same effect could have been achieved by increasing the size of the IMF's gold tranche without requiring new payments into the Fund. But the SDR now holds the spotlight. By the rules of the IMF, the position of the SDR will be reviewed and possibly modified every five years. This process ensures that its future will include long negotiations and acrimonious debates.

For the IMF, which administers SDRs as well as conducting its general operations, the next few years are likely to be equally acrimonious. The IMF has been seriously criticized in a number of respects. Some critics point out the need for a world central bank that could expand the international money supply in times of economic slump and contract it in a boom. The IMF has not developed in this fashion. Nor has it been much help in aiding poor countries, in spite of the sale of some of its gold mentioned earlier. Some suggest merging the IMF with its sister institution, the World Bank. There was major criticism that the IMF did far too little in formulating emergency measures to deal with the oil crisis in 1974. And finally, critics pointed to a sense of confusion in the IMF about whether it would support a return to fixed exchange rates, or acquiesce in the present float.

Fixed versus Floating Rates

The main arena of debate during the 1970s on the monetary side of international economics has been which sort of system to support: Fixed rates or floating rates. This topic stands to be one of the most controversial areas of economics for years to come. Every section of this chapter—the position of gold, the place of foreign exchange reserves, the role of the IMF—is more or less important depending on whether exchange rates are fixed or floating. In this, the concluding section of our last chapter on the international side of money and banking, it is appropriate to review the main arguments for and against fixing and floating.

Given a choice, most businesspeople and bankers would probably opt for some system of fixed exchange rates. The fixed rate is convenient in making plans or in handling finance. American exporters of capital goods, for example, might have to give a price quotation two or three years before receiving payment for the goods. Thus in deciding what price to quote, they face the difficult task of determining not only what their own costs of production will be two or three years hence, but also of where the exchange rate will be. They may indeed have some control, or at least some knowledge, about their own future costs. But the calculation of future movements in the exchange rate is likely to go beyond them or any experts they consult.

Uncertainty of exchange rates may also prove very discouraging for small investors. Consider the hypothetical case of a little old lady in Toronto in 1960. Her holdings of American stocks and bonds gave low yields when the U.S. dollar dividends and interest payments were converted into Canadian dollars at the then-current exchange rate of US $1.03 = C $1.00. Turning her complaints into action, she then sold off her U.S. assets, bought Canadian dollars at the high price of US $1.03, and invested in Canadian assets. Then, in 1962, she found the Canadian dollar had fallen in value to US $0.92 = C $1.00. A movement of this size meant that she could have saved over 10 percent on the cost of buying her Canadian assets, or alternately could have made 10 percent by holding on to her United States assets. Understandably, the lady from Toronto becomes a bitter opponent of floating exchange rates. She joins the bankers and businesspeople who insist that floating rates carry a cost and that, all other things equal, fixed rates are preferable to floating.

Supporters of floating rates will be quick to counter these arguments, however. In the main they would argue that uncertainty is not eliminated under a system of fixed rates, because fixed rates themselves are subject to change. Indeed, by postponing the adjustments needed in exchange rates, fixed rates may cause the eventual alteration to be much more precipitous than it would have been otherwise. For example, if in the ten years from 1957 to 1967 the pound sterling had slid gradually from US$2.80 to US$2.40 = £1, the effect on investors would clearly have been less calamitous than was the loss of $0.40 on every pound that occurred in one nightmare weekend of 1967 when the pound was sharply devalued. During the late 1960s and early 1970s, every major currency in the world underwent a parity change in its fixed rate at least once. Investors rightly became skeptical about the long-run stability of any so-called fixed currency parity.

Supporters of floating rates also call attention to the need for large quantities of foreign exchange reserves in order to maintain a fixed rate system. Although willing to admit that floating rates carry the cost of uncertainty, they point out that large holdings of reserves—especially when they bear no interest, as with gold—are equally an opportunity cost.

The more conservative members of the economics and business communities see a wholly different sort of advantage for fixed rates than the ones discussed thus far: Fixed rates may force the government to follow conservative economic policies in the area of inflation and interest rates. Although we shall later return to this point, it is convenient to introduce the question here. Say that Britain is experiencing considerable inflation vis-a-vis its trading partners. As time goes by, imports will tend to become cheaper and exports more expensive, with the result that more pounds sterling will be offered in the foreign exchange market at the same time that less foreign currency is offered.

The overall effect of this increase in pounds offered and decrease in foreign currencies will be a decline in the value of the pound. To support a fixed rate, the Bank of England will be forced to intervene by buying sterling. Such purchases by the Bank, however, clearly depend on how much foreign exchange is available to it. To conserve its limited stocks of foreign currency, the Bank may well adopt a tighter money policy, cutting back the rate of growth of the money supply in an attack on inflation. The more one dislikes inflation, the more one will welcome the "discipline of international payments," which forces the government toward what conservatives would view as the correct policy.

Advocates of floating rates have a response. Even assuming that fixed rates actually *do* a better job of controlling inflation, isn't it a political decision (to be decided democratically) as to how much inflation a country should suffer as a trade-off against unemployment? Much modern theory in the area of macroeconomics postulates that there is such a trade-off, with price stability often accompanying relatively high levels of unemployment, and low unemployment being a companion of inflation. To the extent that this is so, why should it not be the voters who decide? Why should bankers and businesspeople of the conservative stripe be the ones to decide, through the exchange rate mechanism, that inflation is to be opposed more adamantly than unemployment? Advocates of floating rates still argue that, even assuming fixed rates are good for controlling inflation, floating rates may well have the same effect. The decline in purchasing power from inflation will be seen not only in the standard price indices, but also in the decline of the currency's value in terms of foreign monies. With inflation so obvious to all, the government's proper course is as clear in this case as it is under a regimen of fixed rates.

Opponents of fixed rates also argue that the so-called discipline of international payments may be illusory, bringing unnecessary unemployment or needless inflation just as well as it could bring stability. If, for example, recessions and high rates of unemployment among Britain's trading partners were the reason for its balance of payments difficulties, then contractionary monetary or fiscal policies would in essence represent an import of the recessions. Similarly, an inflation can be imported. Price rises in the United States could cause a dollar inflow into Britain as the U.S. imports move. The expenditure of sterling by monetary authorities to keep the pound from rising and the dollar from falling in value would add to the reserves of the British banking system, and in the absence of proper corrective policy this could prove highly inflationary to Britain.

Floating rates dispense with the need to subjugate the domestic economy to international payments. They allow governments to follow expansionary policies when there is recession abroad and contractionary policies when there is inflation abroad. Nearly fifty years ago it was noted that Peru's floating currency and China's silver-based currency (in essence a floating rate against other countries) had served to insulate both countries against many of the more severe effects of the Great Depression of the 1930s. In recent years, the decision to float ordinarily has not meant a fear of importing recession, but a defense against inflation. Such was the case with the floating of the German mark in 1969 and 1971, of the Japanese yen in 1971, and of the Canadian dollar in both 1950 and 1970.

A more recently voiced worry concerning floating rates is that they may in themselves cause inflation. This could occur where there is a "ratchet" type inflation, in which increased costs tend to push up prices but decreased costs do not lower them. As a nation's currency declines in value, the increased cost of imports would be passed on to the rest of the economy, perhaps even in magnified form. As the price level rises, the government will increase aggregate demand to reach fuller employment at the new price level. Clearly such an argument involves a great number of assumptions about the behavior of firms and governments. The argument has some explanatory power and is plausible, but it is by no means proven. The authors of this text remain chary of it.[7]

Has Floating Worked?   Whether or not floating has worked is a difficult question to answer with satisfaction, as it is not always easy to connect a problem or its solution with a system of exchange rates. It *is* clear that floating rates brought the world through the continuing oil crisis without the gigantic flows of hot money that would surely have developed had the old adjustable peg been in use. Speculation against the currencies of countries faced with massive oil import bills simply did not develop on anything near the scale of 1971 or 1973.

One factor that makes it difficult to judge the effectiveness of floating is that the world as of 1979 cannot really claim that floating rates are fully in operation. Dirty floating appears to be the rule rather than the exception; the EEC snake preserves the essence of fixed rates; IMF loans and the use of swaps to support exchange rates are as frequent as ever (the IMF made more loans in 1974 than in any year since its foundation). Whenever dirty floating is carried to the point where it approaches the defense of a fixed rate, then it gives speculators a target to shoot at, and exchange rates are likely to change sharply. The events of March 1976 sounded much like the old days of the Bretton Woods Agreement. The pound lost 5 percent of its value against the dollar in five days, the lira dropped 5 percent in one day and 9 percent in three days, and the franc fell 4½ percent in a day. In the losing game to support the rate, Britain lost almost $1 billion, France lost $1 billion in a day, and Italy exhausted its reserves almost entirely. To add to the difficulty of making an informed judgment, controls on capital movements, on exchange transactions, and even on foreign trade itself are still common. The conference of the IMF, in Kingston, Jamaica, in January 1976, hinted at a return to fixed rates,[8] and many countries still fix their rate against some major currency such as the dollar, mark, or franc. In fact, Mexico's move to floating in September 1976 was a textbook example of how floating ought not to be used. Starting with the Mexican peso tied to the dollar, the Mexican authorities found rapid inflation and capital outflows threatening its foreign exchange reserves. They floated as an emergency measure. Not surprisingly, the peso slumped sharply. Mexico then rounded up emergency support to fix the rate again, but found the peso under continuing attack. How can floating as a theory be judged under conditions like this?

The true tests of the theory are reasonably obvious, but it will take considerable time for their assessment to be made. First, it is unfair to judge floats when the floating is undertaken under crisis conditions. A period of two or three years following the forced move to floating in 1973 is neither enough time nor sufficiently "normal" for a proper assessment to be made. Second, one would want to know whether any long-term changes in the volume of world trade seem to be taking place, and whether they seem associated with floats versus fixed rates. Third, the passage of years should make it clear whether floating rates really do avoid the hot money flows of yesteryear. Fourth, further research should ascertain whether floats do encourage inflation, as some charge. The jury is still out, and the decision is certainly one that ought not to be made on the basis of still-fragmentary information.

What *Are* the Rules Now?

As a final summary, let us review what rules *are* now in effect. They are minimal. Most developed countries have undertaken to keep their currencies convertible; the rules concerning SDRs are still in effect as are those concerning IMF drawings. Beyond this there are virtually no other rules. Reserves can be held as a country pleases, in gold, foreign exchange, or SDRs. There is no official price now for gold or foreign exchange. A country that wants to peg its currency can do so if it wishes: to another currency (now some 30 are pegged to the dollar, 10 to the franc, fewer than 5 to the pound), to a group of currencies (the EEC snake, 9 others to assorted "baskets"), to the SDR (as with some oil states and five or so other countries)—anything except gold. Such pegs can be within any margins; they can creep or be adjusted in large jumps without requiring the permission of any outsider. Or if they float, the float can be as clean or as dirty as a country pleases. The question whether this makes for a better world in international economics is still debated, but there is no debate that it is certainly a different world.

Notes

1. It was illegal for American and British citizens to own gold, except for legitimate industrial uses, and as certified collectors of gold coins. The law making gold ownership illegal, which dated from 1934, was repealed in 1975, and now even contracts can be expressed in gold, just as they commonly were in the nineteenth century.
2. The IMF's profit is the difference between the official price at which the gold was valued in its accounts (on the order of $40 per ounce) and the free market price.
3. In the case of the United States, the reversal of the swap has sometimes entailed agreements for the foreign country involved to purchase U.S. military equipment, or an agreement to hold dollars guaranteed against exchange rate changes (the so-called Roosa Bonds mentioned in this chapter).
4. The sixteen major currencies are averaged in the following relative proportions:

U.S. dollar	33 %	Belgian franc	3.5%
German mark	12.5	Swedish krona	2.5
British pound	9	Australian dollar	1.5
French franc	7.5	Spanish pesata	1.5
Japanese yen	7.5	Norwegian krone	1.5
Canadian dollar	6	Danish krone	1.5
Italian lira	6	Austrian schilling	1
Dutch guilder	4.5	South African rand	1
		Total	100%

5. The interest rate had been a very low 1.5 percent until mid-1974.
6. Had the recipient country already used its $100 worth of SDRs, it would have been obligated to accept $300 worth from others instead of $200.
7. See Janice M. Westerfield, "Would Fixed Exchange Rates Control Inflation?" *Business Review* (July/August 1976): 9. This article is an understandable and short survey of the entire problem. Sometimes the effort is made to blame floating rates for the recent increase in the cost of hedging exchange risks in the forward market. An article in *Business Week*, June 2, 1975, pointed out that the cost of properly hedged foreign exchange transactions was perhaps ten times what it had been in the mid-1960s, and perhaps five times more than in the late 1960s. The implication is that floating rates have caused this. But surely the blame cannot be so easily laid on floating rates. The cost of hedging in the forward market is ordinarily the interest-rate loss a bank suffers from holding a currency such as the dollar rather than a currency such as the pound. While it is true that the spread in interest rates between New York and London has indeed widened in recent years, hence raising the cost of hedging, is this not due to very rapid inflation in Britain, and attempts by the British monetary authorities to control it?
8. The Jamaica Conference provided for a generalized return to par values and fixed rates if so voted by an 85 percent majority of the total number of votes in the IMF. Thus the approval of both the United States and the EEC would be required.

Before the vote, the IMF would have to determine that several conditions for stability had been met. No country would be forced to set a par value. It is most unlikely that any quick return to fixed rates will occur. See Edward M. Bernstein et al., *Reflections on Jamaica*, Princeton University Essay in International Finance No. 115, April 1976.

PART **III**

TRADE
THEORY

Economics is the study not only of the full use of existing resources, but also of their allocation. Chapters 1-9 examined the macroeconomic questions of employment and inflation, yet this is only half the story. Full employment at the expense of improper resource allocation, as in the case of using import restrictions to stimulate the domestic economy, can be a costly policy because it prevents the economy from reaching its full potential—and it can harm future growth. The distribution of income, moreover, with its critical economic, social, and political implications, requires microeconomic analysis. Indeed, many economists feel that the issues of efficient allocation and proper distribution are more important and more fundamental than the macroeconomic questions. In their view, the development of exchange rate systems and of investment markets is only a means to an end—that of the efficient global allocation of resources. While the authors feel that such a view should be modified to include provisions concerning full employment and inflation, they are in accord with its general thrust. It is necessary, in Leland Yeager's words, to see the reality beyond the "veil of money and prices."

10

INTERNATIONAL TRADE THEORY

THE THEORY OF COMPARATIVE ADVANTAGE

To see beyond the veil of money and prices, we need to make many simplifications and abstractions; otherwise, we perceive only the chaos of the world. Hence we enter what is usually called the pure theory of trade. To perceive the shape of trade, we postulate a very simple world of two nations with two products. This world has perfect competition, which is essential to make price equal cost and ensure efficient operation of firms. Within each country there is a free movement of resources, and when trade opens up there are no transportation costs. There is full employment, so that resources displaced through trade are instantly put to work elsewhere. Tastes are assumed to be unchanged as are resource endowments. As in any pure competition model, goods and inputs are considered to be homogeneous. Later, when we modify the model, we can relax many of these assumptions; yet having once seen the shape of things in the abstract, we should still be able to detect the real forms behind the veil.

Ricardo's Exposition

In the history of economics, the pure theory of trade was one of the first great issues faced by the discipline, and the issue is still alive. The questions posed sound simple. Will countries be better off if they trade with one another? What goods will they trade? Will their welfare be greater if they buy only at home from their own producers?

Intuition supplies an easy answer for some goods, an answer ordinarily not contested. One country may have so great an advantage (in terms of cost and availability) in the production of some good that obviously it can export that good to another country that cannot produce the item. It is reasonable and not debated that the United States should import bananas from Honduras instead of trying the difficult task of growing them at home, and equally reasonable that Honduras should import cars from the United States where they are relatively cheap, instead of trying to manufacture them domestically at great expense. This illustrates the principle called *absolute advantage*, wherein each country holds a superiority in the production of some good or group of goods. Absolute advantage may come about because of the quality of land, including natural resources and climate (which is the reason why Honduras produces bananas instead of the United States); because of differences in labor, capital, technology, and entrepreneurship; because of the quantities of these factors available and the skill with which they are combined; and because of political conditions in the countries concerned. For centuries no one has doubted that trade will spring up under these circumstances and that it will be advantageous. The United States gets bananas it would otherwise do without, and Hondurans drive cars that, if produced at home, would be frightfully expensive.

But what if one country can produce any good more cheaply than another country? Would trade occur then? Should it occur? Would it be at all advantageous to that country? Many observers once believed, and some still do, that such a producer would be foolish to engage in trade as long as it can make everything more economically. To be sure, other countries would gain in trade with it, but they would have nothing to offer in return but high-priced merchandise that could not sell.[1]

Logical? No. The opinion advanced in the last paragraph was exploded by David Ricardo, the English economist of the nineteenth century, in the famous Chapter 7, "On Foreign Trade," of his 1817 book *The Principles of Political Economy and Taxation*.[2] It was in that extraordinary, brilliant chapter that Ricardo enunciated the famous law of comparative advantage.

According to this theory, under free-trade conditions each country will specialize in the production of the goods it produces *relatively* cheaply (that is, goods in which it has a comparative advantage) and will import the goods in which other countries have a comparative advantage.

We can illustrate the theory initially by sticking close to Ricardo's original presentation. We assume the purely theoretical world outlined in our opening paragraphs. Our two countries and products are Ricardo's: England and Portugal producing wine and cloth.

The production of wine and cloth will take place in both England and Portugal in the absence of international trade.[3] Ricardo uses labor time requirements to illustrate costs, and we do the same in Table 10.1.

TABLE 10.1. LABOR COSTS OF PRODUCTION IN HOURS[4]

	Wine (per gallon)	Cloth (per yard)
Portugal	80	90
England	120	100

Note that Portugal thus has an absolute advantage over England in both lines of production. (The reason might be better land.) But Ricardo insists that trade can open up anyway, and more, that it will be profitable to both countries.

Numerically, this can be explained as follows. Before trade, internal prices in the two countries will be proportional to the costs of production. Thus with the cost ratio of wine to cloth 120/100 in England, then 1 gallon of wine must exchange for 1.2 yards of cloth. Why is this so? Because of our assumption of competition. If a gallon of wine could be exchanged on the market for 1.3 yards of cloth, instead of 1.2, then people can profit by producing additional wine and selling it for more than it costs. That will lower the price of wine, back toward a ratio of 120/100.

Meanwhile, in Portugal, the cost ratio of wine to cloth is 80/90 (which is equal to 88.8/100). Thus 1 gallon of wine will exchange for 0.88 yard of cloth.

If we now permit trade to open between the two countries, we make a remarkable discovery. Merchants in London are pleased to find they can get more wine for English cloth in trade with Portugal than they could in trade with English wine producers. One cloth used to bring 10/12 of a gallon of wine, but now, in exchange with Portugal, each unit of cloth brings 9/8 of a gallon at the prices that hold in Lisbon. With 100 hours of labor, England can obtain a product that used to cost 135 hours. (The calculation: 100 hours = 1 yard of cloth. 1 yard cloth = 9/8 gallon wine after trade. 1 gallon used to cost 120 hours. 9/8 gallon would thus have cost 9/8 × 120 = 135 hours.) Incidentally, English wine makers will not be pleased. The great dilemma of free trade is what to do about the industries hurt by foreign competition.

Back in Lisbon, Portuguese merchants also make a discovery. These merchants, who formerly had been able to exchange a gallon of wine for only 8/9 of a yard of cloth in Portugal, now find that they can obtain 12/10 of a yard if the wine is brought to England. With 80 hours of labor the Portuguese get what would have cost 108 hours at home. (The calculation: 80 hours = 1 gallon of wine. 1 gallon wine = 12/10 yard of cloth after trade. 1 yard used to cost 90 hours. 12/10 gallon would thus have cost 12/10 × 90 = 108 hours.) Note again that there will also be some disappointment. Portuguese producers of cloth will lose trade.

Note that at any price for wine cheaper than 120/100 (that is, whenever less than 1.2 yards of cloth must be given up to buy 1 gallon of wine), then England should sell cloth and buy wine. And at any price for cloth cheaper than 80/90 (that is, if 1 gallon of wine exchanges for a little more than 0.88 yard of cloth), then Portugal will gain by selling wine and buying cloth. We don't know yet the actual ratio at which the goods will be traded by England and Portugal—Ricardo's model was not advanced enough to show that—nor do we yet know the quantities that will be traded. But we can be sure that the price will settle somewhere between 120/100 and 80/90, since more wine in England will lower the wine price relative to cloth, more cloth in Portugal will lower the cloth price, less wine in Portugal will raise the price there, and less cloth in England will raise the cloth price in that country. By how much these relative prices will change Ricardo could not tell, and we must turn to modern theory for the answer.

The Modern Theory of Comparative Advantage

Opportunity Costs and Trade.   Nowadays (most) scholars reject the labor theory of value that underlay Ricardo's analysis, and restructure his model on an opportunity cost base. Now instead of saying that wine costs 120 hours and that cloth costs 100 hours, and therefore the exchange ratio is 1.2:1, we say only that England must sacrifice 1.2 yards of cloth to get a gallon of wine. We do not need to know just why this relationship exists (whether it is based on labor hours or what), we just "finesse" or by-pass the question. Thus we can rewrite Ricardo on a set of production possibility curves.

For simplicity we shall use the same ratios employed earlier in our Ricardian model. But now times are modern, and we shall see that it is England that now has an absolute advantage in both goods. Table 10.2 shows that if all factors of production in Portugal were assigned to producing wine, they would produce 90 gallons per time period. (Note that the number 90 represents quantity of output and not labor time as it did for Ricardo.) However, if all the factors turned to cloth output, the resulting production would be 80 yards per time period. Meanwhile, in England, all factors could produce 100 gallons of wine, but if transferred to cloth they could produce 120 yards.

TABLE 10.2. PRODUCTION POSSIBILITIES

	Wine	Cloth
Portugal	90	0
	0	80
England	100	0
	0	120

From these data showing production possibilities, we can now set up a production possibility curve for each country. In this first case, let us assume a situation of *constant costs*. Shifts in production do not bring about an alteration in costs. One more gallon of wine can always be obtained in England by giving up 1.2 yards of cloth, and vice versa, whether the shift to wine is small or large; while in Portugal, one more gallon of wine can always be obtained at a cost of 0.88 cloth and vice versa. The two curves are shown in Figs. 10.1(a) and 10.1(b).

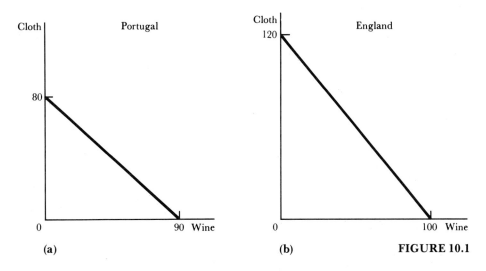

(a)   **(b)**   **FIGURE 10.1**

For Portugal the cost ratio of cloth to wine is thus 8/9 = 8.8/10, and Fig. 10.1(a) does show Portugal with constant opportunity costs, with one more gallon of wine costing 88 percent of a yard of cloth. Similarly, England in Fig. 10.1(b) has constant opportunity costs in the ratio of 12/10, with one gallon of wine costing 1.2 as much as a yard of cloth.

The next step is to show, as in the Ricardo model, that the slope of the production possibility curve is not only the *cost* ratio, but also the price ratio in the two countries. In fact this is true under competitive conditions. In England, cloth and wine will exchange at a rate of 12/10; at any higher price for wine (say 13/10), resources will shift into wine production and away from cloth because wine making gives a clear profit above costs. The result is a decline in the cloth supply and an increase in the wine supply, until a price ratio of 12/10 is restored and abnormal profit is eliminated. The reverse is equally true, with a lower wine price (say 11/10) leading to a shift of resources into cloth production and away from wine until a ratio of 12/10 is restored.

It is now possible to utilize a single diagram showing how, when trade is allowed to open, both countries can gain. Figure 10.2(a) shows Portugal before trade consuming 68 units of wine and 20 units of cloth at point *P* on her price line and production possibility curve, which has a slope of 80/90. If we now put on this diagram the *British* price line, Portugal will find she can improve her position. The British price line is 12/10, but let us reduce the 12/10 to the common denominator 90 for Portugal. Thus $12/10 = x/90$, or 108/90.

If Portugal can trade with Britain at the British price of 12/10, it will see that its position can be improved by producing only wine and exporting it in return for cloth. Say that Portugal produces 90 gallons of wine and exports 20 of these, which is enough to pay for 24 yards of cloth. This gives Portugal more wine (2 gallons) and more cloth (4 yards) at P' than was available at P. (Note that there is no gain to England in this transaction, since England faced a 12/10 price ratio even before trade.)

We can be sure that the scarcity of cloth in England (some cloth is now exported) and the glut of wine (some wine is now imported) will change the price ratio in Britain, and prices will also change in Portugal, where there is now more cloth and less wine. The tendency will be toward a price ratio somewhere between 12/10 and 8/9.

We do not know yet where the price will settle. That depends on demand as well as supply. But suppose it settles at some intermediate ratio such as 10/9, shown on Fig. 10.2(b). In that case Portugal could export 21 units of wine in return for imports of a little over 23 of cloth. Portugal still comes out ahead, and now England gains too. The latter exports 23 of cloth in return for 21 of wine, whereas at the old price ratio of 12/10 it could have obtained at home only 19 of wine. In fact, with constant costs as shown in our diagrams up to now, there will be complete specialization after trade. There is no use in producing *any* wine in England or any cloth in Portugal as long as it is always cheaper to import these items.

The one essential requirement for trade according to this model is that the price ratios between the two countries differ. If they do not, as in Fig. 10.3, for example, where England's 16/12 and Portugal's 8/6 reduce to the same base and have the identical slope, then there will be no profit in exchange.

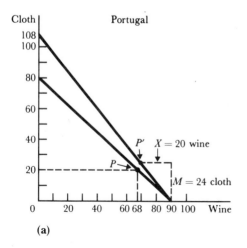

(a)

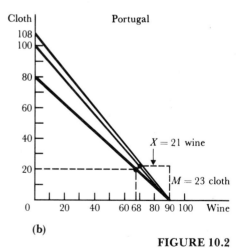

(b)

FIGURE 10.2

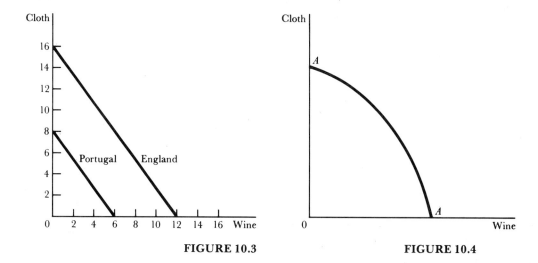

FIGURE 10.3   **FIGURE 10.4**

Now let us drop our assumption of constant costs, and move to the very likely case of increasing costs with the production possibility curve concave to the origin, as on curve *AA* in Fig. 10.4. The increasing costs will ordinarily be due to the fact that some resources are more suited for wine production, while others are more useful for cloth. Society gets more cloth only by giving up more and more wine, moving leftward on the diagram. And society gets more wine only by giving up more and more cloth, moving rightward.

Even though the shape of the curve has changed, we still need to find a cost ratio and a price ratio, as before. And also as before, these two ratios must be the same; if they are not, then prices are not in equilibrium and will change. The cost ratio, showing the marginal cost of obtaining more wine or more cloth, is a line tangential to the production possibility curve. At *X* on Fig. 10.5(a), for example, the cost ratio 3/4 means it costs 0.75 of a yard of cloth to get 1 gallon of wine at that point. And the price ratio must be the same, 3/4, under competitive conditions.

It can be seen from Fig. 10.5(a) that equilibrium is the position where the price line (3/4) is tangential to the production possibility curve. Exactly where along the curve this point will lie is a matter that must also take demand into account, and is a problem taken up later. However, at *X* on Fig. 10.5(a), 0*C* cloth and 0*W* wine are produced at price *PP* (3/4). If the price ratio ever diverges from the cost ratio, as in Figs. 10.5(b) and (c), then adjustments will have to take place. Take the situation at point *Y* in Fig. 10.5(b). Here the relative cost of wine *CC* is cheap (much wine can be obtained for a little cloth if production is moved along the curve), but the wine *price P'P'* is expensive (a little wine sells for a lot of cloth). In response, businesspeople will produce more wine and less cloth. Wine thus becomes cheaper, and cloth more expensive. The price line *P'P'* tips counterclockwise. Point *Y* shifts down and to the right, and line CC tips clockwise to equilibrium, where $P'P'$ and CC have an identical slope.

Now tackle position Z on Fig. 10.5(c). Here the *cost* of wine CC is expensive, but the price $P''P''$ is cheap. Adjustment will involve businesspeople producing less wine and more cloth. Wine gets more expensive; cloth gets cheaper. The price line $P''P''$ tips clockwise; point Z shifts up and to the left to reflect the greater cloth and lesser wine output. As a result, CC tips counterclockwise to equilibrium where CC and $P''P''$ coincide, both just tangential to the production possibility curve.

We have now reached the point where we can see how trade will affect our diagrams. Before trade, as seen in Fig. 10.6, the price ratio in England between wine and cloth is PP. Wine is relatively expensive, but large quantities are being made. *After* trade, the price ratio changes. Cloth if exported will buy more wine than at home, as shown by the slope of $P'P'$. (Information on demand is necessary before we can know exactly *why* the price settles at $P'P'$.) Or, said in another way, the price after trade shows wine relatively cheaper and cloth relatively more expensive. There will then be a shift in production from wine to cloth, which here has the comparative advantage. Production moves from X to Y as England sees it can buy wine more cheaply abroad.

Without further information on demand, we do not know yet exactly how much will be exported and imported. But we are sure that consumption will be to the right of Y, say at point Z on Fig. 10.7. If consumption is at Z, then England produces $0C_2$ of cloth and $0W_1$ of wine at point Y; exports C_1C_2 of cloth and imports W_1W_2 of wine; consumes $0C_1$ of cloth and $0W_2$ of wine; and thus pushes itself out beyond its own production possibility curve.

Note that with increasing costs, England will probably not specialize completely in cloth production, nor Portugal in wine. Wine cheapens in England, as shown on Fig. 10.8(a); cloth cheapens in Portugal as on Fig. 10.8(b); and the lines swing toward one another. As shown in these figures, it is very likely that the price ratios in the two countries are equalized long before complete specialization takes place.

Aside from constant costs and increasing costs, which analysis we have just completed, there is only one further possibility: decreasing costs, of the sort brought about by mass production and large-scale enterprise. Naturally enough, the existence of decreasing costs is even more likely to lead to trade and specialization, because concentration on one product will cause comparative advantage to become even greater. This is an important feature of trade since World War II, sufficiently so that we postpone its discussion here and take it up again in the next chapter.

Adding Indifference Curves. To examine the theory further, we need some concept of what goods the community prefers, given the limited amounts that can be produced. Production possibility curves define the range of combinations open to the economy. The reason price and production settle at any one point, however, is related to community preferences. The tool generally used to demonstrate this is the indifference curve. Some readers will already have encountered such curves and others will have not. Basically, an indifference curve for an individual serves to introduce demand into the determination of comparative advantage. On Fig. 10.9, cloth and wine are shown along the two axes. The curve IC_2 identifies all the various combinations of wine and cloth that would result in the same level of satisfaction for an individual. Thus a person might be completely indifferent to consuming 3 units of wine and 5 of cloth (as at A), or 6 wine and 3 cloth (as at B). Higher indifference curves such as IC_3 represent the same situation but at a higher overall level of satisfaction, while lower indifference curves such as IC_1 represent lower satisfaction.

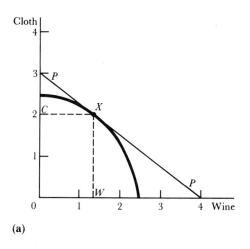

(a)

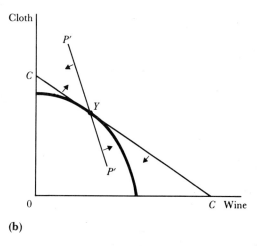

(b)

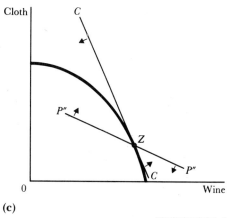

(c)

FIGURE 10.5

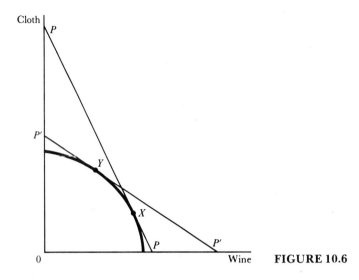

FIGURE 10.6

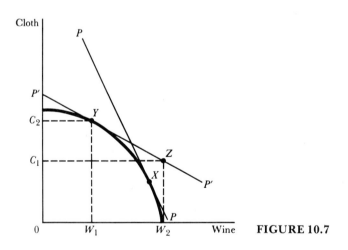

FIGURE 10.7

   In international trade theory it is necessary to use *community indifference curves*, which combine the curves for the nation as a whole. At once difficulties present themselves. Some individuals will be cloth lovers and some will be wine lovers, and furthermore some people will have stronger preferences than others. A movement along an indifference curve, as from *A* to *B* on Fig. 10.9's *IC₂*, will leave some people better off and others worse off. What to do? Economists have invented a principle that takes account of this problem, called the *compensation principle*. It assumes that if the gainers gain enough to compensate the losers and still have something left over, then society is better off than it was before.

The *slope* of an indifference curve, as shown in Fig. 10.10, is called the marginal rate of substitution in consumption. The slope shows, at X for example, that the community is willing to substitute cloth for wine at a rate of 4 cloth for 7 wine, meaning that at that point (X) on the indifference curve, consumers get the same satisfaction from 4 cloth that they do from 7 wine.

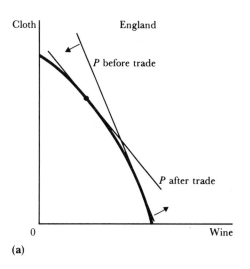

(a)

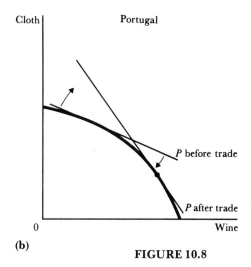

(b)

FIGURE 10.8

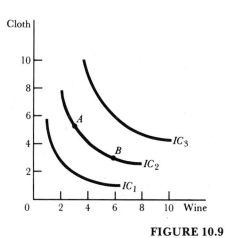

FIGURE 10.9

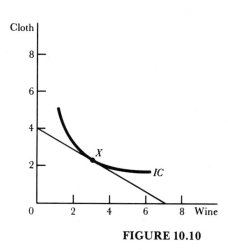

FIGURE 10.10

Putting production possibility and indifference curves together on the same diagram is no problem. An economy will produce where the exchange ratio of wine for cloth desired by the community is the same as the exchange ratio of production possibilities. On a diagram this is at a point where the slope of the production possibility curve matches the slope of an indifference curve—that is, the point where the production possibility curve and an indifference curve are tangential, as at point *W*, Fig. 10.11(a). Now let us examine several variations of trade involving two sets of these curves.

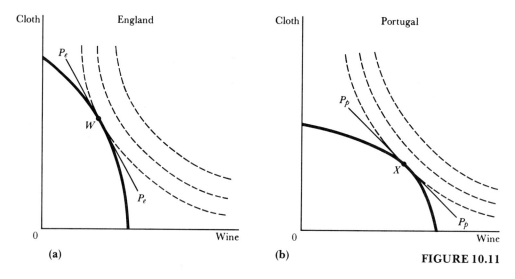

(a)   (b)   **FIGURE 10.11**

The Model Showing Similar Tastes but Different Production Possibilities. Figures 10.11(a) and (b) are drawn carefully to show that Portugal and England have exactly the same pattern of demand for wine and cloth. Their indifference curves are identical. Their production possibility curves differ, however, with England's productive factors more efficient in cloth production, and Portugal's more efficient in wine. The aim is to ascertain how much trade will take place and at what price.

In England, before trade, production and consumption will take place at point *W* on Fig. 10.11(a). Here is the point where the English production possibility curve just touches the highest attainable indifference curve. The equilibrium price is shown by the slope of the line $P_e P_e$, which is tangent to both the indifference curve and the production possibility curve. Should the price not be in equilibrium, both prices and production will tend to adjust toward $P_e P_e$ and a tangency at *W*, as already explained earlier in this chapter.

Similarly for Portugal in Fig. 10.11(b), production and consumption will be at *X*, and the equilibrium price ratio is shown by the slope of the line $P_p P_p$. Only at *X* is Portugal's production possibility curve just touching its highest possible indifference curve.

As trade opens up, Portuguese exports of wine and British exports of
cloth increase. We know that the price ratio will end up somewhere between
the British and the Portuguese; the exact ratio and the exact amount of trade
need not concern us to make our basic points. What is clear is that trade allows
each nation to operate on an indifference curve higher than any that can be
achieved without trade—there is a gain from trade.

We can see this gain by focusing on the "triangles" in Figs. 10.12(a) and (b).
These triangles represent the amount of trade and the price ratio at which
trade takes place. We have postulated in Fig. 10.12(a) that England would
export X_e of cloth. Clearly this must match the Portuguese imports—M_p of
Fig. 10.12(b). Similarly, British imports of wine M_e must equal Portuguese
exports, X_p. The price ratio developed in trade—or the *terms of trade*—is the
slope of the line $Q_e A$ or BQ_p. Since price is the same, these are also the same
slope. Geometrically, of course, the two hypotenuses must be the same length
if the two sides are the same.

Note how the English triangle pushes out beyond its production possibility curve, enabling consumption on an indifference curve tangent to the slope
of the hypotenuse at A. Then the Portuguese curve sticks out above the production possibility curve to touch another indifference curve at B. The gain
from trade is, in essence, the ability to consume beyond one's own production
possibility curve through the use of trade. It is the ability to move to a higher
indifference curve.

Note that this model shows directly the production change in the two
countries. Both countries move toward more specialization in production, at
Q_e and Q_p respectively, and toward less specialization in consumption, as at
points A and B. The expensive item can be imported more cheaply than it can
be produced at home.

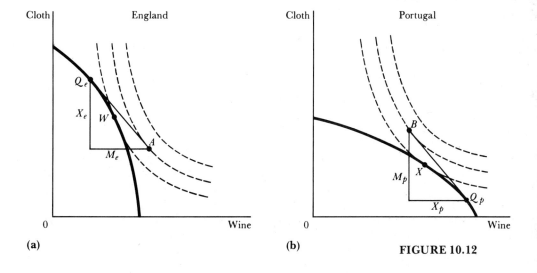

(a) (b) **FIGURE 10.12**

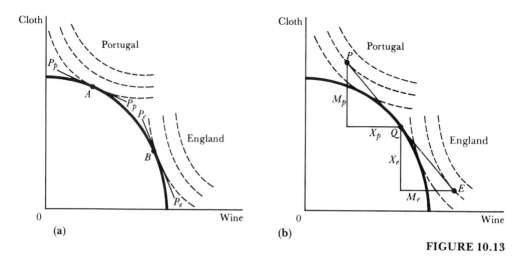

FIGURE 10.13

The Model Showing Similar Production Possibilities but Different Tastes. Up to this point we have assumed a similar pattern of demand in the two countries, and the different price ratios that made trade possible were caused by dissimilar production possibilities based on factor supplies and quality, or technological differences. The result was two different production possibility curves. However, a price differential may also spring up even if production possibilities are the same, if the patterns of demand are different. Thus trade can take place advantageously even when countries are noticeably similar in their factor endowments and their technologies.

Examine Fig. 10.13(a). Here England and Portugal have identical production possibilities, but two different sets of indifference curves reflecting their dissimilar demand patterns. (Portugal is shown with a strong preference for cloth, England for wine.) Before trade Portugal produces and consumes at point A, England at point B. Relative prices are P_eP_e in England and P_pP_p in Portugal.

After trade, prices equalize in the two countries as shown by the line PE in Fig. 10.13(b). Output is at Q in each country. England exports X_e cloth in return for M_e wine, leaving it consuming at point E. Portugal exports X_p wine in return for M_p cloth, hence consumption is at point P. Then $X_e = M_p$, $X_p = M_e$, and the two triangles in the diagram are identical. Both England and Portugal are able to move outside their own production possibility curves, consuming more than would have been possible without international trade.[5] By moving away from the more extreme ends of the production possibility curves, each nation can produce more of both goods. While this would have been wasteful before trade because consumers desired more wine in England and more cloth in Portugal, it is quite helpful when trade is available. As the triangles show, both nations can move outside their own production possibility curves.

***The Model Showing Similar Production Possibilities and Tastes but Differences in
Scale.*** One last difference between countries can cause international specialization and trade. Assume that tastes (demand) are the same in England and
Portugal, and also that factor endowments are such that the factors are available in the same ratio to one another, with the same technology being used.
The only difference is in the scale of production, as in Fig. 10.14, where England's production possibility curve *EE* is located further out from the origin
than Portugal's *FF*. If demand patterns are the same, as we assumed above,
then the identical map of indifference curves must touch these similar production possibility curves along a ray from the origin $0A$. (To keep the diagram simple, the indifference curves are not drawn in.) Relative prices, shown
by the tangent lines P_eP_e and P_pP_p, are the same. In this restrictive situation
no trade would take place, because comparative costs and prices are identical.
However, underlying this statement is a further assumption about income
elasticity of demand. Obviously England's higher position on the diagram allows it to enjoy a higher level of real income. Since its relative preference
between cloth and wine is unchanged as compared to lower levels of income,
its income elasticity of demand for both goods must be unity; that is, cloth and
wine are demanded in the same proportions as income rises. If however the
income elasticity of one good (say wine) is higher than that of the other (cloth),
then at point W on Fig. 10.14 there will be a shortage of wine and a surplus of
cloth. In response, production would swing somewhat lower and to the right
of W (more wine production, less cloth); the price of wine would rise relative
to cloth in England; and if trade were opened, Portugal would find it profitable to export wine to England in return for cloth.

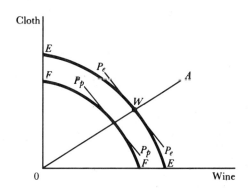

FIGURE 10.14

Thus, when scale economies are present trade will spring up, with the
good whose income elasticity of demand is greater than unity exported by the
smaller country, and the good whose income elasticity of demand is less than
unity exported by the larger country.[6]

A Flaw in the Argument

One flaw in the models must be reiterated. Trade will cause movements along a country's production possibility curve. Income distribution within that country will be altered in favor of the factors of production employed in producing the exported good, and against the factors employed in producing the imported good. Recall the problem with community indifference curves: *Only* if the gainers can compensate the losers can we say, unambiguously, that a country gains from trade.

Ricardo and the other classical economists overlooked this point. It means in practice that only if governments pursue policies of income redistribution through taxes and subsidies will free trade guarantee welfare improvement.

Offer Curves

We have not yet indicated how the price ratio and the quantity of trade are determined in pure theory. It is in fact not necessary to know the exact amount to demonstrate a gain from trade. Nonetheless, to complete the theory (and to read more advanced material), many readers may wish to explore the question further.

The problem in handling the production possibility and indifference curve diagrams such as those of Figs. 10.11 and 10.12 is finding a triangle that has just the right slope and shape to fit the production possibility and indifference curves in both countries. Just geometrically, it takes a keen eye and some imagination to draw it. The tools used to determine it in pure theory are known as "offer curves"; they should get us the right slope and size by spelling out the underlying conditions.

So far in the chapter, all price ratios have been shown as in Fig. 10.15, where a 12/10 ratio runs from axis to axis. However, exactly the same ratio can be shown as in Fig. 10.16, running out from the point of origin. This too shows the quantity of cloth that will exchange for a quantity of wine, and thus it too is a price ratio.

The 12/10 ratio was, you will recall, England's cloth/wine price before international trade. Starting from this line in Fig. 10.16, we can construct an *offer curve* that shows the amount of cloth England is willing to give up (export) in exchange for imports of wine from Portugal. In short, we will soon have for ourselves a curve showing simultaneously the supply and demand for the two commodities entering into trade. Assume now that trade opens between the two countries. For a short time, until the pressures of supply and demand change relative prices, assume that the price in England stays at 12/10. For the time being it will make no difference to English consumers whether they buy their wine at 12 units of cloth for 10 of wine at home or abroad. So a little trade may spring up, as at point *A* in Fig. 10.17.

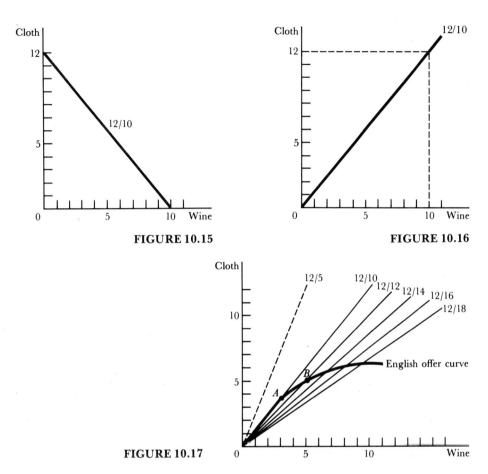

FIGURE 10.15

FIGURE 10.16

FIGURE 10.17

But if the prices had been different, there would have been more trade. (Obviously we need not consider a price movement in England in the direction, say, of 12/5 or higher, as along the dotted line. That would mean that cloth had become cheaper and wine more expensive after trade—and who would give up *more* English cloth in exchange for Portuguese wine than one must give up in England without international trade?) However, a *reduced* price of wine and an *increased* price of cloth, say to a ratio of 12/12, will cause England to want more trade, as at B, where a larger quantity of cloth will be offered for a larger quantity of wine.

As that same point B shows, the development of trade will make more wine available than before, and the English will offer less cloth per unit of wine—in other words, a doubling of wine imports will less than double exports of cloth. See how B, at a price ratio of 12/12, shows England giving up more cloth to get more wine, but not quite so much as it was willing to give up before. The twin reasons for this are (1) England wants wine less, and (2) each unit of cloth is now more valuable because some of it is being exported.

If the price ratio were to change further, say to 12/14 or 12/16, with cloth more expensive and wine cheaper, the same process would occur. More cloth will be given up for more wine, though again not so much per unit. Finally, say at a price ratio of 12/16, England will not give up *any more cloth at all* for wine, no matter how much more wine could be obtained. The offer curve may even bend back far toward the right in the diagram as huge wine stocks lead to superfluous supplies and problems of drunkenness, and consumers refuse to reduce their cloth consumption any further. England would then take more wine only if it had to give up less cloth.

Now we turn to Portugal's offer curve. Portugal's price ratio before trade was 8/9, with 8 units of cloth exchanging for 9 of wine, as in Fig. 10.18. Portugal too would be willing to underake a little trade with England even if the price ratio stays unchanged, as at *A* in that figure. It too would have preferred to get 10, 12, or 14 wine for 8 cloth, but England would not trade with Portugal at those prices because Portugal is already the cheapest winemaker.

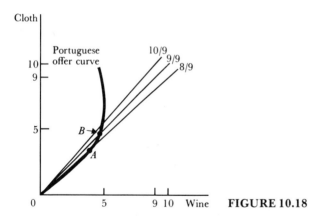

FIGURE 10.18

Thus with trade, the price line swings counterclockwise. At a higher price for wine and a lower price for cloth, Portugal will be eager for more trade. See how point *B*, at a price ratio of 9/9, shows Portugal willing to exchange more wine for imported cloth. The analysis is the same as that for England in Fig. 10.17, except the Portuguese offer curve swings around in the opposite direction.

Our next step is to put both offer curves, one for England and one for Portugal, on the same diagram, Fig. 10.19. Notice that the two curves cross at point *P*. This crossing is important. Only there, at a price ratio shown by the line running from the origin 0 through *P*, will Portugal want to export just the amount of wine that England wants to import, as read off along the horizontal axis. Also at a price 0*P*, and *only* there, will Portugal want to import just the amount of cloth that Britain wants to export. The price 0*P* is thus called the *equilibrium terms of trade*, and at that price the value of English imports equals the value of Portuguese exports, both in turn equal to the value of Portuguese imports and English exports. A country's exports exchange for an equal value of imports at the equilibrium terms of trade.

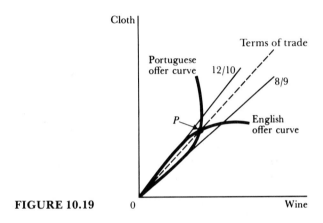

FIGURE 10.19

The connection of offer curves to the production possibility diagrams is straightforward: The offer curves define the size and shape of the triangles used to determine the gains from trade. The reading on the vertical axis gives us the amount of cloth traded by both countries—and is thus the height of the triangles—and the reading on the horizontal axis gives us the length of the triangles. The price ratio gives us the slope (though it must be reversed). If drawn carefully, all should work out well.

The Model Showing Many Countries and Many Commodities. In the real world of many countries and many commodities, the fundamental predictions of the two-country, two-commodity model are not changed. What emerges is a *chain of comparative advantage*, with each country having a list, as it were, of all goods potentially exportable and importable. At or near the upper end of the list will be goods where factor endowments, demand, and/or technological differences combine to give a comparative advantage so great in terms of relative costs and prices that the country is sure to be an exporter of those commodities. At the other end of the list are goods where the cost/price comparative disadvantage is so great that the country is certain to be an importer of those goods. In the center of the list is a "grey area," where costs and prices are so similar between countries (or transport costs so prohibitive to trade, as will be considered shortly) that trade cannot take place. The dividing line between what is imported and what is exported will be a function wholly of relative costs and prices.

Changing Comparative Advantage

Up to now we have been operating within a strict *ceteris paribus* assumption, with no allowance for changes in taste (demand), changes in factor endowments, or changes in technology. Our theory of comparative advantage has thus far been a *static* one, applying at some moment of time. What changes in the predictions of the theory occur when tastes, or factor endowments, or technology are allowed to alter?

First, consider tastes. If tastes are not fixed, then not only may demand patterns change in their own right but international trade may itself alter tastes. This familiar phenomenon includes such examples as the sugar and muslin cloth brought to Europe in the Crusades; the new crops discovered in the Americas after Columbus—pumpkins, squash, beans, tomatoes, peanuts, coffee, cocoa, and so on—which revolutionized the diets of Europe; and the "demonstration effect" so named by the Columbia University economist Ragnar Nurkse, wherein consumers in underdeveloped countries acquire new tastes as they are exposed to the whole medley of goods available in international trade. The upshot is that changing tastes can cause a change in the chain of comparative advantage. As relative prices shift, it becomes more profitable to switch to the export of something else. Japan was once the world's major silk exporter, but as fashions moved away from silk Japan looked for other alternatives. The African country named the Ivory Coast was once a major source of ivory, but changing fashions in interior decorating, occurring at the same time that the Victorians were developing the modern breakfast, led the now-misnamed Ivory Coast into coffee and cocoa production. Comparative advantage constantly undergoes a dynamic process of change, some old goods being replaced by new ones in the list of a country's most profitable exports.

Now consider changing factor endowments. Take the case of large-scale and continuing investment in industries that are capital intensive. The stock of capital grows relative to the labor force and the supply of natural resources. As a result, comparative advantage changes steadily.[7] Two examples of this case of changing comparative advantage might be the United States and Germany, originally exporters of agricultural commodities and then later, toward the end of the nineteenth century, both acquiring new comparative advantages in the export of manufactures. Changing technology has the same effect, and was particularly important in the German case.

THE FACTORS OF PRODUCTION, TRANSPORT AND THE TERMS OF TRADE

Trade and Transport Costs

Throughout this chapter, our analysis has proceeded on the basis that there are no transport costs, and that trade will equalize the prices of the traded

commodities in the countries engaging in trade. But of course differences in
price can and indeed do exist between countries, owing to the costs of transport. Tariffs, quotas, taxes, and other trade restrictions can have the same
effect, but a consideration of these is delayed until the next chapter.

It is easiest to show the effect of transport costs by examining the supply
and demand for just one good (say cloth) before trade, and then after trade
opens. In Figs. 10.20(a) and (b) we see the domestic supply and demand for
cloth in England (a) and Portugal (b). The price of cloth is lower in
England ($0P_e$) than in Portugal ($0P_p$). If trade opens between the two countries, in the absence of transport costs England will export cloth to Portugal,
raising the price in the former and lowering it in the latter until an equality is
reached. A "back-to-back" diagram of supply and demand such as Fig. 10.21
shows this. Here, Portugal's supply and demand is shown in the normal way
on the right side of the diagram. On the left side is shown England, with its
curves rearranged. Now the horizontal axis runs from zero leftward; as usual,
higher prices bring higher quantities supplied and lower quantities demanded, but the curves to show this must have a slope opposite to the customary one—the supply curve rising upward and to the left, the demand curve
falling to the left. An equality of prices in the two countries is shown at a price
$0Z$. England's exports AB are the excess of its own domestic supply over
domestic demand; while Portugal's imports CD are the excess of its domestic
demand over its own supply. As the exports of the one must equal the imports
of the other, $AB = CD$. England produces AZ, consumes BZ, and exports AB.
Portugal produces ZC, imports CD, and consumes ZD. $0Z$ is the equilibrium
terms of trade. The start of trade has lowered the price in Portugal and raised
it in England, just as the theory predicted.

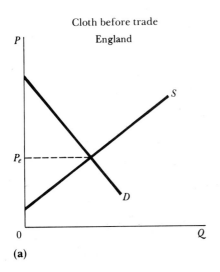

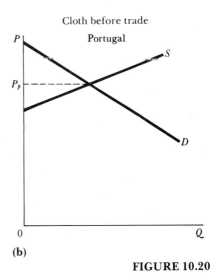

FIGURE 10.20

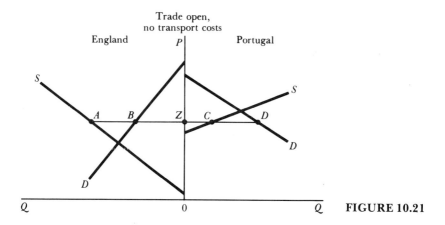

FIGURE 10.21

Now we allow for the existence of transport costs. Transport is here defined broadly to include not only carriage, but also insurance, handling, commissions, and so on. The more encompassing term "transfer costs" is actually more applicable. Transport costs mean that the prices in the two countries will not after all be equalized. Trade will raise prices in the exporting country (but not so much as if there had been no such costs) and lower them in the importing country (but not by so much as when transport costs were absent). In Fig. 10.22, *AB* again represents English exports while *CD* is Portuguese imports. Transport costs per each unit traded are measured by the distance along the vertical price axis. Costs are such on Fig. 10.22 that trade is noticeably reduced. English exports *AB* are equal to Portuguese imports *CD*. If transport costs had been sufficiently high to exceed the difference in price before trade, as in Fig. 10.23, then there would have been no international exchange of this commodity.

This analysis of transport costs is widely applicable. Where no such costs exist, international trade would take place in all commodities as some country would have a comparative advantage (excepting the case of identical tastes, identical factor proportions, identical technology, and hence identical price ratios between the countries). But transport costs when high leave us with the possibility that some goods will be *naturally protected*, with international trade difficult or impossible.

Location Theory. Where will industry in fact be located, taking into account the existence of transport costs? There is more to it than comparative advantage alone, and natural protection helps to explain the existence and siting of industry because transport costs modify comparative advantage.

Transport costs lead to a division of industry into three separate categories: (1) supply-oriented, (2) market-oriented, and (3) footloose. The connection between transport costs and these three categories is traced below.

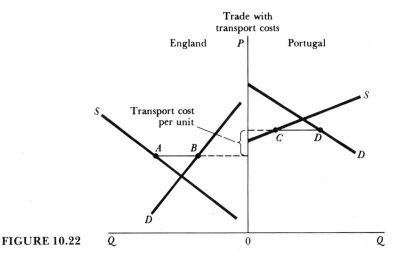

FIGURE 10.22

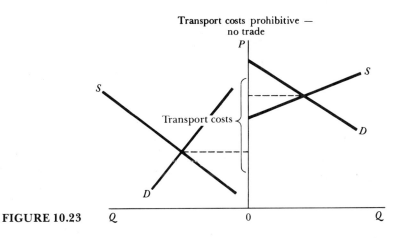

FIGURE 10.23

1. Supply-oriented industry. Such industries must for reasons of transport be located near raw materials or fuel. Typical examples are those whose raw material inputs lose weight in processing. The ores of zinc and copper, for example, contain much waste material and lose much weight in the refining of the metal. It is thus more economical to refine at the site of the mining rather than to ship heavy, useless waste material. Similarly, large-scale fuel consumption can mean economies in producing at or near a source of fuel. This is most true of fuels that are hard to ship, and applies in particular to coal. Coal can be a tremendous attraction for industry, as seen in the German Ruhr, Polish Silesia, the English Midlands, and the region around Pittsburgh in the United States. Finally, agricultural goods requiring immediate preservation or grading are supply-oriented in the sense that canning, freezing, and processing must often be carried out near the source of production.

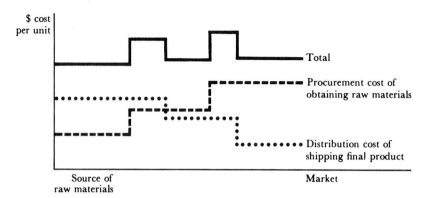

FIGURE 10.24

2. Market-oriented industry. The cost of transport requires that some commodities be produced near the market. Perishable goods such as bread or fresh strawberries are examples. Services, including tourism, haircuts, and the like are also obviously market-oriented. Finally, any commodity that acquires weight or bulk in processing is cheaper to produce near the market. The bottling of beer and soft drinks is a case in point, as is the assembly of prefabricated units such as furniture.

3. Footloose industry. Transport costs are not so important with footloose industries, which can locate at the source of supply, at the market, or in between. Generally, such industries produce products that neither gain nor lose weight in processing. Textile manufacture or petroleum refining are good examples. With petroleum, it makes little or no difference whether the crude oil is refined at the wells, and then shipped in tankers as refined gasoline, kerosene, motor oil, tar, and so forth; or whether the crude is shipped in the tanker and then refined at the market. As little weight or bulk is lost in the refining, there is no cost advantage to be exploited in locating the refinery.

The firm analyzing the effects of transport costs on its operations will presumably have in mind the sort of data shown in Fig. 10.24. This figure, taken from the well-known work of E. M. Hoover, shows us how to sum up the procurement costs of obtaining raw materials and the distribution costs associated with shipping the final product.[8] Procurement costs, shown by a dashed line, are highest at the market, lowest near the source of supply. Distribution costs for the final product, shown by a dotted line, are highest at the source of raw materials, lowest at the market. When added vertically, the two together indicate the total cost of transport—seen in Fig. 10.24 to be lowest when production of the good is undertaken at the source of raw materials supply. This good is therefore supply-oriented.

Factor Proportions—The Heckscher-Ohlin Model

Modern trade theory, you will recall, by-passes the question of why opportunity costs—and hence comparative advantages—are what they are. Why does, in fact, one bottle of wine exchange for 1.2 yards of cloth? Ricardo had thought of this as being connected with the cost of labor. Labor as the sole determinant of value fell out of favor among non-Marxists as superior tools were developed late in the nineteenth century. Economists came to distinguish three factors of production—land, labor, and capital. Using such tools, it is possible once again to address the determinants of comparative advantage.

The Swedish economists Eli Heckscher and Bertil Ohlin (who won the 1977 Nobel Prize in economics) did this, using the factors of production to explain comparative advantage. Basically, the Heckscher-Ohlin idea is quite simple: Nations export goods that use their most abundant factor heavily and import those goods that use their scarce factors heavily. Thus a nation with much labor and little capital exports labor-intensive goods and imports capital-intensive goods. The formal model, however, is rather more elaborate because it is necessary to spell out in some detail the conditions under which the Heckscher-Ohlin proposition would hold.

As with the other pure theory models, we will assume a two-country world of pure competition, homogeneous goods, full employment, no transport costs, and fixed factor endowments. We will not, however, limit ourselves to two products. Furthermore, our concern is with the factors of production; so we need more limitations. At present we will limit factors to the three standard ones—land, labor, and capital. The factors will be homogeneous—one man-hour, one dollar of capital, one acre is as good as any other. Last, we will not allow any factor movement between countries, but we will allow trade—the Mexicans cannot cross the U.S. border, but they can export all they want.

To make the theory work we need another pair of provisions, more difficult to understand. We assume that any good can be made with a wide variety of factor inputs. As an example, rice can be cultivated intensively by hand and water buffalo, as in Asia; there much rice can be produced with little capital or land through hand planting, terracing, and careful attention during the growing season. As the price of labor rises, however, the technique of growing rice changes. Labor-saving machinery is added. Finally, one reaches the highly capital-intensive rice farming of Arkansas. The choice of technique depends on the relative costs, which are determined by the relative endowments of capital, land, and labor. Despite the possibility of producing rice in many different ways, any nation will choose only that particular way that fits its factor endowments.

The matching provision is that, for any given factor mix, some products will use more of one factor than others and that these are ranked in the same order in any country. Textiles will always use more capital than rice in any given area. Rice may very well be grown in a more capital-intensive way in America than in Thailand, but American textiles are also made in a more capital-intensive way. We would expect American textile manufacturing to be more capital-intensive than American rice production. It is even possible for American rice farming to be more capital-intensive than the Thai textile industry; our conclusions are unchanged so long as textiles are more capital-intensive than rice in both countries. Hence it should be possible to rank all products by their relative degrees of capital intensity, as in Fig. 10.25.

Country	Low K-intensity				High K-intensity
Thailand	rice tobacco textiles automobiles electronics				
United States	rice tobacco textiles autos electronics				

FIGURE 10.25

Applying the Heckscher-Ohlin theory, we can say that in Thailand rice, tobacco, and probably textiles are heavy users of Thailand's abundant labor ($1.00-$1.50 a day); they will accordingly be exported, while automobiles and electronics goods, using heavy inputs of capital, will be imported. The United States will have the opposite pattern.

Limitations and Problems with the Heckscher-Ohlin Model. The Heckscher-Ohlin model, despite its great popularity among economists until quite recently, has a number of limitations that restrict its use.

1. The assumption that industries can be ranked by capital intensity (or land or labor intensity) is a troublesome one. In the case of rice, for instance, the order of rank by capital intensity does not seem to hold—in other words, rice production may be either less or more capital-intensive than textiles or automobiles. As the industries become more capital-intensive, their response to the increasing capital varies. Instead of all moving in a row like cars on a train, they may switch positions, as in Fig. 10.26.

Country	Low K-intensity				High K-intensity
Thailand	rice tobacco textiles automobiles electronics				
United States	textiles automobiles tobacco rice electronics				

FIGURE 10.26

Hence we find such anomalies as the fact that both Thailand and the United States export both rice and corn.

2. The role of demand is not considered in the model. A country may produce a labor-intensive good (rice), but consume it all, while that might not

be true of textiles. Hence, it would not necessarily export the product heaviest in its abundant factor, though it would produce it. The United States, for instance, does not produce an enormous amount of rice by world standards, but it consumes very little of it and is hence a major exporter. Thailand, a traditional exporter of rice, is also a minor producer but a heavy exporter of corn (maize). Part of the explanation lies in demand—Americans eat little rice; Thais eat little meat or corn.

3. The model in practice uses only two variables—mostly capital and labor. Three-factor models are difficult to handle. Land especially gives problems, except on a most abstract level. The factors are supposed to be homogeneous, but land certainly never is.

4. The three factors may in themselves be too abstract for practical uses, lacking the homogeneity of the model. Often additional factors are added. Bela Belassa, for instance, is working on models dealing with skilled and unskilled labor as different factors. The United States, in his sense, is an exporter of skilled-labor-intensive goods and services (electronics, computers, management services) and an importer of unskilled labor goods (textiles, shoes, and radios). Sometimes, too, other factors are added to the three basics, such as technology (see Chapter 11).

5. Lastly, as we will see in the following chapter, econometric attempts to prove the Heckscher-Ohlin theory have been disappointing; indeed, they have not as a whole sustained the theory in its classic form.

Factor Price Equalization. The Heckscher-Ohlin theory has a corollary of some interest. Consider the pure theory world of the model. Then consider this question: When will trade be in equilibrium? In the labor-abundant country the export of labor-intensive products will increase the price of labor. The import of capital-intensive products lessens the need for capital, hence lowers its price. (If Peru imports steel, it can free all the capital that would otherwise be tied up in the steel mill.) In the capital-surplus country, the opposite occurs: The need for labor is lessened by the import of goods that otherwise would use a lot of labor, while the price of capital rises as export activities demand more capital-intensive investments. The result is that the factor prices move toward each other. Presumably, the two nations will be in equilibrium when labor and capital costs are the same in both.

One obvious conclusion from the analysis above is that trade can substitute for migration and free capital flows. The theory suggests that the United States will not succeed in stemming Mexican immigration with the aim of protecting American labor. Instead of Mexican immigrants, the United States would see an inflow of labor-intensive Mexican goods; these would tend to depress the price of U.S. labor. Moreover, the increase in the price of U.S. capital that will result from the Mexican demand for American goods that were capital-intensive will also tend to depress the price of labor.

The Terms of Trade

The terms of trade are, quite simply, the conditions of exchange of commodities or the "price" in physical terms of one good for another—for example, the number of gallons of wine for the number of yards of cloth. The terms of trade between two countries entering into trade do not always end up squarely in the middle. A small country trading with a large country, for instance, will not affect the large country's prices (or terms of trade) as much as its own prices. A country with an inelastic supply of exports (like Guatemalan bananas) is likely to see its prices change greatly from year to year (this is analyzed in Chapter 8). Worry about worsening terms of trade has been endemic in many developing countries, leading economists to attempt to move from pure theory to econometrics.

To measure terms of trade, one must reduce all exports and imports to a single "product," so to speak. The way to do this is to create a price index such that one gets the typical export and the typical import. This method can be used to find the commodity terms of trade, also called the net barter terms of trade.

The construction of the commodity terms of trade for a country involves price indices giving the average price of exports and imports. An index constructed for this year is then compared to an index for some previous year in order to detect a trend. The actual formula used is

$$\frac{\text{price index of } X_2}{\text{price index of } M_2} : \frac{\text{price index of } X_1}{\text{price index of } M_1}$$

with the numbers 1 and 2 referring to an earlier and a later period, respectively. For example, set the price index of X and M equal to 100 in some base year, say 1970. Then if export prices, as reflected in the index, rise to 150 in 1979 while import prices rise to 200, the terms of trade are said to have moved against us. If we call the terms of trade in the base year 100, then in 1979 the terms have fallen to 75. This most common form of the terms of trade is published frequently; movements above 100 are said to be favorable, movements below 100 unfavorable.

A major objection to the commodity terms of trade as published nowadays is that an index of prices alone says nothing about revenues earned. High and rising prices for exports may be reducing rather than increasing earnings, depending on the elasticities involved. Lower export prices may stimulate sales sharply. The "best" position is presumably some optimum commodity terms of trade that maximizes earnings, not simply some very high ratio of export prices to import prices. For another thing, productivity may have increased in a country's export industries. A lower price for exported goods may be reflecting superior productivity and higher profitability, yet declining terms of trade suggest the reverse.

Economists are sufficiently critical of the commodity terms of trade that for a number of years they have tried to calculate a version that *does* take into account productivity changes. This so-called *single factoral terms of trade* is the ratio between the income accruing to a country's factors of production that are engaged in export production, and an index of the price of imports. The formula is, for a base year and the year to be measured,

$$\frac{\text{index of income to a factor producing a given quantity of exports}}{\text{price index of imports}}$$

A formula like this enables us to identify the situation in which the prices of export commodities may be falling, but in which there are stable or rising factor incomes in these industries because productivity has risen.[9] Unfortunately, the factoral terms of trade are extremely difficult to calculate because of the pitfalls in defining and measuring an adequate index of productivity. But work is advancing and the factoral terms of trade are now calculated for a number of countries.

All terms of trade figures have important statistical limitations, which become particularly critical when primary products are compared with manufactured goods. A ton of rice today is the same as a ton of rice twenty years ago, but a ton of automobiles is not. National income statisticians have a very difficult time in handling quality changes, and it is generally felt that these are understated. Trade statisticians have an even worse time because their data base is worse—for example, numbers of cars under 1,500 pounds, tons of machinery (in some cases it is measured that way), pairs of socks. The customs people cannot make quality judgments. Hence there is a strong tendency to overstate the price increases of manufactured goods relative to those of primary goods.

Conclusion

The pure theory of trade provides a basis for perceiving the real exchanges of goods or (under Heckscher-Ohlin theories) of the fruits of our labors, our savings, and our natural resources. It is, of course, rather abstract. But as with any model, it is an aid to our perception, not a reproduction of reality. It makes a strong case for free trade—one that, interestingly enough, appears to survive virtually all the challenges thrown at it that we shall see in the ensuing chapters. It is, in short, an extremely useful and durable theory.

One of trade theory's most important lessons is frequently overlooked in public discussions—comparative advantage compares the ratios *within* countries with each other. We do not compare American shoe manufacturing with the Spanish shoe manufacturers, but with other American industries. We find that the shoe industry is weak; it, like most highly protected American industries, is low-paying relative to American industry as a whole, and under-capitalized. Often the companies are poorly managed, but that is incidental rather than part of the theory. In New England, the shoe industry is losing labor rapidly to the more vigorous industries located in the Boston megalopolis. Import competition applies the coup-de-grâce because it further emphasizes the advantages of the efficient (exporting) industries over the inefficient. Thus what one has is not a "cheap wage" argument, but a "cheap capital" argument, as factor proportions analysis can illustrate.

Certainly, the difficulties of the shoe industry in the United States are related to foreign low wages. But they are equally related to low U.S. capital costs. The inability of shoe manufacturers to automate means that they cannot take advantage of low U.S. capital costs. The ability of other industries in the United States to move to more capital-intensive procedures improves labor productivity and wages, drawing labor away from shoes. Abroad, the high costs of capital discourage the building of capital-intensive factories, so that the workers stay with the shoes. Hence while American laborers worry about cheap foreign labor, foreign laborers worry about cheap American capital. Both sides should remember that we are talking about comparative advantage—and the first comparison is made within national boundaries.

There are some important political implications that emerge from the analysis above. Industries under attack from import competition are already troubled. Most tariff law, as we shall see, is concerned with "injury" from imports. Yet the "injury" to the American shoe industry is as much due to the American capital and skilled-labor-intensive industries as it is to foreign imports. Do away with America's most labor productive industries (ones using highly skilled labor and much capital) and shoe manufacturing would not find it hard to borrow money or pay low wages. When, under the 1962 tariff law, the U.S. Tariff Commission had to decide if injury to specific industries came mostly from imports, they rarely did so because there were so many other reasons why the industry was weak; it is no wonder, given the competition in America for the resources they use.

A second important and often overlooked conclusion of trade theory is that trade is *supposed to* shift resources from one use to another. It means not an idling of workers, machinery, and land, but a redistribution of those resources to other purposes—in other words, it operates under the assumption of full employment. From a practical point of view we know that idled resources do not go instantly into productive occupations. Textile machinery and plants, cleared farmland, or aging workers are not particularly mobile. Increased trade will stop new capital from entering weak industries and the bulk of the work force will find other employment. Much land can be put into other uses, so that the economy may still gain from efficiency despite the idling of some resources. Yet there still remains a hard core of immobile resources. Policy makers and economists recognize that two sets of policies are needed: (1) macroeconomic policies emphasizing high levels of employment, and (2) specific measures designed to promote speedier reallocation and/or compensation for those idled for the community's gain. These issues are explored at greater length in Chapter 13.

Finally, we should recognize that the pure trade theory, durable as it is, is not always the best tool to analyze trade. It lacks dynamic elements, and it relies heavily on assumptions of pure competition and the homogeneity of products and resources. Thus in Chapter 11 we turn to some supplemental theories of trade.

Notes

1. This introduction is taken largely from Jan S. Hogendorn, *Modern Economics* (Cambridge, Mass.: Winthrop/Prentice-Hall, 1975), p. 456.
2. Ricardo was one of history's greatest economists. He was also one of the richest, making a large fortune on the London stock exchange within 30 years of his birth in 1772. Public spirited, he used part of his fortune to buy a seat in Parliament, in which he served with distinction. His parliamentary seat was Old Sarum, a large earthwork just to the north of the present city of Salisbury. Old Sarum had been a town in the Middle Ages, but it had been abandoned for centuries and the inhabitants had all moved to Salisbury. Change in England was and is slow, and for all those centuries Old Sarum retained a vote in the British House of Commons. By the early nineteenth century it was the easiest seat for a prospective politician to buy in the whole of the British Isles. A handful of farmers (very rich, of course, given what they had to sell) owned the land and were the only voters. At each election they could be bought. In Parliament, Ricardo was a progressive, championing the reform of Britain's disgraceful "poor law" system of relief for the unemployed, who were confined in so-called workhouses under harsh conditions. Thus political corruption for once had a beneficial outcome. Very few tourists tramping around the mound of Old Sarum know that it was the political base of one of the world's greatest economists.
3. Impossible, one might say. Wine cannot be produced in England! But it can. English wines were indeed produced along the warm southern coast, and a little is even today. If the authors may be permitted a prejudicial comment, its taste bears a resemblance to turpentine.
4. Ricardo actually uses years of labor rather than hours, but the principle is the same.
5. Our models of the gains from trade imply that in equilibrium several conditions are satisfied. They include the following:
   a. At any point along the production possibility curve, the slope of that curve is the relative marginal (opportunity) cost of producing a greater quantitiy of one of the goods.
   b. Because of competition, marginal cost equals price ($MC = P$). Thus a line tangent to the production possibility curve also shows the price ratio.
   c. At any point along the indifference curve, the marginal rate of substitution in

consumption (or marginal utility) of shifting consumption from one good to the other is shown by the slope of the indifference curve at that point.

d. Thus equilibrium in foreign trade as shown on our diagrams will involve the marginal cost ratio equal to the price ratio equal to the marginal rate of substitution in consumption. All these equalities are shown by the slope of the *PP* lines in our Fig. 10.13(a) and by *PE* in Fig. 10.13(b).

6. This analysis is taken from Ronald Findlay, *Trade and Specialization* (London: Penguin Books, 1970), pp. 44-45.

7. The theorem that an increase in the available quantity or quality of one factor of production relative to the others will change comparative advantage in favor of goods embodying the increasing factor is called the Rybczynski Theorem, after its originator, T. M. Rybczynski.

8. See Edgar M. Hoover, *The Location of Economic Activity* (New York: McGraw-Hill, 1963), p. 39. The diagram is simplified in the text.

9. There is also a double factoral terms of trade,

$$\frac{\text{index of income to factors producing a given quantity of exports}}{\text{index of income to factors producing a given quantity of imports}}$$

but this is of less interest because we would much prefer to know what quantity of imports we can buy, not what quantity of foreign factors. Two other terms of trade are sometimes calculated, a gross barter terms of trade,

$$\frac{\text{volume of } M}{\text{volume of } X}$$

and an income terms of trade,

$$\frac{P_x Q_x}{P_m}$$

These are little used.

11

TRADE
BETWEEN INDUSTRIAL
NATIONS: NEW
APPROACHES

Problems of Modern Trade

Observers have noted for some years a rather unexpected pattern in international trade—a great deal of trade occurs between nations that are rather similar in factor proportions and demand patterns. The labor-plentiful nations do not trade exclusively or even predominantly with the labor-scarce, nor do the resource-rich trade that much with the resource-poor. For example, trade in the old European Free Trade Association, consisting of such diverse nations as the United Kingdom, Ireland, Iceland, Denmark, and Norway, never expanded like that of the European Economic Community, whose economies were much less complementary. Trade between the United States and Canada, which share high labor costs, is over five times the value of trade between the United States and Mexico, despite Mexico's low labor costs. (Indeed, U.S. exports to Canada of automobiles alone exceed U.S. exports to Mexico in all categories.) In global terms, the twelve most industrialized nations do 66 percent of their trade with one another.[1] A substantial portion of world trade, it appears, involves like trading with like, which is not exactly what the factor proportions model of the last chapter suggested would happen.

Closer examination of trade figures has done nothing to dispel the puzzlement over the trade of developed countries. Astonishingly, a great deal of that trade has turned out to consist of nations exporting and importing similar products. To give an example from a recently completed survey by Herbert Grubel and P. J. Lloyd, based on 1967 data, the value of French exports of photographic supplies was within 2 percent of its imports of the same supplies.

The figure is higher than average, but not all that rare. Nearly two-thirds of the trade of the main industrial nations in 1967 was in goods produced in both the exporting and the importing country. Much of the *growth* of trade in recent years has been in such "intraindustrial" trade. Many people have asked whether the trade theories of the sort developed in the last chapter could adequately explain such curious statistics.

Another puzzle arose about twenty-five years ago. From the late 1940s the Nobel Prize-winning economist Wassily Leontief had been working with input-output tables for the United States, and he decided to test the Heckscher-Ohlin factor proportions model with them. Expecting confirmation of that model, he was intrigued to find strange results: U.S. exports were more labor intensive than U.S. imports. More precisely, the U.S. ratio of man-hours to dollars of capital was higher in exports than in imports. The publication of these results in 1951 caused a great stir, and the statistical conclusions—reproduced several times for later years—were dubbed the *Leontief paradox*. Literature on the paradox would fill a good-sized bookshelf. How could these various problems be reconciled with traditional theory?

There were two possible directions to go. The theory of comparative advantage and factor proportions could be elaborated, refined, or patched up to handle the new problems. That theory, after all, is effective in analyzing many critical problems, from English importation of wheat to American importation of shoes. Could it not be adjusted to explain trade with rather smaller cost differences? Or were they the wrong tools with which to explain twentieth-century trade? They work, to be sure, but they lose their extraordinary clarity. Perhaps one should look for a superior explanatory model. The balance of this chapter explores the issue. Some of this material is new, speculative, and controversial, yet we trust nonetheless interesting and useful to the reader.

Variations on Traditional Approaches

Traditional approaches can handle the trade problems discussed above through several methods: (1) through discussing border trade, which fits some of the statistics into regular theory; (2) through asserting that the differences in cost are too fine to be measured statistically—that factor proportions work, but just cannot be proven; and (3) through adding additional factors to the model, particularly those called technology and human capital.

Intraindustrial trade can be ascribed partly to the transportation costs that give rise to border trade. If Canada needs fertilizer in Alberta and has a surplus in Quebec, it certainly is not going to haul it 2,500 miles to get it there, but will instead export the Quebec fertilizer to the eastern United States and import the fertilizer for Alberta from the western United States. Similarly, the United States is considering exporting Alaskan oil, which cannot be easily shipped across the country, and importing an equivalent amount to the East Coast, a procedure Canada has followed for years.

The use of "industry" statistics as a measure of the actual exchange of factor proportions has also brought cause for concern. We think of an "industry" as being a group of firms making similar products, technologically related to one another. Normally, the factor mix within the industry is fairly standard; for example, most automobiles and their parts use roughly the same proportions of labor and capital. The difficulty is that the available statistical measures do not necessarily define an industry according to such terms. The classification system—the Standard Industrial Trade Classifications—must make simplifications and distortions. There are catch-all categories and categories that contain products made with very different factor proportions. Consequently, some economists feel that statistical measures of intraindustrial trade do not say much about factor proportions.

To the authors, such arguments against the importance of intraindustrial trade seem too strongly stated. Even in categories such as chemicals or automobiles, with production methods quite standard, there are high levels of intraindustrial trade. We must look further for an explanation.

It is possible to shore up factor proportions theory by adding two more "factors": human capital and technology. Leontief himself felt that his paradox could be explained through examining human capital. The American level of education was for many years higher than those of all other countries, meaning that U.S. labor may have been more productive. In addition, the education of American managers is considerably greater than that of those abroad. Education is a form of capital in that it involves a saving from current consumption to improve productivity later on. Wealthy nations have the ability, in essence, to "save" the labor of millions of high school and college students and direct the labor of smaller numbers of teachers into their training, making them in the end considerably more productive. Hence *educated* labor is more akin to capital in the plant than it is to labor. There are difficulties with this position, however: (1) All education is not "investment"—some is clearly consumption; and (2) It becomes hard to measure labor that is qualitatively different. Nevertheless, the human capital argument does serve to salvage to a considerable extent the Heckscher-Ohlin theory of factor proportions.

Technology can also be treated as a factor of production. Like human capital, it alters the relation of land, labor, and capital. Unlike human capital, which makes labor more productive, technology could make land, labor, or capital (or a combination of all three) more productive. Like human capital, technology is to some extent the result of past investment in research, and may be a form of capital. One can then explain a particular pattern of industrial trade by pointing out that, say, the United States is exporting sophisticated telecommunications equipment, while it imports unsophisticated radios and television sets. Or we can assert that the Leontief paradox may be caused by American technology, making labor relatively more productive than capital. (We should recognize, however, that the opposite is also possible—capital could become more productive than labor.)

One must be careful with such arguments, however, and not treat technology as a "fudge" factor that serves to explain everything that is otherwise inexplicable. It is difficult to define exactly what constitutes "technology," either statistically or conceptually. Research and development can be measured, of course, but it is not clear whether the expenditure in research and development can be directly correlated to technical advances. Technology, moreover, is dynamic. Technological leads and "gaps" appear and disappear. By contrast, land, labor, and capital are fixed. The next model presented makes an attempt to deal with these problems.

Learning Curve Analysis

One way to consider the increasing skill of both technology and labor is through learning curve analysis (LCA). LCA originated in management economics and has been used principally for domestic analysis. It relates the increasing skills of labor and improved technology not to investments in education and research (which are assumed to be constant), but to the total number of products of any given type produced over time.

As long ago as 1925, analysts noted an interesting pattern in the rate of labor's ability to learn. The man-hours spent on manufacturing a given product tended to fall by some regular percentage every time production doubled. Suppose a shipyard found that it took 10,000 man-hours to produce the first tugboat it made and then discovered with the second that it took only 8,000 man-hours. From these two points management could project that the fourth tugboat would take only 6,400 man-hours, the eighth 5,120 man-hours, and so on, with man-hours falling by 20 percent for each doubling. This produces a *learning curve*, as in Fig. 11.1. Learning curve analysis has become a standard procedure in Department of Defense contract negotiations and is in occasional (but not widespread) use in industry. The model, however, has some international economic implications: The nation that has produced the most tugboats uses its labor more efficiently, an efficiency that is not related directly to capital expenditure on education or research, but only to production experience.

A bold extension of learning curve theory was made by a private firm, the Boston Consulting Group. BCG analysis suggests that not only labor costs, but *all* costs (capital and management costs too), decline according to cumulative experience. The rate of technological innovation, change in scale, shop floor improvements, and the like apparently relate more to total production experience than to elapsed time or research expenditure itself. While such changes can be hastened by good management and perhaps higher expenditures on research and development, and slowed by the opposite, the production experience was still the most important variable. The statistical and research techniques involved are still not completely accepted; indeed, many of the data remain proprietary and have not been generally examined by scholars. In any case, the BCG claims that, on the basis of its studies of the automobile and electrical generator industry, a reasonably managed firm should expect to see costs decline 20 to 30 percent for every doubling of production. This produces a chart looking much like that of the learning curve, but with "real costs," not "man-hours," on the vertical axis.

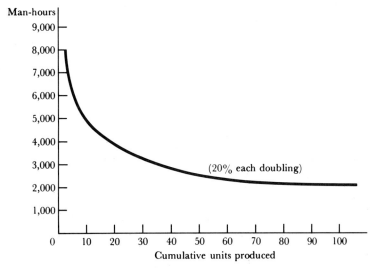

FIGURE 11.1 Learning curve

If one extends BCG type analysis into international economic analysis, the conclusions are interesting. Suppose there are two nations, the "pioneering" nation, which first started the manufacture of a labor-intensive product, and the "late entry" nation. The "late entry" began to develop economically later than the "pioneer" and hence has lower labor costs, which for this labor-intensive product should give it a comparative advantage. Because, however, the late entrant is inexperienced, it cannot initially compete. This is shown in Fig. 11.2, with two experience curves. Curve E_P represents that of the pioneer nation, while curve E_l represents that of the late entrant. Curve E_l lies below E_P, indicating that at any point at which two nations had the same experience, the late entrant's costs would be lower.

What is intriguing about the model is this: The pioneering nation can keep the gap between it and the late entrant only so long as it can keep doubling its production as fast as the latter. But it becomes increasingly difficult for the pioneering nation to continue doubling its production because the base grows so large. (Consider how long it would take for General Motors to produce the amount of cars equal to all it had produced since its founding.)

Accordingly, the rate of cost decline in the pioneer slows, while the late entrant's costs fall rapidly. In Fig. 11.2, suppose that the pioneering nation is at point *a* on curve E_p when the late entrant (with a bit of borrowed technology) starts at point *c* on its curve. Both nations now raise their sales equal amounts of the product (20,000). The pioneering nation's new sales move it down its experience curve from *a* to *b*; for the same sales, however, the late entrant has moved from *c* to *d*. Unfortunately for the pioneer, point *b* and point *d* reflect the same cost of production. Comparative advantage and factor proportions reassert themselves once the technological overburden is weathered away.

The pioneer may even be worse off than implied above if there is a "penalty for taking the lead." High-cost capital equipment that takes a long time to

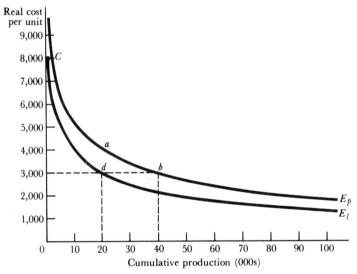

FIGURE 11.2   Learning curves of pioneer and late entrant.

depreciate may eventually become obsolescent and hence a drawback to the pioneering country. Britain's industrial revolution in the first half of the nineteenth century saddled it with an inadequate railway system compared to the later networks of the United States and Germany. Boxcars were (and are) small, with carrying capacity limited. Similarly, the British iron and steel industry was trapped for many years by its heavy investment in Bessemer converters at a time when Germany had gone on to the more efficient open hearth method for steelmaking, supplemented by the Thomas-Gilchrist treatment of iron ore.

Abstract? Consider the behavior of the Japanese Ministry of Trade and Industry. MITI decided to move into automobile production in 1950. Very quickly, the U.S. firms in Japan were forced out of production there. The

Japanese companies then made various licensing agreements with American and British firms to buy some technology. The country was virtually closed to imported cars; if the growing Japanese market was to have cars, they would be Japanese. Japanese production of automobiles doubled many times. By the early 1960s costs had fallen to a point at which the Japanese were competitive at world prices, and they began to export. Later, they agreed to open their borders to imports, but by then their costs were below world costs. Considering Japan as the late entrant, the closing of its borders allowed the doubling of production in a shorter time, and a more rapid fall from c to d. MITI tried the same thing with televisions and cameras, both with equal success. In all these cases the capital stock of the industry was more modern than that of its overseas competitors.

Before generalizing this to a policy recommendation, however, note four considerations rather particular to Japan: (1) The Japanese market was very large and was expanding very rapidly. (2) The United States, which took the brunt of the effect of the trade policies, had strong political reasons for encouraging a prosperous Japan. (3) The pioneering nation must still demand the product by the time the late entrant catches up. (By the time Brazil catches up, perhaps the automobile as we know it will be out of style.) (4) The late entrant's wages must not rise too fast. If the wage gap between late entrant and pioneer closes, shifting E_l upward, then the late entrant is delayed or stymied in its pursuit of the pioneer.[2]

Linder's Model—Markets and Invention

Faced with the problems of analyzing trade between industrial nations, the Swedish economist Staffan Burenstam Linder looked at the invention of new goods and the way in which their use spread, rather than at cost differentials among products whose use was already widespread. New product inventions and introductions, Linder held, are closely tied to national markets. To come up with an invention one must perceive a need, have an inspiration, and then work and rework that initial idea to "tune" it to the market. Often this means not only making the product, but informing people about it and making it accessible to them. Hence the key factor in determining where goods are initially produced is not the cost of the good, but the market for that good, because only by working closely with the market can one invent and develop the good.[3]

An illustration of a typical Linder process can be drawn from the annals of American business. In the year 1851, I. M. Singer saw a primitive sewing machine and recognized its potential in labor-scarce and thrifty New England. Inspiration was not long in coming, and within a few weeks Singer had designed a much superior machine. Invention, in keeping with the Linder thesis, took place in response to a clear market need, and inspiration followed. Yet it took Singer several years before he could figure out the most effective way to sell his machine. The machine underwent few adjustments during the next decade, but the methods of selling it did. By the late 1850s, Singer had developed an elaborate scheme in which the average family could purchase a machine on time (most unusual in the mid-nineteenth century), receive free lessons, and pay a bill collector out of the savings created either from not having to buy clothing or from earning money sewing for neighbors. Thus when he began to sell abroad in earnest (1860s), Singer took not only his machine, but his selling methods. Extensive market feedback, then, characterizes the early stages of product development. Learning curve analysis would reinforce Linder's model here because Singer's early development in the United States would have given it cost advantages over foreign competitors.

As inventions are developed for national markets, consumers in other nations with similar needs discover the new products. Mr. Jones, who wanted a four-cylinder station wagon that handles well yet has plenty of room for carrying belongings, looked at the whole range of American cars but found them all too big or too small; a Volvo wagon, however, suited his needs precisely. Mrs. Jones failed to find a carpet to her liking among American-made ones, and chose one made in Belgium. Young Jones favored the Danish Lego blocks over American toys. In these cases, the manufacturer originally designed a product for a home market but soon discovered that there were large segments of foreign markets that wanted a similar product. Hence exports rose with the discovery of similar markets abroad.

This illustrates a second idea of Linder's, namely that trade begins between nations that are similar in market structures and needs. Typically, they have expensive labor and cheap capital and therefore tend to demand many consumer goods of technical sophistication or high style, and many labor-saving capital goods.

Note another curiosity Linder saw: The importing country is the most logical next entrant into the export market. Having a large market for imports of a good, it also has the conditions for the establishment of variants of the imported good. Typically, in market-oriented goods, domestic production follows imports, and often exports follow domestic production. Thus Singer began production in Glasgow, the center of its largest foreign market, in 1868, somewhat more than a decade after its founding, and was exporting from Britain soon thereafter. Hence we should not be surprised that a large portion of the world's trade is between developed nations or that a high proportion of that trade is intraindustrial.

Product Life-Cycle Approaches

Both the Linder and the learning-curve approaches lay the foundation for a more elaborate analysis based on product life cycles (PLCs). PLC analysis is commonly used by American business managers as a way of predicting and assessing sales, technological, and competitive conditions that face their products and in planning appropriate marketing strategies. Besides being practical, though, PLC models have some highly interesting economic implications and can contribute to the analysis of trading patterns.[4]

Basically, a PLC model sketches the relationship of a product's sales per year to its age. A company's sales per period of time are shown on a vertical axis, while the years (or months) are shown on the horizontal, as in Fig. 11.3. The sales curve itself depends on changes in the potential market, in the technology, and in the competition that develop over time. The following are the major factors that influence that shape.

1. The technology involved in manufacturing or embodied in the product may start out as highly secret and well protected by patents, but this technical edge is gradually lost as other firms analyze the product, engineers change firms, and further research is done. Patent protection is often limited because of the narrowness of the patentable process; slight variations enable the patent to be bypassed. Such a process, called *technological maturation*, may take years (Polaroid's patents protected it for decades) or just months (Schick "knocked off," to use the industrial vernacular, Gillette's two-track razor in a matter of months). Furthermore, declines in real costs are sharpest during the early years of a product's life but slow down as it gets older, as is demonstrated by learning curve analysis.

2. Sales of successful products usually follow a pattern. Initial introduction to the market, often at high prices, attracts relatively few customers. There is often an uncertainty, with many changes and adjustments in both product and sales methods. Witness, for instance, the high prices and varying

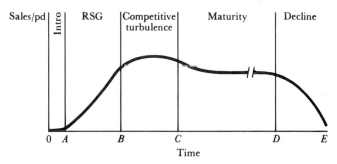

FIGURE 11.3   Product life cycle.

styles of hand calculators when they first came on the market. Then there is often a point of "take-off," when the sales of the new product begin to rise sharply. If this is accompanied by declining prices, the rise may be precipitous. After a point, however, the major markets become saturated—everyone who can afford one and wants one has one—and the market becomes largely a replacement market. This is described as *market maturity*. Finally, sales fall away as the product is supplanted by another.

3. Competitive conditions relate to the technological and sales variables. Initially, only one firm introduces the product. Competitors usually enter in numbers after sales have begun to rise sharply and the pioneering firm's profits look attractive. A period of growing competition follows, aggravated by the leveling off of sales as market saturation is reached. The industry finds itself overpopulated and several firms fall by the wayside. (Remember the Bowmar Brain, which was a notably nonsuccessful calculator.) Then the industry settles into some form of oligopoly.

The curve for the PLC attempts to reflect these three separate aspects. The first stage (0*A* of Fig. 11.3) is called the *introductory* state and is usually characterized by low sales, little or no profit, and little competition. The second (*AB*), or *stage of rapid sales growth* (RSG), is characterized by (naturally) rapid sales growth, declining costs, and the entry of competition. The intensification of competition brings to an end the RSG stage and brings on a third phase (*BC*), described as *competitive*. Here the pioneering firm's sales cease growing and often falter; industry-wide sales fall as the market ceases to expand. Eventually a competitive "shake-out" occurs and the remaining firms live on through a period of *maturity* (*CD*). With some products the process lasts for many years, hence the break in the line; then there is an eventual decline in demand (*DE*), leading to product death.

Product life cycles come in many shapes and sizes. Some products fail after introduction, such as the Edsel. Some have short lives, as with fads or minor product modifications like new cigarette brands or new cake mixes. Others have lives lasting centuries (coffee), or at least decades—brands such as Procter and Gamble's Crisco, Tide, or Crest have been around for years.

PLC analysis can be applied to international trade to explain what is being exported, what is being produced abroad, and what is being imported. Instead of relying on given factor inputs and constant technology, it deals with changing technologies, costs, and competitive conditions. Thus it is a useful tool for dealing with intraindustrial trade.

The first attempt to relate PLC models to international trade came from Louis Wells and Raymond Vernon of the Harvard Business School.[5] The *Wells-Vernon model* provides a thought-provoking historical analysis of U.S. trade. For many years the United States had the highest per capita income in the world, and with that high income came the introduction of many new consumer goods plus a great quantity of new capital goods. In appliances, U.S. consumers saw first the refrigerator, the radio, the clothes washer, then later televisions and dishwashers. Initially, sales of these products abroad were small because few foreign consumers could afford them. Thereafter, as income rose abroad, export markets grew. We show this as two product cycles, one Home (meaning United States) and the other Foreign, with the foreign cycle starting at a later date (see Fig. 11.4).

As foreign markets grew, however, foreign producers were tempted to enter the market. By this time some of the technology was more widely available and the technological lead of U.S. firms was shrinking. Though the foreign production may have been initially more expensive, trade barriers, transportation costs, and local preference served to protect the foreign producers. Costs also began to fall for foreign producers, as suggested by learning curve theory. It is no wonder that American manufacturers at this stage also moved their production facilities abroad to be close to the expanding market.

To this point, the Wells-Vernon model is not controversial. The difficulty comes in the next step. Wells and Vernon go on to suggest that, following the competitive phase both at home and abroad, the foreign producer now has the advantage. Why? Because the technological gap has been closed or is at least quite small, but foreign wages and incomes are still below the American, such that in the mature stage the foreign country will export and the United States will import. This matches the learning curve model suggested earlier,

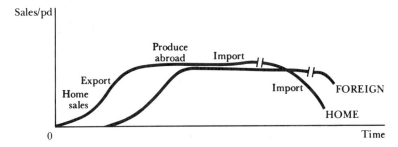

FIGURE 11.4 Product life cycles in home and foreign nations.

and would explain America's imports of radios, televisions, and automobiles. It also serves as a means to predict which products will soon be imported.

The problem with the Wells-Vernon model is that there is very little supporting evidence that the United States becomes a net importer in the mature phases, or that, indeed, any nation with the pioneering product loses its early advantages so completely. For instance, in the trade category "Road Motor Vehicles," American intraindustrial trade stood at 94 percent both in 1967 and in 1975. The supposedly embattled telecommunications industry did surprisingly well, with intraindustrial trade running at 85 percent of total trade.[6] Hence even in the area where penetration is fairly large, exports continue strong. On a micro level, a recent detailed study by Georges Leroy of five multinational manufacturers, examining the development of several hundred products, failed to find a single instance of the sequence described by Wells and Vernon—invention at home, production at home followed by export, production abroad, and *then* export back home. Where there are products sent back to the home nation, they almost always embody foreign technology, or else firms go abroad and begin exporting back home without developing the local market at all.[7]

The reasons for the difficulty with the Wells-Vernon model may stem at least partially from changes in world economic conditions. Both the technology and wage gaps among Europe, Japan, and the United States are closing— in some nations wages are at a par with, or higher than, American (for example, Switzerland and Sweden). By the time one calculates worker benefits and the like, it becomes extremely difficult to make precise judgments about who has the higher wages.[8] Foreign nations are more and more the technological pioneers. We drive on radial tires, manage four-cylinder engines with synchronized shift, ride ten-speed bikes, shave with double-blade razors, light up disposable lighters, and even watch foreign TV commercials. Increasingly, U. S. firms are buying out foreign firms for their knowledge. Royal Typewriter (Litton) purchased the German Triumph-Adler because it could not itself develop an electric typewriter to compete with IBM or SCM. Leroy's study, for instance, showed extensive exchange of products and know-how between foreign and domestic sources of information.

The mature stage of the PLC, rather than being a stage of importation, appears to be a stage of *interpenetration*. Variations on old products (with mini-life cycles of their own), like new razor blades, detergents, or car models, increase the amount of differentiation. Oligopolists seek market shares on a worldwide basis, and a series of investments and counterinvestments in exports and counterexports begins (see Chapter 16). Trade at this point becomes a matter not so much of technology, but of specialized consumption and production goods. These trends are analyzed in the next section.

Trade in Differentiated Goods

High levels of interpenetration with mature products lead us to a closer examination of what has been only lightly touched on—the division of markets into many small pieces with a product specially designed for each. Both supply and demand conditions encourage this. Affluent consumers are less interested in the "economy" of price alone, and more anxious to get a product that accurately meets their own tastes and needs. Rather than saving $50 on a washing machine to spend elsewhere, they buy a machine with extra washing cycles. Firms accommodate them to get their business. Since each consumer is somewhat different, the firm produces a "line" of goods with various features to serve various groups of customers. Complete personal customization is impossible, but the firm can divide its market into "market segments" and manufacture products meeting the needs of each segment, a procedure usually described as *market segmentation*.[9] Inevitably, this adds to costs, but consumers also receive benefits. Hence even under highly competitive conditions, one could expect a degree of market segmentation as firms try to answer the economic question of what to produce.

In most oligopolistic situations, price competition is limited because of fear of retaliation. If Ford cuts its price, GM will follow. In situations where firms have some market power (called monopolistic competition and analyzed in Chapter 15), the market is just not responsive enough to price cuts to make them worthwhile. If *Better Homes and Gardens* lowers its price, it is unlikely to gain customers from *House Beautiful*. Under such conditions (developing in the competitive phase of the product life cycle and continuing through maturity), firms speak of "deepening their market," and they move to heavier advertising and—of more concern here—toward a greater effort to identify market segments and produce goods specifically designed for each. The result is often that consumers are not even offered the choice of a single multifunctional product at a low cost. Instead, they get a great variety of models to choose from, but, if they are to buy at all, they must pay the cost of such customization.[10]

Cost pressures of market segmentation, however, cause firms to seek market segments that are large enough to warrant special production. With a new automobile model, for instance, it would not be out of line for the firm to spend $100 million before the first car was sold. In many cases this means that production is justified only if there are international markets—for example, taken alone, neither the European nor American sales of the Granada, or the Rabbit (the Golf in Europe), would justify its production, but the combined sales in both continents do. A vigorous trade then arises among differentiated goods. As with Linder's model, there are market segments in similar countries that want each other's goods. Accordingly, firms are increasingly designing products for international market segments, virtually planning a vigorous trade among differentiated goods.

Trade in differentiated goods provides considerable advantages to the trading countries. The advantages differ in kind, however, from those associated with *interindustrial* trade. The latter is determined more by comparative advantages, which allocate scarce resources. Intraindustrial trade, by contrast, is based on scale economies. To see this, one must examine the kinds of costs that accrue to firms engaging in extensive market segmentation.

Industrial Rationalization

The Costs of Market Segmentation. Typically, the making of multiple products in a single plant involves a number of costs.[11]

1. *Changeover time.* "Down time"—periods when machines are being changed over for new production runs—can be very costly in terms of both idle machinery and the manpower needed to set up the machine. One Australian factory, for instance, reported that the set-up time on a machine was eight hours—the machine was used for two hours to turn out a supply of parts that would last many months, and was then reset for something else.

The American parent, with its larger market, used the same machine for weeks after the set-up. The more the models, the more the down time.

2. *Equipment usage rates.* Specialized dies and machinery are needed for each of the different models. Many of these must be left idle while other products are run, giving low usage rates.

3. *Automation and the use of specialized equipment.* Many kinds of specialized equipment are justified only with high volumes of particular items. An Australian subsidiary of a U.S. firm used a turret lathe, the British affiliates used a twelve-spindle lathe, and the American parent used a highly advanced multistation loading lathe to make the same item. With smaller markets, specialized equipment is idle so much of the time that a more general machine is needed. Automation is economical only with longer production runs. Workers can be taught to switch tasks, but the machine that replaces them has a more limited range. If there are many different models to turn out, the process cannot be extensively automated, and labor costs remain high.

4. *Size of inventory.* More models mean a larger inventory both of parts and finished goods.

5. *Marketing costs.* The costs in advertising, service, and distribution rise with additional models.

6. *Labor's learning curve.* The repetition of tasks leads to a decline in labor costs, but if there are many models, repetition is lessened and costs do not decline after all.

International trade reduces the number of market segments a firm must service. Foreign production provides products that satisfy quite closely the needs of important groups of customers. Domestic producers, in search of export markets, ignore the imports from abroad in favor of foreign invasion. In other cases, the foreign production may be in a subsidiary of the same firm. We can see both patterns in the automobile industry. European car firms tend to produce a limited range of models. Volvo produces just two basic models, both expensive. A Swede who wants an inexpensive car can buy a Volkswagen or a Fiat, neither of which is a luxury car. The large American firms, in contrast, tend to sell full lines in most countries, but "source" the models from different subsidiaries. The Granada is made in England, the Capri in Germany, the Dodge Colt in Japan. Whatever the case, the net effect is to reduce the number of models each nation produces.

As the number of models declines, costs decline. If Ford is making both Torinos and Pintos and decides (or is forced) to produce only Pintos, it saves all the costs noted above. Note also that most of the costs involved are fixed costs, downtime, unused machinery, planning, and development. Costs of forgoing a more specialized machine are constant, no matter how many of each model is produced. Thus as Ford shifts away from Torino and into Pinto production, fixed costs per unit fall on the Pinto and rise on the Torino. The marginal costs of producing Pintos, measured in units of Torinos, keep falling. The cheapest Pinto would be the last one turned out on a production line of a factory that was 99.999 percent devoted to Pintos; the most expensive Torino would be the first and only one turned out in the factory. This produces an unusual production possibility curve—one convex to the point of origin (see Fig. 11.5(a)). This contrasts with the normal interindustry curves seen in the last chapter, such as the one between cloth and wine, which is concave (Fig. 11.5(b)).

Looking closely at the two production possibility curves in Fig. 11.5, you will note a very interesting phenomenon: In interindustrial trade like wine and cloth, prices start apart and move together. Each additional gallon of wine costs more bolts of cloth. With *intra*industrial trade, prices can start together and move apart. While a nation trading cloth might move from point *A* to point *B* in Fig. 11.5(b), the advantages of trade gradually taper off. The auto production more desirable and will continue until Torino production is eliminated. The trading partner will move in the opposite direction, and both nations end up with costs that are farther apart than at the starting point. (Clearly, the process is easier if, like Ford, you happen to own your trading partner.)

Other Gains to Specialization. Inplant scale economies may be supplemented by firm and plant-size economies. The firm saves the costs of designing and planning the marketing of each model. In many industries these are very high costs: The automotive industry has already been mentioned, but high costs are also characteristic of agricultural equipment, engines, generators, and many electronic goods.

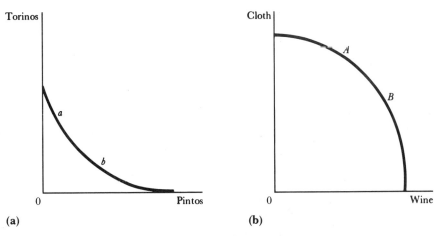

(a) **(b)**

FIGURE 11.5   Inter- and intraindustrial production possibility curves.

Discussion of plant scale economies has been out of favor since the work done by Joe S. Bain in the early 1950s indicated that they had been much overrated. Most major countries could afford several optimal plants in most industries; the very existence of multiplant firms demonstrated that. Bain concluded that the discussion of scale economies was largely a smokescreen for firms wishing to protect oligopolistic profits.

It is clear, however, that in some industries plant scale economies have become more important since the 1950s. An average petrochemical plant in the 1950s, for instance, might produce 10,000 tons a year of ethylene, while today production under 350,000 tons a year would be uneconomical. The Australian chemical industry, to give an example, is operating at twice the cost of "world-scale" chemical plants, being both terribly under scale and, because of overly optimistic market forecasts, under capacity. More sophisticated products, too, sometimes demand larger scale—automatic transmissions, for instance, need to be produced at the rate of nearly one million units a year for a plant to be efficient, in contrast to regular transmissions, which can be made at a rate of well under 100,000. Modern typewriters need 100,000 units a year, up from the 25,000-50,000 or so that used to be standard. Hence it is uncertain today the extent to which Bain's figures would be reproduced, and there are a number of cases in which scale economies are important.

Plant scale economies have also contributed to intraindustrial trade. General Motors has, for instance, one automatic transmission plant for all of Europe (in France), and every GM car in Europe with an automatic transmission is equipped from it. Borg-Warner's European plant supplies the same product to most of the other car manufacturers in Europe. Many producers have a considerable degree of specialization of plants on a worldwide basis, due to both scale of plant and inplant economies. This is especially important in agricultural equipment, where one nation may produce all the diesel engines, another all the transmissions, and a third all the plows. The tendency is also notable in the appliance industry.

The benefits to be reaped through such intraindustrial trade can be considerable. Canadian economists have long been concerned with the high costs of the Canadian manufacturing industry. In chemicals there is a serious problem of plant scale. The market is too small—or too spread out—to warrant "world-scale" plants. In automobiles and appliances, the problem has been inplant economies. Sophisticated Canadians want a product suited to their needs, which encourages market segmentation. Yet at the same time, the production runs tend to be very short, as would be expected of an economy one-tenth the size of the American. Detailed econometric studies have suggested that the gain to Canada from economic integration with the world (meaning the United States) would be in the nature of a 15 percent decline in costs.

Policy and Intraindustrial Specialization. There is one formal trade arrangement that can be directly attributed to ideas on intraindustrial trade and inplant economies of scale. This is the Canadian-American auto agreement of 1965, which allows free trade between the United States and Canada in automobiles, automobile parts, and agricultural equipment. (Only the companies themselves may trade freely—individuals purchasing cars or parts still have to pay a duty.) Until the pact, the American automobile companies had been producing a full range of models in Canada at a cost estimated to be 10-15 percent above U.S. costs. After the pact was signed, the Canadian factories were made as specialized as the American. All production of the Maverick for Northern and Eastern North America, for instance, was placed in Canada. Costs in the United States, too, have fallen as Canadian plants took over the production of models and parts made in the United States, but the percentage decline has not been so great. Cost savings, however, could be as large since a 1 percent saving in the United States on production ten times as large as the Canadian amounts to the same as a 10 percent saving there. Similar pacts have been suggested for appliances and chemicals, but rising Canadian nationalism has prevented action on them.

The process of intraindustrial specialization is interesting from another aspect: It involves little dislocation of labor. The Canadian-U.S. auto pact, for instance, led to no particularly serious dislocation of workers. (There were, in fact, specific provisions in the agreement to protect Canadian workers, but these were considered superfluous by the automobile firms, which had no intention of closing down their extensive Canadian operations.) The reason can best be shown by example. Contrast an interindustrial situation with workers transferred from textiles to electronics with an intraindustrial specialization like the automobile pact. Assume in both situations that after specialization, 9,000 workers can produce what used to take 10,000 workers, and that the remaining 1,000 workers are employed productively elsewhere. In the interindustry case, all 10,000 have to find new jobs, with 9,000 in electronics and 1,000 elsewhere. In the intraindustry case, 1,000 workers will be laid off as a result of fewer changeovers, the use of specialized equipment, and the like. The remaining 9,000, however, would stay employed within the same industry and most within the same firm.

Politically, intraindustrial trade is more acceptable because it involves less dislocation. The old models of international economics are thus not only inappropriate for a great deal of modern trade, but can be politically dangerous. Displacement—even if it is for the greater good—is not politically popular. The most liberal-minded senator is going to defend his or her state's industries if they feel threatened. Arguing that specialization will take place within the plant may not only be more realistic, but is more acceptable politically.

Notes

1. In 1975 the twelve leading industrial nations (United States, United Kingdom, Austria, Denmark, France, Germany, Netherlands, Norway, Sweden, Switzerland,

Canada, and Japan) exported some $425 billion worth of goods, $282 billion of which was to one another (*Direction of Trade,* United Nations, Oct. 1976).

2. The Japanese wage gap is beginning to close. In 1965 the Japanese hourly wage was US$0.51. In 1973 this had risen to US$2.22, a 335 percent increase. U. S. wages in the interim rose from $3.16 to $5.10, a 61 percent rise. At this rate, the gap will soon disappear.

3. Staffan Burenstam Linder, *An Essay on Trade and Transformation* (New York: Wiley, 1961).

4. PLC analysis is explained in most introductory marketing texts. A good advanced treatment of the subject is in Chester R. Wasson, *Dynamic Competitive Strategy and Product Life Cycles* (Austin, Texas: Austin Press, 1978).

5. Raymond Vernon, *Sovereignty at Bay* (New York, Basic Books, 1971), Louis Wells, Jr., "A Product Life Cycle for International Trade?" *Journal of Marketing* (July 1968): 1-6.

6. In 1975 the United States exported $10,036 million worth of "Road motor vehicles and parts," and imported $11,417 million. Roughly half this trade was with Canada.

The telecommunications industry is important because of American manufacturers' claims that the "TV industry" is being hurt by imports and deserves protection. The breakdown is as follows (for 1975)

Description	Exports (in thousands)	Imports (in thousands)
Telecommunication apparatus and parts	1,573,821	2,098,306
TV broadcast receivers	175,735	420,436
Radios	37,378	660,978
Telephone and telegraph equipment, loudspeakers, microphones, and amplifiers	1,360,709	1,016,891

Source: Dept. of Commerce, Bureau of Census, *U.S. Imports and U.S. Exports* 1975.

7. See Georges Leroy, *Multinational Product Strategy* (New York: Praeger, 1976).

8. The following figures compare U.S. and key foreign average wages, in U.S. dollars.

Country	1965	1973	Rise (percentage)
United States	$3.16	$5.10	61%
Sweden	1.89	5.15	172
West Germany	1.42	4.66	288
France	1.15	3.20	178
Great Britain	1.13	2.36	109
Italy	1.12	3.11	178
Japan	.51	2.22	335

9. Market segmentation is sometimes contrasted with "product" or "benefit" segmentation. In the former, customers are divided up according to such criteria as in-

come, age, sex, or life-style. In the latter, products are divided according to perceived benefits—for example, outboard motors with horsepowers of 5, 7½, 9½, 15, 20, 25, 35, 45, 50, 65, 75, 100, 125, 150, and 175 horsepower all have slightly different uses. It is not that the young or the wealthy prefer one or the other; rather their purchase is determined by the function they are to perform. For present purposes the authors prefer to use the phrase "market segmentation" to cover both processes.

10. Surprisingly little work has been done on the optimal number of products per firm. See Kelvin Lancaster, "Socially Optimal Product Differentiation," *American Economic Review* (September 1975): 567-585. Lancaster demonstrates, however, that under monopolistically competitive conditions, there will be more than an optimal number of models produced.

11. See Wilson Brown, "Market Segmentation and International Competitiveness," *Nebraska Journal of Economics* (Summer 1972): 333-348, for development of a list.

PART **IV**

BARRIERS
TO TRADE

12

BARRIERS
TO TRADE: ANALYSIS

All our analysis in the last two chapters has suggested that considerable benefits arise from trade. Yet governments persist in erecting or maintaining numerous barriers to the free flow of trade. Broadly speaking, the barriers to trade are divided into two groups: (1) those created by taxes, principally taxes on imports, or "tariffs," with an occasional export tax in a less developed nation; and (2) those not related to taxes, called nontariff barriers, or NTBs. NTBs include principally quantitative restrictions on imports—"quotas"—and a host of governmental regulations and laws that interfere (sometimes on purpose, sometimes incidentally) with the free flow of trade. This chapter examines the nature of these barriers and presents the basic economic analysis. The following chapter examines the public policy implications of the analysis.

The Effect of a Tariff

We already know from the analysis in Chapter 7 that tariffs affect a country's level of national income and its balance of payments. These are but two of seven tariff effects. Tariffs also alter the *terms of trade* between countries, *protect* domestic industries that shelter behind them, *decrease consumption* of the good, *redistribute income* between consumers and producers, give governments *revenue*, and cause *efficiency to decline* in the allocation of resources, both in *inter*industrial and *intra*industrial trade. Let us examine each of these economic effects in turn.

1. The Terms of Trade Effect. Anytime a tax is put on a product (and of course a tariff is a tax), one expects changes in both the quantity supplied and the quantity demanded. These in turn will alter the price of the product so taxed. Analysis of the terms of trade effect can predict these patterns of alteration. Figure 12.1 is a back-to-back diagram of supply and demand, with the country on the left (say, Ghana) exporting *AB* of some product (cocoa) to the country on the right (England), which imports *CD*. *AB* = *CD*. We will not consider transport costs and as yet there are no tariffs. The equilibrium price is 0*Z* per ton. The diagram is identical to Fig. 10.22, which was used to show what happened when transport costs were introduced. Tariffs are in fact similar to transport costs in their economic effect on the terms of trade. Suppose the tariff is $50 per ton of imported cocoa. On Fig. 12.2 that would move the export price on the left downward and the import price on the right upward so that they would end up varying from each other by $50. Consumers in England cut their cocoa imports, as on the right of Fig. 12.2, to *C′ D′*. Ghana's exports would fall to *A′ B′*.

Note the effect of this on the price of cocoa. The reduction in England's imports (which is really a reduction in the demand for Ghana's exports) means that Ghana cannot charge as high a price as before. The price of cocoa in international trade falls to 0*Z′*. This is not, however, the price that English consumers pay. That price is 0*Z″*, made up of Ghana's price 0*Z′* plus the $50 tariff (*Z′Z″*). The moral of the story is that with "normal" demand and supply curves, a tariff lowers the price charged by the exporter and raises the price paid by consumers in the importing country, with the difference between the two being the tariff revenue collected by the government of the importer. In this sense the tax burden is shared between exporter and importer.

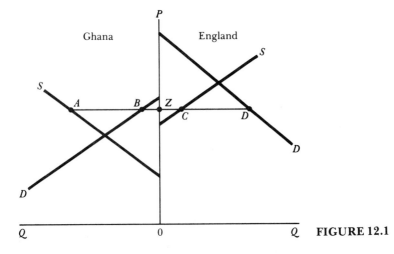

FIGURE 12.1

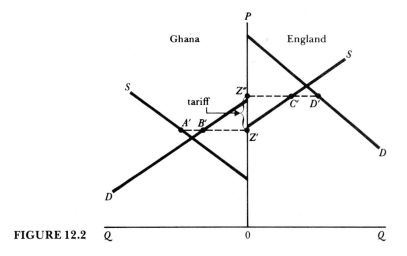

FIGURE 12.2

Depending on the elasticities involved, the burden may fall more heavily on one or the other country. This can be seen in Fig. 12.3. There, very high demand and supply elasticities in the importing country on the right mean that any slight rise in price cuts quantity demanded drastically and quickly increases domestic supplies. The tariff cannot raise prices very much in that country. The exporting country on the left has very low supply and demand elasticities, however. A price fall in that country does not increase the quantity demanded domestically much at all, nor will it cut back much on the quantity supplied. The result is that a decline in the demand for that country's exports will cause prices to fall far. In this case the terms of trade effect is very strong; prices in the exporting country are much reduced, and most of the burden of the tariff is borne by the exporter.

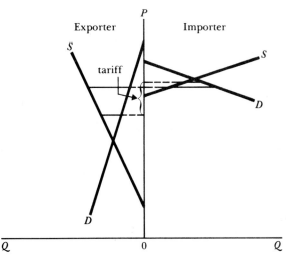

FIGURE 12.3

By contrast, had the elasticities been high in the exporter and low in the importer, prices would have fallen only slightly in the exporter and risen considerably in the importing nation. The terms of trade effect would have been small, and the burden of the tariff would have been borne largely by the importer.[1]

Some supporters of tariffs have argued that this terms of trade effect might be used as policy. An importer might so force down prices in the exporting country as to end up in a more advantageous position. If the terms of trade were large enough to offset the loss in trade volume, the importing country would be ahead. Presumably, then, the nation could calculate an optimal tariff level for its welfare. Such "optimal tariff" arguments, despite their technical validity, overlook the likelihood that one tariff to improve the terms of trade will beget another in retaliation abroad. The risk of a trade war is high. Furthermore, there is generally little practical knowledge available about the elasticities involved in export and import supply and demand curves (and politicians tend to pick the numbers that suit what they want to do anyway). Without very exact knowledge of both its long- and short-run effects, the manipulation of tariffs for terms of trade ends is senseless.

2. Protective Effect.   The tariff also provides protection for domestic industry.[2] This protective effect can be viewed directly in Fig. 12.4, where with no foreign trade the equilibrium price for the good shown is $0P_{nt}$ (the nt standing for no trade). After trade the world price (including transport costs) is lower than our original home price, so that we now import a good deal of the commodity, shown by the distance Q_1Q_3. At the world price $0P_w$, our country's own domestic producers manufacture a quantity $0Q_1$ of the good (indicated by the point at which the international price cuts the domestic supply curve).

Now imagine that a tariff equal to P_wP_t is enacted. To keep the diagram simple, we presume that the supply elasticity of the exporter is virtually infinite so that there is no terms of trade effect and the export price is not lowered. (This would be appropriate for describing a small nation's imports from the United States.) Under this circumstance, the domestic price will rise by the full amount of the tariff. As price is now $0P_t$, our domestic production will rise. (It would rise even more if our supply elasticity were higher.) This rise in production, Q_1Q_2 in the diagram, is the protective effect of the tariff. Protection will be total, with no imports at all, if the tariff is raised as high as P_wP_{nt}.

3. Consumption Effect.   Tariffs lower total consumption of a good. As shown in Fig. 12.4, the higher price will lead to reduced consumption, back along the demand curve from Q_3 to Q_4. In short, consumers pay higher prices because of the tariff and end up with less of the good because of the higher prices. They are forced to buy other less satisfactory substitutes, or do without altogether.

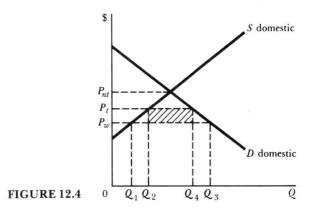

FIGURE 12.4

4. Revenue Effect. Historically, and in many countries even today, the main aim of tariffs has been the collection of revenue for the government. The first U.S. tariff of 1789 was a revenue tariff, and in fact most of the U.S. government's budget was financed from its proceeds. Until the 1850s, 90-95 percent of U.S. government spending was paid for from the tariff, and as late as 1900 the figure was still 50 percent. (It is only 1 percent today.)

A *pure* revenue tariff is one levied on a product not made domestically. There is thus no protective effect. Revenue tariffs can also avoid having protective effects if a tax equal to the tariff is placed on domestic production.

The revenue effect is shown in Fig. 12.4. Here, without the tariff, the price is $0P_w$ and no government revenue is collected. *With* the tariff, government collects P_wP_t on each unit of imports. The quantity of imports is equal to Q_2Q_4. Multiplying the vertical distance P_wP_t by the horizontal distance Q_2Q_4 gives the shaded area of the rectangle in Fig. 12.4. This shaded area is the government revenue collected.

5. Redistribution Effect. There will ordinarily be a redistribution of income from consumers to producers when a tariff is levied, though in the process some income is lost completely (the *deadweight loss*). This too can be pictured by means of standard supply and demand curves.

We must first review the concepts of consumers' and producers' surplus in order to analyze the redistribution effect. Figure 12.5(a) shows consumers' surplus. At a very high price such as $0P_h$, some people would still be willing to buy the product pictured. But in fact they do not have to pay a price as high as $0P_h$, because the market price is much lower at $0P$. Hence the shaded area PAB is all a surplus to consumers. The price is set for the marginal consumer, not the one that is sure to buy. The thirsty and the almost satiated pay the same price for drinks, even though the thirsty would be willing to pay more.

Similarly, the new price entices not the committed producer, but the marginal one. As the supply curve indicates, much production would still occur at

lower prices; the higher price is necessary to bring in the marginal production. Figure 12.5(b) shows that at a very low price such as $0P_L$ some supply
would still come to the market. But the market price is much higher at $0P$, so
these suppliers obtain a surplus equal to the area PBC.

The redistributive effect of a tariff involves the changing sizes of these
respective surpluses. In Fig. 12.6 with a tariff of P_wP_t, the price of the products is raised to $0P_t$. Producers' surplus is thus *increased* by the shaded area
marked A. Consumers' surplus was originally large, made up of the total area
P_wXZ. Now, however, it is reduced to P_tXY. Income has been redistributed
from consumers to producers.

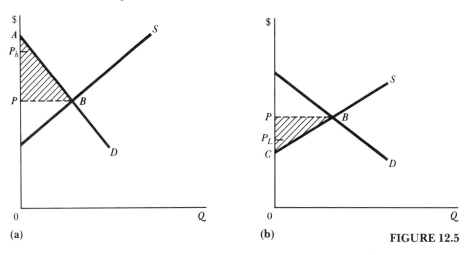

(a)   (b)   **FIGURE 12.5**

6. *Deadweight Loss Effect*. Unfortunately for society as a whole, the gains to
producers are smaller than the losses to consumers. In Fig. 12.6 the reduction
in consumers' surplus is equal to the areas $A + B + C + D$. A has been gained
by producers as the new producers' surplus. C is government revenue (a
transfer to the government). But the triangles B and D are lost consumer
surplus not gained back by anything or anybody. How can this be?

Note the area A in Fig. 12.6. Price actually rose enough to give producers
additional income of that plus the triangle B. Producers, however, cannot "enjoy" all of their gains because in order to expand production they must attract
resources away from increasingly valuable alternative uses. This is, after all,
the meaning of the supply curve: It traces the increasing opportunity costs of
the resources used. Hence triangle B represents additional costs to the producers. That same triangle means that consumers are deprived of the alternative goods those resources could be used to make.

On the demand side, consumers were willing to purchase $0Q_4$ at the
higher price, so we presume it is worth at least $0P_t$ to them. Consumers in the
Q_3Q_4 area found, however, that other products suited their purposes better
when the price was raised—in other words, to get the same amount of satisfac-

tion they had to spend more money on other goods. Or perhaps they simply took their satisfaction in added savings. Whatever the alternative, some buyers (those just to the left of Z) had ready substitutes and took little loss. They were almost, but not quite, indifferent to whether they wanted the protected product or something else. Others (just to the right of Y) found substitutes, but they were hardly indifferent, clinging to the protected product until finally driven away by the price $0P_t$. Consumers to the left of Y, however, suffer no loss of satisfaction from not consuming the protected good, but suffer a loss of income (meaning, of course, they cannot purchase some other goods.) However, their income loss is transferred to the producer, so it is not a net loss.

More broadly speaking, the deadweight loss of the tariff demonstrates what Chapter 10 showed with production possibility and indifference curves—producers move to a less efficient mix of goods, and consumers shift to a lower and less satisfactory indifference curve.

In another, more general, sense, the redistribution means a higher return to the factors of production that are relatively scarce (that is, that produce what otherwise would be imported) and a lower return to the abundant factors of production producing exports and nontraded goods. The tariffs that protect a labor-intensive industry when a country's abundant factors are land and capital will raise the return to labor and lower it for land and capital. This argument, first propounded by Wolfgang Stolper and Paul Samuelson and named after them, is that the protection benefits the scarce factor at the expense of the abundant ones.

7. Intraindustrial Trade Effect. Tariffs prevent the specialization characteristic of intraindustrial trade. As has been amply demonstrated for both Canada and Australia, the high tariff structure of those countries has led to high-cost industry, unable to build the world-size plants or operate the optimal-length production runs that are needed to supply the complex needs of affluent societies.

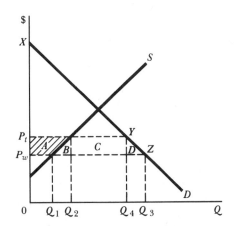

FIGURE 12.6

Nominal and Effective Tariffs

When referring to a tariff, one normally speaks of the amount of the duty compared to the cost of the import; thus a $25 tax on a $100 item would be a 25 percent tariff. In the last decade or so, economists have come to refer to this as the "nominal" tariff and have devised a new concept called the "effective" tariff to measure more accurately the degree of protection offered by a tariff. An *effective tariff* compares the import duty to the *value added* in the importing country. The tale of the pearl stringers illustrates nicely the difference between nominal and effective tariffs. The tariff on "strung pearls" in the United States used to be around $50 when the cost of importing a pearl necklace was around $100—hence a 50 percent nominal tariff. But notice the fact that a pearl importer could buy the pearls in Greece, have the pearls sized and matched for color, have holes drilled in them, and place them on a temporary thread. Pearls so arranged were not considered "strung pearls" and came in with zero tariff. (There is very little pearl fishing done in the United States.) The importer could then string the pearls on a permanent string with a clasp for about $1. The value added is $1 and the tariff is $50—a 5,000 percent tariff. There is no way a Greek company would string the pearls itself, for another dollar's labor would cost it $50 in tariffs.

When economists recognized this phenomenon, they set to work measuring it. To do so one needs to know the tariff on the imported raw materials or semifinished goods. Thus if temporarily strung pearls had paid a duty of $25, the Greek exporter would have faced only a $25 disadvantage, not a $50 one. This would lower the effective tariff from 5,000 percent to 2,500 percent. While few effective tariffs are as high as that, many are high enough to encourage such wastefulness as building furniture, then taking it apart and shipping it so it can be reassembled by protected labor abroad. Table 12.1 shows how significant the difference can be between nominal and effective rates:[3]

TABLE 12.1. NOMINAL AND EFFECTIVE U.S. RATES OF DUTY (before Kennedy Round)

Commodity	Nominal rate	Effective rate
Chemicals	10-19%	25-47%
Plastics	23	65
Plywood	16	99
Iron and alloys	3	14
Manufactures of metal	19	75
Cutlery	28	59
Domestic electrical equipment	14	47
Electric motors	13	56
Cotton fabrics	19	113
Clothing	27	136

Source: Theodore Morgan, *Economic Development* (New York: Harper & Row, 1975), p. 319.

The case can also be reversed, with tariffs higher on imported inputs than on finished products, so that effective protection for finished goods is actually negative. This amounts to a tax on the finished product rather than protection. The table's continuation shows this:

Poultry processing	6%	−10%
Rice milling	14	−28
Textile bags	10	−16
Paper mill products	0	− 7
Fertilizer	0	−24

In most developed countries, effective protection tends to exceed nominal tariff rates by a wide margin. Bela Balassa has calculated average nominal tariff rates and average effective rates of protection with the following results: United States, 11.6 percent and 20 percent; Great Britain, 15½ percent and 28 percent; Sweden, 7 percent and 12½ percent; Japan, 16 percent and 29½ percent; and the EEC, 12 percent and 18½ percent.

Quotas and Their Economic Effects

Now let us turn to the related area of quotas. Quotas are a relatively simple device. They involve a government ruling that just so much and no more of a good will be allowed into the country during a certain time period. The quota might be defined by volume (as, say, six cameras) or (less commonly) by value ($100 worth of cameras). Usually a license will then be necessary for importation to take place.

Quotas were virtually invented during the First World War; they had been very uncommon before that time, and were again dropped in the 1920s. France resurrected them in 1930-1931, largely for protection of its farmers and for defense against low-price Japanese imports, which could not be excluded by high tariffs because of preferential nation clauses in its tariff agreements. France became famous as the land of many quotas. By 1934, more than half the items on which France charged tariffs were now subject also to the new quota limitations. These limits were strict, with many goods subject to quotas of less than half the quantities formerly imported. The situation internationally grew so serious in the 1930s that the term "free trade" soon came to mean tariffs alone, used without quotas or other import controls.

The economic effects of quotas are as many and varied as the effects of a tariff. Figure 12.7 shows the world price of a product (cameras) as $0P_w$ before a quota is imposed. At that price, imports are equal to Q_1Q_4. Now say a quota of 1,000 cameras per year is imposed, 1,000 being equal to the distance Q_2Q_3. The price rises through market forces to $0P_q$, because only at that price will the quantity demanded domestically exceed home supply by the requisite

1,000 (Q_2Q_3). Incidentally, there are those who believe that a tariff must raise prices because it is a tax, but that a quota will not do so because it is not a tax. This position is dead wrong. It forgets that any measure that makes something scarcer will have to push prices up.

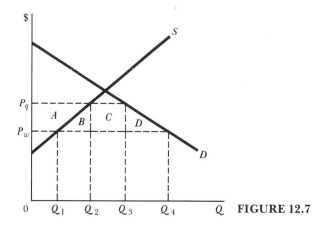

FIGURE 12.7

The protective effect is the same as for a tariff, with domestic industry benefiting from a price increase from $0P_w$ to $0P_q$ and a resulting production increase from $0Q_1$ to $0Q_2$. The consumption effect is also the same, with domestic consumers forced to reduce their consumption from $0Q_4$ to $0Q_3$.

The revenue effect, however, is much different. Note in Fig. 12.7 that at the new high price $0P_q$, the quantity of imports allowed in under the quota (Q_2Q_3) is worth more than before. Increased revenue equal to the price increase P_wP_q times the amount imported Q_2Q_3 (area C) is being received by *someone*. Who is it? Actually, the answer is seldom certain under a quota. The official giving out licenses to import may capture part or all of this revenue as a bribe. (Although uncommon in the United States, this is frequently encountered in many countries of Asia, Africa, and South America.) The importer fortunate enough or with enough political clout to obtain the required import license may obtain the revenue. This is ordinarily what happens in the United States.

The case of the American quota restrictions on imported oil (1954-1973) illustrates this. In those long-gone days, a barrel of oil could be purchased and landed on the East Coast for about $2.00. Oil interests, fearful of the flood of cheap Arab oil, had persuaded President Eisenhower (and his three successors) that the American oil industry could not survive at that price. So to "reduce American dependence on foreign oil," a quota on imports was declared under the Defense Act. This meant in effect that U.S. prices rose to about $3.25 a barrel. Oil companies were given import licenses according to 1953 import shares. Later, other companies, not importers, received licenses on the grounds that, were it not for the quota, they would be abroad. Since not all recipients of licenses actually used them and many companies wanted to import more oil than they had licenses, a vigorous market grew up for spare licenses. The price, of course, was the difference between the domestic and international price, or $1.25.[4] As Chapter 17 notes, Americans pay heavily today for their earlier independence.

Foreign exporters may capture the revenue by raising their prices if they have sufficient market power to do so. In practice, some combination of all three of these may be found. In no case does the public share in this revenue, although theoretically there is a way for this to occur. The government *could* hold an annual auction of import licenses, with importers bidding against one another and the collected revenue then becoming equivalent to the revenue paid under a tariff. Quota license auctions have been suggested for the United States, but have never been implemented. Brazil and some other South American countries have in the past tried the auction method.

Redistribution of welfare also occurs, similar to the situation under a tariff. In Fig. 12.7, consumers lose surplus equal to $A + B + C + D$, while producers gain A as surplus and somebody, we know not who, gains C as extra revenue. There is a deadweight loss from the quota equal to the two triangles B and D. There is also a terms of trade effect, with the imposition of a quota serving to lower the price the exporting country can charge. Figures 12.2 and 12.3 serve to illustrate this. Here, instead of a tariff, a quota $C'D'$ is imposed by the importing country; this then causes the price in the exporting country to fall from $0Z''$ to $0Z'$, basically because demand for that country's exports have been cut back.[5]

Quotas provoke unusual reactions. Very often, businesspeople seeking protection prefer quotas to tariffs. But professional economists are usually adamantly opposed to quotas because they believe them to have disadvantages for society more serious than those already discussed for tariffs. These economic disadvantages are as follows:

1. Quotas are by their nature very rigid. They limit imports to a fixed quantity no matter what the foreigner chooses to do about price. Compare Fig. 12.8(a), showing a tariff, to Fig. 12.8(b), which portrays a quota. In Fig. 12.8(a), domestic demand D has risen to D'. Even though there is a tariff P_wP_t, the quantity imported can still rise—in this case from Q_1Q_2 to Q_1Q_3. But with a quota, a higher domestic demand leads to no further importation at all. In Fig. 12.8(b), new demand D' serves only to raise the price charged at home from $0P_q$ to $0P_q'$, with imports remaining limited under the quota to a fixed quantity $Q_1Q_2 (= Q_{1'}Q_{2'})$. Businesspeople interested in protection naturally prefer this high degree of certainty. It is far preferable from their point of view that foreigners will not be able to cut their prices in the face of a quota the way they can do for a tariff. It is far preferable that a change in buying

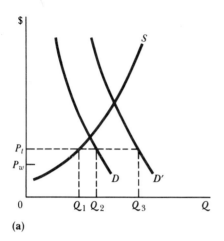

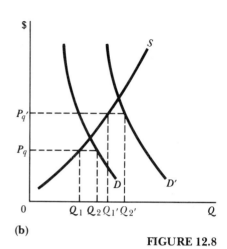

FIGURE 12.8

habits that leads consumers to prefer imports cannot result in a greater quantity imported. With no additional competition permitted from abroad at all, any latent or real monopoly position can be exploited. And the stimulus to higher efficiency that stems from competition is lost.[6]

2. Government loses the tariff revenue; in the United States this usually goes to the importers who have gained a share of the quota. The obvious solution, as pointed out earlier, is for the government to auction the licenses awarded under the quota, but such action is extremely rare. Importers would decry auctions as "unethical," and perhaps argue that their high overhead would allow fly-by-night competitors to underbid them at the auction. Why the importing companies should have any special rights to the revenue is usually not stated.

3. Quotas are difficult to administer. If a so-called global quota is imposed, say 1,000 cameras per year, then importers rush to bring in the cameras at the beginning of the quota period. To counter this indiscipline, licenses are ordinarily issued, most often on the basis of past performance. If imports in 1978 were 10 million pairs of shoes and you want to cut that figure to 8 million in 1979, then just issue an order that all firms importing shoes in 1978 can import 8/10 of their 1978 figure in 1979. This method freezes the patterns of trade, lessens competition, and does not allow new and cheaper sources of supply to enter the market. Nonetheless it is very common. One possibility for avoiding the problem is to save a part of the quota, say 10 percent or 20 percent of the whole, for new applicants. Even so the old producers will have a vested position, and will be much more protected under the quota than they would have been under a tariff allowing in an equivalent quantity of imports. And much political infighting is likely to develop as firms jockey for import licenses.

Quotas, moreover, tend to get ever more complicated. Quantity limitations in steel, for instance, encouraged foreign exporters to shift from supplying inexpensive "cold rolled sheets" to specialty steels, which brought more per ton; then specialty steels too had to be protected by a quota. Textile agreements become ever more complex with each passing year. Governments cannot hope to administer international trade, yet they continue to try.

When all these factors are taken into account, it is not difficult to understand why economists have tended to consider quotas a greater problem than tariffs. The case has been well put by Michigan State University's Walter Adams:

> In summary, import quotas are inimical to the public interest. Quotas undermine the competitive discipline of the marketplace. They encourage price escalation and cost-push inflation. They penalize industries using quota-protected products as raw materials, thereby reducing the cost-and-price-competitiveness of those industries in domestic and world markets. Finally, like any scheme of protectionism, quotas have a narcotic effect on the patient they are ostensibly designed to help. A sick industry no longer has to face up to its problems—to reform if it is to survive. Under a quota system, it can luxuriate in inefficiency and backwardness without penalty, knowing that a permissive government will support its catatonic refusal to face up to reality.[7]

Other Nontariff Barriers and Distortions to Trade

Quotas are the most familiar of the nontariff barriers to trade, as they are known in the jargon. But there are many others—Robert Baldwin's book on distortions to trade notes hundreds of further examples—and they are becoming more visible as the average rates of tariffs drop through international negotiations. The most important of these barriers and distortions are:

Government Buying Policies. Many countries give limited or total preference to domestic producers where government purchases are concerned. It is difficult to gather information on such practices, but they are pervasive. Federal and national governments, states (United States, West Germany, Australia), provinces (Canada, Italy), counties (United States, Great Britain), departments (France), cities, wards, even school boards, frequently engage in preferential buying. The public sector of any modern economy is already large and usually growing. The overall impact of the practice is thus probably intensifying. Note, incidentally, that even if one were to track down every example of preferential legislation, the full magnitude of the problem would still not be apparent because officials and agencies frequently buy at home through habit even when not required to do so. The procedures for announcing contracts, bidding, and finally drawing up agreements may be unclear, complex, and difficult for foreigners to follow. Some European governments and publicly owned firms have frequently been known to invite bids only from domestic concerns. Other governments and agencies put out offers only a short time before contracts are awarded, and provide very little information with the offer so that insiders have a distinct advantage in bidding.

An excellent example of preferential buying is the U.S. federal Buy American Act of 1933. The present wording of this act requires the federal government to buy U.S. products instead of imports whenever the U.S. price does not exceed that of the import by more than 6 percent, or 12 percent for areas of high unemployment, or 50 percent for goods purchased by the Department of Defense. The latter category, defense, may not be as obvious as it seems. Recently it was widened to include hand tools. Thus the lonely American visiting the Munich PX of an American army base finds California and New York wine in the heartland of Riesling and Rheinwein, and Budweiser instead of Lowenbrau. True, lots of Gallo and Bud would be there anyway as a matter of taste, but the Buy American Act requires it.

Then take the 1934 Ship American Act. Under its provisions, 50 percent of the U.S. government cargoes shipped to foreign countries must be carried in merchant vessels under the U.S. flag. The act applied only to government shipments (Food for Peace, military aid, and the like), but in 1977 it was proposed to extend the principle to the private sector, with American-flag tankers guaranteed the right to carry 4½ percent of the country's oil imports, rising annually for five years to 9.5 percent. Congressional supporters of the merchant marine had been pushing for a figure of 30 percent, and such a bill was indeed passed by Congress in 1974. But it was not signed by President Ford,[8] and the 1977 bill died also, "of embarrassment," said the London *Economist*. A full 50 percent of the oil imported for the new U.S. government reserves being stored underground as insurance against another OPEC embargo must be carried in American-flag tankers. Another relatively obscure law dating from 1920, the Jones Act, requires that all ships used in domestic trade (that is, in traffic between American ports) be built in the United States. Thus the big tankers needed to carry Alaskan oil to the West Coast must be built in American shipyards at much higher cost than if they were purchased abroad—in Japan, for example.

Domestic Subsidies and Taxes.   The shipping industry is also a good example of how government subsidies can play a large role in international trade. American-flag ships currently receive a 35 percent construction subsidy (formerly 55 percent) that makes American yards more competitive at a current cost to taxpayers of $236 million per year, with 87½ percent of the credit for building the ships guaranteed by the government. The shipowners also receive an operating subsidy covering repairs, maintenance, and higher wage and insurance costs in the United States. The operating subsidy in the 1976 budget was $403 million. Construction subsidies for shipping are a common occurrence throughout the world, and in one form or another, ranging from direct cash grants to government-sponsored credit, most important ship-building nations use them.

Under the General Agreement on Tariffs and Trade (GATT, discussed in the next chapter), direct subsidies for exports are illegal. But, as with the shipping industry, *domestic* taxes and subsidies can commonly be used to have an important impact on international trade. A familiar example is the regional development assistance used to promote industry via direct cash subsidies, or tax relief, or tax relief for certain lines of production or on certain inputs, or the provision of special credit facilities. Examples include the Italian Mezzogiorno project, the French regional development program, and the Common Market's identification of various areas (parts of Ireland and Britain, for example) as development areas aided by EEC money.

Aside from shipbuilding, no area of international trade is more affected by domestic subsidies and taxes than is agriculture. The EEC's protection of agriculture with subsidies is enormous, with the average level of protection about double what it was in the early 1960s. The Common Agricultural Policy (CAP) cost the EEC about $6½ *billion* in 1977 in direct budget expenditure and about as much again in the cost to consumers paying prices above those in the world market. (In the United States, the old farm program cost only about half the EEC's, and even that is now much reduced because U.S. subsidies were scaled down when Earl Butz was Secretary of Agriculture.)

The EEC program was not set up to have a direct effect on international trade. It and its huge expenditures are there because a powerful 20 percent of the electorate in the EEC is dependent on farming, and price supports have been set up to allow the highest-cost producers to survive. Farmers get about two-thirds of their income from the support program. But the implications for international trade have been grave. Enormous surpluses of agricultural commodities have been one result. In 1973-1976, with the EEC-subsidized price for butter over three times the world market price, farmers responded so actively that the Common Market was forced to accumulate huge butter stockpiles held in storage, the famous "mountain of butter." In early 1977 the butter mountain had passed 190,000 tons and predictions were that at current rates of growth it would soon reach 300,000 tons. Attempts to clear away the mountain had their impact on trade. Special negotiated sales to Russia at below world prices in 1973, and additional sales of surplus butter to Russia in 1976, were cases in point. Meanwhile there grew an even greater "mountain of milk." Stored in powder form, the milk mountain hit 1.3 million tons in 1976. Attempts to whittle it down took the form of forcing farmers to include milk powder in their cattle food, and indeed, 380,000 tons of milk were thus disposed of before the scheme ended. But Americans found their soybean exports, in place of which Common Market farmers used the milk, were also whittled away in the process. Soybeans, incidentally, are less expensive, contain more protein, and are easier to handle than powdered milk. Hence the objections from Common Market farmers.[9]

Among the many results for international trade has been a decline in U.S. agricultural exports to the EEC. These were actually down 19 percent between 1966 and 1969. The percentage of total U.S. agricultural exports going to the EEC was 35 percent in 1960 and only 25 percent in 1975. A high export subsidy must be paid by the EEC to its own agricultural exporters so that they can successfully trade abroad. Without such export subsidies, the EEC would export very few farm commodities. The cereal grains support price, for example, though not as high relatively as the butter and milk prices, is still twice the world price level. The whole question of these subsidies is one of the great bones of contention between the United States and the EEC, the United States arguing that the Common Agricultural Policy distorts trade severely. The United States has even retaliated from time to time. There has been a U.S. lard subsidy, a subsidy on chicken exports, retaliatory tariffs during the "Chicken War" of the 1960s, and talk of a "Soybean War" from time to time. Certainly the whole question is a difficult one, and the situation calls urgently for reform.

Domestic taxes can also distort trade. The automobile industry is a good example of this. Vehicle license and road-use fees often apply to a car's horsepower or weight in Europe and Japan, and not to the price of the car as in the United States. As American-produced cars tend to be higher in horsepower and heavier, they often labor under a substantial tax disadvantage when imported by foreigners. France, for instance, has a special levy averaging about $200 per year on high-horsepower U.S. cars. Britain also taxes cars on horsepower, and the financial penalty on American cars is nearly as bad there. Japan has been notorious for its tax discrimination against imported vehicles. Now readers, and the authors as well, will say that laws penalizing high horsepower and weight are fully justified as a measure for conserving scarce fuel. The authors personally support such laws in the United States. However, the French, British, and Japanese tax laws were passed *not* to conserve fuel, but to protect the domestic car industry. They had been in effect for many years, long before roads became cluttered and long before OPEC became a reality.

Export-credit Subsidies and DISC. As we saw in the preceding section, direct subsidies for exports are prohibited by GATT. But most governments do subsidize the *financing* of exports, through finance facilities, credit guarantees, and low-cost insurance. Exporters are thus able to offer lower interest rates to foreign importers by comparison with domestic importers, with resulting distortions to trade. U.S. export credits are given by the Export-Import Bank (Eximbank) in Washington, established in 1934 and equipped with a "discount window" allowing for loans to exporters backed by their commercial paper. This in turn allows the American exporter to grant easier terms to foreign buyers. However, Eximbank loans dropped from $3.8 billion in 1974 to $2.1 billion in 1976 because of a legislative attack that forced the bank to pay higher interest rates to the treasury for its funds. European and Japanese credit subsidies are much more liberal.

Much more controversial has been DISC, standing for "domestic international sales corporations," which have been permitted under American law since the U.S. Revenue Act of 1971.[10] The whole DISC scheme amounts to a huge indirect subsidy of American exports, and it was initiated to counter the severe balance of payments problems facing the country when it was established. Under the DISC law, U.S. exporters could establish subsidiary corporations called DISCs, to which authorized parent corporations could allocate up to 50 percent of their profits on exports. The DISCs were then permitted to defer indefinitely 50 percent of the tax payments due on these profits, provided that the proceeds were used to promote exports or invested in export-related commercial paper.

This impressive tax incentive led to the establishment of 4,000 DISCs by the middle of 1974, rising to over 8,000 by 1976. The great majority were owned by a single corporation engaged in exporting. Alas for them, a GATT ruling in November 1976 declared them to be nothing more than a colossal, albeit disguised, export subsidy, and thus illegal under GATT rules. The whole issue is now up in the air, with President Carter advocating their abolition, and Congress favoring retention. In the authors' opinion, however, there is little doubt that the original reason for establishing the DISCs—namely, a deteriorating U.S. balance of payments position—has long since become obsolete because of the adoption of floating exchange rates, which themselves are the adjustment mechanism for balance of payments surpluses and deficits. That being the case, the DISC must be seen as a transfer of income from taxpayer to exporter, representing a fine windfall gain for the latter. (The greater part of the DISC benefits, incidentally, accrued to a small number of very large corporations. These firms lobbied hard for its retention.)[11]

Border Tax Adjustments. Nontariff distortion to trade can be a complex topic, and no part of it more so than the complicated question of border tax adjustment. Notwithstanding the complication, it has been one of the more crucial trade issues of the 1970s. GATT has a rule, dating from early in its history, that depends on the belief that indirect or sales-type taxes are shifted forward fully to final users of a product in the form of higher costs and prices for that product. GATT thought, at the time it implemented its rule, that it would be unfair for country A to charge a 10 percent sales tax, which then would figure in the final price of the good, while country B, its trading partner, did not have any sales taxes and so would be in a favorable position. GATT therefore tried to promote competition on an equal footing in the country where exports were to be sold, no matter what the differing rates of sales tax were. To accomplish this, countries were permitted to give tax rebates at the border on their exports, and to charge a special compensatory tax of the same amount on imports. Thus the distorting effects of the sales tax would, in the theory of the time, be eliminated. Meanwhile GATT, again following current economic theory, assumed that income and profits taxes were not passed on to final buyers, being absorbed instead by the seller. Thus the GATT rules did not permit a border tax adjustment on these types of taxes.

For reasons that may be related to the issue of rebates, but probably were not, the Common Market in the 1960s began to standardize its taxation with sales-type taxes. Their direct corporate-profits taxes were largely replaced with a system of indirect taxes called the VAT, for Value Added Tax. Almost all of Europe, including the whole of the EEC, now uses the VAT, although its imposition has been delayed for technical reasons in Italy. The EEC has sought a common rate of about 15 percent for the VAT, meaning a reduction in such taxes in France and an increase in Germany. Japan uses similar taxes. Some readers may not be familiar with the VAT because its use has been very rare in the United States—though the state of Michigan used a similar levy for some years. VAT works as follows: A sales tax is calculated on only the value added by the firm being taxed. This is determined by subtracting the money value of purchases from other firms from the money value of sales, this equaling the value added. It is usually charged by taxing all sales and then rebating the tax paid earlier on all purchases.

Say $750 in VAT has been charged in all on a $5,000 German automobile. It is this $750 that under GATT rules may be rebated at the border when the car is exported. Imports of similar cars may legally be taxed an identical $750. Or if U.S. steel is used in the manufacture of the German car, VAT can legally be charged on the imported steel. Thus, according to plan, the price of exports will be free of indirect tax, and the price of imports will be equalized with domestic production.[12]

The U.S. government and private firms have long protested against the GATT rules on border tax adjustments. The tax rebate on exports has been called an unfair subsidy; the imposition of tax on imports has been called an unfair form of tariff. In fact one of the reasons the United States established the DISC subsidy system described in the preceding section was apparently an attempt to even the game with the Common Market and Japan.

Obviously the GATT rule's equity depends on the economic theory of who bears the burden of a tax. If GATT is indeed correct in arguing that indirect VAT-type taxes are passed on to the final consumer via prices, while income taxes are borne by the producer, then the rebate of VAT is logical and fair. If, however, indirect taxes are *not* fully passed on to the consumer, and are partly absorbed by manufacturers—which appears to be the prevailing opinion in most principles of economics textbooks nowadays—then rebates of VAT do discriminate in favor of countries employing that type of tax. Also, if corporate income and profit taxes *are* in part passed on to consumers and not wholly absorbed by the manufacturer of exports, then the VAT rebate again discriminates in favor of countries employing it. Traditional theory has held that profits taxes are not passed on, but numerous economists have argued otherwise in recent years. Administered markup pricing, with taxes considered as a cost and made part of the markup, may result in the corporation tax being passed on through prices to the final consumer. Some scholars are placing more and more emphasis on the position that *both* indirect and direct taxes are largely passed on in this manner.[13] The upshot would then be that the GATT ruling is indeed inequitable, discriminating in favor of countries with the VAT and against countries, such as the United States, that rely heavily on income and profits taxes.

The issue has been in doubt for some years now, and is unlikely to be settled soon. Americans tend to argue that GATT rules should be changed to stop the rebate of VAT, or to allow the rebate of direct corporate taxes. Europeans tend to reply by saying the United States too could have rebates if only it would adopt the VAT. This leads Americans to counter with charges that VAT is not progressive, and as a fixed percentage tax it hits the poor harder than the rich. Then, like a *deus ex machina*, there swung into this rather airy debate a momentous court decision in New York City. The case was initially very obscure. It was brought by the Zenith Corporation into the U.S. Customs Court, which sits in New York. Zenith charged—and no one denies it, as seen above—that Japan was rebating sales-type taxes to exporters of Japanese color TV sets. Zenith brought its case under an American law of 1897, which protects against secret subsidization of exports by foreigners. Zenith claimed that the Japanese tax rebate was a disguised subsidy, illegal under the 1897 act. The Customs Court agreed and ordered importers to pay a special tariff of 15 percent to offset the presumed advantage accruing to the Japanese. Since perhaps 60 percent to 70 percent of all imports to the United States receive rebates, the court's decision put the United States in violation of GATT agreements, would almost certainly have led to broad retaliation, and could possibly have caused a trade war. The Supreme Court, however, working faster than its wont, struck down the ruling in June of 1978. VAT rebates thus continue to be legitimate in American law.[14]

In a world of floating exchange rates, the debate is really quite academic. If a 15 percent rebate increases France's exports, then, other things being equal, the franc will appreciate by 15 percent, wiping out that advantage. When such rebates are across the board, as is VAT, there is no problem that a floating exchange rate will not rectify. If, however, some exporters get larger rebates than others, a distortionary factor is introduced that the exchange rate change cannot handle—a 20 percent rebate to automobiles alone will not change the exchange rate by 20 percent. The automobile manufacturers in other countries have the right to complain about unfair—and uneconomic— discrimination. That, however, has not been the argument to this point.

Technical and Health Regulations. Worldwide, there is a maze of technical and health regulations imposed by government, many desirable in their own right, but also fully capable of distorting trade. There are barriers to importing fruits, plants, and animals.[15] Hoof-and-mouth disease precautions are particularly strict in the United States against beef imports from Latin America;

an outbreak of hoof-and-mouth disease in a remote part of Argentina was enough to cause fresh meat to be embargoed from all areas of that country. There are hygienic requirements in food production. Then there are different manufacturing standards. Some countries produce products with nuts threading counterclockwise, using pole instead of knife-type electrical connections, with steering wheels on the right rather than the left, and a myriad of other variations. These would in any case be inconvenient for export, but they also often violate some national, state, or local law. Perhaps the most familiar of such regulations are now the U.S. and Canadian safety standards for automobiles, which, justifiable as they may be, effectively prevent the importation of many foreign makes and models.[16] There are similar safety standards for tractors and electrical equipment. For sheer discrimination, the greatest offender among regulations is probably the mark-of-origin requirement under which an import must have a label announcing where the good was made. "Made in USA," "Made in South Korea," "Made in Singapore," presumably give some information, but also presumably are intended to stir patriotic feelings and allow Americans to by-pass products from countries not well liked. Also, the problem of printing or stamping "Made in Spain," "Hecho en Espana," "Fabriqué en Espagne," and so on can increase costs of some goods substantially.

Administrative Regulations. Dozens of administrative regulations exist as nontariff barriers to international trade. Mordechai Kreinin has pointed out that the French ban scotch and bourbon advertising, and that the British limit the showing of foreign films on the BBC.[17] The U.S. grading requirement for tomatoes effectively discriminates against tomato imports from Mexico. These are micro measures applying to specific products. There are also macro measures used as substitutes for tariffs and quotas in an attempt to improve the exchange rate or the balance of payments, most of which have been discussed in Chapter 7. The British pioneered the use of *deposit advances* against imports. (There was some earlier use of the idea in less-developed countries in the 1950s.) The original British scheme of 1968 required importers to deposit with the Treasury an amount equal to half the value of their imports for six months at no interest. Such regulations spread rapidly and were introduced during 1974 in Iceland, Israel, Italy, Yugoslavia, and Greece, among others. In 1975-1976, nine more countries established such schemes. A last macro measure is the *import surcharge*, a flat percentage tax charged across the board on imports. President Nixon's 15 percent surcharge of 1971 is a good example. Other current examples include Bolivia, Brazil, Ghana, and Spain, among many others.

Conclusion

As Chapter 1 noted, the very existence of nation states with their various laws, regulations, and taxes creates the field of international economics. Nowhere is this clearer than in the observation of tariff and nontariff barriers. But we are dealing with governments, conscious to some extent of the interrelationships of their various laws affecting trade. Accordingly, governments have tried to create trade *policies*—that is, reasonably integrated and consistent approaches toward their laws governing trade. Hence when dealing with trade, we do not necessarily deal with a series of isolated causes and effects, but with governmental policies that in some measure integrate and shape tariff and nontariff measures. It is to this subject that we turn in the following chapter.

Notes

1. The terms of trade effect can be seen using offer curves. Take the case of Britain putting tariffs on cocoa imports from Ghana. Figure 12.9(a) shows the offer curve of Britain shifting upward as a tariff is imposed, improving Britain's terms of trade. In Fig. 12.9(b), however, Ghana retaliates, putting a tariff on British machinery. The terms of trade return to their original relationship—but total trade is less.

2. A splendid example of lobbying skill leading to total protection was the Onondaga Salt Company, one official of which was the speaker of the house in the New York legislature and another a member of the U.S. House Ways and Means Committee, which framed tariff legislation. In the mid-nineteenth century this company backed huge duty increases on salt. Three such brought the tariff to $0.40 a

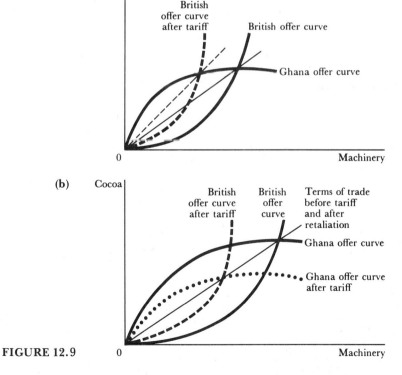

FIGURE 12.9

bushel, after which almost no foreign salt entered the country. The company more than doubled its price, and within five years it had paid out over $5.8 million in dividends on an invested capital of $160,000.

3. The actual calculation of the effective tariff involves several things:

    x = international price of the finished commodity;
    y = the domestic price, including tariff protection;
    a = the international price of the imported components; and
    b = the domestic price, including tariff protection of the same component.

    Take the case of a U.S. levy of 30 percent on clothing, when the imported cotton or wool and other materials are duty free. Assume that these inputs are half the final value. A $100 suit consists of $50 in imported raw materials and $50 worth of home inputs like labor and capital. The $30 duty is 30 percent of the suit, but 60 percent of the domestic value added. If no components are in fact imported we would use the formula:

    $$\frac{y - x}{x}$$

    and get

    $$\frac{130 - 100}{100} = 30 \text{ percent.}$$

    When some components are imported we must change the formula to include those:

    $$\frac{(y - b) - (x - a)}{x - a} \quad \text{or} \quad \frac{(130 - 50) - (100 - 50)}{100 - 50} = \frac{30}{50} = 60 \text{ percent.}$$

4. The oil quota begat its own evasion. It was not designed to apply to Canada, so all oil arriving by pipeline was excluded from the quota provisions. There was at the time no pipeline from Mexico. It was not long before oil firms built a very short pipeline of less than a mile in length extending from Mexico into the United States. Oil trucks would come up from Mexico, enter the United States with their cargo "bonded" and sealed (so it would not be used there), and then travel on the good U.S. roads, leaving the country again at the pipeline. Once on the Mexican side of the border they would empty their cargoes into the pipe, where it would flow into the United States, free of the quota. The trucks would then return to Mexico. This operation was known as "El Loophole."

5. Quotas also have a balance of payments effect and an income effect, similar to a tariff.

6. It is possible to show that a quota can convert a potential monopoly into an actual one. (The proof is provided by Charles P. Kindleberger in his *International Economics*, 5th ed. (Homewood, Ill.: Irwin, 1973), Appendix E). Say that as in Fig. 12.10(a) a firm faces a world trade price $0P_w$, and is protected by a tariff $P_w P_t$. Since customers can buy abroad any quantity they want at a price $0P_t$, no one will pay our domestic firm more than that. $P_t MR_t$ is thus a horizontal demand curve for the

firm's product, and $P_t MR_t$ is the marginal revenue curve for the firm as well. The firm produces where marginal cost MC equals marginal revenue MR, or $0Q_t$. The remainder of the country's demand $Q_t Q_w$ is supplied from imports. Now see the changes introduced by a quota. Let us establish a quota equal to $Q_t Q_w$ on the quantity of imports. At the very top of the demand curve, shown in Fig. 12.10(b), with high domestic prices, we can say that the cheaper imported good will be preferred. In effect, the domestic demand curve is moved to the left by the amount of the quota, down to the price below which the foreigner cannot go ($0P_w$). Anywhere below that, our domestic firm captures all the demand. This new demand curve D_q is shown as a heavily shaded line. The end result is that the same quantity of imports as permitted under a tariff ($Q_t Q_w$), when brought in under a *quota*, worsens consumers' welfare. The new curve for marginal revenue MR_q shows, at $MC = MR$, a price far higher at $0P_q$ than it had been under a tariff ($0P_t$).

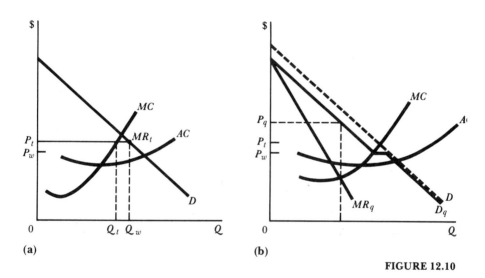

FIGURE 12.10

7. Walter Adams, "The New Protectionism," *Challenge* (May/June 1973): 10.
8. Under American law, if Congress is not in session, the president need not send a formal veto message to Congress or give Congress the opportunity to override the veto. Instead, by "putting the bill in his pocket," so to speak, and not bothering to sign it, the bill does not become law. This is known as a *pocket veto*.
9. One of the mountains, for all its huge size, was actually larger some years ago. In 1968-1969 the EEC butter price was five times the world price, and in 1969-1970 six times larger. Farmers responded with a butter mountain of 400,000 tons of surplus held in storage in the latter year. In that year, older butter was being fed to cows!
10. A good, concise description of DISCs is an article by Joseph G. Kvasnicka and Jack L. Hervey, "Promoting US Exports through DISCs," *Business Conditions* (October 1976): 3-9.

11. There is an account of the GATT ruling on DISCs in the *Economist*, November 20, 1976, pp. 101, 103.
12. On occasion, alterations in VAT and hence in the amount of rebates have been used as a substitute for alterations in the exchange rate. They can certainly have a similar effect. For example, long before France actually devalued the franc in 1969, her VAT rates were increased by a maximum of 5 percent. This meant a stimulus to her exports (increase in rebates) and discouragement for imports (border taxes increased). In the opposite direction, Germany in 1968 kept her VAT rate constant at 11 percent, but reduced the border adjustment, lowering the rebate on exports and the border tax on imports, to only 7 percent. This neat device was a disguised form of changing exchange rates, difficult for most people to understand and thus attracting far less attention than a significant mark revaluation would have.
13. For a full theoretical discussion of these issues, see Marian Krzyzaniak and Richard A. Musgrave, *The Shifting of the Corporation Income Tax* (Baltimore: Johns Hopkins Press, 1963).
14. A similar case, not yet decided, has been brought by U.S. Steel, Inc., against EEC steelmakers. The Zenith decision presumably settles the issue.
15. Many American tourists crossing into Canada have experienced loss of fruit to eagle-eyed Canadian customs inspectors. The favorite tale of many an American family choosing to move household possessions through Canada is how customs seized its houseplants, or how (as with one of the authors) such seizure was avoided only by turning back and traveling on the south sides of Lakes Erie and Ontario.
16. And woe betide the unsuspecting owner of a nonstandard vehicle who tries to cross the border. One of the authors, assured that his beloved Peugeot 304 coupe met American and Canadian standards but then finding that after all it did not, was told that the closest markets to New England for disposing of his car were the tiny French islands of St. Pierre and Miquelon, lying just off the coast of Newfoundland and presumably a final home for dozens of rare and exotic foreign cars—no doubt acquired rather more cheaply than their original puchase price.
17. Mordechai E. Kreinin, *International Economics: A Policy Approach,* 2d ed. (New York, Harcourt Brace Jovanovich, 1975), p. 335 to p. 448.

CHAPTER

13

PUBLIC POLICY
AND
TRADE BARRIERS

Tariffs Before the 1930s

Artificial barriers to trade seem as old as trade itself. An ancient caravan entering an Arab area had to offer a *ta'rif,* in Arabic merely a "notification," to be allowed entry; but since that explanation also involved a tax, *ta'rif* came to mean a tax on trade.[1] Still today in most Western languages the word *tariff* generally means an import tax—although occasionally it simply means any tax. Travelers to Hadrian's Wall, the Roman defense work running across the hills of northern England, find at almost every gate in the rampart the remains of a little room that once housed the tax collector who imposed the tariff on goods moving in and out of the Roman empire. Today, walls may be absent, but there are still gates and little houses for tax collectors at borders.

Tariffs were originally designed for revenue, with little thought being given to their protective effects. Only in the late eighteenth and early nineteenth centuries were the protective effects recognized and employed. In England, the repeal of the "Corn Laws" (the English called any grain "corn" in those days) was based on the recognition that farming interests were being protected and industry was being hurt by these tariffs on imported grain. In the United States, Alexander Hamilton, the first secretary of the Treasury, recommended protective tariffs. Southern export interests, however, dependent on imported goods, managed to block substantial protective tariffs until the Civil War—with one exception, the short-lived "Tariff of Abominations" of 1828. This high tariff so angered the South that one state (South Carolina) threatened to secede, forcing a new tariff law a scant four years later.[2] The

283

ascendancy of northern manufacturing interests after the Civil War, however, led to a long period of high tariffs—often with some forty to fifty cents out of every dollar's worth of imports going for the tariff. In Germany, industrialists and economists successfully advocated the protection of infant industries by tariffs, asking how Germany could ever develop industry in the face of floods of low-priced British manufactures. Thus by the end of the nineteenth century, the use of the protective tariff was well established.

The First World War gave tariffs an additional boost. Britain, which had been virtually tariff free since the 1840s, turned to tariffs as a means to finance its skyrocketing war costs. The United States, having finally lowered the tariff under the Democratic presidency of Woodrow Wilson, found that the Europeans, engaged in total war, were unable to ship the goods the Americans otherwise would have taken. (Or to put it in economic terms, the war reduced the elasticity of supply of European exports.) Europeans, however, still demanded American goods (though with the British blockade Germany and Austria were unable to get them, even when America was neutral), and America had a strong balance of trade position. Moreover, the war stimulated new, burgeoning industries in chemicals and pharmaceuticals. When the war ended, these "war babies" demanded protection.

The world began to slide into greater protectionism. In the United States a curious bargain was struck in Congress. American agriculture had changed much during the war years; high prices due to the European demand and increased mechanization had expanded output greatly. As European agriculture began to recover, there was a sharp drop in grain prices, causing severe dislocation. To aid the farmers, Congress first increased duties on agricultural imports. This was, however, a futile task because there were so few imports anyway. The tariffs were largely "excess tariffs." Figure 13.1 shows the United States with low wheat imports; world price, $0P_w$, is barely below the nontrade equilibrium price of $0P_{nt}$. A tariff of P_wP_t cannot improve the price of agricultural goods beyond P_{nt}. Moreover, there is no revenue once imports fall to zero at P_{nt}. Hence the part of the tariff—$P_{nt}P_t$—that lies above the equilibrium point is an "excess tariff."

Farm states received their "protection" (such as it was and it wasn't much) in 1921; the next year the manufacturing interests claimed their part of the bargain, and the farm bloc voted for high manufacturing tariffs. Unfortunately for the farmers, the high tariffs on manufacturing were not excess tariffs, but had a large impact on price. The farmers had traded something for nothing.

In Europe, revenue tariffs of the war turned into protective tariffs. Fear of competitive devaluations (justified in many cases) and a rise in economic isolationism encouraged more protectionist tariff policies. In Canada, protectionist interests grew stronger. Just before the war the United States and Canada were set to sign a free trade treaty. In advocating legislation that would implement the treaty, an over-enthusiastic U.S. congressional leader suggested that this would be the first step in annexing Canada. In turn, the agreement became an election issue in Canada, which led to a new government that never passed the necessary legislation. This action diverted Canada back into a development policy of attracting American branch plant manufacturing through levying high tariffs, and the policy was renewed with vigor after the war.

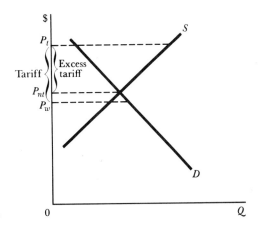

FIGURE 13.1 The excess tariff.

By the end of the 1920s many people of foresight felt that the tariff situation was out of hand. Some farm senators realized that in fact the tariff was not doing them any good. Surely the time was at hand to lower tariffs. There was, however, no mechanism for negotiating tariffs. American tariff policy was securely in the hands of Congress; the president could promise a nation to ask Congress to cut the tariff, but Congress would not necessarily go along. (It was not like a parliament, which would always agree to the cabinet's wishes or force a new government through a "no-confidence" vote.) President Hoover asked Congress in April of 1929 for a revision of the tariff—seemingly to decrease manufacturing tariffs somewhat and to increase agricultural ones. The world waited for that decline in manufacturing tariffs. The House of Representatives, in which revenue bills must always be introduced first, voted through a bill sponsored by Representative Hawley with higher agricultural tariffs and more moderate manufacturing protection. But month after month in the Senate, under the leadership of the arch conservative Reed Smoot of Utah, new tariffs were tacked on—eventually totaling 800 items in all fields, at rates over 50 cents per dollar of imports, nearly twice the 1913 figure. Meanwhile the Great Depression had begun. But Hoover suggested no changes in the Smoot-Hawley legislation. In March 1930, after many months of congressional "log-rolling," the bill went to the White House. One thousand economists sent the White House a statement that the bill not only would fail to help agriculture, but would certainly invite retaliation by foreign governments on American exports.

To the dismay of the thousand and to the shock of world leaders, who had been hoping to be able to export more to the United States and thus stimulate their economies, Hoover signed the bill. The psychological effect was enormous, further weakening business confidence abroad. The precise evil results predicted for the bill came to pass. Twelve large trading countries retaliated almost immediately with heavy tariffs of their own. Trade in farm commodities fell to one-third its former level. The total exports of the United States declined more than those of any other major nation, and were only 53 percent of their 1929 volume in the year 1932. Although much of that decline can be laid to income effects of the Depression, even the income effect was connected because of the psychological impact of Smoot-Hawley on investment. This was surely America's second "Tariff of Abominations."

A Turn in Trade Policy

When the Roosevelt administration assumed office in 1933, it took rapid (and belated) steps to undo the harm. It attacked the agricultural problem through subsidies to farmers and the creation of buffer stocks. It then turned to the question of lowering tariffs. Roosevelt's secretary of state, Cordell Hull, was convinced that trade and commercial ties between nations would discourage war and pursued his ideas with evangelical zeal. The result was the Reciprocal Trade Agreements Act of 1934, which has formed the basis for all subsequent American trade policy. Since it is so important, it is worthwhile to examine some of its provisions closely.

The basic features of the RTA Act were the following:

1. Reciprocity was the key. Trade concessions to other countries could be extended only in return for concessions to the United States.

2. The president was given *prior* authorization by Congress to cut tariffs. These could be cut on an item-by-item basis anywhere between zero and 50 percent, depending on the product. Such authorization was renewed by Congress eleven times between 1934 and 1961. This provision avoided the earlier problem of the United States being unable to negotiate for fear Congress would not agree. Similar prior authorizations have been provided in RTA renewals and in the 1962 and 1974 trade acts.

3. All tariff concessions were to be on a nondiscriminatory basis. If the United States cut a tariff to one nation, it would cut them to all. This provision, known in diplomatic language as "the most-favored nation" (MFN) clause, was even in 1934 an old principle of tariff legislation. For a brief period early in the century the United States had departed from this tradition, setting higher tariffs on certain nations' goods, but the provisions proved unworkable. The problems of defining and enforcing separate tariffs for each of the thousands of product classifications would be compounded greatly by multiplying all those by the number of countries in the world. Hence the 1922 (Fordney-McCumber) tariff reestablished the MFN principle that was retained in the RTA.[3]

An exception to the MFN provision was made after World War II when the Communist bloc refused to enter into negotiations on tariffs. Rather than grant its members something for nothing, they were exempted from the new tariff levels. Tariffs to Russia today are often double the MFN rates. Another exception has been made recently for developing countries (see below).

4. Undue dislocation of labor was to be avoided by two provisions: Peril points and escape clauses. Under the RTA, the U.S. Tariff Commission, the group then supervising tariff matters, had to decide in advance of negotiations how low the tariff could be without harming domestic producers. If the president reduced the tariff below this "peril point," he had to explain his action to Congress. This meant extensive hearings on hundreds of products and limited the president's ability to negotiate.

In addition, there was an "escape clause." If an industry could show injury after a tariff cut, the president could order a return to the old tariff levels. Again the appeal was made through the Tariff Commission, which then made a recommendation to the president. The escape clause, seldom successfully invoked (only twelve times in twenty-eight years), was the only recourse available for firms seeking relief from tariff-cut injuries.

The problem of displacement has been one of the most serious difficulties in tariff legislation since the RTA. From an economic viewpoint, tariff cuts are *supposed* to displace resources, moving them from low to higher productivity occupations. From a political point of view, tariff cuts are not supposed to be disruptive. What in fact occurred was that Congress left a political decision up to the president and the Tariff Commission. In general, the Tariff Commission rejected the bulk of the complaints and the president rejected most of the Tariff Commission's recommendations to increase duties.

Under the leadership of the United States, moves were made to cut tariffs internationally. Only slight progress was made during the first ten years; the United States in 1934 was so mired in the Depression that it could hardly stimulate export-led growth elsewhere. World War II followed, imposing its own restrictions on trade, so that most of the major negotiations came in the postwar period. By 1962, there were reciprocal agreements with fifty-four countries, and the average tariff for the United States had fallen from a high of about 53 cents on the dollar in 1934 to 11 cents. Roughly half of this fall can be attributed to RTA-inspired negotiations. If you take a 1930 list of imports and tax them with 1960 tariffs, you get a rate of 24 percent, about half of the actual 48 percent rate of 1930 and twice the actual rate of 12 cents on the dollar in 1960.

What accounted for the other half? Run 1960 imports through with Smoot-Hawley rates. Behold, another 24 percent tariff. The answer lies in the nature of the tariff itself. Until 1962 the vast majority of U.S. tariffs were expressed as "specific duties"—$0.10 a pound, $0.05 a yard, $2 a pair, and so on. What this meant was that as the price of goods rose due to inflation, the tariff remained the same. While in 1930, $2 a pair might have been half the cost of a pair of shoes priced at $4, by 1960 those shoes would be going for $8 and the tariff would be down to 25 percent. Hence inflation was as helpful as negotiation in bringing down the level of tariffs.[4]

Today, however, specific duties are much rarer, and inflation can help little. The vast majority of duties are expressed in ad valorem (Latin for "to the value") terms. This means that the duty is stated as a percentage of the import price. Occasionally the two are even combined.[5]

Each type of tariff has its own characteristics. Specific duties are easier to administer, because imported goods do not have to be valued as they enter the country. All the customs official has to do is to decide what category the item is in and how much of it there is. Specific duties also provide more protection against price cutting. If textiles from Hong Kong cost $0.20 a yard and the duty is $0.05 a yard or 25 percent ad valorem, then a big cut in the Hong Kong price—say $0.10—means that the specific duty provides more protection than the ad valorem. The old price with a specific duty is 20 + 5 = $0.25. The new price under the specific duty is 10 + 5 = $0.15, but under the ad valorem it is now 10 + (.25 x 10) = $0.125. Earlier in this century specific duties were very popular as protection against cheap imports from Japan.

Specific duties have other problems. They mean that a low-priced good will pay more tax as a percentage of the original price than will a high-priced good of the same kind. Assuming it is low-income consumers who buy the low-priced good, then they are taxed more heavily than the wealthier. As mentioned above, specific duties lose their protective effect during inflations. Finally, specific duties cannot be used to tax art-works, antiques, or other "unique" goods.

Ad valorem duties overcome these problems. They are not regressive (but not progressive either), there is no need to alter them as prices change, and they can be used for unique items. But they suffer from a serious disadvantage: Each and every item imported must be valued by a customs official. The invoice or bill of sale is, of course, not to be fully trusted, and the checking and documentation are a nuisance to traders and customs officials alike. Facing ad valorem tariffs, an importer sometimes understates the price on the invoice. The valuation by the customs official may thus become more important than the actual percentage tariff itself. A country could appear generous by assigning a low tariff to goods and then instruct customs inspectors to place high valuations on those goods. The over or under valuation, incidentally, would find its way into trade statistics, introducing another inaccuracy in payments accounts.

GATT

The most important change in tariff policy after the Reciprocal Trade Agreement Act was the formation of an organization called the General Agreement on Tariffs and Trade (GATT). This deserves more recognition than it gets from the general public, for it has been a powerful force in furthering the goal of tariff reduction.

In 1944 at the Bretton Woods Conference in New Hampshire (the same at which the adjustable peg and the IMF were established—see Part I), it was decided to found an organization called the International Trade Organization (ITO) to liberalize tariffs and quotas following World War II. A charter signed at Havana, Cuba, in 1947 formulated rules for the ITO, and the organization had real teeth for enforcing those rules. Unlike the other organizations created by Bretton Woods, however, the ITO failed to come into full operation, largely because the U.S. Congress did not ratify the Havana Charter. Congress withheld its consent for several reasons, but mostly because of fear that other countries would not abide by the various rules of the ITO.

ITO, however, had already set up an agency under the name General Agreement on Tariffs and Trade to tackle its initial teething troubles. GATT as an administrative working agreement did not require U.S. congressional ratification—and never got it in spite of several attempts. But GATT remained in existence nonetheless because the need for it was seen and appreciated. GATT has regularly arranged conferences that negotiate worldwide reductions in tariffs. The first of these occurred in 1947, the very year the parent ITO was being debated. GATT's small and elite staff is based at Geneva, Switzerland. As at the nearby Bank for International Settlements, its well-dressed doorman is said to read the London *Financial Times*.

Members of GATT agree to a number of conditions, among which are the following:

1. The most-favored nation principle will apply to all tariffs, quotas, licenses, and so on. The "legitimate" exception is allowed for less developed countries, which do not have to reciprocate their MFN status with developed countries. One other exception is the United States, which does not extend MFN treatment to some communist countries.

2. GATT forbids quotas, except temporary ones for reasons of balance of payments adjustment and quotas on agricultural imports when a country already restricts its home output. GATT has thus had little effect on farming, and in any case the prohibition against quotas is violated often enough—not least by the United States, as we shall see.

3. GATT members agree to consult together on trade problems at meetings of the GATT Council of Representatives. It was this council that settled the 1963 Chicken War between the United States and the EEC. The EEC

socked the United States with a sudden high tariff on frozen chicken. The United States threatened immediate tariff retaliation. Tempers were raw until the Council negotiated a compromise, with the United States being permitted to raise tariffs on $26 million worth of Common Market goods.

4. GATT *permits* customs unions (like the Common Market). This provision is so important that it is the subject of a separate chapter.

5. GATT has no power whatsoever to apply independent sanctions or to use force, in spite of its very large membership. (A two-thirds vote of the old members is needed to admit new ones.)

GATT has had substantial influence on the development of world trade, as might be expected from the fact that the original twenty-three member nations have now grown to eighty-four plus twenty-one associates, accounting for considerably more than 80 percent of all world trade. Quotas, for example, are far less important now than they were just after World War II. By far the most impressive activity undertaken by GATT, however, has been its sponsorship of many conferences (called "rounds" in the jargon) that have led to negotiated multilateral tariff reductions. Rounds have been sponsored in Annecy, France, in 1949; in Torquay, England, in 1950-1951; and in Geneva in 1956 and again in 1960-1962 (the Dillon Round) and 1962-1967 (the Kennedy Round). The latest negotiations currently underway were called originally the Nixon Round and, after that president's political demise, the Tokyo Round or the "Multilateral Trade Negotiations" (MTN). These talks were agreed upon at a foreign ministers' meeting in Tokyo in 1973, commenced in Geneva 1975, and are continuing at a slow pace with about one hundred countries participating.

The Trade Expansion Act of 1962

The growth of the European Economic Community (see next chapter) and the expected inclusion of Britain in that group spurred the most important round of tariff discussions to date. As of the early 1960s, the United States, though generally pleased with the economic success of the EEC and the growth and stability it brought to its allies, was perturbed by a number of its actions. The United States had hoped for large markets for its agricultural goods, but was frustrated by the evolution of a highly protectionist agricultural policy. Since the policy was not yet completed, the United States hoped that by offering industrial concessions, it could deflect EEC agricultural policy into a less protective track. (Alas, this was not to be.) The United States hoped that if it offered large enough tariff cuts it could protect its interests—not only in agriculture but in having an independent and prosperous Europe.

President Kennedy accordingly threw his full weight behind new and more vigorous U.S. trade proposals. To do so, however, he needed a new trade act. Tariff-cutting authority under the last RTA renewal had expired. It might have appeared that 1962 was a very bad year for an important trade bill. Unemployment was high, there was a serious balance of payments deficit, and it seemed difficult to convince voters that tariff reduction was necessary. Furthermore, the president's position was relatively weak, with a narrow majority in Congress. It was one of the surprises of the Kennedy administration that the bill passed anyway, by large majorities, giving the president more than most observers had expected.

The 1962 Trade Expansion Act (TEA) had four main provisions:

1. The president was authorized to cut any U.S. tariff by 50 percent. This differed from the old RTA acts, which had provided detailed product-by-product negotiation, often with several countries at the same time. Now, however, across-the-board tariff cuts could be negotiated. Instead of, say, a 5 percent cut on cars, 10 percent on trucks, and 7 percent on buses, all bargained tediously and separately, the president could press for a 10 percent reduction on all transport machinery and equipment. This provision made it more difficult for individual firms to exert political pressure to object to a tariff cut, because any one product was now lumped in with many others in large-scale negotiations. To get the bill, however, President Kennedy had to make some exceptions. The oil and cotton textile industries were two major examples.

2. For the first time in U.S. tariff history, the president was empowered to cut some tariffs to zero. These included (a) cases where the Common Market plus the United States supplied over 80 percent of the world's exports of the goods in question (airplanes were the major example); (b) tariffs where the U.S. tariff rate (on an ad valorem basis) was already low, at 5 percent or less; and (c) tropical primary products of the agricultural or forest type, which were not much produced in the United States—thus providing a helping hand to the less developed countries.

3. All tariff cuts were to be on a most-favored-nation basis for all countries. The exceptions were the Soviet and Chinese blocs, and initially (until 1963) Yugoslavia.

4. The TEA tried a new means of dealing with the problem of displacement—adjustment assistance. Instead of assuming there would be no displacement, the law arranged to ease the burden of those who faced adjustment. The firm that could show that the tariff cut had injured it could receive federal "adjustment assistance." Under the law, the burden of proof was on the firm to show serious injury. "Injury" was defined as a direct cause-and-effect relation between the tariff reduction and idle plant and equipment, reduced profits, and growing unemployment. A firm making such a case was eligible for technical and managerial assistance and loans to aid it in becoming more competitive through finding new products or new markets. The firm could get tax relief of a minor sort, and its employees could get special unemployment compensation. The workers were eligible to receive 65 percent of their former average wage for up to one year; they were also eligible for training in new jobs (with twenty-six extra weeks of pay for this), and for the cash allowances to cover the costs of moving to a new location. (Note that the workers who were unemployed as a result of federal decisions other than tariff decisions—for example, to cancel an airplane order or move a military base—held no such privileged position but had to fend for themselves.)

With adjustment assistance in the package, the cumbersome peril points and escape clauses were narrowed. Under the 1962 law the Tariff Commission reported privately to the president about the impact of tariff cuts, thus doing away with peril points. The escape clause still could be used, but only if adjustment assistance did not work.

Unfortunately, in the light of later events, adjustment assistance did not work out well in practice. After ten years of operation, only eight companies and fifteen thousand workers had received any adjustment assistance. Compensation for workers was, in some states, little more than unemployment insurance, and the retraining provision was rarely used. The reasons for the smallness of the benefits were two: (1) The tariffs proved extremely difficult to negotiate. The EEC insisted on completing its agricultural policy first, leading to bitter bargaining. Many observers expected that the talks would fail, and the negotiations took the full five years to the time the act expired. Then the tariffs were to fall by only 20 percent of the negotiated cut each year, so it was at least five years anyway before the tariff cuts were felt. (2) More serious, the attempt to close the escape clause was "too successful." The Tariff Commission had to find "serious injury" that was due "in major part" to imports that had increased *because* of TEA tariff concessions. Most import industries that fall victim to import competition are already weak; after all, it is because they are less efficient than other domestic firms that they lack a comparative advantage. Hence it was very hard to prove that imports caused the injury and virtually impossible to prove that those imports were due to TEA tariff concessions. The result of the rather narrow interpretation of the law was the alienation of labor—which had supported the 1962 act.

The Resurgence of Quotas

Labor's dissatisfaction with American trade policy was expressed in nearly four years of campaigning in favor of the provisions of a bill submitted by Representative James Burke of Massachusetts. The bill, narrowly defeated or maneuvered off the calendar in two Congresses, called for quantitative limitations on imports in a number of key industries. (Further aspects of the bill are discussed in Chapter 16.) Most quantitative restrictions on imports had disappeared from the industrialized world in the mid-1950s as the postwar exchange control systems were dismantled, so the suggestion of their reimposition shocked many economists and statesmen.

The United States, it is true, already had a few quotas—the oil quotas mentioned in the previous chapter, and some in the agricultural area. Of principal concern was a sugar quota, which limited the importation of sugar in order to maintain a high domestic price—often as much as twice the world price. This quota was ended in the Nixon administration. Other agricultural quotas were unimportant because the United States was the low-cost producer anyway. The administration, however, was not anxious to establish a system of quotas on industrial goods and invented instead an even more insidious plan (but one leaving the administration, not Congress, in charge)—the "voluntary" export quota.

This alternative to the direct import quota has, understandably, achieved wide and sudden popularity. Import quotas as such are not always easy to impose. Congress must legislate them, and these days consumer interests there are strong. Also, as seen earlier, the imposition of a quota on manufactured imports would in most cases be in violation of GATT agreements. A neat way out—with no need to go to Congress, and legal as far as GATT is concerned—is to negotiate a "voluntary" agreement with some trading partner wherein that partner undertakes to cut its *exports* to the United States.[6] The agreement would usually be with a foreign government, but it also would be possible to negotiate directly with foreign firms.

Dating from the 1950s, when the first was negotiated with Japan (which agreed to restrain its exports of cotton textiles), these agreements have proliferated. In 1962 the Kennedy administration pushed to extend this to most major supplying nations, and the result was the International Cotton Textile Agreement, now supervised by GATT, which controls increases in imports—some countries have agreed to limit these increases to 5 percent per year, others to 7½ percent. In 1971 these voluntary agreements were extended to synthetics and woolen textiles. Of course the word "voluntary" in these arrangements is a ludicrous illusion. As far as the exporting countries are concerned, they are voluntary to about the same extent as is the act of an outlaw raising his hands in preference to being shot by the sheriff. The United States in particular has put enormous pressure on exporters to conclude such deals. President Nixon, for example, welcomed the 1971 extension of the textile agreement as a "cooperative working out of differences." But before Japan finally signed, it was threatened with a unilateral quota on its exports, to be imposed under the old First World War "Trading with the Enemy Act." The present textile agreement, incidentally, has an expiration date of 1978. It has been renegotiated every three to four years since its establishment.

Another "voluntary" export quota was the steel agreement (negotiated in the Johnson administration and implemented in 1969), which cut back steel imports from eighteen million tons in 1968 to fourteen million in 1969, and limited growth in imports thereafter to 5 percent per year and later 2½ percent following renewal of the pact in 1972. The steel agreement was between the U.S. government and individual firms abroad. It expired in 1975.

1977 saw a sudden resurgence of such agreements, the establishment of which now appears to take up much of the time of the American special representative for trade negotiations, Robert Strauss of Texas. In May, the Japanese agreed to reduce their exports of color television sets to the United States by 40 percent. They did so rather than face the punitive 5-25 percent tariff increases recommended to President Carter by the U.S. International Trade Commission. This agreement is particularly stringent. Japanese exports were to be cut at once from 2.6 million color sets a year to 1.56 million. No increases in imports will be allowed for the life of the agreement, three years. But the Japanese ought not to count on the resumption of unrestricted imports of their TVs after 1980. The textile agreements of the 1950s and early 1960s were also supposed to be temporary, but they look as healthy as ever.[7]

The TV agreement was followed by a shoe pact with South Korea and Taiwan, taking effect July 1, 1977. This four-year agreement rolled back shoe imports from the two countries by about 22 percent, from 200 million pairs a year to 155 million. It also curbed the growth of imports to about 10 percent per year. In case of difficulty, outright quotas can be imposed in place of these agreements. Thus, in 1976 the United States replaced its voluntary restraint agreement made earlier in the year with straight quotas on beef, veal, and mutton.

The Trade Reform Act of 1974

While voluntary export quotas were developing, the Nixon administration faced some other very serious trade legislation problems. The tariff-cutting authority of the president granted in the Trade Expansion Act had expired in 1967, and the last percentages of the Kennedy Round tariff cuts, bringing the total of world trade affected to $40 billion, had been made in 1972. Thus the Nixon administration had to turn its attention toward getting a new trade bill in a far more hostile and less promising environment than that which Kennedy had operated in.

The first problem any new trade bill would have to solve was the labor displacement difficulty. The second problem was to find a way in which the president could cut nontariff barriers. How could Congress give the president prior authorization in such matters? It could not just say that he should harmonize auto safety standards by 50 percent.

The third problem was that of coping with unfair practices. Under the RTA acts, such problems had been handled under the "antidumping" provisions, a kind of international Clayton Act, preventing the foreign producers from selling in the United States at prices lower than they sell for in their home countries. In such cases, the United States can put on a countervailing duty to raise the price up to the price in the producer's home market. Retaliatory tariffs were also allowed. Congress, however, felt that the United States should be able to act more strongly in this area.

The Trade Reform Act of 1974, given the environment in which it was written, is a surprisingly liberal piece of legislation. Its provisions are as follows:

1. The president gets the authority to reduce tariffs by up to 60 percent on goods where the ad valorem rate is over 5 percent, and to eliminate them entirely when the ad valorem rate is less than 5 percent. Showing its concern for unfair practices and a bit of a protectionist tinge, Congress also authorized the president to increase tariffs up to 20 percent as a bargaining weapon. Thus, whether or not the law is protectionist, as the French prime minister has recently claimed, depends on whether or not the president is; Jimmy Carter is not. Tariff cuts would be spread over ten years (twice as long as the 1962 provisions), falling by 10 percent of the total each year.

2. The president could also negotiate reductions in nontariff barriers. The problem of prior authorization was "solved" (and we don't know yet if it really has been) by giving the president general authority, but requiring Congress to then approve the legislation. The ability of Congress to disapprove is hamstrung by the fact that it has only sixty legislative days in which to veto the presidential action. This is rather a short time to get a move going against the president, particularly if he has cleared his provisions with congressional leaders. Foreign governments are leery of this provision, but it is hard to see how Congress could do otherwise. Congress also called for "balanced concessions" from other countries; it remains to be seen how these can be implemented. (What would "balance" the adoption of 220-volt electrical standards in the United States—foreign adoption of seat belts?) When concessions have been made, the newly renamed U.S. International Trade Commission (formerly the Tariff Commission) must report within six months about the economic effects of the concessions.

3. Adjustment assistance was much liberalized. No longer was it necessary to show that tariff reduction was a *major factor* (more important than any other cause) in the injury to a firm or industry. After 1974, it was enough to show that the reduced tariffs were a substantial, or important, cause. If the International Trade Commission finds that imports are a substantial cause of serious injury, the president must within sixty days either raise the tariff (to any desired level), impose quotas, negotiate "orderly marketing arrangements" (the so-called voluntary export quotas), proffer adjustment assistance, or announce that he is taking no action at all. If the president's decision differs from that recommended by the commission, Congress can require the president by majority vote to adopt the commission's suggested form of relief. The president can offer concessions to foreign countries if import restrictions are imposed against them. All protectionary measures are temporary, to expire five years after passage though with the possibility of a three-year extension. This latter clause is designed to reduce the possibility of American industry sheltering permanently behind tariff barriers.

Adjustment assistance is much modified under the 1974 act. It has been separated from the escape clause provision and procedures. Workers qualify if the secretary of labor finds, within sixty days after the workers, their union, or their firm files a petition, that new imports "contributed importantly" to their unemployment. Eligible workers receive fifty-two weeks of compensation (longer for older people and those in training), which is equal to 70 percent of the weekly wage that had been earned but limited to a maximum of $180 per week. Workers are also entitled to retraining and allowances for job search and relocation, the latter two up to 80 percent of costs incurred to a maximum of $500. Firms can also obtain technical, managerial, and financial assistance, as under the 1962 law, except for the liberalization of the "serious injury" clause. When whole communities are adversely affected by increased imports, community adjustment assistance is provided. A "trade impacted area" can receive technical assistance, and direct grants for acquiring and developing land plus improvements in public works and public services. Loans and loan guarantees are available to applicants who wish to construct or modernize plants within the affected area.

Clearly, the 1974 act has made it easier for firms and workers to obtain relief. Labor unions, while not accepting that adjustment assistance was fully adequate for the import problem, have moved aggressively to the use of the expanded provisions for relief. From the time the new law took effect in early April of 1975, until November 1976, over 1,000 petitions were filed (although many covered very small numbers). About half of the petitions were certified as eligible, while the other half were rejected on the grounds that imports were not the cause of the unemployment. In all, 179,000 workers have received benefits in some form, while the petitions of another 231,000 have been denied. The major problem has been with funding, with projected expenditures of about $150 million per year being much in excess of what was actually appropriated. By March 1976, only some $30 million had been spent for unemployment benefits and $1.9 million for relocation and retraining. (There is a special adjustment assistance program for the shoe industry, dating from July 1977, and to last three years. It has additional provisions for the evaluation of troubled firms by government management experts, the planning of a recovery strategy, government assistance for management development and technical training. It is funded with $56 million in federal funds.)

From firms themselves, the 1974 act has not received unanimous praise. Supporters of tariffs and quotas for import relief have been disappointed to find that quotas have been imposed in only one case—stainless and other specialty steels—and even this caused loud protests, especially from Common Market steel exporters. In March 1977, President Carter chose not to follow a Trade Commission recommendation for tariff increases against shoe imports. (As mentioned earlier, a "voluntary" shoe pact was negotiated with South Korea and Taiwan.) Claims have been rejected for, among others, metal fasteners, cigar wrappers, and fresh and processed asparagus. Congress in April of that year was deliberating an override of the president's decision, the forces of protection being led not surprisingly by Representative Burke of Massachusetts. Actually, the small number of requests for added protection is probably an indication that not very many domestic producers have been badly harmed by imports, or at least not sufficiently so that they can prove their case or make their effort worthwhile. However, the Trade Commission has recommended tighter sugar import quotas (rejected by President Carter, who opted for direct payments to producers), and large tariff increases for color TV sets (resulting in a "voluntary" agreement with Japan).

American shoe, steel, and TV manufacturers have certainly made the most well-known pleas for protection. The steel industry has sought controls on imports covering the whole industry. By the summer of 1976 it had received only a quota on stainless and specialty steels. Imports of these steels rose from 11 percent of domestic sales in 1974 to 18.5 percent in 1975, but opponents of President Ford's decision to impose a quota pointed out that this was in part due to the business recession, with foreign firms more willing to cut prices than American firms in the face of declining demand. Such steel imports had even declined between 1970 and 1974, and many thought the case for a quota in this instance was weak. In any event, the amount involved is small, with specialty steel imports in 1974 amounting to only some $200 million, 5 percent of steel imports in value and 1 percent in tonnage.

Late in 1977, a major move toward protection of the entire steel industry was made by the Carter administration. The move involved a new tool—the so-called trigger price system. This significant innovation involves sixty categories of carbon and alloy steels (but not the stainless and specialty steels already covered by the quota discussed in the last paragraph). A "trigger price" is calculated on the basis of production costs in Japan, currently the world's lowest-cost producer. Added to this is a nominal profit margin of 8 percent and transport costs. Steel sold in the United States above this price faces no problems. But sales below that figure will "trigger" a special fast-track investigation taking sixty to ninety days (the usual delay nowadays in such investigations is more than a year). If sales below cost are proved, the imposition of a tariff will follow. Clearly the trigger price system is more attractive than an outright quota. If a competitor's low prices are genuine, then it will be allowed to compete. But there is some suggestion that the trigger will be adjusted on a quarterly basis, which would introduce sufficient uncertainty about what prices will be permitted to cause foreign exporters considerable difficulty. The first adjustment (a hike of 5½ percent) occurred in May 1978.

Meanwhile, steel was also receiving new protection in the EEC during 1978. The Davignon Plan, named for the EEC's industry commissioner, Viscount Etienne Davignon, is a combination of new antidumping rules, establishment of EEC minimum prices for steel, and a freezing of the share taken by imports in the EEC markets. Steel is, internationally, the sharp cutting edge of the new protectionist surge.

Damage in the shoe industry has been much greater than in steel. In this $2 billion industry, imports rose from 15 percent of American sales in 1963 to 40 percent in 1975, and have continued to mount. The problem seems to have been straight out of Heckscher-Ohlin theory—shoes are relatively labor intensive in production, and cheap labor bestows a cost advantage. Thus Italy, traditionally the largest exporter to the American market, is being challenged by new exporters such as Taiwan, Brazil, Spain, South Korea, and Argentina. Actually, some portions of the American shoe industry are not all that sick. 1976 was prosperous, and employment outside New England (the traditional bastion of the industry) actually climbed in the areas where newer, more efficient plants are being located. U.S. shoemakers retain an advantage in transport costs, quality controls, quick reaction to style changes, and greater ease of delivery. (Many domestic retailers are unfamiliar with the paperwork of foreign trade and prefer to pay a domestic company a premium rather than to import. Also, some shoe companies themselves import part of their product lines from abroad.) Thus some plants in the United States that are mechanized are prospering, while the older small and labor-intensive operations are just getting by. Each group sells about half of the U.S. output. Whatever the merits of the issue, the Trade Commission proposed a combined tariff and quota arrangement on shoe imports. It is estimated that the combination would have cost consumers $185 million a year in higher shoe prices. The likelihood that this would have saved the portion of the shoe industry damaged by imports was small, because the protection under the 1974 act could legally last only five years plus a short extension. The special adjustment assistance for the industry mentioned earlier appears to promise much more. But the battle has been much in the news.

The case made for protection by the TV industry is that the American producers have been blitzed in recent years by foreign competition. The market share of imports was less than 20 percent for color sets in 1975; by 1977 it was over 40 percent. Of the black-and-white market, 75 percent was in foreign hands. Five U.S. companies had quit manufacturing TVs since 1968; 60,000 workers had been laid off since 1971. The Trade Commission recommended tariffs that would raise the price of an average foreign-made color set by $56, thus costing American consumers perhaps $280 million in higher prices. President Carter did not accept the recommendation, and instead negotiated the 1977 "voluntary" export quota with Japan discussed earlier.

4. Though the protectionist wave it generated is perhaps the chief point of economic interest in the 1974 act, there are other sections worthy of mention. One relates to so-called countervailing duties. For many years (actually since 1897), U.S. law required that countervailing duties (tariffs) be imposed in instances where it was proved that foreign governments were paying subsidies to support certain exports. It was not even necessary to show any harm to American industry. This law was recently used against Canadian-manufactured Michelin tires and Italian refrigerators. Now, however, as an aid to trade negotiations, the president is allowed *not* to impose these countervailing duties for up to four years while talks are going forward, although countervailing duties can presently be imposed even on goods that had come into this country free of tariffs, on services as well as goods, and on imports from countries paying subsidies in support of their trade elsewhere even though not in their trade with the United States. Finally, the act gives the president authority to impose a temporary import tariff surcharge, up to 15 percent of the value of imported goods, to defend against balance of payments problems. (President Nixon levied such an overall surcharge for three months from August 1971, but his authority for doing so was disputed at the time. Now the authority is clear.)

5. Perhaps most controversial was the bitter fight over MFN treatment for communist countries. Led by Senator Jackson (then running for nomination for president), Congress wrote into the act a human rights clause requiring Communist countries to relax their restrictions on Jewish emigration and watch their step on various other issues of humanitarian concern as a condition for MFN status. Rumania agreed, sped up emigration to Israel, and allowed Rumanians more freedom to visit and entertain overseas relatives, and was duly rewarded with MFN treatment. Hungary "joined the club" in 1978. But the Soviet Union and several other Eastern European countries refused to agree, taking umbrage at what they considered meddling in their domestic politics, and thus are still excluded from MFN status.

6. The act also offers preferred treatment for manufactured goods imported from less developed countries. This honored a pledge made by President Johnson in 1967 and further commitments made under Nixon. It is called the *Generalized System of Preferences* (GSP). Such preferential imports are now duty free. But the good effect is much diluted by a long list of exceptions to GSP. Many primary products and semiprocessed agricultural products are excluded. Preferences are denied to countries supplying 50 percent by value of total U.S. imports of a particular product, or $25 million annually of imports of that product. The president can limit, suspend, or withdraw preferences at any time. Retaliation is authorized against countries that restrict supplies or join in cartels. Thus GSP has not been available to OPEC nations and could be denied to many other (indeed virtually all) developing nations on those grounds. The EEC, incidentally, under the Lomé Convention has similar GSP preferences, but it too is hedged by many quantity limitations.

Negotiating Problems in the Tokyo Round

The entry ticket into the ongoing Tokyo Round of GATT tariff negotiations is, of course, the 1974 act. The major problems to be faced in this round are wider and perhaps more intractable than in the GATT rounds of the past. They include the following:

1. Agriculture. Past rounds said very little about trade in agricultural commodities. It is a can of worms. The Common Market insists on ironclad protection for its expensive programs that aid farmers. Free trade would make these programs almost impossible to operate. Meanwhile the United States would like to see immediate easy access for American grain and other farm products into the lucrative EEC markets. Less developed countries are seeking trade concessions on their agricultural output. In February 1978, one of the first sessions on agriculture broke up in failure, and negotiations are likely to be protracted.

2. Tariff disparities. The United States has many high tariffs as well as lower ones. The Common Market's tariffs have fewer peaks, and are lower on the whole (see Fig. 13.2). The Common Market thus claims that it would be unfair to cut tariffs linearly, by a fixed percentage across the board, because that would still leave some American tariffs quite high, and would provide a greater degree of effective protection for American industry. U.S. negotiators counterclaim that when tariffs are recalculated on a trade-weighted basis, then the EEC has slightly higher tariffs after all. (Notice in Fig. 13.3 how tariffs are calculated; about 30 percent of U.S. imports are subject to a duty of 5-10 percent, compared to 45 percent of Common Market imports.)[8] The upshot is disagreement on how to cut tariffs, with the Europeans supporting the idea of bringing everybody's rates down to a uniform level. One possible compromise is to cut high tariffs by large percentages, low tariffs by small ones—cut a 50 percent tariff by 50 percent, for example, and a 5 percent tariff by 5 percent. In September 1977, the United States accepted a Swiss proposal close to the Common Market position—reduce big tariffs by more than small ones—but much remains to be ironed out.

3. Retaliation against trade offenders. Present law requires a country retaliating against another country's trade offenses to apply the retaliation against all trading partners, in accordance with most-favored-nation provisions. This does not seem to make much sense, and the Tokyo Round will be taking up the problem. GATT also currently permits retaliation only when imports are rising. But in recessions, imports may possibly fall much more slowly than domestic production, causing substantial injury. This too will be examined.

4. One last major sticking point finds the Americans the villains. This involves the ASP, not the snake that bit Cleopatra in a tender spot, but instead the American Selling Price method for calculating tariffs. This highly controversial concept is a half-century old, and involves only a very few goods—most importantly about 200 benzenoid chemicals, which comprise some 10 percent of all U.S. chemical production and are used in the manufacture of solvents, pesticides, explosives, and dyes; and some other products such as tennis shoes, canned clams, and wool knit gloves. This very odd assortment is protected by tariffs levied on the American selling price of the item, not on the price of the import. (In keeping with the ASP acronym, Australia also has used the ASP system.) Ridiculously high duties of 100-200 percent have been reported under ASP, with the overall duty on benzenoid chemicals about 50 percent. Such duties are very erratic from the foreign point of view, changing when the U.S. price changes. In the Kennedy Round, American negotiators promised to give up ASP in return for certain Common Market concessions. But Congress refused to concur, and as of 1978 U.S. negotiators in the Tokyo Round were again promising to get rid of the device. This minor concern of tariff policy has become a major psychological barrier to trade talks.

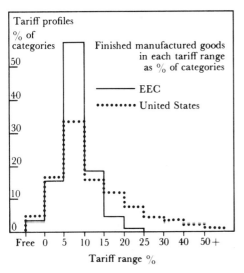

FIGURE 13.2

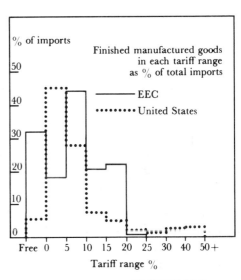

FIGURE 13.3

Why Protectionism?

We saw in Chapter 10 that the argument underlying the theory of comparative advantage is very strong. It demonstrated that with international trade, a country can attain a point beyond its own production possibility curve, with resulting higher levels of real income. Tariffs, quotas, and the other nontariff barriers to trade lead to a less efficient use of the factors of production, so argued that chapter, with resulting restrictions on consumption and choice. Why then would any rational person support protectionism? Many reasons have been advanced over the decades, some of them becoming almost a tradition in politics. We shall now consider the claims of those who support protection.

Self-interest. The easiest argument to understand is pure self-interest on the part of management and labor in industries threatened by foreign competition. Economists can talk all they want about comparative advantage increasing real incomes for society, but to those threatened the harm is real and in the here and now, while the promised benefits are spread among the whole population and do not appear to compensate for the loss of a job. Even good retraining and adjustment schemes involve sacrifice for workers and managers possibly forced to move from their old homes, finding their old skills obsolete, subject to uncertainty about the future. Psychology here is fully as important as economics. Economists have come to realize that it is not enough to show the overall benefits of freer trade. The costs to those whose jobs are lost must be understood and treated with compassion, with efficiency, and without the condescension that sometimes plagues our unemployment and welfare systems. Consider your own reaction if told that in the pursuit of benefits for all, your job will be the one sacrificed. Who then is the free trader? Much of the support for protection is thus an understandable reaction on the part of those who distrust and fear change, and for the most part rightly so because, as we have seen, the United States has been slow to adopt comprehensive plans for adjustment assistance. The vehemence of the steel interests, the TV producers, and the shoe manufacturers is in part due to their belief that protection will *serve their self-interest* more than will reliance on the mercies of the market system or on our small-scale adjustment assistance programs.

The Infant Industry Argument. The "infant industry argument" was used to justify tariffs throughout the nineteenth century in Europe and America and is still in use today throughout the developing world. Chapter 11's argument about experience curves also showed a possible reason for protecting an industry. When an industry is small, new, and inexperienced, its products will naturally be expensive and it may be unable to compete with well-developed foreign industry. Infant industry tariff protection will allow new firms to operate, to obtain the knowledge required to train their labor, to accumulate capital (capital markets may themselves be in their infancy), and to improve production processes. When this point is reached, the infant industry tariff can be removed, as it will no longer be necessary.

As reasonable as this sounds, there are some problems with the argument. It is all too easy to extend infant industry protection to firms that have little or no chance of ever growing up; literature on development is legion with examples of steel mills, automobile assembly plants, and petrochemical complexes built in nations whose markets could never under any conceivable circumstance support such operations. Import substitution as a development strategy has been much criticized in recent years because of this rather indiscriminate approach to choosing protected industries. Then again an industry may grow up, but due to its political clout the tariff is somehow never removed. A case in point is the American pharmaceutical industry, which gained protection in the 1920s in order to mature. Its adulthood was achieved long ago, but it is still protected.

A third problem with the infant industry argument concerns who bears the cost. Even if tariff protection is removed after an industry grows up, there has still been a cost to the country's consumers. Only if the industry eventually has sufficient earnings to repay consumers for their initial sacrifice can the tariff be said to have succeeded. Finally, on political and economic grounds, most economists would prefer an infant industry subsidy to a tariff. Tariffs once embodied in law do not come up for annual review by legislatures. They can go along without examination for a long period of time. Since consumers don't pay the tax outright (though they must pay for the higher cost of the goods), they rarely question the tariff. Subsidies, however, are reviewed frequently—in the United States they must be reviewed every year in the budgetary process. Therefore, there is less chance that the protection will be permanent. Economically, a subsidy has further advantages. Prices will be lower, and the market for the infant industry's goods will thus be wider. The previous argument still applies, however, and the infant industry should repay the consumer (say, by paying a bounty to the government and thus cutting taxes).

The National Defense Argument. It is said that protection must be made available to industries manufacturing such products as aircraft, firearms, shipping, electronics, ocular glass, petroleum, and the like. If foreign competition were to drive these industries out of business, so the argument runs, our potential for national defense would suffer. The national defense case dates back at least to Adam Smith and his *Wealth of Nations*, and it has always had a certain logical appeal. But the objections to it are strong. As with infant industries, subsidies for this purpose are much to be preferred because Congress can assess exactly how much is being spent and has an annual opportunity to reconsider its policies. Everyone wants to be considered valuable for the national defense, and at various times and places claims for protection on that ground have been made by the watch industry, by candlemakers (emergency lighting), by textile manufacturers (uniforms), and by toothpick makers (good dental hygiene for the troops, of course).

The argument once had some merit—and presumably it still does in some cases such as Israel's, where sudden boycotts could have an even worse impact on small arms and ammunition supplies, tanks, aircraft, and the like than they would have now with production of these strongly subsidized by the Israeli government. But for a major country like the United States to base part of its trade policy on the defense argument seems to strain logic in most cases. It is hard to conceive of a modern war so serious that it halts international trade without that war being very serious and very short! If those military scientists who believe any big future war will be short are correct, then protecting domestic production of goods essential during wartime is less vital than it used to be. Actually, in the history of war, modern countries like the United States, Germany, Japan, and the Soviet Union have shown themselves immensely able when it comes to converting productive capacity from one use to another, or building new capacity, even under the most stringent wartime conditions. For example, the United States converted almost its entire automobile-making capacity into tank, truck, and airplane production during 1942; Germany's plants for manufacturing warplanes were bombed to rubble during 1943, but it took a deep breath, rebuilt and retooled underground and dispersed small factories, and in 1944 produced more aircraft than in any other year of World War II; while the Soviet Union in 1941-1942 relocated most of its heavy industry in the area of the Ural Mountains far to the east of Moscow when the western part of the country was overrun by Germans in the same war. In view of immense successes such as these, in time periods of a year or less, most claims to the need for protection in the name of national defense are pale indeed.[9]

The Cheap Labor Argument. Surely the most familiar of all the reasons for protection is the cheap, or "pauper" labor argument.[10] Generations of businesspeople, voters, and members of Congress have been sold on its logic, which holds that American industry is at a disadvantage when competing against the manufactures of foreigners who pay very low wages to the workers they employ. Now it is true that evidence shows many low-wage manufacturing countries are rapidly closing their wage gap with the United States. The differential in wages among South Korea, Singapore, Hong Kong, and the like is much less than it was in the beginning of the 1970s. Japanese average monthly pay in the early 1960s was only one-fifteenth the figure in an American factory. That had risen to one-third by 1970, and was more than one-half by 1977.[11]

But let us give the devil his or her due by ignoring the closing of the gap, and by using the comparative figures for 1970, which truly *do* demonstrate a very large pay differential between the United States and cheap labor countries. In that year, the figures were as shown in Table 13.1.

Proponents of the cheap labor argument use facts like these to make two claims, both of which have a serious ring. First, goods manufactured by the cheap labor will so undersell American products that domestic producers cannot compete. Second, American firms will be tempted to transfer their operations overseas so they too can employ cheap labor. Either way, most people find the argument highly persuasive on first hearing.

TABLE 13.1. APPROXIMATE AVERAGE MONTHLY EARNINGS OF LABOR IN INDUSTRY, 1970

Country	Earnings	Percentage of U.S. wage
United States of America	$600	100%
Japan	$190	32
Taiwan	$105	17½
Singapore	$56.25	9
South Korea	$46.25	8

But the case contains grave weaknesses, some of which can be clarified with the theory of comparative advantage, others of which can be handled on political and pragmatic bases. Consider this question: If indeed labor is so much cheaper abroad, then how is it possible that we can *export* anything at all in competition with such low wage rates? The fairly obvious answer, after a moment's reflection, is provided by the theory of comparative advantage and its underlying Heckscher-Ohlin logic of factor proportions. Labor is not the only factor of production, and thus not the only component of costs. There is capital, technical change, the natural resource endowment, *skilled* labor, and the talents of management. Industries producing goods that are capital intensive, technology intensive, and the like will not fear the lower wages abroad. If anything, the workers of Singapore or Taiwan may attend study groups where they view with alarm the cheapness of capital in more developed countries, the ease with which technology is improved, and the cost advantage conferred on a country (like the United States) with a substantial stock of natural resources. This is indeed why the United States in 1977 was able to *export* a record high $120 billion worth of merchandise—a record high not only for it, but the highest export figure ever recorded by any country in the world. True, some industries in the United States will be labor intensive, with wages the most important cost of production. These industries may well be harmed by foreign competition.[12] But to protect them by tariffs and quotas is very risky. It is estimated that about nine million Americans (about 10 percent of the labor force) make their livings in jobs connected with exporting. Keeping out the labor-intensive products of foreigners is an open invitation for them to limit entry of our own capital-intensive or high technology products. A trade war of this type is no solution to our problems—though it probably would benefit the owners and workers in the labor-intensive industries being harmed. Hence the importance given to the "self-interest" argument at the start of this section.

All this is not to say the U.S. labor-intensive industries cannot survive against low-wage competition. One must know more about productivity in these industries. A simple example will show this: What if wages in some American industry were four times those in Poveria, and American workers turned out four times as many units of output per hour of labor time as did the Poverians? Under these circumstances, the two countries might well be able to compete on even terms. The much higher productivity of labor in one country than in another might be due to better food and health, better education, higher literacy rates, and more amenability to modern factory methods, among many other possibilities.

Lastly, even where foreign labor is both less expensive and equally or more productive than U.S. labor, and forgetting for the moment the comforting consolation of comparative advantage, it would be impossible for this to have a catastrophic effect because of "natural protection." It is remarkable to find that the majority of the American labor force is in occupations naturally protected by the very high transport costs (and sometimes the impossibility) of importing the finished product. Table 13.2 illustrates this relative invulnerability. In 1976, total U.S. employment outside agriculture was 79 million. Of this 79 million, those working in the sectors shown are subject to little or no competition from imports.

TABLE 13.2. U.S. EMPLOYMENT, 1976, BY SECTOR (in millions)

Construction	3.6
Mining	.7
Transport, communications	4.5
Wholesale, retail trade	17.7
Finance, insurance, real estate	4.3
Services	14.6
Government (federal, state, and local)	14.9
Total	60.3

That 60 million total is 76 percent of 79 million—a 76 percent that is fully protected from foreign competition, and includes the service sector, which tends with economic growth to expand as a proportion of the labor force. The perspicacious reader might ask: But what about the possibility of foreign construction firms moving into the United States? What about the rise of the British Barclay's Bank in the United States as mentioned earlier in this book? What about an Arab purchase of a motel chain or an insurance company? Or a foreign takeover of an American airline or department store chain? Would not all these weaken the claim of natural protection? Not at all! The immigration laws alone would require that such firms hire mostly American citizens rather than foreigners. At the worst some home high management or technical positions might be lost. The natural protection remains intact. (True, huge illegal inflows from Mexico might someday alter the picture, but this is a far different case from claiming tariff or quota protection because of cheap labor abroad.)

The only segment of the nonfarm labor force that does not benefit from natural protection, then, appears to be manufacturing. And this remaining 24 percent of the labor force includes a large proportion of workers who earn their livings by producing that $120 billion in merchandise referred to earlier. (Specifically, 9 percent of the jobs in manufacturing are export related, according to the Labor Department.)

In short, protection against cheap labor is unnecessary as far as the vast majority of the American labor force is concerned. Further, it would jeopardize American exports, which would surely be retaliated against. Exports are as vital to the United States as imports, and the latter could not be halted without ruin for the former.

The Total Efficiency Argument. This argument holds that some nations are becoming more efficient than the United States in every way, including labor, capital, technology, and management. Protection is needed, say the real pessimists, because clearly the Japanese, the West Germans, the Swedes, the Swiss, and their ilk are growing so efficient in all ways that American industries will not be able to survive without barriers to trade. This argument, which has its parallel in many an underdeveloped country, is not persuasive. The theory of comparative advantage demonstrates that trade is advantageous even when one trading partner is the lowest-cost producer of all commodities. Furthermore, consider what would happen to exchange rates if one country started to import everything and export nothing. The exchange rate for that country's currency would fall and fall, until imports were very high in price and exports once again were potentially profitable. A country *cannot* permanently pay out more of its currency than it receives in foreign currency. What would foreigners do with their excess stocks of American money? There is only one thing they *can* do: Spend it on American goods.

The "Dumping" Argument. Few words in economics sound quite so horrid as dumping, and even those who do not know what it is could hardly be expected to defend anything so nasty. *Dumping* is the practice of selling in export markets at a lower price than in home markets. Note carefully that this by no means implies selling *at a loss*, although in ads and in newspaper articles the impression is frequently given that foreign dumpers are selling at a loss. Very few significant cases of this latter practice have been reported.

The standard form of dumping, called "persistent dumping" in the literature, is rather easy to explain with the familiar curves for demand, marginal cost, and marginal revenue. Say Watanabe Radio, a very large Tokyo firm, has markets for its product in both Japan and the United States. The firm is a profit maximizer. It may well find—in fact it will almost certainly find—that the demand curve for the product is not the same in the two countries. The difference in shape and elasticity may be due to dissimilar tastes, habits, national traits, levels of income, and degrees of competition in the two markets.

Assume Watanabe Radio has some degree of market power, that is, a demand curve that slopes downward but with a different slope and elasticity in each of the two markets (D_1 and D_2), as in Fig. 13.4(a). What price will Watanabe's managers decide to charge in the two markets? They might do the obvious thing, combining marginal cost and marginal revenue in the two markets and producing where the two are equal. Figure 13.4(a) is drawn on the assumption that marginal cost is the same in both markets but that demand and hence marginal revenue are different.

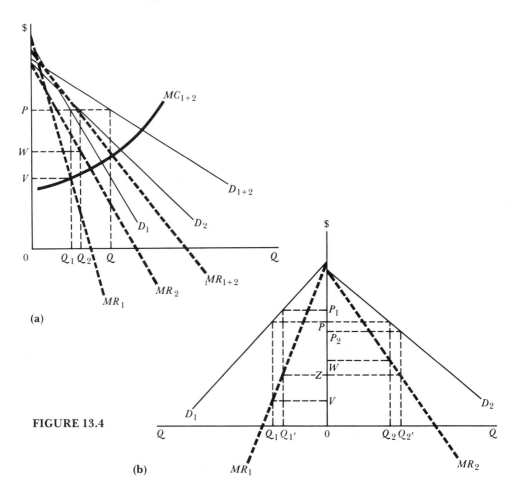

FIGURE 13.4

The decision to equate the combined marginal cost (MC_{1+2}) with the combined marginal revenue (MR_{1+2}) means that the company will produce a quantity $0Q$ and charge a price in both markets of $0P$. The price $0P$ will mean that a quantity $0Q_1$ is sold in the first country, and a quantity $0Q_2$ in the second country. $0Q_1 + 0Q_2 = 0Q$. But it immediately becomes apparent that some profits are being lost. Look at the diagram again. Identical pricing has led to a marginal revenue $0V$ in the first country, and a marginal revenue $0W$ in the second. There is a higher marginal return per unit sold in the second market than in the first. Additional revenue would be earned, with no alteration in cost, by transferring some sales from the market with low marginal revenue to the market with high MR. This means, in our example, from the first market where $MR_1 = 0V$ to the second where $MR_2 = 0W$. As sales are transferred, each extra unit (radio) sold in the second market brings more revenue then it did when sold in the first. However, this action has its own repercussions. Selling fewer goods in market 1 raises prices there, and selling more in market 2 lowers prices there. Extra revenues continue to be earned from shifting sales until $MR_1 = MR_2$, at which point it does not matter where a sale is made. Equality of marginal revenues means maximization of profit in the two markets taken together.

The final outcome is seen most conveniently on a two-sided diagram, Fig. 13.4(b). Here the demand and marginal revenue curves for the first market (D_1 and MR_1) run downward and to the left rather than to the right. The quantity produced, $0Q_1 + 0Q_2$, is the same as the total output $0Q$ for both markets seen on Fig. 13.4(a). Since an identical pricing policy ($0P$) gives lower marginal revenue $0V$ in the first market than in the second $0W$, transfer a quantity Q_1Q_1' to the second market ($=Q_2Q_2'$), thus equalizing MR_1 and MR_2 at $0Z$. The resulting price in the first market will be higher at $0P_1$, and lower in the second market at $0P_2$. In short, an industry with some market power will maximize profits by equating MR in its markets. This in turn means charging more in markets where demand is less elastic.

Thus we see the logic of why a seller might choose to sell at different prices in different markets. It is easy enough to understand where the complaints come from. Exporters get accused by their foreign customers of exploitation when they sell abroad at a higher price (due to more inelastic demand) than at home. Or if they sell abroad cheaper than at home, due to more elastic foreign demand, then foreign competitors accuse them of dumping. It is not easy to win, and in fact, rather than risk trouble, many firms that could sell at different prices in different markets often choose to charge a flat price. That way publicity and possible retaliation are avoided.[13]

In U.S. practice, antidumping duties, quotas, and other penalties have been common. The basis for this in law has for many years been the antidumping act of 1921. Under it, the U.S. International Trade Commission is authorized to investigate charges of dumping and to recommend action. If the Commission finds "material injury" to a domestic firm or firms from

dumping, it can recommend to the Treasury the imposition of special retaliatory duties. Such cases are sometimes hotly argued: How do you tell whether
Watanabe Radio's American model is the same as the one sold at home in
Japan? (In 1972 the case of electric transformers *made to order* by a foreign
manufacturer was defined as dumping.)

Without doubt, persistent dumping by a foreigner provides competition
for American producers, and these producers, following their self-interest,
may well inveigh against the practice. But it is equally true that consumers in
the United States will benefit from the foreign competition, and it is difficult
to see why for so long the public has been so fully persuaded that antidumping is an unmitigated evil. Be that as it may, sixty antidumping duties were in
effect as of mid-1977—the latest a 32 percent levy on Japanese steel plate
imposed in October 1977, after Japanese steelmakers refused to open their
books to American investigators. Since 1974, six other dumping duties had
been removed after proof that the dumping had stopped.

Sometimes two other types of dumping are distinguished. The first of
these, "sporadic dumping," is sale abroad at prices below those charged at
home because of some temporary overstock. It resembles the clearance sales
held by department stores. Since its nature is so temporary, by definition, it
has seldom attracted much attention. Much more serious is so-called "pred-
atory dumping," defined as cutting prices to the point where they are actually
below the average costs of production. Here the intent may be to drive competitors out of the industry, with the predator presumably raising its prices
again to a new level higher than the original once the deed is done. Such
warlike tactics have seldom found much support, whether perpetrated by a
firm in domestic operations or in international trade.

The Argument that Trade Perpetuates Underdevelopment. This last argument,
which has a strong and growing appeal, is sufficiently important to receive
treatment in a chapter of its own, Chapter 17.

An Exception to All the Rules on Tariffs and Quotas. Here, at the conclusion of
our two chapters on tariff and nontariff barriers to trade, it is time to call
attention to one major exception to the whole discussion thus far. Under
GATT rules it is perfectly proper to designate a certain geographical area as
a zone of free trade, even when the rest of the country is subject to normal
tariffs and quotas. Typically, such zones are isolated by fences or other
obstructions, and sometimes access to them is limited only to citizens of
foreign countries. The most familiar examples of this phenomenon are the
"duty-free shops" found mainly at international airline terminals. You can buy
freely there, without being subject to a panoply of trade restrictions. You then
can depart the country freely. But if you try to leave the zone and enter the
home country, you then run up against the smiling (or frowning) customs
inspector.

Such zones may be large in size: the whole of Gibraltar, Shannon Airport in Ireland, Hong Kong, the waterfront of Monrovia, Liberia, and many others. In the United States, free trade is permitted in so-called Foreign Trade Zones established under the 1934 act of that name. These "isolated, enclosed, and policed" pieces of U.S. territory are useful mainly to companies that wish to import components or raw materials free of duty, and then export them again. (There is no tariff advantage in selling to U.S. customers, for then the duty would have to be paid after all.) Zones are granted after application to the Department of Commerce. In 1975-1976, there were twenty-six such zones ranging from Port Everglades, Florida, to Seattle, Washington, with the one at the Brooklyn Navy Yard the largest. In that year, some 750 firms were using them on a permanent basis, accounting for less than $600 million in goods. They are like greenhouses sheltering rare plants. Beyond their confining fences lies the real world of restricted trade.

Notes

1. One of the authors used to write this on the blackboard as ‏تعريفة‎. But he stopped doing so when an Arabic-speaking student laughed uproariously at his first view of Arabic written from left to right.
2. The Confederate States of America were so angry at northern use of the protective tariff that they made it unconstitutional to protect any specific industry with a tariff.
3. Other countries have also tried to weasel out of MFN commitments. The most famous dodge of all times was the German tariff of 1905 on cattle. The Germans wanted to give Switzerland a favorable rate, but did not want to give the rate to other countries. Hence this wording was adopted: The (favorable) tariff shall apply to dappled mountain cattle or brown cattle, "reared at a spot at least 300 meters above sea level, and which have at least one month's grazing each year at a spot at least 800 meters above sea level."
4. Don D. Humphrey, *The U.S. and the Common Market* (New York: Praeger, 1962).
5. Specific duties can also be on a sliding scale, thus avoiding the problem of coping with inflation. The famous English "Corn Laws" against grain imports were a good example of a scaled specific duty. For example, under the legislation of 1791, when grain brought 54 shillings in England, the tariff was only a nominal 6 pence; between 50 and 54 shillings the duty was higher, at 2 shillings 6 pence; while under 50 shillings the duty mounted to a staggering and prohibitive 24 shillings 3 pence.
6. Americans often call them orderly marketing arrangements; the Japanese use the term voluntary export restraint agreements.
7. There was a new wrinkle in the TV agreement with Japan. If 40 percent of the labor costs embodied in a set are American, the set is not subject to the quota. This is expected to promote partial manufacture in the United States by Japanese firms. Matsushita, Sanyo, and Sony have already established plants here, while Mitsubishi and Toshiba are expected to join them.
8. See the London *Economist*, October 12, 1974, p. 56. Complicating the issue, U.S. and Canadian tariffs are usually calculated on an fob basis (free on board, not

including transport costs), while most European and many other countries use cif prices (cost, insurance, freight, and thus transport costs) in figuring the tariff. As a result, any given American tariff expressed in percentage terms is likely to be slightly lower in its protective effect than a tariff calculated on a cif basis.

9. Remember that war that blocked *imports* would also block *exports*, freeing vast quantities of productive factors for a war effort. Sample this passage from p. 164 of Norman Stone's *The Eastern Front, 1914-1917* (New York: Charles Scribner's Sons, 1975): "In September 1914, there was 40 percent unemployment in Nuremberg because the Franconian pencil-makers and pencil-sharpener-makers, who supplied the world, were deprived of markets. But the pool of skilled labour that this created, and still more, perhaps, the quantities of now unusable raw materials, were of utmost service to the war effort, and areas such as Franconia became important centres of the munitions industry overnight, and to everyone's surprise. It would be interesting to speculate how much less war-goods Germany would have produced if the British had allowed her to go on exporting."

10. Most interestingly, a recent article by Norman S. Fieleke shows very little correlation between low wages of labor in a given American industry and the degree of tariff protection accorded that industry. (The same claim of low correlation is also made for industries involved with defense contracts, incidentally.) See *New England Economic Review* (July/August 1974): 15-17.

11. The average rate of pay for Swedish factory workers in 1977 actually exceeded pay in the United States.

12. The admission that some industries will be hurt by free trade (in the United States meaning in particular labor-intensive industries, with labor not sufficiently productive to offset its comparative disadvantage based on costs) was the main factor behind the adjustment assistance built into the acts of 1962 and 1974, and discussed earlier in this chapter. From an economic standpoint, the U.S. firm in trouble would presumably detect declining sales revenues and falling profits, these leading to lower wages for workers. Or, if unions are strong enough to keep wages fixed, the result will be unemployment.

For industries where this happens, it would be very advantageous if the relative downward pressure on wages did not have to proceed very far before workers in labor-intensive industries were hired by other industries unharmed by foreign competition. The greater the labor mobility, defined as the willingness of workers to move and the ability of other firms to use more labor, the less will be the problem. The same point applies to the other factors of production in the declining industry. Fortunately for the United States, it is generally believed that countries attain higher factor mobility through economic development. This still does not excuse it from the slowness and lack of funds that have affected U.S. adjustment assistance programs.

Japan is now in much the same position. Its once powerful textile industry has been crippled by the cheap labor of South Korea, Hong Kong, Singapore, and so on. Some 817 Japanese textile firms went into bankruptcy in 1976. Textiles were nearly 40 percent of Japan's exports in 1955; but only 5 percent in 1976. The government is having to cope with a massive transfer of labor out of this industry. Some firms are moving their operations to Southeast Asia.

13. In an important case decided February 1978, the European Court of Justice found United Brands (the American multinational once known as United Fruit) guilty of charging different prices in different EEC countries. The court ruled that the practice must stop.

14

ECONOMIC
INTEGRATION

Economic integration is the process of joining together two or more countries into a closer economic union than either has with the rest of the world. Typically, economic integration is begun with a customs union, in which tariffs are abolished between the nations involved, but not with the rest of the world. Economic integration, however, can also involve freedom of resource movement, common economic policies, even a common money. Both in theory and in practice, integration raises economic questions that are less than obvious, but of considerable importance, so it is well to examine them in this short and separate chapter.

Integration in the Non-Communist World

EEC and EFTA. Economic integration is hardly new. The U.S. Constitution of 1789, by abolishing the separate tariffs of the thirteen states, created a customs union out of these loosely federated entities. (Under the Articles of Confederation, New York actually charged some tariffs on imports from Connecticut.) The nineteenth-century unification of the various German states into one nation was accompanied by customs union arrangements among sovereign states. The connection between political unity and economic unity was not lost on the statesmen of Western Europe and America who sought to rebuild the Western World after the Second World War. These leaders did not want a divided Europe to continue; rather they envisioned a Europe united politically, economically, and militarily, a Europe that would no longer fight with itself, but would be strong enough to resist the threats from Russia and from radical dissidence within. The first and most practical step would be to create a customs union. Not only did a customs union make economic sense, it would force the countries into regular political consultation. Thus the creation of the European Economic Community in 1957 had more than economic purposes: Its economic behavior—and the tolerance of the United States toward some of its excesses—must be understood in this broader political context. A mixture of lofty ideals and hard economic and political realities can produce some unusual reactions.

The European Economic Community (EEC) was founded in Rome in March of 1957 by six nations—France, West Germany, Italy, Belgium, the Netherlands, and Luxembourg. It was based partially on an earlier cooperative effort known as "Benelux," a customs union among the last three nations named above. It was also based on experience gained in tariff-free trade in coal and steel in the ECSC, the European Coal and Steel Community.[1] Tariffs on industrial goods were cut with great speed, and a common external tariff, somewhat lower than the weighted averages of European tariffs, was erected. In contrast, agricultural policy developed slowly and painfully, and not until the mid-1960s did agricultural goods flow freely.[2]

The EEC is one of the two exceptions to the most-favored-nation provisions allowed under GATT (Chapter 13). Free trade within the customs union is accompanied by a *common* external tariff for all goods entering any of the member countries. This is shown in Figs. 14.1(a) and (b). In 1(a) the nations all have separate tariffs; in 1(b), they have no tariffs among themselves but have the same tariff in each country for goods from the outside. The EEC goes beyond being only a customs union, however, in that the factors of production are free to move; for example, Italian workers move to Germany and German capital moves freely to Italy.

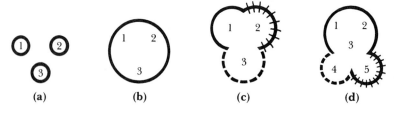

(a)   (b)   (c)   (d)

FIGURE 14.1

In 1960, seven nations outside the EEC came together to form the European Free Trade Association (EFTA). A "Free Trade Association" is also allowed under GATT. In this type of organization all members cut their tariffs to one another, but maintain their own tariffs against outside nations, as in Fig. 14.1(c). Such a system requires supplementary regulations applicable with respect to the country of origin of goods, such that goods from outside the group are not shipped into the lowest-tariff country and then from there to a high-tariff nation. When those imports are a component or raw material for a product made in the low-tariff country, and then exported to a high-tariff nation, the law must specify how much value must be added to qualify for the zero tariff. (It could also tax just the components, but that is administratively very difficult.) This, of course, creates economic inefficiencies by encouraging processing within the low-tariff country.

The EFTA administrative arrangements lack the closeness and supranational authority characteristic of the EEC. There is no need to decide on a common tariff, common agricultural policy, or immigration laws. Hence EFTA appealed more to the traditionally nonaligned or reluctant-to-align Britain, Switzerland, and Sweden, and to those nations that had to contend with Soviet objections—Finland and Austria.[3] On January 1, 1973, however, three founding EFTA members left that organization to join the EEC—Britain, Denmark, and Ireland.[4] EFTA in the interim had picked up new members so that at present its membership includes Austria, Finland, Iceland, Norway, Sweden, Portugal, and Switzerland.

The present arrangement between the EEC and EFTA is like that of a larger free trade association. The EEC keeps its common external tariff, but extends zero tariff provisions to EFTA; while the EFTA nations grant zero tariffs to the EEC, but maintain separate tariffs for outside nations, as illustrated in Fig. 14.1(d). This process is still in transition. At present virtually all tariffs are down to zero except for those on agricultural goods and some key products such as steel, pulp, and paper.[5]

Other Customs Unions. Although the EEC and EFTA are by far the most familiar of the customs unions, they are by no means the only ones. The biggest geographically in the Western world has been the Latin American Free Trade Area (LAFTA), including Argentina, Brazil, Bolivia, Chile, Colombia, Ecuador, Mexico, Paraguay, Peru, Uruguay, and Venezuela. The guiding principle of this organization has been to allocate certain industries to certain countries, then to trade these goods freely. But LAFTA's ambitions have been thwarted by political discord. Local interests supporting protection have proved very strong. The Andean Pact subgroup of LAFTA (Bolivia, Chile, Colombia, Ecuador, Peru, and Venezuela) at first had especially ambitious goals. They were to achieve a common external tariff in 1975, completely free trade in the same year, and a plan for the integrated long-term allocation of industry. All of these have fallen through; and in the infighting, Chile withdrew from the pact.

Even so, LAFTA has had more success with industrial allocation than the Central American Common Market (CACM). After a promising start, CACM suffered severely from the short war between Honduras and El Salvador in 1969.[6] Intraregional trade shrank for years thereafter; a new accord between these two countries promises a brighter future for the union.

Two unions have broken up completely: the West Indian federation because of political hostility among the various island members, and the East African union of Kenya, Tanzania, and Uganda largely because of antipathy between Idi Amin, Uganda's president-for-life, and the other two members. Another, however, is progressing rapidly. This is ASEAN, the Association of Southeast Asian Nations, founded in 1967 and including Indonesia, Malaysia, the Philippines, Singapore, and Thailand. The move to make this a common market dates from 1976. General tariff cuts and some industrial allocation have already been agreed on, and in the summer of 1977 Japan announced it was willing to give ASEAN very substantial financial support.

The Great Debate: Trade Creation versus Trade Diversion. For a very long time the general opinion was that any customs union would be beneficial. Free trade was the optimum, according to economic theory. A customs union was a movement toward free trade, therefore a customs union must increase welfare. This proposition lay in some part behind all the nascent customs unions of the past: Napoleon Bonaparte's Continental System of Trade, the Swiss Confederation of cantons, or the nineteenth-century German Zollverein. At the time, and well into the twentieth century, there was no adequate theory to explain the economic impact of a union. Few questioned the conclusion that unions were a good thing; but in fact there had been no rigorous study of the subject and there was virtually no literature covering it.

This picture changed in 1950, when Jacob Viner showed in his book *The Customs Union Issue* that the standard opinion was not necessarily correct, and that under certain conditions a customs union might result in a reduction of welfare. Viner's conclusions soon became a famous illustration of what came to be known as the "paradox of the second best." This paradox, put in print by Richard Lipsey and Kelvin J. Lancaster of the London School of Economics, states that although a "first-best" course of action *must* optimize welfare, the "second-best" course of action may *not* increase welfare (as in jumping 99 percent of the way across a canyon).

How can it possibly be so? All along, people have been assuming that a customs union would allow lower-priced imports from a trading partner to replace higher-priced domestic output, increasing welfare. Here, with modifications, is how Viner illustrated the case. Table 14.1, Case 1, shows the cost of wheat in three countries, X, Y, and Z. To protect its domestic producers, X has a tariff of 200 percent. At that tariff not even Z, with its costs of $1.00, can compete in X with X's $2.00 wheat. Assuming constant costs for the present, we can conclude that all of X's wheat is purchased at home. Now a customs union with Y, as shown in the bottom part of Case 1, lowers Y's price to consumers in X so that they shift their purchases to Y, leaving X's farmers to grow something else. Assuming full employment, X is clearly better off producing something else and importing wheat from Y, the low-cost producer. Another way of saying this would be to point out that X could produce $2.00 worth of goods for every bushel of wheat it ceased producing and only use up $1.00 worth of resources to get the wheat from Y.

TABLE 14.1.

	Case 1 (200% tariff)			Case 2 (90% tariff)		
Before Customs Union	X's	Y's	Z's	X's	Y's	Z's
Cost of wheat	$2.00	$1.50	$1.00	$2.00	$1.50	$1.00
Tariff in X	- -	3.00	2.00	- -	1.35	.90
Price in X	2.00	4.50	3.00	2.00	2.85	1.90
After Customs Union						
Cost of wheat	2.00	1.50	1.00	2.00	1.50	1.00
Tariff in X	- -	- -	2.00	- -	- -	.90
Price in X	2.00	1.50	3.00	2.00	1.50	1.90

Viner calls this type of customs union a "trade-creating customs union," and so it is, with trade in wheat replacing domestic production. Today we would speak of it as being a customs union in which there was only a "trade creation effect." Note, not so incidentally, that X would have been even better off if Z had been included in the union. Still, it is certain that the welfare of X is improved, while the welfare of Z remains unaffected.

Case 1, however, is only one possibility. Consider the same situation with the tariff changed. In Case 2, a 90 percent tariff has been substituted for the 200 percent tariff. Before the customs union, the cheapest wheat in X was that imported from Z, hence X's farmers did not grow wheat and Z enjoyed X's wheat market. With the signing of a customs union agreement with Y, however, a curious thing occurs: Y's price to X's consumers falls below Z's so that X *diverts* its trade from Z, the lowest-cost supplier, to Y, a higher-cost supplier. People in X may think that they are getting wheat more cheaply—the price for them is down $0.40 per bushel from the $1.90 they used to pay for imports from Z. But they have forgotten that their government was collecting $0.90 a bushel in tariff revenue, $0.50 of which is now lost, and $0.40 of which goes to the consumer. The world has seen wheat that cost $1.00 supplanted by wheat that uses up $1.50 in resources. Viner called this a "trade-diverting customs union," in which trade has been diverted from a more efficent to a less efficient producer.

Research in the 1960s concentrated on further explorations of trade creation and trade diversion. Viner had focused attention on changes in production, but diagrammatical analysis soon made it apparent that the effects of a customs union could be more complex. Fortunately, we already have developed the basic material needed to understand customs union effects (Fig. 12.6), and the reader may wish briefly to review it and the entailed concepts of producers' and consumers' surpluses.

Figure 14.2 of this chapter illustrates the "customs union" effect. It shows Country X's demand and supply curves, along with the prices of wheat from Y and Z. As the positively sloped supply curve indicates, Country X has increasing costs. For illustrative clarity, we endow Y and Z with constant costs. P_z is the price of Z's wheat before a tariff, P_y is Y's wheat price. The tariff (a specific duty in this case) can be added onto both P_z and P_y, giving us $P_z + T$ and $P_y + T$.

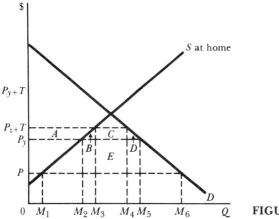

FIGURE 14.2

With no tariff at all, we can see that M_1 would be produced in country X, M_6 consumed, and $M_1 M_6$ imported. All imports would come from Z, which is a much cheaper supplier than Y—indeed, Z squeezes out most of X's production. After the tariff, Z, at $P_z + T$, still remains the low-cost supplier. X's production expands to M_3, and its consumption declines to M_4. These are the usual effects of a tariff, but our principal concern will be with the revenue effect, represented in Fig. 14.2 by rectangle $C + E$—the tariff times the imports of $M_3 M_4$. This, then, is our starting point for examining the effects of the customs union.

Now, a customs union opens up between X and Y. The price of Y's wheat falls to P_y, below $P_z + T$, and thus trade is diverted to Y. The lower price and greater quantity traded lead clearly enough to a gain in consumers' surplus, which, we recall from Fig. 12.6, is the triangular area above the price but below the demand curve. This triangle of consumers' surplus has expanded to an area larger by $ABCD$, because the price has fallen and the quantity has increased. But this is not an unadulterated gain for society. Do not forget country X's own domestic producers, who are hurt by the lower price. Their producers' surplus is reduced, in this case by area *A*. There is also lost tariff revenue. Country X had been collecting tariffs on its imports, but does so no longer on the imports from Y, its fellow member in the customs union. This lost tariff revenue is equal to areas *C* + *E*. *C* is redistributed to consumers, but not *E*, which must be used to pay Y's higher costs. In short, the welfare gain may be shown by the size of *A* + *B* + *C* + *D*. The welfare loss is equal to *A* + *E*. This boils down to a comparison between the little triangles *B* and *D*, and the rectangle *E*. If *B* and *D* together are larger than *E*, then gains in consumers' surplus outweigh lost producers' surplus and lost tariff revenue. The customs union thus creates more trade than it diverts. But the reverse case, with *E* larger than *B* + *D*, shows the reduced welfare of a customs union that is heavily trade diverting. In our Fig. 14.2, trade diversion obviously predominates, with *B* + *D* significantly smaller in size than area *E*. Rectangle *E* represents not only country X's loss, but world loss. It shows the additional resources used in producing wheat in Y; or, to use Viner's numbers, the $0.50 a bushel additional cost for Y's wheat.

In contrast, Fig. 14.3 shows a trade-creating customs union. Take note of the characteristics of the figure that made the trade creation exceed trade diversion.

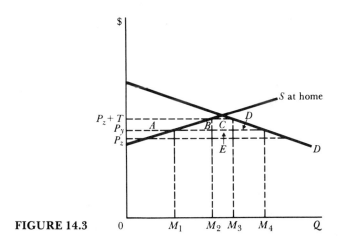

FIGURE 14.3

1. The supply and demand curves are very flat. Any decrease in price along these elastic curves will cut domestic output sharply and also increase consumption greatly, thereby increasing imports by a substantial amount.
2. There is a big difference between the home country (X) and the partner in the customs union (Y); at the same time there is only a small difference

between the partner and the lowest-cost nonmember in the outside world (Z). See in Fig. 14.3 how imports rise enormously after a customs union (from M_2M_3 to M_1M_4). Again the gain in consumers' surplus is $A + B + C + D$. Again the lost producers' surplus is A; again tariff revenue falls by $C + E$. But here the net gain is large because triangles $B + D$ are far larger than area E. Trade creation predominates.

There are additional theoretical conclusions. The first is that the larger the customs union, the less possible is trade diversion. This is reasonable, given the limiting case where *all* countries are members and there can be no diversion at all. Fine, but there is a dark corollary: The harm to the outside party is greater the larger the customs union. How can there be little diversion but much harm? The reason is that the trade of the outsider is not diverted, but the outsider takes a beating with respect to terms of trade. Consider the circumstance of the last nation in the world left out of the World Economic Community. If this pariah is to trade at all, and is being underpriced because of competitors' tariff-free privileges, it must cut its prices to absorb the tariff itself. (If it were country Z, for instance, it would lower its price to be competitive with Y, absorbing most of the tariff.)

Take Spain, for example, in relation to the EEC. Spain wishes to export oranges but finds that many other producers now have to pay the tariff. When the EEC was smaller, Spain could export successfully to England, Ireland, and Denmark. Now it finds itself at a disadvantage compared to Italy, and to associated members of the French Community (ex-colonies) who now have duty-free access to former Spanish markets. Spain is clearly worse off. If it is to trade at all, it must lower its prices to pay the bulk of the tariff itself.[7] This is one of the reasons why the EEC also cut tariffs to EFTA—to prevent such serious dislocations and discrimination. Nonetheless, that may just pass the problem of being an outsider on to the remaining nonmember nations, this time with an even larger customs union to face. (Spain's problem could be even worse, as illustrated in the following section.)

A third important generalization is that unions among rival or similar economies will create more trade than unions between complementary economies. This is because the demand and supply curves are flatter. Indeed, as the discussion of intraindustrial trade suggested, the supply curves may even be negatively sloped. Hence the EEC, with its economies that compete with each other, saw a much steeper rise in trade than did EFTA, whose members had largely complementary goods.[8]

Trade Diversion and Trade Creation in the EEC. Probably the major illustration of trade diversion and trade creation effects may be found in the EEC. In manufacturing, the model that emphasizes trade creation seems to fit the case best. EEC members have economies that are competitive with one another, in itself suggesting greater trade-creation effects. Both demand and supply elasticities for many industrial commodities tend to be large. Substitution among industrial commodities is easy, leading to highly elastic demand. Mass-production techniques that allow large increases in output at little or no increases in cost lead to a highly elastic supply. Indeed, our theory in Chapter 11 suggests declining costs in intraindustrial trade, and therefore downward-sloping supply curves. Professor Bela Balassa of Johns Hopkins University has found considerable evidence of vigorous intraindustrial trade with large trade-creation effects in chemicals, machinery, fuels, and transportation equipment. Lastly, the trade diversion is unlikely to be large because many of the industries in the EEC were already the world's lowest-cost producers (meaning there would be no trade to divert), or close to it (meaning only a small loss in diversion).[9]

By contrast, agriculture in the EEC appears to approach the heavy trade diversion model of Fig. 14.3. The members of the EEC are not very similar in agricultural production. The British emphasize the raising of livestock, the French labor-intensive farming, the Danes capital-intensive production. In the main, the lowest-cost producer within the union is by no means the *world's* lowest-cost producer. This certainly applies to grains, dairy products, and tropical commodities such as cocoa, coffee, and oilseeds. Demand is relatively inelastic for many agricultural commodities such as meat and grain. Supply is also notoriously inelastic in the short run, as production is difficult to increase or cut back during the life cycle of animals, or during a crop year. There is thus the possibility of substantial trade diversion, especially from the United States and the British Commonwealth, in particular Australia, New Zealand, and Canada. Balassa found diversion to be especially strong in beverages, to-bacco, and some raw materials as well as food. The main impact of the diversion appears to be felt by Britain and West Germany, both of which formerly imported a great portion of their food supplies from the cheapest sources overseas, and now import from high-cost sources within the EEC.

The agricultural difficulties stem in part from the political structure of the Common Market itself, and in part from inherent contradictions within European agriculture. In the early 1960s, bargaining over agricultural policy pitted Germany, a high-cost producer and importer (Country X, so to speak) against France, the medium-cost producer (Country Y), with the United States, Canada, Argentina, Australia, and New Zealand being the onlooking Country Zs. Germany did not want to sustain both revenue losses from trade diversion and the displacement associated with trade creation. France was not eager to pay the high level of German agricultural support prices, but it did want the German market. In the resulting bargain, Germany agreed to accept French imports (and the trade diversion and loss of revenue that it entailed) in exchange for the French acceptance of high agricultural support prices. Thus German farmers could continue to produce; and the trade creation effect did not occur in the sense that German resources were not displaced.

At German support prices, the Germans continued to produce, but the French farmers could produce a lot more. To handle this increasing surplus, the EEC limited imports of agricultural goods more severely—causing an even larger trade diversion effect and displacing outsiders almost entirely from agricultural trade in many products. When no more trade was left to be diverted, the surpluses we spoke of earlier began to build. Hence the difficulties in making decisions within the EEC resulted in hardship to outside parties.

In fairness to the EEC, we should note that the agricultural problem is extremely difficult. Unlike North American farms, the vast majority of European farms are small. The average U.S. farm is 159 hectares; the average farm in the EEC is only 17 hectares. Moreover, that farm may be in three or more separate fields, interspersed among fields of other farms, reflecting ancient patterns of land tenure and inheritance. No American dairy farm is economically viable with fewer than fifty cows, and one hundred or more is common; the average European farm has fewer than four cows. In an era when U.S. chicken production was highly industrialized, with massive chicken houses crammed with specially bred, specially fed chickens whose days and nights were controlled by optimal artificial light conditions, European chickens were still scratching around the farmyard. Moreover, the farm population is not mobile. The average German farmer is well into his or her sixties; all the young have indeed been reallocated. The social and psychological cost of closing down the farms would be enormous, and many resources would simply be idled. Thus there is a situation analogous to some of the American textile and shoe "industry towns"—but on a scale involving 20 percent of the population. It is not that the EEC leaders do not want to be efficient or to have the world become efficient in agriculture; it is that they do not want to pay the price. They thus pursue the highly protectionist policies described earlier, in Chapter 13.

We will mention briefly only one of the special tools the EEC uses to keep foreign imports out. In defense of their support prices (called "intervention prices" in the EEC), the Common Market managers use a particularly effective form of tariff called the *variable levy*. This is a tax equal to the difference between the (cheaper) price of imported farm commodities, including transport costs, and the price the EEC wants to defend for its farmers. Unlike a regular tariff, this variable levy will rise if the price of the imported goods falls, or if the EEC's intervention price is raised. Also unlike the case of a regular tariff, it is not possible for exporters to the Common Market to maintain their sales by cutting their prices so as to absorb a part of the tariff themselves. The only result is to increase the size of the variable levy. Protection under this system is ironclad. That is the reason why a nation like Spain could be hurt by being outside the EEC even more than customs union theory suggests. That is also the reason why EEC prices for agricultural commodities exceed world market prices by the large margins shown in Table 14.2.

TABLE 14.2. PRICES AT EEC FRONTIERS AS PERCENTAGE OF WORLD 1975-1976 PRICES

Country	Percentage
Wheat	124%
Husked rice	137
Barley	117
Maize (corn)	128
Sugar	109
Beef, veal	158
Pork	113
Olive oil	207
Butter	320
Milk powder	266

Dynamic Effects of Economic Integration. So far we have examined economic integration only in terms of its static effects—as if the production possibility curves of the member nations were unchanged by economic integration. It is likely, however, that there are also *dynamic* effects serving to push out the production possibility curves of the members. If the creation of a customs union caused the introduction of new technology, for instance, the entire production possibility curve would shift outward. In terms of our typical goods, the nation could produce more of either wine or cloth. The dynamic effects usually cited are in two categories.

1. Competition effects. These include higher levels of investment, improved marketing, greater efficiency in production, and the introduction of new technology.

2. Scale effects. A larger market means that industries can introduce economies of scale impossible in the smaller market, also expanding the production possibility frontier.[10]

Holland's Philips Lamp case illustrates a number of these points. Philips was well placed to enjoy the benefits of the EEC because it operated in all the original six countries. Yet Philips's tradition of strong national subsidiaries prevented it from organizing efficiently on a community-wide scale. American corporations, however, were able to design and produce goods in one center for the entire common market, achieving greater production efficiencies. Philips, in maintaining its market share, had to cut costs and thus saw an almost disastrous fall in its profit margins. As a consequence, it was forced to become more efficient in both production and organization.

The dynamic effects of a customs union are often called on to buttress the arguments for such unions. Defenders of the EEC, for instance, point out that its dynamic effects have far outweighed any negative static effects, citing impressive growth statistics on EEC imports from other nations. It would be odd indeed, to complain about a diversion of 10 percent of trade if the selfsame force had produced a doubling or tripling of trade.

Such an argument about integration's dynamics has, however, a serious weakness: One must show that the customs union was *necessary* to have the dynamic effects. All the effects categorized under "competition effects" can be achieved with a unilateral tariff cut. If a country wants the bracing wind of international competition, all it has to do is to cut import barriers. The end of exchange control and import licensing in Britain in the late 1950s, for instance, provided such a wind to the domestic economy. If all six original EEC nations wanted more competition, there is no reason why they could not have lowered their tariffs to everyone. Such a mutually agreed on lowering of tariffs to all nations would also have provided the opportunities for scale economies, albeit with more international competition.

In the specific case of the EEC's growth, one gets into treacherous statistical waters in ascribing the dynamism and growth of its members to the customs union itself. The nations were already growing by 1956; Sweden and Switzerland, outside the EEC, grew just as well. The authors are rather inclined to accept the dynamic arguments as being generally valid, but are uncertain about attempts to quantify them. It is not at all clear by how much customs-union-induced growth expanded trade, nor is it easy to say if that extra boost to growth overcame the very substantial static effects of the EEC's agricultural policy.

Last, not all dynamic effects are necessarily positive. In particular, a customs union may increase regional disparities within member countries. Its location effects can cause a drain on the more distant regions. Northern Italy draws resources away from the South. A customs union between the United States and Canada would probably increase the drawing power of Ontario or British Columbia over the Maritimes or even Quebec. Harmonization of social policies may limit the abilities of governments to use traditional means to subsidize regions—for example, the Norwegian agricultural subsidies designed to keep farmers in the north. This is one of the reasons why the EEC has a compensating regional policy to counteract some of the negative dynamic effects of trade.

One of the most important advantages expected in the long term is the dynamic effect of eventual currency unification. In Chapter 3 we saw that the EEC's snake has been an attempt to keep exchange rates of the member countries from varying outside a narrow band. The vagaries of the scheme were discussed at length there. For our purposes at this point, it is enough to say that many officials of the Common Market are strong supporters of eventual monetary unification, perhaps with a common currency in the end. The moves to similar taxes (the VAT) and similar tax rates have also been prompted by the same sentiment. Eventual monetary unification is lauded on several grounds by its supporters. The advantages are wholly obvious, and the United States is often used as the best example. A single currency, the units of which are exactly equal and interchangeable, is highly desirable for safety and convenience. There then would be no necessity for foreign exchange transactions, or for maintaining numerous separate currencies and central banks. There would be no risk of fluctuation in rates, no need for a forward market in currency. Any American knows how nice it is that a dollar is a dollar in New York, in Chicago, and in Los Angeles. Trade in the EEC would indeed be much more simple and convenient if the currencies were unified.

But the goal of monetary union is still a long way in the future for the EEC. The economies are subject to very different rates of unemployment, and lower mobility of factors compared to the United States (few Italians, for example, are willing to move to Denmark to escape chronic Italian unemployment, and there are social and legal barriers to large population movements). There are also national jealousies to consider on a political level. Keeping separate floating currencies is the proper prescription if countries wish to pursue independent fiscal and monetary policies for the fight against inflation and unemployment, or for reasons of nationalism. The urge for monetary unification seems as strong as ever, but it will surprise the authors if the goal is attained before the mid-1980s to late 1980s, if indeed it is achieved in this century.

A long-term EEC goal that is showing more progress is the elimination of nontariff barriers. As noted previously, the Common Market moved to a common tax arrangement, based on a value added system. Even Britain, which like the United States emphasized direct taxes, has moved toward "harmonization" with the rest of the EEC, adopting VAT taxes. The tax rates are not the same between the countries, but the tax systems are similar. Thus there is relatively little question about the distortion to trade caused by the border tax adjustment problem since such adjustment is roughly the same for all. This is particularly important given the desire to have fixed exchange rates between the countries, because the countries are deprived of the services of an exchange rate mechanism for making adjustments to different tax systems.

Progress is also being made in lowering other nontariff barriers, particularly in the health, safety, labeling, and administrative fields. Even the size of trucks is standard (so that goods do not have to be transshipped or put into especially small trucks to move from one nation to the other); thus heavy European trucks have been annoying the English in their small towns. Although this may be burdensome, there are many balancing benefits. NTB elimination means, for instance, that a lathe or radio made in England can be sold without modification in any of the nine member countries.

Conclusion. It is difficult to summarize the overall effects of customs unions in the West, partly at least because our sample size is so small. We cannot always distinguish what is inherent in customs unions from what is unique to the EEC. It is clear that there has been immense trade creation and considerable growth in the EEC. But at the same time, that organization has demonstrated pronounced trade diversion in agriculture. It is difficult to separate political elements unique to the EEC from more general theoretical conclusions. One result deriving from both theory and politics does, however, stand out: Customs unions are not necessarily beneficial. The discovery of the trade diversion effect in the 1950s followed by the EEC's trade-diverting actions in the 1960s made economists far more aware of the economic burdens that customs unions place on non-members and far less certain that customs unions are the best path to a more efficient world.

Integration in the Communist World: COMECON

One very different union has not yet been discussed. This is the trade organization of most of the Soviet bloc countries. COMECON, which stands for the Council for Mutual Economic Assistance (also called CMEA) includes Mongolia, Cuba since 1972, and Vietnam since 1978, in addition to the senior partner, the Soviet Union, and the six countries of eastern Europe, excluding only Albania and Yugoslavia. COMECON has made an attempt to rationalize trade among its members, but this has been very difficult to achieve. The main problem is that central planning is a major facet of all these nations' economies, and foreign trade has usually been held subservient to the domestic goals of the national plan. Exports have often been thought of as surpluses unnecessary for the requirements of the plan, while imports have been viewed as a way to avoid planning bottlenecks. Pricing has been especially difficult. Prices in all these countries are fixed by a planning agency to a large extent, rather than established by supply and demand on the world market. Pricing has thus become a matter of delicate bilateral negotiation, often at the ministerial level. Currency problems have also given difficulties, as neither the ruble nor the other currencies (Polish zloty, Hungarian forint, and so on) are traded internationally. "Transferable rubles" are now used as the unit of account of such trade, these rubles not really existing except as an artificial yardstick with which to measure the value of bundles of goods exchanged. Hence, if the Soviet Union sends oil to Poland in exchange for tractors, the transaction is ordinarily to establish the tons of oil and the quantity of tractors first, then to place a "transferable ruble" value on them, and then to credit the accounts of the country that exported the greater value with a net ruble balance. But these rubles cannot be spent in the normal way. Another bargain involving goods must be struck before the ruble balance can be expended.

Prices in trade among COMECON members have been the subject of many disputes, focusing on complaints that the Soviet Union charges higher prices to members for its raw material exports than it does to the outside world. But this question of unfairness is not an easy one to resolve, given the system's reliance on arbitrary prices not fixed by market forces. COMECON's progress has been slow.

East-West Trade

It is appropriate to consider at this point "East-West trade," the term used to describe commerce between the communist (East) and the market (West) economies. This commerce is sufficiently different both in background and in structure to require special attention.

Two significant points about East-West trade stand out, one historical, the other theoretical: (1) For the biggest Communist nations, trade is not now, nor has it ever been, an important part of GNP; (2) Western trade theories and legislation are based on concepts of cost alien to the theory and practice of the communist states.

Historically, trade between today's Eastern countries and the rest of the world was relatively small even before communism. When Peter the Great opened Russia to the West in the early 1700s, foreign trade expanded ten times, but from extremely low levels. Peter set the future for Russian imperial policy with very high tariffs and an intensely national program of protection in which serfdom spread to industry and many of Russia's machines were manned by drafted labor. By 1891 Russia had a prohibitive tariff against many manufactured goods. Soviet policy, particularly under Stalin, favored industrial autarchy even more strongly. The volume of Soviet foreign trade in 1928 was less than half its 1913 level, falling further to only about a quarter of the 1913 level by 1938. The 1913 level was not attained again until the 1960s.

Albania, most of Yugoslavia, Bulgaria, and Romania were well into the nineteenth century part of the economically stagnant Turkish Empire. Poland was largely part of Russia; Hungary and Czechoslovakia (part of the Austrian empire) were the only areas much involved in trade at all. None of these countries, of course, became communist until after the Second World War.

China's experience with trade was unfavorable, to say the least. The largely self-contained dynasties had not one-tenth the interest in foreign goods that the "foreign barbarians" had in theirs. The Chinese bought some furs, some mechanical items, and considerable amounts of silver specie. (China was then on the silver standard.) One thing the Chinese did like, however, was opium. Recognizing the difficulties of opium, the Manchu Dynasty had forbidden its sale in 1729, but imports of the drug rose steadily with the connivance of corrupt officials and British merchants who shipped it from India to Portuguese Macao. There they bought tea, silk, and cotton goods in return for silver specie and opium. When the Manchu government took vigorous action to halt the trade in 1839, the British went to war. China lost this first Opium War of 1839-1844 and trade in opium continued and flourished as the British had taken the occasion to seize Hong Kong as their new port of entry. China lost a second Opium War in 1856-1860, and, as a condition of settlement, was forced to legalize the drug trade. Shipments of the highly addictive and debilitating drug were not curtailed until the present century. In the meantime, the political disintegration and disorganization that occurred in the latter days of the Manchu Dynasty, and the chaotic conditions that followed its collapse, served to restrict the growth of both the Chinese economy and trade.

In Europe, trade revived to some degree in the inter-war period, but the Great Depression, World War II, and the ensuing Cold War left little room for growth. The Soviet Union was embargoed in 1947, China in 1949, and most of the Eastern European countries in the same period. Trade from that point on required the approval of Western governments on a deal-by-deal basis. Then the Korean conflict turned Cold War to freeze, and East West trade as a percentage of world trade shrank from a small 2.6 percent to half that, 1.3 percent, between 1948 and 1952.

With the partial thawing of Cold War tensions in the 1960s, trading restrictions—particularly those of the Western European countries—were relaxed. The communist countries, China excepted, also showed more of an interest in trade.[11] By the end of 1970 such trade had reached 2.9 percent of world trade, just above the 1948 level. By 1975 the figure hit 5 percent, $48.8 billion in all, and the annual growth rates (30.8 percent in imports, 22.8 percent in exports to and from seven Eastern countries, 1971-1975) are among the most dynamic ever recorded.

Unfortunately for the East, exports have not grown as rapidly as imports. One of the chief difficulties in such trade is a chronic balance of trade deficit for the East, made worse when recessions strike the West, because then Western imports decline while imports to the East are stable or grow because their planned economies are not subject to the same cycle. Financing the deficit has been up to now a matter of Soviet exports of newly mined gold, and large grants of credit (rising from $2 billion early in the 1970s to $20 billion by the end of 1976) by Western banks. Eastern countries have traditionally tried diligently to maintain their credit ratings with prompt payment of outstanding bills and scrupulous attention to the liquidation of loans. In this they have been largely successful, with the exception of North Korea, which has defaulted on loans.[12]

There are undoubted obstacles to the growth of East-West trade. Many special restrictions on imports from the East still exist in the West, including refusal by the United States to grant most-favored-nation treatment to the Soviet Union. But such obstacles are rather mild compared to the difficulty encountered in exporting *to* the East. How to enter the market, how to service products once they are sold, how to get and keep in touch directly with sellers, how to compete with prices when prices are largely fixed, how to overcome the problems of strict currency inconvertibility? These are the problems for the manager in East-West trade. The degree of difficulty differs among countries. The Soviet Union, East Germany, and Bulgaria give priority to the planned output in the national plan, with international trade then serving as a residual—further needs can be imported, surplus output can be exported.

Hungary and Poland are more liberal: A Hungarian firm with a license to import can actually use foreign currency and make many of its own decisions on what to import, subject only to the approval of the Technical Ministry, and over 30 percent of Hungary's foreign trade is now with the West. Yugoslavia, as we shall see, is a special case; its dinar is convertible, and its worker-managed firms are free to import or export as the market moves them, or to join with Western firms in production and trade.

In the 1970s, new forms of East-West trade have rapidly developed. The old barter arrangements (wheat for petroleum products, trucks for sugar) and payment in gold or hard currency seem old-fashioned now. The new methods take a good deal of bargaining, often initiated at one or another of the international trade fairs such as the famous one at Leipzig in East Germany. Their forms are as follows:

1. Licenses are granted by a Western firm to an Eastern producer, along with technical help. The Eastern firm pays by shipping to the West a portion of the good manufactured under the license.

2. Complete factories are delivered by a Western company to the East, paid for as in (1) above by a portion of the goods manufactured by the new factory. These buy-back arrangements are now most common between West Germany and the Soviet Union, and they are massive. For example, in chemicals, Montedison's eleven new chemical plants in the Soviet Union will be paid for with 250,000 tonnes of ammonia per year; ICI and Klockner will be paid about 300,000 tonnes per year of methanol starting in 1981.

3. Coproduction is undertaken, with one partner (the Western one, almost always) furnishing the technology, research and development done jointly, each participant reserving its home market for itself and with the markets shared in other countries.

4. Participation by a Western firm takes place in an Eastern firm. This is most common in Yugoslavia, less so in Hungary and Romania, still rare in Poland and Czechoslovakia, and almost nonexistent elsewhere. In Yugoslavia, for example, the basic law of 1967, amended in 1971, guarantees against expropriation or nationalization, and allows foreign ownership to reach 49 percent. The Western participant is legally entitled to repatriate 33 percent of the profits in hard currency to the home country, and the 1971 law abolished the requirement that at least 20 percent of profits had to be reinvested in the firm. As of 1974, there were eighty joint enterprises, the biggest involving Italy's Fiat, the second biggest East Germany's I.G. Farben. Befitting Yugoslavia's maverick status, any Eastern participant in a Yugoslav firm must cough up hard currency to do so. Some Yugoslavian enterprises have quite a stable of foreign participants.

Take, for example, Genex, which not only runs the Communist world's only private airline (Avia Genex) but works jointly with General Electric, Monsanto, British Leyland Motors, and Goodyear Tires.

Finally, there is a very new idea of cooperating in the joint building of enterprises for the underdeveloped countries of the Third World. Active in this have been Poland (low-cost labor), Yugoslavia (intermediate technology), Romania (petroleum-based industry and mining), and Czechoslovakia (dependable technology in chemicals and electrical equipment). Nearly two-thirds of such joint projects have been established in the Middle East and North Africa, with India also an important target.

As a percentage of their total trade, East-West exchange is now significantly more important for the Communist nations than for the West. By 1975, COMECON exports to the West made up 22 percent of their total exports, while imports from the West were 30 percent of their total imports. East-West trade by value is far less important for the West: In 1975, it accounted for 6 percent of France's exports, 5.8 percent for Italy, 9 percent for West Germany, 2.9 percent for Great Britain, 1.5 percent for the United States, and 3.7 percent for Japan. One must not exaggerate the size of the trade even for the East. The *total* exports for COMECON were lower in 1975 than those of West Germany alone, and the Soviet Union's foreign trade is only about 4 percent of the world's, about the same as for the Netherlands. But it must also be said that East-West exchange from the West's point of view is often in the critical areas of raw materials and energy. Take, for example, the list of Soviet projects with the West due for completion in or before 1981-1982. Included in that list are $3.5 billion in petroleum and natural gas, $2 billion in chemicals, and $2 billion in uranium for nine Western countries. Soviet exports to the United States are overwhelmingly (83.1 percent in 1974) nonferrous metals and petroleum products; the traditional caviar, vodka, and fur coats take a distinct back seat. The largest joint project between the Soviet Union and the United States is in energy. Called "North Star," it involves natural gas produced in north-central Siberia: 3.2 billion cubic feet per day (equal to 10 percent of the natural gas used in New York, Pennsylvania, and New England) is to be exported from the new port of Peehengue north of Murmansk on the Arctic Ocean to Deptford, New Jersey, where it will be distributed by a U.S. consortium of Tennessee Gas, Texas Eastern, and Brown and Root. Of the $8.2 billion cost of this immense twenty-five-year project, the greater part is being financed by American private banks and the government's Eximbank.

By contrast to this rapid growth of trade among many of the Eastern countries and the West, China's trade is still extremely limited, less than 1 percent of world imports and exports, which is less than South Korea's, and less even than Taiwan's. It is as if the Manchu dynasty's initial total lack of interest in "foreign baubles" (as imports were called in an imperial letter to

King George III nearly 200 years ago) and its century of unhappy memories dating from the Opium Wars have made antipathy to trade a permanent part of Chinese thought. As of 1978, China's trade totaled just over $13 billion, but negotiations on a whole series of important new trade agreements also began that year.

Nowadays China's main Western partner is Japan. The new 1978 Sino-Japanese trade pact, an eight-year deal, calls for Chinese oil and coal to be exchanged for complete factories and construction equipment, particularly tractors and bulldozers. Trade with the United States is especially small; in 1977 it equaled only about 8 percent of Japan's total. Chinese trade with the West is unlikely to surpass that of South Korea or even Taiwan for some years to come.

It is safe to conclude that East-West trade will continue to grow unless politics intervenes. Even the United States, slower than West Germany, France, and other European countries to encourage such trade, granted most-favored-nation treatment to Hungary in 1978. Yugoslavia and Poland have had MFN treatment for a long time, and Romania got it in 1974. For several years, Congress has linked MFN to emigration policy and human rights in general, and there was a brouhaha in 1978 when President Carter stopped a Sperry-Rand computer sale to the Soviets in protest against the conviction and sentencing of several Soviet dissidents.

The growing size of East-West trade presents a number of difficulties because of the very uncertain relation of cost to price in communist systems. Marxist theory, based on the labor theory of value, does not allow for returns to capital or land. Used indiscriminately, the theory can lead to underpricing of capital-intensive goods. Soviet exports of oil in the 1950s, for instance, have been linked with an undervaluation of the capital used in the development of the oil fields. Most communist nations—particularly the Eastern European ones—are generally more careful in their use of capital, recognizing its scarcity at least, but the costing of capital remains very difficult in nations wedded to the labor theory of value.

More serious, perhaps, are the pricing errors that occur as goods pass through a state-controlled distribution system from one state corporation to another. As has been noted even of large vertically integrated American corporations, where the problem is generally on a smaller scale (see Chapter 16), pricing becomes a matter more of bargaining and politics than of expressing costs. With tightly controlled exchange rates (generally overvalued), the correspondence between domestic and foreign prices is distorted. As a result, the prices quoted for export markets—or the bargaining terms decided on—may appear considerably lower than prices in domestic markets.

If prices do not represent costs, does East-West trade improve world welfare? Suppose the Soviets consistently undervalue their capital. Resultant trade would encourage more wasteful use of capital in the Soviet Union and, by depressing the price of capital in the West, a heavier use of Western labor than optimal allocation would suggest. In turn, world production would be lower than it could be.

Note in this situation that the goods and services available to Western nations increase. It is the lower price of Soviet goods that enables the Westerners to get more for their goods through trade than they could get at home. The East, however, unaware of its error in pricing, would pay a penalty in reduced goods and services available to it, as costly and scarce capital was mistakenly devoted to securing goods through trade. (It is not that trade itself is bad, but that the wrong goods are traded.) The key factor, then, in assessing the gains from East-West trade is the quality of the East's pricing. If we assume the East knows what it is doing and can reasonably expect benefits from trade, then we can assume that East-West trade improves world welfare. If we believe that the Eastern bloc is generally erroneous in its pricing than we might well suspect that trade does not bring any net gains for the world.

While East-West trade brings gains for the West, whether or not it improves the lot of the East, it may not be acceptable for other valid political-economic reasons. The Western manufacturer hurt by imports from the East may be able legitimately to claim protection from dumping. Russian fish trawlers operating off the Pacific coast of North America are willing to process fish caught by American fishermen at prices considerably below what American processors can charge. Clearly, this would free American capital from fish processing and increase goods and services available in the United States. But, by American standards of fair competition—and American law—firms are not to be driven out of business through cut-throat price discrimination or subsidies of governments. Thus, although this process is beneficial from the point of view of providing a gain to trade, there is still a question of whether the United States should allow its processors to lose out to Soviet competition when that competition is on a basis that would ordinarily be considered unfair and illegal in domestic trade. This is a difficult problem to resolve and could be a major block in the further development of East-West trade.

Notes

1. The EEC was an outgrowth of the drive for European unity in the dark days following World War II. Led by Jean Monnet of France, who is often called the father of the Common Market, the drive led first to the formation of ECSC in 1951. ECSC involved the six original Common Market members in a customs union covering coal and steel only. Another forerunner of the EEC was Euratom, the organization devoted to atomic energy development. Finally, the EEC was preceded by the Benelux union, a full customs union set up to cover Belgium, the Netherlands, and Luxembourg. The Benelux union remains in effect, and in some ways has stronger bonds than the EEC itself, as seen in the abortive attempt in the 1970s to keep the Benelux currency exchange rates closer to one another than required by the EEC's snake.

2. In the EEC, the establishment of the common external tariff by the original six members took ten years (1958-1968) to accomplish. The external tariff raised West German and Benelux barriers, because these countries originally had relatively low tariffs, and lowered the high French and Italian tariffs. The effect on outsiders was very different, depending on whether they traded more with the former four countries or the latter two.

3. The agreement under which the Russians removed their occupation army from Austria stipulated that Austria should not join in close alliances of the EEC sort. Finland, similarly, feels constrained to bow to Soviet wishes on such matters.

4. In 1973-1977, the tariff-cutting process was carried on again for the EEC's three new members, with tariffs falling in five steps. The target for internal free trade was achieved on July 1, 1977. The EEC's common external tariff, now in full effect, averages 9 percent on industrial goods.

5. On July 1, 1977, tariffs between EFTA and the EEC were eliminated with the exceptions noted in the text. These are to disappear in the 1980s.

6. This war is worth remembering for its novelty value. It started over a disputed soccer game, and hence was called in English the "Soccer War." It presented airplane buffs with their first and presumably only opportunity to see the two greatest American World War II fighters, the Navy's F4U Corsair and the Army Air Force's P-51 Mustang, in action against one another (Honduras' Corsairs won). Last (and apparently least in the opinion of newspaper writers, who hardly thought it worth mentioning), it effectively dismembered the CACM.

7. This case cannot be shown with figures like Figs. 14.2 and 14.3, which show completely elastic supply curves for outside suppliers. More sophisticated models use supply curves with positive slopes. In such cases trade diversion may be only partial as costs rise in Y and fall in Z. In the Spanish example, one must consider the additional element that the Spanish supply curve to any one nation or group of nations is only part of that nation's supply curve, and is therefore flatter. When, however, the lone outsider faces the same tariff everywhere, its supply curve is just as steep as with a two-country world.

8. Adverse dynamic effects might also be realized. An Italian firm protected by tariffs might set up in southern Italy. But when free trade is established with Germany, transport costs might force this firm to locate in northern Italy if it wants to export. Indeed, the EEC has taken steps to aid peripheral areas (southern Italy, Gascony and Brittany, western Ireland, and so on), which are termed development regions and are granted subsidized credit and other forms of assistance.

9. In his textbook *International Economics*, 2d ed. (New York: Harcourt Brace Jovanovich, 1975), Mordechai Kreinin gives a rough estimate of the money value of trade creation and diversion caused by the Common Market's enlargement through 1977. He suggests that the larger market will cause trade creation of about $5.3 billion and trade diversion of about $3.8 billion.

10. This case can be distinguished from the convex production possibility curve situation of Chapter 11. There, the production possibility frontiers were limited eventually by total specialization in either of the two goods represented. In the present case, any given combination of the two goods could be produced more efficiently in a larger market, hence the production possibility frontier, with whatever shape it has, will move outward.

11. A large conference on East-West trade was held in France in April 1977, under the sponsorship of the Association Internationale des Etudiants en Sciences Economiques et Commerciales. The papers of that conference have now been published under the title *Le Commerce Est-Ouest* (Angers, 1977), and the information provided there has been especially helpful in the writing of this section of the chapter. Lina Veilleux of Colby College helped in translating the book for the authors. Readers might also consult J. Wilczynski, *The Economics and Politics of East-West Trade* (New York: Praeger, 1969); P. J. D. Wiles, *Communist International Economics* (London: Oxford University Press, 1968), and V. N. Bandera and Z. L. Melnyk, *The Soviet Economy in Regional Perspective* (New York: Praeger, 1973).

12. One facet of this credit has been the extension of loans eastward by the Eurocurrency market. Recently Eurocurrency loans to the East were 14 percent of all operations in that market. The duration of bank loans to the East is usually 5 to 6 years (Euromark loans commonly extend for 10 years); often these loans are guaranteed by the Western governments and supplemented by government credits, with France currently the largest supplier of direct credits.

INDUSTRIAL STRUCTURE
AND TRADE

15

THE INTERNATIONAL ECONOMICS OF IMPERFECT COMPETITION

In contrast to introductory economics, international economics has generally been little concerned with the nature of the competitive structure, and has usually treated monopoly, oligopoly, and monopolistic competition as peripheral matters. To some extent, this lack of interest is justified. Unlike the monetary and national income models, microeconomic models do not need to be modified to fit international situations. They can be more or less lifted whole, without special discussion. Even so, the role of imperfect competition in international economics is certainly great. There are probably several monopolies, certainly a number of oligopolies, even cartels, and a great number of firms that could be described as monopolistic competitors. Hence this chapter examines the important international aspects of imperfect competition, as well as the international aspects of antitrust regulation. It also examines another question of fundamental theoretical importance. Given that under imperfect competition costs are not the same as prices, how do we handle all the comparative advantage theory that assumes that they are? Do we modify our stance on the benefits of free trade?

Monopoly and Monopsony

Pure monopoly, like pure competition, is more an ideal concept than a model of reality. Every product has some sort of competition, both in the sense of competition for "the consumer's dollar" and in the availability of imperfect substitutes. Indeed, it can be argued that some of the examples given here are closer to monopolistic competition than to monopoly, because of the availability of substitutes. Nonetheless, there are some important lessons to be learned by examining the hypothetical monopolist and the monopolistic elements involved in actual situations.

Perhaps the closest thing we have to a monopoly today is in diamonds. There are synthetic diamonds used, particularly in industry, and other gems are also available. But few would deny that the prestige and the unique quality of the real diamond give it an untouchable place in the market. The company that sells 85 percent of the diamonds in the world is deBeers of South Africa. Ten times a year, deBeers packs up its diamonds in bags, each labeled at a certain price ($20,000, $50,000, and so on). Buyers may examine the bags and the contents—and within they find a mixture of uncut diamonds of varying qualities. A buyer either pays the price or leaves without buying; no haggling, no alternatives. If the price of diamonds goes up, this means that poorer diamonds are put in the bag, but deBeers generally doesn't raise the prices of the bags.

Few firms are as privileged as deBeers. Generally monopolies require enforcement by governments, few of whom are willing to do so. A glance over the history of monopolies will show this. A great deal of European trade with the rest of the world was begun on a monopoly basis. The establishment of good stable trading links with overseas areas involved considerable expense. To be sure, a ship could be outfitted and filled with trading goods to call at some distant port—and indeed such was characteristic of much sixteenth-century trade. But as trade grew, a need developed to have permanent trading posts, known as "factories." (One still speaks of factoring in the financial market in referring to trading assets.)

Factories needed regular supplies, personnel, and generally some military protection, all of which made them expensive. Money for the establishment of factories would flow forth only if the crown itself was interested, as the Spanish Crown was, or if the crown would grant the company monopoly rights to trade. Even with such privileged status, a company would spend large sums opening up trade only to find that "interlopers" followed in its path and lowered its return. Both the British East India Company and the Dutch East India Company for many years claimed exclusive rights, although beset at times by such private traders. The same was true of the still extant Hudson's Bay Company, which claimed a monopoly over much of northern Canada from 1670 to 1869, and of several other similar firms.

But what did it mean to have a monopoly? Generally it meant that ships from the company's own nation could not be outfitted to trade in the areas of monopoly, but that was no guarantee of protection. Any ship captain once at sea could turn his vessel anywhere—and captains did so with frequency. Other "interlopers" simply set up their own operations outside the reach of the monopolist or under the protection of some local ruler. An Englishman known as "Siamese White," for instance, constantly challenged the British East India Company's monopoly as he operated under the supposed protection of the Thai king. Nor could the company always defend itself against other nations seeking a monopoly. Malacca, on the Malay coast, and key to the only safe passage from India to China, changed hands from a native kingdom to the Portuguese in 1511, to the Dutch in 1648, and to the English in 1795. In Canada, the Hudson's Bay Company was raided sporadically by the French until late in the eighteenth century, and also suffered from the rivalry of fur traders coming up the inland routes.

What, then, did monopoly mean? In general in the East Indies, the Europeans had to pay at least "market prices" in the context of a vigorous trade among the various oriental kingdoms themselves. Since Europeans did not bid directly against one another, there were elements of monopsony—sole purchasers tending to keep prices lower than they might otherwise be. Matching the limited monopsony was also a limited monopoly in the home nation—no other companies were supposed to be bringing those products from the same part of the world. Thus while no other company could bring furs to London from the Hudson Bay area, furs could be brought from Russia, or from Montreal.

A more recent venture serves to illustrate further the problems of international monopolies. United Fruit, now United Brands, established itself in Central America in 1899. Up to that time, the shipping of bananas had been a rather haphazard operation of ships pulling into small ports and buying whatever happened to be available. "Unifruit" was anxious to sell bananas throughout the United States, and to do so needed a regular supply of quality controlled fruit. To achieve this, the company established its own plantations (draining unused lowland areas) and built ports, railway lines, and communication facilities. Occasionally, though not as often as some of its harsher critics suggest, the company resorted to violent tactics to oust competitors. The result was that Unifruit ended up with a monopoly over the sale of bananas in the United States and a monopsony over the purchase of bananas in Central America. Its critics saw it as *El Pulpo*—the Octopus—controlling every important aspect of the economies of Guatemala and Honduras.[1]

These combined monopoly-monopsonies (which one wag once called, but was never again able to pronounce, "monopolopsonies") present some interesting analytical problems and may serve as the foundation for further discussion of other forms of imperfect competition. Monopoly theory demonstrates that the firm will hold supplies back from the market in order to keep the price up. Marginal revenue equals marginal cost at a point which always lies below the demand curve (Fig. 15.1).

There is a parallel phenomenon on the monopsony side. Rather than buying according to the average revenue product, as one would under pure competition, monopsonists recognize that their own purchases drive up the cost of supplies and hence pay attention to the marginal revenue product, stopping where marginal revenue product equals marginal cost. This point is above the *S* curve (Fig. 15.2).

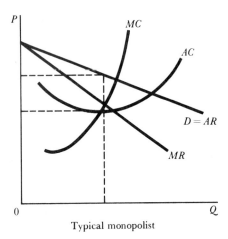

Typical monopolist   **FIGURE 15.1**

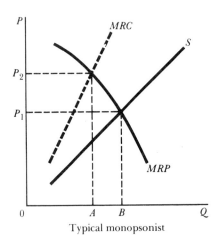

Typical monopsonist   **FIGURE 15.2**

The allocative and income effects of this monopoly-monopsony can perhaps be best shown on a diagram that shows the demand and supply without the cluttering marginal curves. We may even consider this more realistic because monopolists are rarely able to calculate their marginal costs and revenues with any precision. What we show, then, is a "quota" imposed on the market by monopolists such that their costs do not rise to meet their prices and they retain their economic profit (Fig. 15.3).

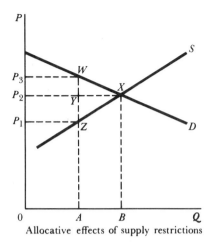

Allocative effects of supply restrictions   **FIGURE 15.3**

The diagram shows two important things: (1) The profit of the monopolist is P_1P_3WZ. (2) The misallocative effects are represented by the triangle WXZ. They can be explained in this way. $0A$ would be produced and $0A$ would be consumed, so those resources are allocated correctly. Potential suppliers of AB, however, are not asked to produce because the monopolist does not want those additional goods. The potential suppliers, accordingly, have to make or grow something else (for example, corn instead of bananas), which is not as profitable. The supply curve shows us that those producers just to the right of Z have rather poor alternatives, since they would sell to the monopolist at a price just above P_1. In contrast, producers just to the left of X would need a major price incentive of just under P_2 before they would supply the monopsonist. This reflects the valuable alternative uses for their resources. The misallocative effects due to higher supply costs are therefore the triangle YXZ.

A similar exercise shows the loss that occurs through misallocated purchasing decisions. Take the example of the effects of an oil monopolist. Consumers just to the left of X are almost neutral between coal and oil, so the high price of oil causes them only some slight problems as they shift from coal. Consumers just to the right of W, however, find oil much more convenient but still feel compelled to buy coal. That decision to buy coal accordingly induces coal mines to so provide it to consumers, despite the fact that the amount of resources needed to satisfy them with oil are fewer. Hence the cost of the misallocated purchasing decision is the triangle WYX.

Figure 15.3 can also be used to show what happens when producers get together to bargain against the "monopolopsonist." First, note that the monopolist's restriction on the market creates, in essence, a "rent" that the monopolist collects. One can speak of a rent on a piece of land meaning that all the money paid to use the land can be removed and the land will still be there. Note in Fig. 15.3 that above Z and below W the same situation prevails: No matter what price between W and Z producers and buyers settle on, the quantity supplied and that demanded are unchanged. Hence WZ represents a rent.

Now, the suppliers recognize the price discrepancy between what they are paid (P_1) and what the monopolist is getting (P_3) and would like to obtain a piece of the rent for themselves. To do so, they must seek power against this monopsonist. Workers create labor unions; agricultural suppliers create producers' associations. Often the government steps in to help local suppliers, a move that is particularly likely if the buyer (like United Fruit) is a foreign company, exercising its monopoly on foreign consumers and its monopsony on domestic producers. Thus arises what Galbraith called "countervailing power." Others call it "bilateral monopoly."

The interesting thing about countervailing power is that it does not move to a "free competition" solution. On the contrary, the monopolistic position of the international company can be used to the advantage of the suppliers. As the latter increase their powers, they can bid the price of the products all the way up to P_3 before the international firm would start to run a loss. Hence the monopolist's profits become a prize over which both the suppliers and the international firm battle. The ultimate price can range anywhere from P_1 to P_3. Galbraith suggested in his discussion of countervailing power that prices would come out close to P_2, the free market equilibrium price. Note, though, that a price of P_2, however fair or satisfactory it may be to the bargaining parties, does not end the economic misallocation. The triangle WXZ remains, and both the ultimate consumers and the excluded suppliers still suffer losses. All that happens is that the monopolist and a limited number of suppliers share in the spoils.

Oligopoly and Cartels

The idea of monopolistic rent developed above leads directly into a discussion of oligopoly and cartelization. The oligopoly model, the reader may recall, demonstrates that members of an industry in which there are few firms generally eschew price competition. Because of the likelihood of retaliation for price cuts, a kinked demand curve emerges. For each firm, the "kink" is at the industry price, though the volume sold may differ. Any increase in price will not be imitated by competitors and will consequently lead to a sharp decline in sales. But any decrease will be copied and lead to no expansion of market share and little if any expansion of total industry sales. The diagram is usually shown for only one firm, but for present purposes it is best to examine the entire industry as shown in this "triopoly" of Fig. 15.4.

The three firms shown all charge the same price, though each has a different market share and a different cost structure. Typically, the largest producer is shown with the lowest cost, though this need not always be the case. The effect of the oligopoly is to impose a fixed market price of $0P$. With a given demand curve, this creates the same "rent" situation discussed earlier. The industry demand curve is shown as a summation of the three demand curves below the kink (when it is assumed all will move together). This line is then projected above the kink to indicate where the demand might be if the three firms also raised their prices together. (The diagram, of course, assumes that they only lower their prices together.) We show no supply curve for reasons developed below.

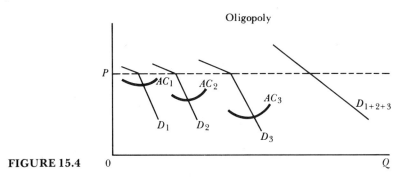

FIGURE 15.4

Under price competitive conditions, firm 3 would take an even greater share of the market. It would lower prices, but see its costs rise. As its costs rose and with that its prices, firm 2 might eventually be enticed to enter, and perhaps later firm 1. Thus the rising price level would "turn on" each firm as it became economical for it to produce. Oligopoly, however, does not work that way. Firm 3 tolerates the less efficient firm 1 because it wants the price of $0P$, and that high price has induced firm 1 to enter. It is true that firm 3 could eliminate firm 1, but to do so it would have to lower its prices below $0P$, and take that loss all across its production. It therefore tolerates the loss in market share. Such a high price, because it protects the less efficient firm from the rigors of international competition, is called an "umbrella price."

Cartels differ from oligopoly in that there is a formal agreement on price and market share. Rather than depending on the threat of a price war to discourage price cutting, the oligopolists draw up some rules. Hence our cartel diagram in Fig. 15.5 dispenses with all demand curves and simply portions out the market shares. In addition to fixing prices and market shares, the cartel must also prevent "cheating" by high-cost producers who use the umbrella price to sell larger amounts of their products. The latter can be especially galling to low-cost producers who find that, to keep prices stable, they must cut back their own production, as we demonstrate.

In Fig. 15.5 we show just two members of the OPEC oil cartel, Saudi Arabia, a low-cost producer, and Ecuador, one of the higher-cost producers.

If Ecuador seeks to expand its share of the market from $0A$ to $0B$ and Saudi Arabia seeks to hold the price at $0P$, Arabia ends up decreasing its production from $0D$ to $0C$. It could, of course, drive Ecuador back to a production of $0A$ by lowering price to $0P_1$, but the loss encountered in so doing (PP_1 times the volume $0D$) exceeds the loss in market share. Clearly, Saudi Arabia would want to reach some accommodation with Ecuador and Ecuador can only push so far.

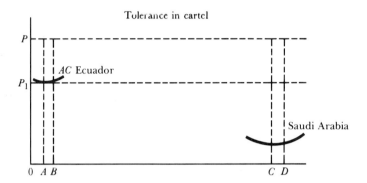

FIGURE 15.5

To have a successful cartel, producers must agree on market shares. Otherwise, the low-cost producer drives the others out of business but does not enjoy the benefits of a high rent while doing so. The process by which agreement is reached is a political one, not an economic one. In the old days in the oil industry it was the producing companies that made the decision. The decision, incidentally, was never so neat an example of collusion as some might believe. There were, however, very important elements of outright collusion.

In 1928, the presidents of Exxon (then Standard Oil of New Jersey), Royal Dutch Shell, and British Petroleum went grouse hunting together on a Scottish estate. Amid such innocent conviviality, the three men decided to leave world market shares as they were. This became known as the "As Is" agreement. In addition, a base point pricing system was set up in which all crude oil prices were based on the price in Gulf of Mexico ports plus freight charges. Even if oil from Iran were to be delivered to Greece, its price would be figured on the basis of what it would have cost to buy oil at a Gulf port and ship it there. Hence there was no incentive for price wars. In addition, several agreements were devised for controlling the companies' shares of key oil fields. The Texas Railway Commission was given the authority to regulate the East Texas field, which became a source of downward price pressure in the 1930s. The Iraqi fields were controlled by the Iraq Petroleum Company, which was made up of a number of U.S. and foreign companies that extracted oil according to their shares. Finally, in 1952, after Iran nationalized its oil fields but then turned their management back to the oil companies, a market share agreement was worked out for those fields. (Both the "As Is" and the Iranian deal remained secret for many years.) Thus if, for instance, Exxon pumped 10 percent less than the previous year, the whole of Iranian production might be down, say, 3 percent and all other firms would have to cut their quotas accordingly. Such agreements were occasionally broken, and the history of the industry has been characterized by confrontation and accommodation. As one maverick oilman put it, "Oilmen are like cats; you can never tell from the sound of them whether they are fighting or making love."[2]

The oil companies themselves were anxious to reduce their political risks and thus drew oil from both high- and low-cost fields. As a result, there has developed a kind of "grid," with (1) the low-cost *companies* not driving out the high-cost ones, and (2) the low-cost *countries* operating side by side with the high-cost ones. Even within low-cost countries there may be both high- and low-cost producers operating. The OPEC takeover of the oil cartel has not altered the basic questions. Now, instead of the companies deciding what the price is and what nation will produce what, it is the cartel itself that is supposed to make that decision. So far, OPEC has been efficient at deciding price, but the difficult question of assigning quotas has been handled less smoothly. Indeed, the oil companies still carry out much of that decision.

Handling the distortionary effects of a cartel is more difficult than handling those of a monopoly. The general principles are the same. The consumer pays a higher price, but it is difficult to define exactly where the supply curve would cross the demand curve. As we have shown, there is no single supply curve, but a montage of supply curves of individual producers, each operating under the umbrella price. Unlike the monopoly situation, where all the low cost production would be used first, the oligopoly uses both high- and low-cost production. Hence it is impossible to speak of *a* supply curve.

Other Oligopolies and Cartels

Petroleum is hardly the only cartel. There have been (and still are) numerous others. A short survey is worthwhile to try our model further.

Copper cartels have existed for brief periods, but have as a whole been unsuccessful. There were perhaps half a dozen attempts to hold price and market share over the last century. The cartel arrangements appeared to work for short periods, usually when demand was strong, but participants were reluctant to hold excess copper when demand fell off. Sooner or later one company would unload its surplus at the umbrella price—leaving its former cohorts holding a broken umbrella. The problem with copper stems from its general availability, from the low cost of processing (which encourages many smelters), and from the widespread existence of substitutes. It has thus been an extremely difficult industry in which to exercise market control.

In contrast, aluminum has approached the oligopoly model, but has never had or needed a formal cartel. Until 1945 there were only three aluminum producers—Alcoa, Allusuisse, and Pechiney. After the U.S. Justice Department broke up Alcoa in 1945, these firms were joined by Alcan, Kaiser, and Reynolds. Until that time, the processing of aluminum was controlled by patents, of which only two were recognized as legal. Because aluminum ore cannot be smelted but must be dissolved and separated electrolytically, it is highly capital intensive, discouraging entry of new firms. Refining costs are 10 percent of the cost of a bar of copper, but they are nearly 40 percent of the cost of a bar of aluminum. While the aluminum companies do compete—in service, in delivery, and in cost cutting—they rarely engage in head-on price competition.

Tin presents us with another case of relatively "successful" cartelization. Tin ore in commercial quantities is found today mainly in Malaya, Indonesia, and Thailand, where it is mined in large open pits, and in Bolivia, where it is mined in shafts and tunnels. Bolivian tin is considerably more expensive to extract (due both to the process and to the excessive number of miners), but the Southeast Asian producers tolerate high-cost Bolivian tin so that they can keep their umbrella price. Within each country, too, some low-cost operations are closed and some high-cost operations continue, so it fits our model nicely. Three major factors have led to the success of the tin ore cartel: (1) The demand for tin is highly inelastic. Tin is a necessary but small ingredient in a number of items—notably tin cans, solders, and various alloys, including brass. The cost of tin in cans is a very small portion of the cost of canned food, and although it represents a large portion of the cost of electrical solders, it is only a tiny portion of the cost of electrical appliances. In addition, there are no substitutes for tin (although the use of tin in cans was cut to one-fifth of the old amount by an electroplating process developed during the Second World War, when the tin mines were largely in Japanese control). (2) Tin is not generally sold as a pure metal, and is rarely used that way. This has meant that the industry has been concentrated at the mining level, with little tug-of-war between mines and smelters. (3) There are relatively few large tin producers in each country, and the opening of any new tin mine, being capital intensive, is an occasional and well-known event. This has meant that each government can fairly easily control production within its own borders.

Agricultural production presents more difficulties in control than does mineral production. With few exceptions, agricultural production is spread among many producers. Nor does agriculture require as extensive financing. The capital invested tends to be of the kind that smallholders can generate themselves—the accumulation of seed, the growth of trees (initial planting of coffee may not be expensive, but every year the trees are larger and more valuable), draining, terracing, the leveling of land. Widespread production and easy entry complicate considerably the problems of maintaining any quotas. Yet the same factors make it socially important for governments to try to keep a steady and predictable price. The result is usually widespread but only partially effective government intervention.

We would move into much tangential material if we tried to describe the import quotas, the export taxes, and the government purchasing arrangements and target prices that proliferate in the agricultural sector. Nonetheless, one must understand agricultural "cartels" against this background. World prices in such situations often do not reflect costs. If the EEC buys wheat from its farmers at $3.00 a bushel and sells it at $1.50 a bushel, undercutting the North American price of $2.00, this does not mean that the EEC is a lower-cost producer than North America. It does mean that the taxpayers of the EEC are willing to subsidize a lot of wheat growing. Surely the governments want some consultation, and this may then lead to establishing world prices and quotas in an attempt to make some kind of political solution that at least takes some economics into account. Such consultation and arrangement have sprung up from time to time with wheat, sugar, and coffee. Anyone familiar with the roller coaster prices of those commodities, however, cannot be impressed with the ability of governments to maintain stable prices.[3] (The current attempts at cartelization are further described in Chapter 19.)

Cartels and oligopolies in manufacturing industries have been much more complex and have generally not survived the post-Second World War economic changes. There have been (and perhaps are still in secret) cartels in incandescent lamps, magnesium, synthetic rubber, explosives, and a number of chemicals.

The chemical cartel is perhaps the most important of these. In the 1920s and 1930s there was an informal understanding that DuPont or one or another American producer was to have the American market; Imperial Chemical Industries (ICI) was to have the British Commonwealth; and I.G. Farben, the European continent. (Canada was shared in a DuPont-ICI joint venture.) A series of complex licensing deals on patents assured this market arrangement. (The licenses would not allow production outside a stipulated area.)

One of the more unseemly consequences of these various licensing arrangements occurred with synthetic rubber. There were three processes for producing the product: butyl, being developed by Exxon's chemical division for its Atlas tires; buna, being developed by Germany's I. G. Farben; and neoprene, developed by DuPont. Butyl and buna processes could be combined to give a good rubber at low cost. Throughout the 1930s, I. G. Farben played off the two American companies against each other, finally making an agreement with Exxon for exchange of patent information. Exxon ended up telling I. G. Farben how to make butyl rubber in 1938 but did not get the buna patents until just before the U.S. entry into the war, when I. G. Farben knew the patents were lost anyway. Exxon planned to license its production in the

United States and charge a high fee. By that time, Exxon had become so stalled on its development of butyl rubber, waiting to get the buna process, that the United States could not produce the synthetic rubber needed for the war effort. (The Southeast Asia plantations, of course, were in Japanese hands.) In December of 1941 the U.S. government seized Exxon's buna patents and made them available for any American company to use at a nominal fee. Exxon was sued in court and did not contest the suit, paying fines for Clayton Act violations.

For one familiar with the rough-and-tumble, highly aggressive price competition in chemicals today, it seems amazing to see *Fortune*'s 1937 remarks on the chemical industry: "The chemical industry has seldom been bedeviled by overproduction, has had no private depressions of its own, and has not involved itself in long and bloody price wars. . . . By and large, the chemical industry has regulated itself in a manner that would please even a Soviet Commissar."[4]

What could have happened between then and now? (1) On the antitrust front, I.G. Farben was broken up into several firms by the Allies right after the war, while the U.S. Supreme Court broke a restrictive licensing pact between ICI and DuPont, as well as the earlier Exxon-I. G. Farben one. (2) Perhaps more fundamentally, the pace of technical change accelerated, particularly with petrochemicals, leading to rapid declines in costs and aggressive pricing. (3) The number of competitors increased with the growth of older firms (like Dow and Monsanto), and the diversification of nonchemical firms into chemicals (Kodak, W. R. Grace, and the major petroleum firms). (4) Finally, the lower transportation costs and the geographical dispersion of the producing facilities of each firm prevented any geographical division of the market.

Cartels and the Law

In Chapter 1 we noted that international economic rules allow a rougher game than do the domestic. This is apparent with antitrust laws, where, under a rule that is less than golden, it is proper to do unto foreign consumers what you do not do unto your own. The Sherman, Clayton, and Federal Trade Commission Acts in the United States protect U.S. consumers but they do not make it illegal to conspire against foreign consumers. Foreign antitrust legislation, most of it written after World War II, also protects consumers abroad, but foreign laws are not generally enforced very rigorously, nor do the laws prevent price fixing against foreign consumers.[5]

One example of the "Leaden Rule" above is the Webb-Pomerene Act of 1919, which allows U.S. corporations, under some rather restrictive conditions, to join together to exploit a foreign market. Thus Calso (Chevron) and Texaco have joined together to form Caltex, which sells gasoline in the Far

East; and Pet and Carnation formed the General Milk Co. for purposes of selling to Europe, undoubtedly reducing competition abroad. To balance this view of the Webb-Pomerene Act, it should be noted that courts have used its rather narrow definition of what mergers may be allowed for foreign market entry as the only circumstances under which such mergers are legal.

If, then, it is not illegal under British law for companies to join together to monopolize the American market, or vice versa, what defenses do nations have? Therein lies a tale involving the concept of *extraterritoriality*—those who use the word more than twice a day call it extrality. Extrality is the extension of domestic law beyond a nation's boundaries. An example is the law that used to prevent American citizens from holding gold while abroad, even when in countries where it was legal. (The word goes back to the "unequal treaties" with China in the nineteenth century, in which Westerners in China were tried according to Western, not Chinese, law.)

American law has seen a steady extension of antitrust law outside the U.S. jurisdiction. In 1909, the U.S. Supreme Court held that United Fruit was not guilty of monopoly under American law because the offenses occurred outside the United States. By 1927, in *U.S.* v. *Sisal Sales Corporation*, a suit almost parallel to the banana case, the Supreme Court declared the conspiracy to monopolize sisal (used for cordage and twine) illegal, even though all the sisal was produced abroad. This time the court noted that there was a strong "effect" within the United States and that there was some "act" in the United States (namely, its discussion). The key cases, however, came after the Second World War. In *U.S.* v. *National Lead Co.*, the court found a conspiracy in titanium pigments to be illegal, even though nothing took place in the United States, the grounds being only that its *effect* was felt in the United States. Similarly, in a case against Timken Roller Bearings, the Supreme Court said: "The fact that the cartel arrangements were made on foreign soil does not relieve the defendant from responsibility . . . they [the arrangements] had a direct influencing effect on trade."

The Clayton Act, similarly, has been extended overseas. Section 7 requires only that anticompetitive effects be felt within "a section of the country" and can accordingly be applied internationally. Perhaps the ultimate in extrality was reached, however, when a U.S. district court ordered the Swiss watchmakers to end all restrictive practices, not only against Americans, but against other nations as well. The Swiss government had to send lawyers to U.S. courts to argue its sovereignty. The United States, of course, could never enforce such a decree.

What happens if an agreement is legal under foreign law and illegal under American law? Are corporate leaders damned (or at least fined and imprisoned) if they do and damned if they don't? In breaking up the chemical cartel, a district court ordered ICI to retransfer British patents to DuPont for licensing, but the British court refused to carry out this order. The eventual decision, carried through to the U.S. Supreme Court, was that the United

States could not order the company to violate foreign law. To avoid potential conflicts, the United States has a number of treaties of "Friendship, Commerce, and Navigation," which contain clauses calling for consultation between the "High Contracting Parties" about any restrictive practices. There is also a consultation "procedure" (not a treaty) with Canada.

All of these laws govern private corporations. Where governments themselves are the cartel participants, as with OPEC, tin mining, or some agricultural products, there is not much the United States can do. No sovereign nation can sue another sovereign nation without the other's consent; moreover, that would be under international law, not U.S. law, and international law on antitrust is a matter of conjecture. The moral of this, if anything, is that it is probably not wise to form a cartel against U.S. consumers, unless you are a sovereign state, but your chances are better if you decide to restrict some other nation's commerce.

Monopolistic Competition

One of the best models for analyzing the behavior of international firms is not oligopoly, but monopolistic competition. This model, often described briefly in introductory texts, is important for understanding a number of aspects of international investment behavior (see next chapter), and for understanding trade (Chapter 11) and the flow of technology.

Monopolistic competition is a mixture of monopoly and competition. Edward Chamberlin, the Harvard economist who originated the theory, had been studying the "duopoly" (two sellers) problem, when he realized that the solution to the problem would depend on whether the products sold were identical or not. As his theory developed, he pointed to a basic weakness of most microeconomic models—the assumption that the products are identical. Automobiles, as he pointed out in the early 1930s, can be a Model A Ford or luxury Locomobile; they do not even compete with one another. What is more, manufacturers consciously try to make their products different. They practice product differentiation, so that each enjoys a rather limited (and sometimes considerable) monopoly. Yet this monopoly is weak. There are always competitors, sometimes in unrelated fields (the Locomobile competed with a trip to Europe), sometimes in related areas (it also competed with the Packard).

Firms create or enjoy their monopolistic position through a variety of means, which we can classify in two groups: those protected by law and those protected by market strength. We have already noted how Alcoa was protected by patents. But consider also the protection afforded such companies as IBM, GE, or RCA by their patents. Or consider the patent and trademark protection for Coca Cola, Kodak, or Xerox. Certainly all of these companies have competitors, but the competitors do not manufacture quite the same thing. With patents on processes, too, the companies have lower costs and undersell competitors.

Even without patent protection, firms can differentiate their products. This involves the creation both of real differences through market segmentation and of artificial differences through advertising. There are also substantial differences in service, delivery, and availability of products.

How, then, does monopolistic competition work? Returning to the idea of rent, we see that the "monopoloid" position allows the firm some freedom in pricing. A small change in price is unlikely to lose many customers; hence firms try to collect the rent on their patents or differentiated goods. They are limited, however, by the fact that there are many imperfect substitutes. If the local supermarket charges too high a price, the customer will go to the next town.

Chamberlin envisaged two possible processes occurring: (1) There would be price competition; or (2) Price would be held stable, but there would be nonprice competition. The price competition model may be familiar from first-year economics. As shown in Fig. 15.6, the firm has a demand curve of D and a cost curve of AC. Naturally, it restricts production to make an economic profit producing, suppose, at $0A$, hence collecting the rent YZ. Competitors, however, enter and engage in so much price competition that the firm's market share slips and the demand curve is driven back toward D_1. While the firm is still charging high prices, the lower volume causes costs to rise, and its rent declines. Finally, it ends up with no profits at all as the demand curve becomes tangential to the AC curve. The firm sells at $0P_1$, which is also its costs.

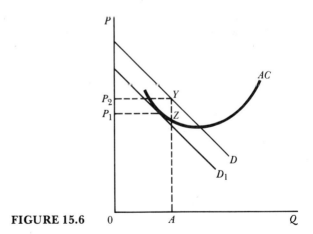

FIGURE 15.6

If price is held stable by, let us suppose, some cartel agreement, firms engage in nonprice competition. Nonprice competition is expensive—

advertising costs may rise, new product models or product proliferation cause factory costs to go up, better delivery and distribution systems are more expensive. The result is that the cost curve rises (and is here shown to shift to the right, reflecting the higher fixed costs of most of these measures).

In Fig. 15.7 we see this process. Firms increase nonprice competition in order to push out the demand to D_t (t for temporary). But competition responds with similar changes, and the demand falls back. In the meantime, average costs have increased. Eventually the AC curve ends up tangential to the demand curve. Any further change would drive the firm into a loss.

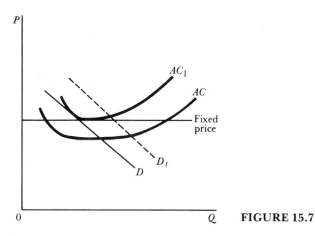

FIGURE 15.7

The "tangency" solution, as it has come to be known, characteristically leaves firms operating with excess capacity, but no profits. Chamberlin was careful to note, however, that in monopolistic competition not all firms have the same costs, so that at industrial equilibrium some firms would be left with economic profits, others with losses, and only some with the tangential position. The reader should also note that, though most first-year texts view monopolistic competition as something between oligopoly and pure competition containing many sellers, Chamberlin developed the model to handle product differentiation in oligopoly.

A good illustration of Chamberlin's second model—in which the AC curve moves—is found in the airline industry. The International Air Transport Association fixes fares and routes. To compete, the airlines characteristically increase the number of flights per day (since flight convenience is generally of great importance to the traveler), add features like movies, increase advertising, and try to reduce costs through adding more efficient (but often capacity-expanding) equipment. Thus "seat miles" increased very sharply with the introduction of jumbo jets on top of the already too-frequent flights, but passenger miles remained unchanged. Planes began flying half empty and airlines began losing money. No airline, however, could afford to do the two things that might have helped. If it cut back on routes, its market share would slip (demand moving to the left of *AC*) and total revenue would fall faster than total cost. If it cut price, it faced cartel action, or oligopolistic reaction.[6]

The monopolistic model is also closely related to the trade problems discussed in Chapter 11. Excessive market segmentation is characteristic of nonprice competition. Factories then are used inefficiently—not in the simple sense that total plant output is below some optimal level, but in the sense that the production lines, tools and dies, and the like, are not used fully. This can be seen in the diagrams of Chapter 11. The *AC* curve moves upward and also to the right, reflecting the added fixed costs involved in product proliferation. If advertising is handled as a fixed cost, it too moves the *AC* curve the same way.

Imperfect Competition and Trade Theory

Most international economic theory is based on pure competition assumptions; yet as we have seen, little if any trade actually occurs under those conditions. We have already noted how imperfect competition modifies the Marshall-Lerner problem. More basic perhaps is its relation to comparative advantage. Comparative advantage requires price to equal both the cost of making the product and the "utility" achieved by the user, and this is not true under oligopoly or monopoly. Is free trade still "a good thing" under these conditions?

Most economists would answer, "Yes, perhaps even more important," although they would reserve the right to make a number of exceptions. International trade itself increases competition, bringing in more sellers to each national market. This tends to increase the difficulties involved in oligopolistic control and in making "understandings." We have noted already how the chemical industry became more competitive in recent decades, due in part to the increased number of participants. Monopolistically competitive behavior has been changed also. To give one example, before imports of automobiles were highly significant in the American market, American car manufacturers had 375 different models and were changing basic styles every three years. With the pressure from imports, the American companies found their consumers less captive (they could not get much of a rent) and were forced to cut costs, looking for fewer models with fewer style changes. This can be seen on the monopolistic competition diagram. The increased number of competitors tends to flatten out the demand curve, indicating a greater sensitivity to price, and moving the point of tangency closer to the bottom.

On a worldwide scale, there also appears to be sure evidence of increasing competition. A recent British survey showed that concentration ratios (percentage of total output controlled by a given number of the largest firms) had declined markedly since the early 1960s.

The increase in competition created by international trade should help make prices reflect more accurately the costs of production. But even without the beneficial competitive effects, it is probable that a good deal of price distortion from imperfect competition is not sufficient to make freer trade cause resource allocation to become less efficient. Hence the cheaper goods that are exported and the dearer goods that are imported probably reflect the true economic cost—plus some rent. Unless the rents are excessively high (as with the oil industry), the traded goods are still those that would be traded under pure competition. Moreover, as noted in Chapter 11, the increased size of the market is especially beneficial under monopolistically competitive conditions because it allows economies of scale, even with much market segmentation.

Where, as with some of the cartels and monopolies discussed, rents are indeed quite high, or where, as with airlines, there are heavy government subsidies, freer trade is not necessarily going to improve economic efficiency. As we have seen in the discussion of cartels, a nation paying the umbrella price may be buying either low- or high-cost products. If some oil nation like Norway chose not to join OPEC and charged a lower price, the United States could end up paying $9.00 a barrel for oil that cost $5.00, instead of $10.00 for oil that cost $0.15. This tends to increase the "efficiency of consumption" (bringing the uses to which oil is put nearer to the cost of the resources to get it), while decreasing the efficiency of production (using up $4.85 more resources to produce the oil). Such results can end up with either a net increase or decrease in world welfare. (The analysis is akin to that of customs unions.)

Such situations present international economists with no easy solution. They recognize that the best solution is to have no restrictions on subsidies and to have free trade. Lacking the first prerequisite, however, they are unsure if freer trade is the "second best" solution. But second best solutions do not always come near to the first best. If you must cross a stream in the forest, jumping nine-tenths of the way across may not be second best. In many situations, the second best solution involves some attempts at government management. International political bargaining replaces economics to some extent. Thus IATA has meetings to decide international rates, the coffee-producing nations meet with the consuming nations, and the price of oil becomes a point of discussion between heads of state. The questions become exceedingly complicated; and, unable to leap the stream, one can get lost in the forest seeking the true second best solution.

Notes

1. Over the past two decades United Fruit has undergone many changes. The U.S. Department of Justice sued in the early 1950s for violation of antitrust laws, leading Unifruit to sell part of its operations to Del Monte. In addition, new banana-

producing lands have been opened in Ecuador. Finally, Unifruit itself sought to reduce its vulnerability to expropriation (and its heavy investment in land) by replacing land ownership and direct management with contractual arrangements with local sellers. Patterning its operation on food sellers in the United States, Unifruit made agreements with local landowners for the sales of banana plants, fertilizers, and insecticides in return for bananas of stipulated quality. It still remains true, however, that Unifruit's transportation lines and shipping routes do not allow for competitive buying.

    Literature on United Fruit is extensive. The classic "attack" on the company, still good reading, is *The Banana Empire* by Charles Kepner and Jay Soothill (New York: Vanguard Press, 1935). The classic defense is Stacy May and Galo Plaza, *The United Fruit Company in Latin America* (National Planning Assn., 1958). A more recent and balanced view of the world market for bananas is found in Jean-Paul Valles, *The World Market for Bananas* (New York: Praeger, 1968).

2. Literature on oil is also extensive. Anthony Sampson, *The Seven Sisters* (New York: The Viking Press, 1973) is a good, readable, though popular, account. John M. Blair, *The Control of Oil* (New York: Pantheon Press, 1973), Chapters 1-5, is a scholarly, but not detached, account of the cartel. See also George W. Stocking, Sr., *Middle East Oil* (Nashville, Tenn.: Vanderbilt University Press, 1970).

3. Cartelization schemes were also frequent in the natural rubber industry, beginning in the early 1920s. The invention of synthetic rubber, however, meant that the manufacturing cost of that substance, not the cost of the natural, tended to determine the price. To put it in a more jocular way, the invention of the synthetic caused the (demand) elasticity of the natural rubber to increase.

4. Quoted in George Stocking, Sr., and Myron Watkins, *Cartels in Action* (New York: Twentieth Century Fund, 1946), p. 396.

5. This discussion is drawn from the U.S. Tariff Commission's report to the U.S. Senate, "Implications of Multinational Firms for World Trade and Investment and for U.S. Trade and Labor," Report to the Committee on Finance of the U.S. Senate, February 1953 (U.S. GPO 5270-01708), pp. 820-867. A more accessible treatment of the topic is in Louis Turner, *Invisible Empires* (New York: Harcourt Brace Jovanovich, 1970) Chapter 4.

    Restrictive practices in the EEC area are controlled under two laws. Iron and steel practices are handled under Articles 60 and 65 of the European Coal and Steel Community Treaty. These are rather similar to U.S. Clayton Act rules. The EEC itself is controlled under Articles 85 and 86 of The Rome Treaty; there has been some enforcement of these provisions, including a noteworthy decision against Continental Can for "abusing" its dominant market position and thereby restricting competition. British competition has been covered by a Monopolies Commission (established 1948) and a Restrictive Trade Practices Act (1956), and now also by the EEC statutes.

    Canadian activities are controlled by the Anti-Combines Act, generally considered rather weak. Japanese antitrust legislation was drafted by the American Occupation Army. Promulgated in 1947, the "Act Concerning Prohibition of Private Monopoly" (a kind of combination Sherman and Clayton Act) was for years not vigorously enforced, and numerous laws were passed exempting cartels in various industries from the act. With the growth of consumerism in the 1960s, however, there has been more attention paid to the law's provisions.

6. As readers are no doubt aware, price competition was restored on the North Atlantic route in 1977. Many airlines did indeed drop the frills. The consumer was given a considerably wider range of choice. Rather to the airlines' surprise, demand for North Atlantic travel proved surprisingly price elastic. Total revenue, rather than falling, increased with heavier passenger traffic, while costs, largely fixed, increased much more slowly.

16

THE ECONOMICS OF THE MULTINATIONAL FIRM

Large international firms pose questions that deal not only with their mutual interaction, as discussed in the preceding chapter, but also with their internal dynamics. These questions are suggested in part by the size of foreign investment: Foreign direct investment (that is, investment where control is exerted) of the U.S. in 1976 was $137 billion. Foreign figures are less easily gathered, but it is safe to say that there are between $200 and $250 billion worth of foreign direct investment in the world today. To give an idea of its distribution, we show a UN estimate by country for 1971 in Table 16.1. Moreover, the vast bulk of this foreign direct investment is made by firms that are in themselves large, often dominant, in their home markets. Indeed, no more than two or three hundred firms account for almost all foreign direct investment, and the domestic holdings of these firms are generally larger than their foreign assets. Half of all American exports are shipped by these large firms (half of these shipments are made to their own subsidiaries) and a quarter of U.S. imports come through American international firms. Foreign figures are similar. These large firms, moreover, are more than just conduits for trade. They conduct both long- and short-term capital movements of considerable size and are probably the most important institutions for transferring advanced technology across borders.[1]

Again, the spirits of market imperfection come to haunt international trade theory, uneasy in its bed of pure competition assumptions. More questions arise. Does the existence of the MNF itself alter existing theories of re-

TABLE 16.1 MARKET ECONOMIES: STOCK OF FOREIGN DIRECT INVESTMENT, 1971 (book value)

Country	Millions of dollars	Percentage share
United States	86,001	52.0
United Kingdom	24,019	14.5
France	9,540	5.8
Federal Republic of Germany	7,276	4.4
Switzerland	6,760	4.1
Canada	5,930	3.6
Japan	4,480	2.7
Netherlands	3,580	2.2
Sweden	3,450	2.1
Italy	3,350	2.0
Belgium	3,250	2.0
Australia	610	0.4
Portugal	320	0.2
Denmark	310	0.2
Norway	90	0.0
Austria	40	0.0
Other	6,000	3.6
TOTAL	165,000	100.0

Source: United Nations, Department of Economic and Social Affairs, *Multinational Corporations in World Development* (New York, 1973, ST/ECA/190), p. 139.

source and factor allocation? If so, by how much? And the complementary question: Can existing theory adequately explain the growth and behavior of MNFs?

The debate is hardly confined to economists. American labor launched a major campaign against American multinational firms in the early 1970s, raising some of the very questions of which we speak. MNFs, labor said, have fundamentally changed the economic situation. Responding to artificial tax incentives, they are channeling capital and technology abroad, in turn moving jobs out of the United States. Moreover, intrafirm sales are bringing goods back into the United States at artificially low prices. Two successive Congresses faced close votes on various proposals of the labor-sponsored Hartke-Burke bill, which would have sharply increased taxes on international corporations and restricted the outflow of technology. In neither Congress did the provisions pass. In nations where the MNFs' subsidiaries are located (the host nations), rather the opposite concerns have surfaced—the fear that the MNFs might be denying the importation of the most advanced technology and that they transfer goods and services out of the country at too high a price. These political concerns provoked a spurt of theory and research.

As a result of such work, the shape of MNF behavior is gradually becoming clearer, the theory more refined. Data have shown some theories to be untenable, others suspect. Considerable controversy and uncertainty remain, however, and one would be hard pressed to come up with a single widely accepted assessment of the impact of the MNF on economic theory or policy. In this chapter we hope to reveal both the emerging shape of our knowledge and the controversies that remain.

A few years ago such firms came to be called *multinational firms* (MNFs), and that phrase, though perhaps not the most accurate (transnational is better), is well rooted in the literature. The multinational firms are a familiar lot; we have met some of them before as imperfect competitors. Many are household names, as an inspection of the list of MNFs in Table 16.2 reveals. How can the existence of such firms affect economic theory? Why are they of concern beyond what we have said in the previous chapter?

Some Historical Perspective

For some years most writers on the MNF were content to examine the growth of foreign direct investment since the end of the Second World War. As can be noted in Table 16.3, American investment abroad expanded 170 percent between 1950 and 1960 and another 140 percent in the next decade. It followed from this limited perspective that the MNF was something "new" and explosive on the world scene. More careful historical work, however, rather dampened the "sudden explosion" theory. American investment abroad in the early 1970s—as a percentage of America's GNP or as a percentage of America's exports—was remarkably similar to pre-Depression and pre-World War II figures. Indeed, U.S. foreign direct investment (FDI) in 1914, 1929, and 1970 amounted to 7 percent of GNP. Table 16.4 relates U.S. FDI to U.S. GNP and Table 16.5 relates U.S. FDI to U.S. exports in selected "watershed" years.[2] Concern in Britain about the "American invasion" was voiced well over seventy years ago by a British writer who noted: "Our babies are fed on American food, and our dead are buried in American coffins." Taking a long view, then, the Depression and war seem sufficient to explain an apparently "depressed" rate of U.S. FDI at the war's end. If the FDI we have today is roughly proportional to what it was in the past with respect to GNP and to exports, how can the problems of the MNF be new? Why, for instance, would not the tax arrangements worked out in the 1920s still work today?

Some writers feel that the type of firm today is different. Size, after all, is just one measure of importance; tightness of control is another. Modern firms appear more tightly managed than earlier counterparts. Hence while their relative sizes may be unchanged, their behavior most certainly is. Modern managerial techniques, modern communications, and modern transportation enable a corporate headquarters to control its foreign subsidiaries much more strictly than it could in 1929. But are they in fact more strictly controlled?

TABLE 16.2. TWENTY-FIVE LEADING MULTINATIONAL FIRMS (1971 figures)

Firm	Country	Total sales (in millions of dollars)	Foreign content (percentage of assets, production, or employment)
1. General Motors	United States	28,264	27e
2. Exxon	United States	18,701	52a
3. Ford Motor	United States	16,433	40a
4. Royal Dutch Shell	Netherlands–United Kingdom	12,734	70e
5. International Business Machines	United States	8,274	27a
6. Mobil Oil	United States	8,243	46a
7. Chrysler	United States	7,999	31a
8. Texaco	United States	7,529	65p
9. Unilever	Netherlands–United Kingdom	7,483	60a
10. ITT	United States	7,346	61a
11. Gulf Oil	United States	5,940	38a
12. British Petroleum	United Kingdom	5,191	83e
13. Philips Lamp Co.	Netherlands	5,189	67p
14. Standard Oil of California	United States	5,143	46p
15. Volkswagenwerk	West Germany	4,967	25p
16. Imperial Chemical Industries	United Kingdom	3,717	25a

17.	Nestle	Switzerland	3,541	90a
18.	Daimler Benz	West Germany	3,460	28a
19.	Union Carbide	United States	3,038	25p
20.	International Harvester	United States	3,016	26a
21.	Eastman Kodak	United States	2,976	27a
22.	Fiat	Italy	2,943	43a
23.	Akzo	Netherlands	2,307	66e
24.	British-American Tobacco	United Kingdom	2,262	82a
25.	Caterpillar Tractor	United States	2,175	25a

a = assets
e = employment
p = production

The problems encountered in developing any list of MNFs are great. Figures can range from the 168 American multinationals used in the Harvard Business School study to the 7,276 multinationals of all nations toted up by the UN (which figured 2,468 for the U.S.). The authors prefer a combined definition involving size and percentage of foreign production, but these figures are often difficult to discover. The table above is based on UN figures, which list, where available, the size and the percentage of sales, production, assets, earnings, and employment outside the parent nation. We have included only those firms whose foreign assets, production, or employment amounted to 25 percent or more of the firm's total. (Hence we do not count firms that are mainly exporters with very limited foreign production.) There are also some firms that probably should be included but for whom there are no foreign content figures. The firms are ranked by their total sales, regardless of whether these sales are domestic or international.

Source: United Nations, Department of Economic and Social Affairs, *Multinational Corporations in World Development* (New York, 1973, ST/ECA/190), pp. 130-132.

TABLE 16.3. U.S. FOREIGN DIRECT INVESTMENT, 1929-1973

Year	Book value (in millions of dollars)	Rate of growth (percent)
1914	2,650	185
1929	7,553	− 7
1940	7,000	68
1950	11,790	170
1960	31,820	145
1970	78,180	37
1973	107,268	

Source:Mira Wilkins, *The Emergence of Multinational Enterprise*, p. 20; Louis Turner, *Invisible Empires* (New York: Harcourt Brace Jovanovich, 1971), p. 5.

TABLE 16.4. U.S. FOREIGN DIRECT INVESTMENT COMPARED WITH U.S. GNP IN WATERSHED YEARS

Year	U.S. FDI (in billions of dollars)	U.S. GNP	FDI of GNP (percent)
1914	2.65	36.4	7.3
1929	7.5	103.1	7.3
1946	7.2	210	3.4
1950	11.8	285	4.1
1960	32	864	3.7
1970	78.1	1155	6.8
1973	107	1295	8.3
1975	133	- -	- -

Sources: Table 16.3; *Federal Reserve Bulletin*, December 1973; *Survey of Current Business*, October 1974, p. 76.

TABLE 16.5. U.S. FOREIGN DIRECT INVESTMENT COMPARED WITH U.S. EXPORTS IN WATERSHED YEARS

Year	U.S. FDI (in billions of dollars)	Exports	Exp./FDI
1929	7.5	7	.9
1941	7	5.9	.8
1950	11.8	13.8	1.2
1960	31.8	24	.75
1970	78	62.9	.8
1973	107	100.4	.9
1975	133	107	.8

Source: Table 16.3; *Survey of Current Business*, October 1973, p. 75; Federal Reserve Historical Chart Book.

Historical evidence suggests that U.S. MNFs have always been rather tightly supervised. The early entrants to foreign production had already devised means to control the geographically diverse American market before going abroad, and generally applied overseas the same rather strict marketing and production controls that they used at home. Such firms as Kodak, Singer, Swift, or Quaker Oats keep today and kept at the turn of the century close control over all marketing operations. With the transatlantic cable in place from 1868 (coinciding with the opening of the first American manufacturing plant abroad—Singer's plant in Scotland), key decisions could still be referred to headquarters.

Evidence on contemporary styles of control shows no dramatic change. Modern managerial theory emphasizes the trade-off between centralization and decentralization. MNFs show many degrees of concentration, depending on the product, market, and corporate strategy. In only a few cases does this call for monolithic centralization. Overly centralized firms tend to lose good managers, to be unresponsive to local market conditions, to be slow to react to changing conditions, and to have difficulty in judging managerial competence. Hence a firm, even though possessing the means to centralize, may not choose to do so. Nor may this choice be made "freely," because the firm choosing the wrong degree of consolidation for its particular operations will lose money.

Some writers also point out that American manufacturing is more footloose than it was in the 1920s because manufacturing has increased as a percentage of total foreign investment.[3] Manufacturing can presumably be done in any number of countries, while mineral exploitation or the operation of street railways and telephone systems cannot. Manufacturing, however, is very highly market oriented. Nearly three-quarters of all products manufactured by U.S. firms are sold in the nations of manufacture. With some exceptions for border activities along the Rio Grande and some electronics work in Southeast Asia, few companies go abroad specifically for cheap labor. Considering all such evidence, the authors' sense of the matter is that, whatever impact the MNF has, it is not new. Whatever we face now has existed for three or more generations.

MNFs and Profit Maximization

The growth of MNFs has brought to the fore a number of concerns previously considered mostly on a domestic level. One idea is that MNFs fail to carry out "the dictates of the market" because they themselves are not interested in making as high a profit as they can. This argument differs from those advanced in the last chapter regarding the extent to which the structure of the industry caused market distortion. In those models, firms were maximizing profits. Here we suggest that imperfect competition *allows* the firm to act in an uneconomic way. Protected from the rigors of tough competition by oligopoly and monopoloid advantages, the firm *need not* maximize profits.

Writers give differing reasons as to why this non-profit-maximizing behavior should occur. The "classic" Berle and Means thesis is that the management and ownership have become separated. With share ownership widely dispersed, the managers have little to fear from a "proxy fight" as long as they pay some dividends. Management's aim, then, is more to keep itself in power, well paid, and comfortable than to work hard getting high profits.

Moving from the Berle and Means view, management theorists have suggested that managers do not normally "optimize," but rather "satisfice."[4] *Satisficing* behavior consists of setting rather moderate goals and, once they are reached, striving no further. As an example, a company may set a goal of 10 percent return on investment after taxes. So long as that is reached it will not strive for a 12 percent return. This reduces the risk to any manager within the company and provides a pleasant, if rather dull, atmosphere. Such behavior is well documented. It assumes theoretical importance when we allow the firm to be insulated from competition.

A third theory suggests that growth, rather than profits, is the objective of most firms.[5] This objective aids stockholders because the stock market often places value on corporate growth over profit. This is reflected in the valuation of earnings per share over return on investment. The firm that grows from its retained earnings can continue to increase earnings per share even if it makes rather marginal investments, so long as it does not issue new shares. Market analysts use earnings per share as a key indicator. Firms are accordingly seen as more growth than profit oriented.

No close observer of business behavior would deny any of these possibilities; they all happen. But the more serious question is whether they are persistent and widespread enough to provide a general theory. Proxy fights do occur. Indeed, corporate raids on other less vigorous companies are frequent. Although the shareholders themselves may not revolt, another corporation may begin a proxy war. And as observed in the previous chapter, many seemingly secure firms have been forced to shape up by new competitors. Procter and Gamble, for instance, spotted a sleeping Unilever in Britain and moved in to take over a large part of its market share in detergents. Growth strategies, particularly in the weak stock market of the mid-1970s, have failed to inspire high market prices as in days of old. Perhaps most tellingly, though, statistical studies have found return on investment the best indicator of share price in the long run. This implies that long-run profit maximization will bring the highest prices and is, or should be, the goal of most firms. The balance of opinion to this date is not so much that non-profit maximization theories can be rejected outright, but that some kind of profit maximization theory is still applicable.

MNFs as a Product of Oligopolistic Forces

Another line of inquiry connects the MNF with oligopolistic theory. As noted above, MNFs are large and dominant, so it seems logical to examine the direct investment process in the light of oligopolistic behavior. Two questions are posed: (1) Why do firms keep accumulating retained earnings rather than distributing them? (2) Why do firms with retained earnings choose foreign direct investment over conglomeration or diversification?

Answers to the first question are connected closely to the "growth of firm" idea suggested above. There is a tax argument. Owners prefer growth because the tax is lower on capital gains and also because the tax occurs when the share is sold, not when the profits are earned. If all profits are paid out as dividends, in contrast, they are taxed not only as profits, but again as personal income. Other answers to the first question deal with the internal dynamics of a corporation that has surplus managers and talent as well as capital and can only keep its good managers by expanding rapidly.

The second question can be answered in managerial terms. Many firms have indeed opted for diversification, among them many MNFs. Of those that did not, or that retreated from diversification, the reason was the inability of top management to handle the diversity of decisions that was necessary. Studies at Harvard University supported by the Ford Foundation revealed, in fact, two quite distinct groups of MNFs. One group concentrates all its production in a rather narrow range of products in one major industrial grouping. These may be called *product-concentration firms*. The other group produces in many industries, both at home and abroad. These are called *product-diversification firms*. The latter have been shown to be more numerous than the former, but we have in any case some evidence that foreign investment is for some firms an alternative to diversification.

Harvard economist Richard Caves connected the firm's oligopolistic excess profits to its foreign direct investment, arguing as above that capital tended to be "industry specific." Logically, if the capital is industry specific, so is the rate of return on investment. Some industries, we know, consistently get higher returns on investment than others. As oligopolists increase foreign direct investment, theorized Caves, the rates of return in each national market will come closer together as a new oligopolistic equilibrium is reached in the industry. This provides at least a partial explanation of the growth of foreign direct investment.[6]

There are a number of problems about any theory based on capital surpluses. New data have revealed the very great extent to which MNFs rely on foreign funds to build their investments. Retained earnings, depreciation, and local borrowings provide the bulk of the funds for foreign investment. For American firms in the period 1966-1970, the transfer of funds abroad for investment almost exactly matched the dividends paid back—one hand giveth what the other hand taketh away. (These were, of course, different firms, some moving capital in, some out.) The Europeans have long complained—correctly, it appears—that American corporations were buying them out with their own money. (They are incorrect, however, to imply that their own savings were used, since it is the American shareholder who forgoes dividends in such instances.)

Why would an MNF borrow abroad at higher rates of interest rather than transfer money from the United States? For one thing, throughout the late 1960s the United States had restrictions on the outflow of capital. This, however, was probably not as important as a number of internal factors. Indeed, the removal of the restrictions has not seemed to make much difference to corporate behavior. A more important reason is the corporation's own degree of decentralization. As noted earlier, the MNF is not necessarily a monolithic structure. In pursuit of the benefit of decentralization it sacrifices some financial gains. Thirdly, MNFs want good relations with local communities and need local banking expertise, so they borrow locally. Finally, the marginal rate of borrowing abroad may not be much higher than it is in the United States. If MNFs tried to borrow all their money in the United States, they would drive interest rates up sharply.

A second oligopolistic theory relates to risk. The firm's goals are, in this view, not solely to gain high returns, but also to minimize risk. Like a bondholder, the firm balances risk against return. Nowhere is this more apparent than it is in oligopoly. Competitors' successful moves can lead to a loss in market share, loss of production experience, loss of opportunities to develop new products, and resulting higher costs. Hence, oligopolists play a close-checking game.

This theory has considerable appeal. There have long been foreign direct investments that apparently did not maximize profits. Some firms entered foreign markets where the return on investment was clearly lower than the domestic. Some firms were investing in other countries despite predictable losses. Interviews with executives often pointed to an oligopolistic rationale behind many investment decisions. In the first place, firms feared that a competitor could get a technological edge in exploiting a new market. Second, they feared that competitors would use high profits in one market to finance low prices in another. By making countervailing investments, the oligopolist can strike at a competitor in the latter's home market. Thus if Philips Lamp Company attempted to use Dutch profits to expand its light bulb sales in the United States, General Electric could counter by lowering prices in Holland. Lastly, they feared missing out on large sources of potential supplies. Note how the oil companies all flocked to the same fields when oil was discovered there.

Emerging data suggest that this oligopolistic explanation accounts for some, but hardly all, foreign direct investment. "Product-concentration" firms do indeed show a high degree of sensitivity to competitors' moves, entering foreign markets "just because" their competitors do, measuring their success by percentage of market share, and being overfearful of competitors' advantages. Product-diversification firms, however, do not as a whole demonstrate the same oligopolistic behavior. We may have explained Exxon or Heinz but we have not explained ITT.

Toward New Explanations—The Internalization Thesis

Charles Kindleberger posed the problem of foreign direct investment in monopolistic competition terms.[7] Why, he suggested, do we have MNFs at all? Consider the problem.

1. The MNF has been seen as a conduit for capital transfer. Yet in itself, capital is transferred very easily through banks and other private capital markets. Most capital moves without the necessity of an MNF.

2. MNFs are equally unnecessary for the transfer of goods. Three-fourths of the world's manufacturing trade still takes place between independent companies.

3. Managerial services can be rented out. This has been the traditional mode of operation for construction companies for many years, but has become increasingly common in a number of other industries. As noted in the last chapter, United Brands (nee United Fruit) has in large measure shifted from owning its plantations to making contractual arrangements with farmers. The widespread use of franchising (now moving internationally) in restaurants and hotels provides additional examples of contractual obligations being used instead of direct ownership.

4. Technology and brand names are licensed regularly. The corporation itself does not have to introduce them directly.

Kindleberger's answer to the question of why MNFs existed was to look for imperfections in the capital market, in the goods market, and in the technology and managerial services market, giving special attention to monopoloid advantages provided through branding, patent control, and vertical integration. Each firm attempts to collect a rent on its monopoly control of a brand, a technical process, or skilled marketing services. Monopolistic competition, however, explains only why high *rents* exist, not why the firm cannot or does not rent its monopoloid advantages to foreign firms.

The problem is this: Being an oligopolist, being large, or having product differentiation or technical advantages are not in themselves sufficient conditions for foreign direct investment. Indeed, of the Fortune 500, well over 300 did not qualify as MNFs under the Ford-Harvard definitions. Market structure must be combined with something else. The search for "something else" takes us back to the theory of the firm—in particular, a branch of it associated with a seminal article by Ronald H. Coase, which has in recent years served as the foundation for a new theory of international investment. We shall refer to this as the *Coasian model*.[8]

To begin with, note that a firm and a market can both allocate resources. The market uses the price mechanism; the firm uses administrative fiat. Professor Smith in the classroom did not come because the students paid him more than another to come but because the administration decided he should be there. The gasoline you bought did not get to the station through the processes of independent stations bidding for surpluses in wholesalers' hands. Rather, it was planned and programmed by the oil companies. Allocation in our economy is in fact a mixture of administrative and market decisions. Ultimately, we trust, the market puts the check on the administrative decisions. If they often prove wrong, the market will not take the final product. Nobody takes Professor Smith's course. Too little gasoline is used or a shortage develops.

Our attention at this point focuses on the internal mechanics of the firm. Why are some allocational decisions made by administrative fiat and others by market mechanisms? The answer lies in the cost of using the market mechanism itself. To use a market one must know the price and one must know what one is buying or selling. For some goods and services, those pieces of price information can be extremely costly. Technological inventions, brand names, and marketing methods are cases in point. All of these are extremely difficult to "cost," let alone price. Companies do not know what they should charge or pay for these. Hence one cost, known as the *brokerage cost*, is that of finding relevant prices to charge a matching buyer and seller. A second cost is the *contractual cost*, or that of drawing up a mutual contract. In a large joint venture of several mining and steel companies recently, the books of contracts spelling out the mutual obligations were nineteen inches high, doubtless with correspondingly lofty lawyers' fees.

A third cost or "risk" is the risk of selling at too low or buying at too high a price. Some companies have ruefully admitted to licensing some brand or invention with the expectation of modest sales and then have witnessed the licensee make a veritable mint. Or they have licensed a product and then discovered that the licensee did not market it in the appropriate way. Long-term contracts typically fail to give the flexibility needed to change policy or products, thus increasing risk to signers. If, however, the single firm sells its goods abroad itself, it faces only the risk that the good will not sell well. It does not suffer if the good sells better than anticipated.

Allocation by administrative fiat also has costs. The bureaucracy must exist to make the decisions, and that in itself is costly. Management functions well to a point in making allocational decisions, but if there are too many decisions to be made, efficiency declines. Decisions take too long and opportunities are missed. Wrong decisions are taken because management cannot devote enough time to studying any single one. The increasing complexity of the firm isolates the decision maker from the operating level, resulting again in incorrect and delayed decisions. Thus as the number of decisions increases beyond some optimal point, the cost of making them increases. Note that we say "the number of allocational decisions," not just the size of the firm. Relatively simple firms such as petroleum firms need relatively few allocational decisions to generate a lot of sales. Firms such as ITT, however, operating in a dozen industries, face a multitude of allocational decisions. These product diversification firms tend to be more decentralized in an attempt to reduce or avoid the high costs of administrative decision making. But decentralization is only a partial solution. Eventually, the firm becomes less efficient than the market at making decisions. Size is limited, then, by a firm's internal ability to allocate resources more cheaply than the market.

From a Coasian point of view, then, the expansion of the firm depends on the relation of the costs of market allocation to the costs of managerial allocation. Where market costs are higher, the firm will "internalize" what would otherwise be a market decision. Our concern, then, is to determine what situations would carry firms across national borders.

The international market is not efficient in the pricing of new technology. Although there certainly is abundant licensing of technology, recent data show that licensing of independents does not substitute for the easy flow of technology within a corporation. Licensees get just what they pay for and nothing more. Subsidiaries generally get full access to the parent (or other affiliate) technology. One problem with licensing technology is that it is very hard to price it. Its cost is difficult to figure. How do you allocate the expenditures on basic research among 100 inventions? (Most firms, in fact, do not allocate basic research to specific products.) Technology's worth to the buyer is very hard to estimate. Contracts expire after a specified number of years (often seven), but at their expiration the licensee may well have the knowledge to develop some slightly different version (separately patentable) of the invention. Hence the costs of finding relevant prices, of negotiating and arranging contracts, and ultimately of the risks involved in accepting contracts discourage the licensing of technology.

Management's ability to coordinate activities transnationally is exceedingly difficult to value. This problem has long been recognized in relation to vertical integration. Consider Kindleberger's classic example of the three different owners of, respectively, West Virginia coal, an unbuilt railway, and unprepared port facilities, all wishing to export coal. All three want to ship coal to Europe, but (1) the coal mine operator will not open the mine without a railway and port to ship the coal; (2) the railway will not put in new tracks until it has coal and a port; and (3) the port owner will not put in coal-handling facilities until it has coal and a railway. As separate agents they do nothing because the firm that finished first would take losses on unused facilities. Under one company, however, the losses due to unscheduled delays would be spread among the three component groups. United Fruit provides such an example of a single company integrating an entire process as it began to move bananas from Central America to the United States. Oil companies, similarly, claim that their ability to plan oil from exploration to automobile allows a smoother flow of oil and a smoother opening of new fields than would occur under more competitive conditions.

Recently, scholars have noted the value of horizontal integration—the coordination of the sale of finished goods. Consider such things as the maintenance of brand names across borders (together with associated quality controls), or the handling of advertising that crosses borders. The need for flexibility and rapid change makes contracts difficult to arrange. The need for consistency makes a strong hand necessary. The marketing of consumer goods in particular involves very extensive coordination from the basic market surveys to the delivery, distribution, and advertising of the good itself. How is the company to price, "package," and sell such services? Rather than to try to do so, it simply internalizes all these allocational decisions.

The process of internalization is closely related to market structure, but the relation is a complicated one. Oligopoly encourages more internalization than there would be under free market conditions. (1) Under oligopoly the risk of loss of market share is higher, hence the risk cost of using the market is higher. (2) The greater the internalization, the smaller the market. For years, oil companies did "everything" for themselves—explored, drilled, shipped, refined, and distributed. There were no independent companies engaged just in exploring or just in refining. Only in later years did such separate companies spring up. With a thin market, brokerage costs rise. (3) The greater the internalization, the higher the barrier to entry—and vice versa.

Monopolistic competition also serves to raise the price of using the market. (1) Product differentiation makes products less comparable, weakening the effectiveness of the market mechanism. (2) The implementation of product differentiation involves extensive market coordination. (3) The drive for new products and new technology creates many goods that are difficult to price. (4) To the extent that monopolistic competition leads also to oligopoly, risks and barriers to entry also arise. Thus we have a mixture of explanations for the high costs of marketing. Some are related to traditional explanations of imperfect competition, but others such as coordination and the difficulty of pricing technology are characteristic of any market structure. Hence, although it seems doubtful that there would be as many MNFs in a more perfectly competitive world, so long as we grant the reasons for the existence of firms, we grant the reasons for MNFs.

MNFs, Trade, and the Allocation of Resources

We return now to some of the original questions posed in the beginning of the chapter. How, aside from the distortions we already know from oligopoly and monopolistic competition, can an MNF affect the allocation of resources?

The Coasian model holds the basic consideration to be this: Administrative allocation and market allocation do not necessarily result in the same thing. Since administrative decision making occurs because the good or service is too costly to price, we do not know *what* the market would say. Just as Newtonian laws do not apply within the atom's nucleus, so Marshallian rules do not apply within the firm. Not everything that moves across borders within the firm, then, is necessarily following classical economic principles.

One conclusion from this is that some goods and services will thus be transferred, goods and services that would not be had the firm not existed. In this sense the MNF aids in the international transfer of resources. We could thus treat the cost of using the market as a barrier to trade, and note that the MNF can bypass this barrier.

Contemplate the possibilities at this point. Technology can travel better from IBM in America to IBM in Europe than it can from IBM in America to Burroughs in America. Coordination in the introduction of new car models can be closer between Ford of the United States and Ford of Canada than between Ford and GM in the United States. The latter set is likely to introduce cars that duplicate each other's functions, the former to introduce complementary vehicles. Hence we find that some resources move better inside the firm than inside the nation, while others act more traditionally and move better inside the nation and between firms. One could suggest, then, a matrix of the sort shown below. High technology would flow better vertically while, say, electrical applicances would flow better within a nation (horizontally). The subject is interesting, but has only been lightly explored.

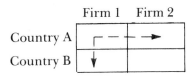

Firm 1   Firm 2

Country A

Country B

Issues Raised by MNFs

The impact of the MNF is more ambiguous than it might at first seem. The internalization of allocational decisions shifts the locus of power from an impartial or at least morally neutral market to the executive offices of corporations. In turn, there is often a shift in governmental policy toward pressuring the corporation directly for benefits rather than simply using the tools of economic policy. There is some merit to a coordinated approach of both policy and direct pressure, but the MNF's freedom must be taken in perspective.

Only a quarter of world trade is intracorporate. Substantial as this is, even in itself much of it takes place at close to market prices (the firm that cannot price technology may have no trouble pricing manufactured products). MNFs themselves are frequently decentralized, with each subsidiary acting in many respects as an independent firm. Much economic analysis errs in its treatment of the MNF as a monolithic, centrally directed entity. A treatment of this nature might be appropriate for a few firms, but quite inappropriate for the majority of international firms. We are still talking about matters of degree—degrees of discretion that in themselves vary from firm to firm and function to function. Unfortunately, we do not know to what extent they vary, and many assessments differ on just that matter.

The Transfer Price Issue.   Central to many discussions of MNFs is the question of the prices charged for intrafirm transactions—transfer prices. Since tariffs, profits taxes, balance of payments policies, and economic assessments of performance are all affected by these prices, they have come in for considerable discussion. Say that an American MNF "sells" its subsidiary a license to use a given technological process, charging that subsidiary $50,000 a year. The U.S. government could claim that it should "really" be $100,000 and tax the parent company on an extra $50,000 (and it has done so on occasion). The host government could claim it was worth only $25,000 and tax the subsidiary on the $25,000 extra profit (and often treaties to prevent double taxation do not provide for the effects of this type of disagreement). If goods are involved, the import duty of the importing nation would be affected. It is, moreover, a common practice for firms whose profits are blocked through exchange control from leaving a host country to pull out some of these profits. This can be achieved through high charges on any imports from the parent country, and low prices on exports from the host.

Although much debate has raged, the authors are inclined to be rather conservative in their assessment of the transfer price question. From a managerial standpoint, effective decentralization requires realistic transfer prices. Otherwise, the divisional managers cannot be held responsible for their profits, a key goal of decentralization. Intracorporate bargaining over transfer prices often resembles market bargaining in bilateral monopoly conditions. The establishment of artificial prices is costly. Companies will set such prices only if the complications are slight (as in pricing crude oil), or where rewards are high. High rewards may accompany great differences in tax rates (which are *not* that different among industrial countries), exchange control, or high tariffs. These are also, incidentally, the same situations under which independent traders might try some of the same tricks. One does not need a MNF to have a false invoice accompany a shipment while the real one goes through the mail.

Governments prefer companies to use "arms-length" prices—that is, to charge subsidiaries close-to-market prices. Yet if the Coasian theory holds, it is the difficulty of discovering the "correctness" of such prices that brings the firm into existence in the first place. As with the countervailing power of a bilateral monopoly, one can only establish a range of prices, some clearly too high and others too low. As an example, suppose an American corporation transfers abroad a product that has been selling on the American market for five years. The costs of research and development on that product have already been written off, presumably on American operations. The firm could charge (1) a license fee of zero based on marginal costs; (2) a fee somewhere near what it can deduce from cost data; or (3) a fee based on what it is worth to the foreign subsidiary. The second choice is probably most acceptable to governments, but that is precisely the figure the firm does not know. A dozen different accounting systems could yield a dozen different costs. The third figure is difficult to estimate, particularly if there is no sense of a going rate for a similar license. As a consequence there is no right price—just prices that are acceptable to the contending parties.

Labor Issues. Home countries usually fear that the MNF is transferring abroad technology and employment. Host countries generally fear the opposite. These concerns are particularly strong among labor unions and the issues demand closer attention.

To some extent, the transfer of technology abroad follows the product life cycle. As industries mature, the rate of development of new technology slows and existing knowledge becomes well known outside the firm. What was once a monopoloid advantage becomes a virtual commodity and can be purchased through contractual arrangements. American labor, for instance, has accused U.S. automobile companies of selling American technology to Japan, leading eventually to Japanese imports. This rather misses the historical sequence. The Japanese forced the American companies out of Japan in the early 1950s, then negotiated with British and French companies for technical knowledge. Only after those agreements were made did American companies sell their knowledge. These arrangements, moreover, were market arrangements—not intracorporate transfers. By 1950, automobile technology was already quite stable and available on the market.

Looking at the development of new technology, we can follow Linder's ideas on market-oriented invention. Invention of this sort is hardly limited to U.S. markets. American firms are bringing in foreign inventions, both by developing them themselves in foreign nations and by purchasing them abroad. (Gillette bought the Cricket lighter by buying a French company. Royal Typewriter's parent, Litton, bought Royal a competitive electric typewriter by buying out a German firm.) Foreign firms investing in the United States, often technological leaders in their own fields, bring technology to the United States. The process of such transfer, it appears, is by no means a one-way street. Nor is it a zero-sum game—both countries benefit from technological transfer, whether or not one "loses" in the sense of transferring more out than in.

The difficulty of the job-loss argument is both theoretical and statistical. As noted in Chapter 7, the maintenance of full employment depends on aggregate demand. Unemployment created by changes in factor shifting should be only frictional. We face a problem no more difficult (and no easier) than we faced when discussing the displacements caused by comparative advantage. If MNFs are in fact moving capital and employment to areas where labor is cheap, this should be improving world welfare. In this sense, the firm is behaving in the same way as would separate national firms. In most situations, MNFs allocate resources in the same direction as would independent firms. Many of the foreign investment decisions in television and textiles, for instance, were defensive in nature: If the American companies had not gone abroad, imports from unaffiliated companies would have increased instead.

Statistically, the studies of MNF effects on U.S. employment have shown that they bring about larger increases in U.S. employment than do non-MNFs. In addition, the U.S. Tariff Commission discovered that only extreme assumptions about "what would have happened" to U.S. exports in the absence of MNFs could support the thesis of a net loss in employment. One has to assume that high percentages of U.S. MNFs' offshore production could have been exported from the United States to produce a net loss for U.S. employment.

Other information also works against labor's case. Relatively little investment is made abroad with the specific purpose of finding cheap labor—this is mostly in electronics in Southeast Asia and in textiles in Mexico. American foreign investment remains market oriented, with only 7 percent of all foreign production sent back to the United States, another 22 percent sold to third countries, and the rest sold in the nation of manufacture. Of the 7 percent sent back to the United States, half of that is in the Canadian automobile trade (more than matched by U.S. exports in the same category), and a good share of the remaining half is probably also intraindustrial.

Foreign labor's fears are just the opposite of American labor's. Both cannot be right. The assumption on both sides is apparently that MNFs have the power (that is, the discretion) to move or not move employment or technology, and that the exercise of this power will harm their particular interests. We have argued that, yes, the MNF does have discretionary power, although it is held in check to some (perhaps considerable) degree by market forces. We are not prepared to say, however, that the firm is going to be capricious in its use of power. The firm tries to act rationally, choosing to produce wherever its various costs are lowest.

Labor unions, fearing that such power would be used haphazardly, or at least be used against them, have tried on a small scale to organize internationally. American and European unions in chemicals and metalworking have formed international secretariats to deal with transnational labor problems. For the most part these organizations have provided useful exchanges of information. For example, a labor negotiator in the United States could know all of Ford's labor practices in all countries, plus the international company's profit picture. Hence he or she could bargain with a worldwide perspective.

The international secretariats have also served to put some pressure on the parent company's head office when the MNF is dealing with labor problems in less developed areas, serving to bring those problems more directly to the notice of corporate managers. They also may be used to prevent the breaking of a strike in one nation by blocking the MNF's attempt to send goods in from another nation. There is little sign so far of any international union developing the same cohesiveness as its domestic counterpart, especially in coordinating large international strikes. Indeed, the only two nations that have such cohesive unions are the United States and Canada—and recent Canadian nationalist militancy has weakened even that.

MNFs and Governments. National governments must take into account any discretionary power an MNF has. Governments may—and do—deal directly with MNFs, asking or requiring them to transfer some technology, maintain or increase employment, or increase exports. Canada's Foreign Investment Review Act and its Australian counterpart explicitly require foreign firms to enumerate the benefits to the host country. If they are insufficient, permission to invest may be denied. Such laws assume implicitly that the firms have the power to deny or to grant what the governments ask. Yet traditional economics would suggest that the governments may be wasting their time. If they want employment, they should follow full employment practices. If they want exports, they should devalue. If they want technology, they should give tax incentives.

Once more we have a question of degree. The greater the difference between the cost of using the market and the administrative cost, the more the discretion. We know that this depends both on what the firm is trying to price and the industrial structure. A firm would have wide discretion in pricing new computer technology or in valuing its services in marketing a new automobile because both the type of service and the industry tend to be high cost in terms of brokerage, contracts, and risk. Conversely, the transfer of a piece of clothing from one nation to another is likely to provide the firm with little room for maneuver, since none of the three costs of using the market is high.

There is a natural political tendency to overestimate the freedom available to the MNF. It is easier to harangue fifty companies than it is to introduce sound economic policy. It is easier to blame foreign corporations than one's own government, so the claims about the MNF's ability to ignore market incentives grow. Yet as we suggested in our discussion of job losses, resource allocation within the MNF may not differ greatly from market allocation. In a pioneering study of American firms in Canada, for instance, Albert E. Safarian demonstrated that in large measure and for a broad range of activities American firms there were responding in the same way as were domestic firms to the same economic pressures. High tariffs and an affluent population encouraged the maintenance of rather small-scale manufacturing with high cost structures. The "evils" of those American firms—lack of exports, high cost structures—were in fact the result not of the MNF's deviousness, but, in large part, of sixty years of Canadian industrial policy.

Direct pressure on the MNF can be *part* of economic policy, reinforcing other measures taken. As an example, when Canada wanted to produce a popular American car model, it arranged for lower tariffs, but it also bargained with the car companies over which models Canada would make. This way one part of the corporate decision—the big part—is a response to changing market conditions, while the other part, remaining within the discretion of the firm, is administrative.

A second area of interest for policy makers is the question of whether the country wants to host MNFs at all. Some nations do not allow any foreign firms (Communist countries) and some allow only joint ventures, held 51 percent by locals (Mexico and Japan). Even leaving aside the questions of politics and national pride, the economic issues are rather complicated. We now examine several economic benefits the MNF may bring to the host nation and what is known about them.

1. MNFs can bring capital to the host countries. There is, however, considerable evidence that they bring little capital with them but instead generate most of it domestically. This has led some people to conclude that governments are incorrect in thinking the MNF will help raise capital. If one assumes a fixed stock of savings, the MNF's borrowings and retained earnings merely crowd out domestic investors.

The issue, however, is more complicated. Retained earnings are in fact savings of the corporate shareholders in the parent company. It is they who direct (or are forced by management to accept) lower dividends than they have earned. Lower dividends mean a better balance of payments for the host nation, hence more goods and services available for domestic absorption and presumably higher savings.

This same matter can be seen in Coasian terms. In a purely competitive no-MNF world, the payments for services presently rendered by the MNF would all be recorded as payments on the current account. What are now retained earnings would be new borrowings and would come in under the capital account. This in turn would allow a larger real transfer into the nation. Hence, while there is little evidence of a capital transfer in the sense of moving large surpluses built up in the parent nation, there is a willingness among the shareholders of the parent company to make savings on the *new* income provided by the host country. MNFs may accordingly help national savings.

2. There is evidence that MNFs use capital and labor more efficiently than domestic competitors. Return on investment and capital-output ratios, as well as sales per man-year, tend to be higher for American MNFs than for foreign domestic competitors. The same amount of capital, then, would tend to produce more when used by an MNF. Hence the MNF may improve the use of existing capital.

3. Advanced technology flows better through MNFs. Older technology moves well through regular market channels. Nations interested in a great flow of new technology need MNFs more than nations with a desire for older technology. The more developed nations have a greater need for advanced technology, hence a greater use for the MNF.

4. Marketing coordination and planning can in themselves save resources and deliver desired goods more cheaply to the consumer. The transnational product policies described in Chapter 11 can be effective only if consumers are also informed of the ways in which the product might benefit them and where to get it, and if the consumers find the good when they go to get it. The marketing services in themselves may be expensive, and can often be done more cheaply on a transnational basis—for example, using the same advertising copy for several countries. Again, it is generally the developed countries who are more interested than the less developed countries in this kind of international product coordination. Yet less developed countries might find increases in such coordination useful too, as in the instance of the Ford *Fiera*. This simple four-cylinder light truck is designed specifically for Asian countries. No one nation has a market large enough to support production, but by producing motors in one nation, transmissions in another, and the like, and making an easily assembled frame, Ford can market these cars throughout Southeast Asia.

5. Vertical integration and coordination still pose many problems. One problem lies in the high brokerage and transaction costs in finding supplies in a thin and unreliable market. Many firms find they can best develop reliable supplies by owning the suppliers. If, however, reliable suppliers are available, contracts can replace direct ownership. We see this in bananas, coffee, cocoa, and in the United States with most canned and frozen vegetables. We see it also in the automobile industry—where a company (particularly General Motors) often goes to great lengths to train suppliers to bring it quality goods on schedule. Once a company can create reliable suppliers, there is no need for ownership—it can use the market instead of administrative allocation.

A second problem is in the scheduling and planning of complex flows of goods. If contractual costs rise with such complexity, the firm will tend to internalize allocation more and more. The third problem is, of course, the risk costs associated with oligopoly.

The question of vertical coordination that the host nation faces, then, is whether such coordination is needed or helpful—or whether the nation has in itself enough managerial and technical skills to substitute contractual obligations for direct ownership. Additionally it must consider the type of industry to see if the latter course is at all feasible.

Conclusion

The recent scrutiny of MNFs has added new and interesting dimensions to international economics. New theory and data enable us to define and to some extent predict divergence between the way in which international firms and domestic firms may react to a particular market situation or policy decision. The degree of this divergence is still a matter of dispute. It appears to be greater the less perfect the competition, and also greater for certain functions or services than for others.

It is the authors' sense of the matter, however, that the amount of variance between MNF and non-MNF behavior is not so large or significant as to cause major changes in the theories of international resource allocation. The questions the MNFs raise are largely those confined to specific situations and specific policy issues, rather than to the basic concepts of trade theory itself. What we have is not a substitute theory, but an elaboration on existing theory.

Notes

1. U.S. Foreign Direct Investment figures can normally be found in the August editions of the *Survey of Current Business*. This one is from August 1976. Worldwide figures are from: United Nations, Department of Economic and Social Affairs, *Multinational Corporations in World Development* (New York, 1973). Figures on trade proportions are from the Tariff Commission study cited below.

2. We compare FDI to GNP because those are more solid figures than "foreign sales of affiliates," which we do not have until quite recently. Roughly, foreign production is about twice the book value of foreign investment. Hence we could say that American firms were producing abroad in 1914, 1929, and 1970, roughly 14 percent of U.S. GNP.

3. In 1914, manufacturing was 19 percent of U.S. FDI; by 1975 it was 42 percent. Mining fell from 29 percent in 1914 to 5 percent in 1975. Agriculture fell from 15 percent in 1914 to 7 percent in 1940 (when the statistics ceased handling it as a separate category). Sales, trade, and utilities fell from 23 percent in 1914 to 14 percent in 1970. The following information is from *The Survey of Current Business*, August 1976:

Percentage U.S. FDI by industry—1975
(total $133,168 million)

Manufacturing	42	Transportation and utilities	3
Petroleum	26	Finance	11
Mining	5	Other	4
Trade	9		

Percentage by area

Developed (68%)		Developing (27%)	
Canada	23	Latin America	17
Europe	37	Other Western	
Japan	2	Hemisphere	4
Australia, New Zealand,		Middle East	3
South Africa	5	Other Africa	2
Unallocated	5	Other Asia and Pacific	4

4. The word *satisficing*, ugly as it may be, is well established in the literature. The concept is associated with H. Simon, *Administrative Behavior* (New York: Macmillan, 1957). See also R. Cyert and J. March, *A Behavioral Theory of the Firm* (Englewood Cliffs, N.J.: Prentice-Hall, 1963).
5. See William Baumol, *Business Behavior, Value and Growth* (New York: Macmillan, 1962).
6. Richard E. Caves, "International Corporations: The Industrial Economics of Foreign Investment," *Economica*, 38 (1971): 1-27.
7. Charles Kindleberger, *American Business Abroad* (New Haven: Yale University Press, 1969), Chapter 1.
8. See Ronald H. Coase, "The Nature of the Firm," *Economica*, Vol. 4, Nov. 1937.

VI

SOME CURRENT ISSUES

17

THE INTERNATIONAL ECONOMICS OF ENERGY

Perhaps no topic draws together so many threads of international economic analysis as does the energy situation, yet is at the same time so topical and important. Microeconomics suggests questions concerning the availability of future energy supplies and the nature of the oligopoly. Macroeconomics leads us to examine the monetary adjustment of the OPEC balance of payments surpluses, the impact on national incomes and on growth of the sudden changes in the price of energy, and, finally, the emerging "real transfer" question. Any model is, of course, an abstraction from reality, and as one applies a model to a specific situation, the model never fits exactly. A good model may accordingly suggest more questions than answers. Yet the questions are better and more analytical ones than would otherwise be asked.

Price and the Supply of Energy

To begin, it behooves us to examine perhaps the most basic question—the relation of price to the supply of energy. Most goods have positively sloped supply curves. In some cases, however, the supply curve is vertical, indicating that no additional supplies are available at any price. In such situations, higher prices just return rents to the owners of the goods. The rent in such cases serves the vital economic function of allocating the good in limited supply to its highest yielding use. One school of thought suggests that the supply curve of energy, particularly petroleum, tends toward the vertical.

Such a pessimistic outlook envisions a very limited supply of energy, at least under current or readily available technologies. It sees as an historical accident, more or less, the fact that current supplies of energy are readily available at low cost. It makes no difference if the man-hours, capital requirements, and land rents needed to produce an "oil barrel's worth" of energy are today low. The marginal costs of producing energy for the next generation are very high. Current high prices reflect entirely proper and completely correct speculation on future prices. The curve SS_1 in Fig. 17.1 represents such a view.

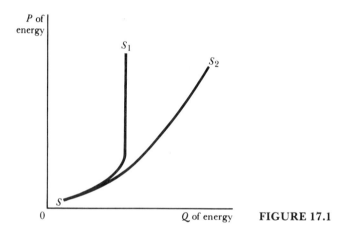

FIGURE 17.1

In caricature, one could picture a colony of shipwrecked economists on some desert isle. Their only oil is in five drums salvaged from the wreck. The cost of getting access to those drums is minimal, yet not even the greenest in the group would suggest that they determine the use of the oil on the basis of "present cost." Rather, the cost of the oil should be its replacement cost—the marginal cost of getting a sixth barrel. Since that cost is beyond the resources of the group, they must regard the supply of the oil as fixed. They then must establish priority uses for the oil, a process that will undoubtedly cause some lively debate. However decided, in the end they would come up with a series of "rents" for the oil. Is this, though, a reasonable caricature of the situation we are really in?

Most economists are suspicious of "quantum leaps" and discontinuities. In the absence of substantial evidence, they presume a gradual movement. They ask: "Does the supply curve for energy really have such a precipitous rise, with marginal costs leaping from very low to virtually infinite? Do we really have something that looks like curve SS_1 of Fig. 17.1, or is curve SS_2 more realistic?" The balance of evidence, in fact, suggests that SS_2 is indeed the closer approximation.

Reserves of oil in the United States, it is generally agreed, are indeed limited. The total of all known petroleum in the continental United States in 1860 was probably about 170 billion barrels. By 1970, 96 billion of those had been used, and it is expected that another 47-50 billion will be gone by 1990. Higher estimates of U.S. reserves were made in the 1950s, but these were suspect and have proven unfounded. These estimates do not include Alaska (5-10 billion) or the continental shelf. The latter is geologically "correct" for oil, though this is no guarantee of its presence.

World reserves, however, do not appear to be in any danger of imminent exhaustion. "Proven reserves"—oil in fields where test wells have indicated its presence—are conservatively figured at more than half a trillion barrels. At present consumption rates of 20-odd billion barrels a year, the oil we know about now should last through the end of the century. But "proven reserves" have little to do with the actual amount of oil in the earth. Rather, they are closely related to expected demand and probably secondarily to interest rates.

No company is going to explore and drill for wells just for the sake of finding them—it has to expect to sell the oil. If it spends a million dollars looking for oil and then doesn't use the oil for twenty years, it has forgone quite a lot of interest. (At 8 percent, the value of a million dollars after 20 years is around $4.66 million.) Even if potential oil-holding geological structures were lying at our doorsteps, companies would not explore for proven reserves beyond a prudent span of years. Therefore, to say that "proven reserves" will only last out the century is merely to say that present price and interest rate conditions make companies uninterested in proving reserves beyond a twenty-year span. Proven reserves accordingly rise with expected demand. If one looks at the statistics on proven reserves outside the United States, one would note that they rose by 111 percent from 1962 to 1972, despite no major new finds.[1] At some point, though, even potential reserves will run out, but most economists working closely with oil do not see that day as particularly imminent. Potential oil-producing structures abound. In the Middle East, Iran is probably the only nation whose proven reserves come close to its actual reserves; the center of Saudi Arabia and most of the offshore areas have been untouched. Political difficulties in Iraq have blocked exploration there. Outside the Middle East large portions of Africa, China, and the Soviet Union are unexplored for oil, as are most of the world's continental shelves. As the technology to explore and produce on continental shelves improves (moving along its experience curve), there will be more (and safer) drilling there. Estimates of world reserves are almost meaningless, but there are several areas the U.S. government feels could produce "100 billion to a trillion" barrels.[2] One is, of course, skeptical of trillion-barrel fields, but the chances of another "East Texas" or "Saudi Arabia" cannot be ruled out. More likely are the chances of finding more oil, but at higher prices, in places such as Alaska or Siberia.[3] Thus we arrive at a curious and difficult position. The reserve situation in some nations—the United States, Venezuela, Iran, and some of the Gulf sheikdoms—does indeed approach the SS_1 curve of Fig. 17.1, while the world situation may be closer to SS_2. This means that many nations will want to charge a rent that the market will not pay. The problem, incidentally, is exacerbated by the oligopolistic trait of working both low- and high-cost fields at the same time, such that the world does not move gradually from exploiting low-cost to exploiting high-cost oil.

Oil reserves are only part of the store of energy in the earth's crust: Chief among the alternatives is natural gas. The discovery of natural gas and the definition of "proven reserves" involve much the same difficulties as with oil: They are hidden, "only potential," until brought to light either by accident (as a by-product of the search for oil) or when they become commercially feasible. Most economists working with gas again feel that there is no imminent shortage of gas, even within the United States. The problem with gas is its transportation; either it goes by expensive pipeline, or it must be cooled to a point where it liquefies and can be transported in special containers. Both methods are technically feasible with current knowledge—but they are, or have been, more expensive than oil.

Coal reserves are very large, and, unlike oil, they do not need to be mined to be confirmed. (In the 1950s, coal was highly competitive when oil was in the $2 price range.[4]) Estimating that only half of the world reserves would be "recoverable" and that the use of energy continues to climb at about 5 percent a year, coal reserves alone would carry the world into the twenty-second century. In addition to coal, the uranium needed for nuclear energy, at least in the amounts projected for its use, is not in short supply.

The evidence, then, does not support the idea of a sharply increasing marginal cost curve for energy—not even for oil. As a study for the Brookings Institution notes: "The world is not about to run out of energy. The known and probable deposits of oil, coal, gas, and uranium are still enormous and there are no insurmountable physical barriers to the expansion of energy production from these sources in order to meet the world's needs though this century and beyond."[5]

If the study is right, then how can the sudden increase (and its maintenance for several years) in the price of oil be explained? (1) Some forms of energy are not easily interchangeable. Automobiles are designed for gasoline and cannot switch to coal. Home heating, while more flexible than automobiles, still takes a considerable investment to change over. (2) Consumers bound to one form of energy often pressure the government to keep that price low—witness the pressures to keep both gasoline and natural gas at below market prices; this delays any changeovers. (3) Energy costs, while in the aggregate high, are still a small part of the cost of most finished products or services. Even home heating and gasoline amount to relatively small portions of the total incomes of most Americans. This leads to inelastic demands.

(4) There has not been time yet for major changes to develop. Changes in consumption due to price, moreover, are hard to assess in a period when income has been fluctuating.

Many believe that the world will be facing not an energy shortage, but an energy glut. One need only make small changes in the projected rates of consumption and production to produce a glut on paper. In one model done for the Brookings Institution, the effect of a $7.50-per-barrel price was tested against some rather conservative changes in pre-1972 projections. Rates of consumption growth were cut 0.9 percent (from 5.4 percent to 4.5 percent), much more conservative than government estimates, and projected additional supplies of other energy, on a source-by-source basis, were made. The result of this exercise indicated a glut of oil developing in the late 1970s.[6]

Such a glut is already occurring. Indeed, since the initial supply shortages associated with the 1973 embargo ended, there have been no shortages of oil and OPEC's main concern has been the prevention of additional production. Hence what we may see in the 1980s is not a shortage, but a very plentiful supply of energy, matching the curve SS_2 of Fig. 17.1.

Some writers go even beyond this, projecting lower energy costs.[7] Such arguments are hooked into historic trends and to ideas of experience curve behavior. Moreover, as many governments pour in funds to hasten the development of alternative energy sources and more petroleum, there may be an overadjustment of the market. Macrae's Law, "Governments produce surpluses of what is expected to be in short supply and shortages of what is expected to be in surplus," may apply. Others, less sanguine about lowering costs, suggest rather that the success of governments in producing alternative energy will leave a high-cost energy structure, which the governments will find necessary to defend through limiting imports of cheaper energy. The higher price structure will thus become institutionalized.

Imperfect Competition and the Energy Crisis

Lacking evidence for a sudden change in the supply curve's shape due to natural factors, the economist then inquires about the nature of the industry, which, as we noted already, is cartelized. Nonetheless, there are special aspects to the cartel and earlier oligopoly that are both interesting and instructive.

The development of the energy crisis is closely connected with the theory of oligopoly as developed in Chapter 15. To reset the stage: The leading oil companies had by the late 1920s achieved a mixture of formal and informal understandings about the nature of their competition; this involved the fixing of shares of output in major oil fields and a basing-point pricing system. Known to oil people as "The Majors" (and after the 1950s to journalists as "The Seven Sisters"), these leading oil firms dominated world markets for several decades.[8] In 1953, for instance, only a handful of companies outside the majors had any production outside their home countries. The five U.S. majors, for instance, had foreign investments of $1,549 million, compared to only $219 million (12 percent) for other U.S. companies.[9] The situation with other countries was even more lopsided.

The majors, moreover, were vertically integrated—that is, they controlled most of the oil from the exploration stage, to the wellhead, and into the gas tank or oil furnace. The majors always made some sales to independents (keeping them carefully in line) and some to each other. Some majors were generally "long" on oil (having more wells than outlets), such as British Petroleum or California Standard; some were generally short on oil, as were Shell or Texaco. The ideal, however, was to have a good balance between the oil being discovered and pumped and that which was sold. This enabled a company to plan a smooth flow of gasoline and oil, avoiding shortages that would alienate consumers, yet not building up considerable overinvestments in storage and exploration activity. Exxon generally had the best balance—both between supplies and markets and on its books.

Vertical integration that allows continuous coordination is economically beneficial, a point often stressed by the oil companies in their attempt to stem U.S. congressional bills to break up the companies. But vertical integration also has a darker side. The integration of the oil companies back into production (a process that began around the turn of the century) led to oligopoly. It discouraged the exploration for oil by independents (who without a marketing network could not sell their oil), while it also discouraged the marketing of oil by independents, who would lack their own supplies. By forcing the independent company to provide both oil and markets, vertical integration raised the barriers to entry (though not, as we shall see, high enough to prevent entry).

Vertical integration also had another aspect bound to cause trouble— transfer pricing. As we have seen in Chapter 16, intracorporate sales are always a cause for some concern, and nowhere has that concern been larger, or more justified, than in petroleum. The majors kept the price of oil high at the wellhead, billing their own refineries and selling to outsiders at or near the "posted" prices they established. As a consequence, the refineries themselves and the gas stations rarely made a large return on investment. This manipulation of prices had several important effects:

1. It shifted profits from the marketing and refining country to the producing nation. This is one of the reasons oil companies frequently paid few U.S. taxes.

2. It made it extremely difficult for independent refiners to earn good returns, thus strengthening the oligopoly.

3. The marketing of gasoline placed little emphasis on profitability (breaking even was about all the companies wanted), and most on the ability to

sell more gasoline. This led to a proliferation of gas stations and retail promotions, many of which were both unsightly and uneconomic.

The power of the majors in their heyday was considerable. In 1936, Mexico nationalized all oil lands in its country, ending some twenty years of unsettled relations. The new Mexican national oil company could find no foreign buyers for its oil. "Fortunately," Mexico's fields were already well past their peak and the national market was taking most of its production anyway, so the nationalization was not disastrous. Nonetheless, the lesson was apparent; none of the majors would buy Mexican oil. Independents, fearful that cooperation with Mexico would hurt their chances of buying oil from the majors, turned their backs; and even the U.S. government, on the eve of the Second World War, turned down Mexican oil.

Then in 1951, Mohammed Mossadeq, radical premier of Iran, seized the oil facilities of British Petroleum in Iran. Iran, unlike Mexico, needed export markets greatly, yet no oil firm in the world would buy Iranian oil. The result in Iran was a severe economic depression, the overthrow of Mossadeq, and the restoration of the powers of the more conservative Shah. One of the Shah's first acts was to invite the major oil companies back to Iran. Ownership of the fields was to remain with Iran, but compensation was paid to British Petroleum, and the consortium of majors was to run the fields. (Unbeknownst to the Shah, the majors prorated the Iranian fields, as explained in Chapter 15.) This was considered a major victory for the oil firms.[10]

Although it was hardly apparent at the time, the Iranian boycott (and a subsequent battle with Italian interests) marked the end of a period, not its high point. The considerable barriers to entry were being hurdled with increasing frequency. In the decades since the oil cartel had been arranged, a number of things had occurred to lower the hurdles. Improved technology had, among other things, made it possible to build smaller refineries producing more gasoline (the catalytic cracking refineries). Independent firms grew up that would design and build refining facilities; others would drill or explore on contract. Shipping companies built their own tankers for hire to any oil company. Hence much of the capital needed formerly to enter into foreign oil operations could be rented. Recalling our discussion in Chapter 16, the reader could note how the market mechanism came to be more efficient than internal allocation. The new entrants to foreign oil operations were of several kinds:

1. First came many of the "smaller" (by oil company standards) American companies. The high rates of profit made by the majors tempted the companies, while the diminishing supplies of U.S. oil goaded them. The names of many of these companies should be familiar to American (and by now some foreign) students—Atlantic Richfield, Cities Service (Citgo), Phillips, Standard of Indiana (AMOCO), Sun, and Union. They had be-

come well established in the United States, but had not before the war invested abroad. Another group of smaller American companies, such as Occidental, Tenneco, and Kerr-McGee, also moved into foreign production. In addition, a number of natural gas and chemical companies went abroad to seek their own sources of oil or to diversify (for example, El Paso Gas, Allied Chemical, Union Carbide).

2. The same phenomenon occurred elsewhere, with some twenty-five private firms expanding abroad—for example, Belgium's Petrofina, England's Ultramar, or Italy's Montecatini.

3. Finally, some fifteen government companies began petroleum operations, each backed by its national government. Some of these were "yardstick" companies, designed to provide a standard of efficiency against which to measure the performance of private companies. Some were designed to pressure the majors into keeping retail prices low. Some, like Iran's NIOC, were foreign marketing companies in their own right. NIOC, for example, has an important interest in New York's Ashland Oil.

The entry of these newcomers to foreign production and marketing fundamentally changed the shape of the oil industry. Recall that in 1952 the U.S. majors held some 87 percent of the foreign assets of U.S. oil companies; by 1972 this percentage had fallen to 65 percent. A similar weakening of the position of the majors is found in exploration, refining, and ownership of proven reserves and sales. Thus the industry was changing from a highly concentrated one to one of far more moderate concentration.[11]

The entry of so many new companies made the oligopolists' problem of controlling supplies considerably more difficult. Many of the new entrants had spent years tangling with the majors. Indeed, their very success was often linked to being noncooperative. Standard of Indiana, for instance, found its first foreign oil in Saudi Arabia only because it had not signed the 1928 Red Line Agreement, which restricted noncooperative ventures in that area. (Standard of Indiana, did, however, later agree to cooperate with the majors in the field's subsequent development.) Occidental's president, Armand Hammer, had fought the majors tooth and claw on more than one occasion.[12] As shown in Fig. 15.5, any expansion of the share of a minor company forces the major companies to cut back production to maintain the umbrella price. The majors' annoyance at the minor companies was understandable, however economically unjustified it may have been.

Beyond the companies' struggle for market share lay the producing countries' struggle for the same thing. In effect, at that time (as well as now) it was the oil companies who decided the market share of each country. Each country put pressure on the oil companies to increase its share. When the majors controlled world markets, there was little a country could do if it failed to get its share. But with new entrants, the countries could turn to independents and pressure them. Thus the already difficult balancing act involving seven companies and a number of producing countries was becoming much more difficult with the new entrants.

Despite such changes, the message of "Iran" still rang in the ears of most petroleum-producing countries for twenty years. In those years the relations among oil companies were hardly harmonious, but some of the noise was love making. The producing countries as a whole managed to increase their "take" of oil revenues. As with most countervailing power situations, however, this led neither to lower prices nor to the inclusion of additional producers.

Most new tax agreements worked in a way that gained considerable significance at that time and later on. Table 17.1 demonstrates the typical tax arrangement, with the posted price being used as the "value" of the oil; this in turn yields a 12 percent royalty and a profits tax based on the difference between the cost of that oil and the posted price, after royalty.

TABLE 17.1. TYPICAL OIL TAX ARRANGEMENT

Price per barrel	$2.00
Royalty (12%)	0.24
	1.76
Cost of oil	0.20
	1.56
Profit tax (50%)	0.78
Company's profit	$0.78

This posted price by the end of the 1960s had become a fiction, since less and less oil was being sold at that price. Increasing sales in the spot market and long-term contract market were being made at prices below those posted—some as low as $1.50 per barrel. Note that if you work over the "cost" to the company of the oil in Table 17.1, you will see that it is the cost of extraction and moving to port ($0.20), plus the royalty of $0.24, plus the "profits" tax of $0.78, or $1.22 in all. Even at $1.50 the company could make a profit.

What occurred in the later 1950s was a considerable number of sales of oil below the $2.00 posted price, reflecting the low cost of Arabian oil. To adjust to the downward pressure on prices, Exxon executives lowered the posted price to $1.80. Other firms followed Exxon's price leadership. While Exxon's management saw this as a technical question, the oil-producing countries were enraged. One boardroom decision, dropping the posted price of oil, had cost them something over $0.13 a barrel in tax revenue. They had, moreover, "understood" that the oil companies would consult with them before any such move. The change in price was a *fait accompli* but the oil nations vowed to prevent a reoccurrence and banded together to form an organization known as the Organization of Petroleum Exporting Countries (OPEC). Initially, its membership was only five countries and its influence was weak, but over the years its membership expanded, though it remained cautious until 1972. Its main achievement through the end of the 1960s was keeping the posted price from falling even further, though that price became less and less representative of the actual transactions made for oil.

The oil crisis began, however, not with OPEC, but with a country not at the time an OPEC member, Libya. Libya had a number of special features that set it apart from its neighbors. (1) It produced a "light" crude—one that was easy to refine, yielding higher percentages of gasoline—hence its oil usually sold at premium prices. (2) It was closer to Europe than the Middle Eastern countries, whose oil came by tanker around Africa. (3) Its pace of development was slow enough that it had accumulated a substantial foreign exchange surplus. (4) It had a relatively large number of nonmajor oil companies operating in its borders—55 percent of its oil, contrasted with 15 percent for other OPEC countries, was produced by nonmajors.

Libya and its producers, particularly Armand Hammer of Occidental (Oxy for short), were by this time thorns in the sides of the majors. The majors were under pressure from Persian Gulf governments, particularly Iran, to increase production. Back in the old days, Exxon would simply have cut back Libya's share to do so, but now no major controlled the Libyan production. Oxy was hardly party to such arrangements and was happily producing under the majors' umbrella. (The more imaginative may picture this.) If Exxon were to keep prices up, it could only do so by reducing its own and the Persian Gulf's market share, worsening its relations there.

The denouement came after the radical government of Colonel Qadaffi overthrew the conservative Libyan king. Soon after taking office, the Qadaffi government demanded $0.40 more a barrel for its oil, enforcing its demands with partial embargoes on the export of oil. Exxon was pleased with this, since it enabled it to increase Persian Gulf production, where it had vastly larger stakes than it did in Libya. Then came threats of nationalization. Armand Hammer, Occidental's president, went to Exxon's president and told him that he would resist this demand if Exxon would supply him with all the oil he would otherwise have taken from Libya at around Libyan costs. Hammer figured that Exxon would agree because otherwise the oil companies would look divided. Hammer was unable to forgo his Libyan oil, as it was necessary to feed his international marketing network. Exxon's reply was not satisfactory: It would indeed supply Oxy with oil, but not at a price anywhere near Oxy's suggestion. To Exxon, the seizure of Oxy's lands would be an easy solution to the oil-balance situation. Oxy capitulated to Libya's demands, and shortly after, all other Libyan independents did the same.

Cooperation of the independents notwithstanding, Libya gradually nationalized all the foreign holdings in the country. Unlike the Iranian case, some twenty years earlier, however, Libya was able to continue to market the oil, partially through the independents, who still needed the oil and were hoping for good compensation, and partly through national companies. The new message was not "Remember Iran," but "Remember Libya."

OPEC was stunned. This unsophisticated Libyan colonel (and his quite sophisticated advisers) had done what OPEC had been unable to do. OPEC itself then demanded improvements in oil prices to match the Libyan and received surprisingly little trouble. Prices were increased in late 1970 (to match the Libyan), in early 1972, and again in 1973. The oil companies—despite a "waiver" of antitrust action from the United States—were unable to present a united front. The concessions in retrospect seem small. The December agreement eliminated "disparities" in posted prices, raising Arabian oil to Libyan prices. Later agreement raised the posted price $0.20 and tied these prices to currency values, which led to another $0.15 raise in June of 1973. The problem with these price increases was that they did not reflect in the least the actual cost of oil. In effect the posted price became a way of raising taxes—for every $0.10 increase in posted price the countries got $0.012 in royalty and $0.055 in profits taxes (which had been raised to 55 percent), and the actual cost in profits to the oil companies of a $0.10 price rise was $0.067.[13]

Negotiated price changes ended in 1973. OPEC wanted to double the price; the companies wanted to let it increase 25 percent. When the companies refused to go along, OPEC raised the price unilaterally from $3.00 to $5.11. Then in January of 1974 the price was raised again to $11.65 and in October of 1975 to $12.38, which is close to its 1977 price.[14]

One can easily overplay the role of the Arab-Israeli war of October 1973 in these happenings. The Arab embargo was never really in itself that effective. Indeed, it was probably the speculation on higher prices that held up supplies more than the estimated 7 percent reduction in shipments. The war and the embargo served to further divide the Western nations and to demoralize its negotiators, but the war became more of a political excuse for an economic action than a political action in itself. This is not to say that the Arab-Israeli problem was not linked to the price increase in any way at all. Some writers have maintained that the U.S. Arab policy, involved as it is with oil revenues, led directly to OPEC's moves. They argue that this was because of the neglect of Arab problems. Others argue that some pro-Arab elements in the U.S. Department of State (and in the oil companies) were happy enough to see at least some moderate price rises because it would strengthen the Arabs' hand in negotiating with the United States and Israel.

Macroeconomic Aspects of the Energy Situation

The macroeconomic questions are of equal interest. The increase in oil's price and the short-term inelasticity of demand for oil meant that there would be large balance of payments deficits in consuming nations and surpluses in producing nations. What impact would these have on aggregate demand, particularly in buying countries? How would world monetary stability be affected? Finally, how, in the long run, would the real transfer of goods and services to the producing countries affect growth rates? Policy makers viewed the situation with considerable trepidation. Even now the outlines of what did happen and what is still happening are just beginning to emerge.

The effect on aggregate demand was perhaps the most serious problem faced by the consuming countries in the initial year of the price increases. With world consumption of oil at roughly twenty billion barrels a year, a price increase of $7.00 (from $3.00 to $10.00) a barrel would at a maximum transfer some $140 billion from consumers to producers. Such a figure is too high, though. In the first place, the posted price was used to figure the tax, not at that time to determine the selling price. As indicated above, a $0.10 price rise costs the company about $0.07. Secondly, much of the oil consumed was not imported—U.S., Canadian, Russian, and North Sea oil all were consumed domestically, and most of this was under price control. More realistically, figures for the amount of income transferred are in the $60-80 billion range— very substantial in any case. Thirdly, there would be some deflection of demand into local oil supplies and substitutes, depending on the elasticity of the import demand for foreign oil. The domestic supplies, at least in the short run, would be highly inelastic and demand about equally unresponsive. This lack of response would be further compounded by governmental policies of holding energy prices at or near precrisis levels. Econometric estimates indicated that the deflection of demand into domestic consumption would provide only a slight stimulus for domestic expenditures.

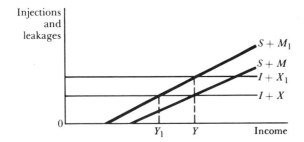

FIGURE 17.2

Figure 17.2, accordingly, shows this decline as an "autonomous" (oil-price induced) shift in the S+M schedule. Income is shown to fall from Y to Y_1.

Standard "Keynesian" economic policy suggests that the governments should restimulate demand, replacing those billions that have gone abroad.

We can show this as a shift in the $I + X$ curve, reflecting, let us say, an easy money policy. Income shifts back to Y. Such a policy has unfortunate side

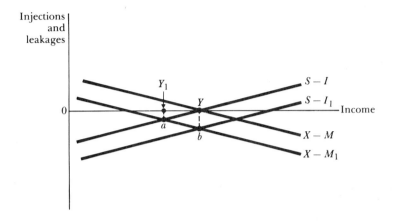

FIGURE 17.3

effects of increasing the balance of payments deficits, as can be seen by Fig. 17.3, where the curves are rearranged into $S - I$ and $X - M$, and the initial deficit Y_1a is enlarged to Yb.

Unfortunately, the world did not appear to be in any "standard Keynesian" situation in October of 1973. Prices had been rising steadily in most developed areas, while there was still substantial unemployment and idle industrial capacity. The United States was extricating itself from a rather unhappy experiment at using price controls and reflationary policy. Conservative and liberal economists alike were recognizing that a decline in aggregate demand does not necessarily prevent price increases. The oil price increases made the problem that much more difficult because the increases were bound to be passed on, yet no one expected that prices elsewhere in the economy would fall as demand was redirected. The balance of payments question, then, was really less important than the fear of rekindling the inflation.

The reaction of the U.S. government was accordingly rather conservative, letting the contractionary effects of the oil price increases take hold of the economy. The oil price increase alone probably contributed to about a 2.5 percent decline in GNP according to a Brookings estimate. (This includes first-year multiplier effects.)[15] In addition, however, the U.S. government actually supplemented that contraction. The "automatic stabilizers" in income taxes caused higher revenues as people were thrown into higher tax brackets (despite no real income increases), while government expenditures actually lagged behind the price increases. The money supply expanded at about half the rate of price increases, increasing the demand for cash balances and helping to drive up interest rates to record levels. The result was the highest level of unemployment in more than three decades—but the inflation rate was slowed markedly. The option taken by the government (not, incidentally, returned to office) was clear; whether it was the right one will be debated for many years. In our context, though, we should recognize that the oil crisis carried two conflicting pressures—an upward pressure on prices and a downward pressure on aggregate demand. The government used the former to contain the latter.

Japanese economic policy was similar to the American—a swift (and even more effective) strangulation of demand in order to hold off a cost-push inflation. In Europe as a whole, the response was more moderate. This is partly because the tax system in Europe has fewer "automatic stabilizers," depending heavily as it does on value-added taxes (which are fixed percentages), and partly because the business cycle itself was in an earlier stage and still carried with it upward momentum.

The effect of higher oil prices on economic activity in non-oil-producing less developed countries was not initially as severe as feared. True, the nations had to face higher oil prices plus declining demand caused by the recessions in developed nations. They were helped, however, by two things. First, they already had considerable revenues from the high commodity prices of the previous years, and sugar prices began to skyrocket in 1973 and 1974. Second, the OPEC nations lent money to many of the hard-hit less developed countries. Longer-term prospects, however, are not as bright, as we shall see below.

The balance of payments surpluses of the OPEC countries were initially rather worrisome. The world had just passed through a series of monetary crises. How would the emerging floating-rate system take these new funds? The answer was, "very well, indeed." Fortunately (in the authors' opinion), the gold standard had ended and there were few fixed rates to attack. The countries that were having balance of payments surpluses did not possess currencies in demand by the international banking community. Solid as the Saudi Arabian riyal is, it is not an international medium of exchange or store of value. Gold was unavailable outside the private market, so most of the surplus had to be placed, basically, in U.S. dollars or in Eurodollars.

The Eurodollar system proved a convenient and efficient way to "recycle" funds from the OPEC countries to borrowers in less developed countries. The demand for medium-term loans by developing countries rose sharply. Arab banks participated in many consortia that handled such loans. Much of the shorter-term Eurodollar deposits found their way, often by intermediation, into medium-term loans. The surprising thing was that the financial system handled these so-called petrodollars so easily.

There was, at least in the beginning, a fear of "sloshing"—a fear that, though most of the petrodollars would stay put, those at the margins would be large enough to cause speculative pressures against whatever currency was weak at the moment. By and large, however, the OPEC bankers have been very conservative with their funds and no serious problems have yet emerged.

The national income effects were further complicated by the capital movements. The funds that were reinvested in the United States or in the Eurodollar market served to lower interest rates there. The United States tried to sterilize most of the inflow, but the Eurodollar market in particular became very much a borrower's market. This would in turn have stimulated investment and, since many of the loans were ultimately used to finance imports, the exports of many countries. Nonetheless, the uncertainty created by the oil crisis discouraged any sort of investment boom, even with money available.

Finally, the surplus money never amounted to as much as feared. Some OPEC nations proved quite able to spend the additional money—Iran and Venezuela, in particular, have appetites for any foreign exchange they can get. Hence even in the first year, expenditures by OPEC countries were higher than expected. Then the price and the recession-induced decline in demand for oil (and a warm North American winter) held oil revenues down below initial projections.

OPEC's Situation

Considering both macro and micro effects, we can see that the OPEC nations face considerable problems in their pricing strategy.

1. The world has not returned to the low rates of inflation and vigorous growth that characterized the pre-1972 period. This has meant that OPEC nations are caught with declining purchasing power *and* stagnant sales.

2. The sales problem has been worsened by the coming on-stream of Alaskan and North Sea oil—and there is more oil farther upstream. Accordingly, there is a widely recognized oil glut for perhaps the next decade (though many predict troubles beyond that point).

3. The failure of the United States to develop a coherent energy policy has worked two ways. While it has helped OPEC's sales, it has depressed the value of the dollar, the main store of value for OPEC's reserves.

4. OPEC nations are accordingly faced with a problem of the exhaustion of their nonrenewable resources while the store of value that they must choose to offset this exhaustion—foreign investment—is also declining in value.

5. Cartels are always more difficult to manage during a glut. OPEC has never quite mastered the political problem of allocating shares and still relies on the oil companies to handle a great deal of that problem for them.

As of the late 1970s, OPEC had responded by doing nothing—that is, by letting the real price of oil decline. At a moderate 6 percent inflation, a price of $12.35 a barrel (prevailing in 1976) is $7.50 in only eight years. This was the price that Henry Kissinger suggested when the oil crisis developed as being a good long-run equilibrium price. There may also arise considerable discounting and cheating, something hard to trace in the byzantine pricing system of oil.

Perhaps in the long run the best policy is to let the real price fall, given the availability of substitutes. Ironically, the greatest aid to the macro climate—a U.S. energy policy emphasizing more production and more conservation—would restore OPEC's ability to raise prices, but would contribute to the energy glut. Ultimately, the OPEC nations may have to recognize that their oil, while perhaps more valuable than it was in the 1960s, does not command the kind of rents they so earnestly desire.

Notes

1. Estimates of world reserves appear in several books, in particular: John M. Blair, *The Control of Oil* (New York: Pantheon Books, 1976); Joseph A. Yager and Eleanor B. Steinberg, *Energy and U.S. Foreign Policy* (Cambridge, Mass.: Ballinger, 1975); Neil H. Jacoby, *Multinational Oil* (New York: Macmillan, 1974). One indication of the way "proven reserves" grow without any spectacular discovery is found in Saudi Arabian statistics. After the fields were found, but largely untested in 1948, the proven reserves were 6 billion barrels, though the wealth of the field was suspected by then. By 1962, the proven reserves were 52 billion barrels. A decade later, with no new big discovery and ten years of pumping out oil, the proven reserves were 138 billion (Jacoby, *Multinational Oil*, pp. 68-69).
2. The U.S. Geological Survey has given such estimates for Saudi Arabia, the Soviet Union, Algeria, Kuwait, and Libya (Yager and Steinberg, *Energy and U.S. Foreign Policy*, p. 194).
3. One estimate for the United Nations guesses well over 2 trillion barrels in the sea beds, mostly on the continental shelf (Jacoby, *Multinational Oil*, p. 271).
4. One of the authors remembers carrying out the coal ashes and stoking the fire through 1952—and he wasn't the last kid on the block to see his coal furnace replaced, either. In a house he later owned, the same furnace had been converted from wood to coal to oil. Obviously such changes take time, but they do occur.
5. The quotation is from Yager and Steinberg, *Energy and U.S. Foreign Policy*, p. 3. Other information on gas, coal, and uranium is largely drawn from that book.
6. Edward R. Fried, "World Market Trends and Bargaining Leverage" in Yager and Steinberg, *Energy and U.S. Foreign Policy*, pp. 231-275.
7. Of particular note among those expecting an energy glut are Herman Kahn, the noted futurist, and Norman Macrae, editor of the influential *Economist* magazine.
8. The majors were: Exxon (then Standard Oil of New Jersey), Royal Dutch Shell, Socony-Mobil, British Petroleum, Gulf, Texaco, and California Standard Oil.
9. See Jacoby, *Multinational Oil*, pp. 146-147.

10. The history of the oil business has been told in many books. From the suggested readings, the interested might try Anthony Sampson's *The Seven Sisters*, or Blair's or Jacoby's books cited in Note 1.

11. See Jacoby, *Multinational Oil*, pp. 120-149, 172-212.

12. Early in his career, Hammer had brought Soviet oil into Europe, much to the annoyance of the majors. Just before the crisis, Hammer had attempted to build a refinery in Maine in an area to be declared a free-trade zone. At that time, oil imports were restricted (to hold up U.S. prices), but refined products were not. Hence Hammer could refine in the "free-trade zone," avoiding the import restrictions, and send out refined products. The proposal was not approved, but it served to focus national attention on the import controls and on New England's energy problems, annoying the majors.

13. Actual price changes are more obscure than posted price changes. To the extent that a company pumps its own oil, the posted price serves only as a tax base and the actual cost is only about 70 percent of any tax increase. The OPEC nations have, however, rapidly taken over the oil wells themselves. Under today's arrangements, the oil is sold to the marketing oil firms at a discount, which presumably pays for their services and managerial aid. At present such discounts are small. Where oil is marketed directly by the producing government's company (as with Iran's NIOC), the old transfer question comes up again. The free market price has been running over $12.00 so there does not yet appear to be widespread discounting. The free market is, however, only for a minority of sales.

14. Much of this discussion is based on Edward R. Fried and Charles L. Schultze, eds., *Higher Oil Prices and the World Economy* (Washington, D.C.: The Brookings Institution, 1975.)

15. Two relevant models are described in Fried, "World Market Trends and Bargaining Leverage," and in George L. Perry's essay in Fried and Schultze, *Higher Oil Prices and the World Economy*.

CHAPTER

18

TRADE AND DEVELOPMENT: THE PROBLEMS OF THE LESS DEVELOPED COUNTRIES

The famed economist Alfred Marshall believed that trade was a major cause of the economic progress of nations.[1] This opinion, more or less standard during the nineteenth and much of the twentieth centuries, fits in well with the Heckscher-Ohlin version of comparative advantage theory. Low-income, less developed countries (LDCs) will benefit from international trade. Rising demand for their agricultural and mineral output (primary products) emanating from the industrial countries overseas will stimulate investment and output. The resultant widening of markets and rise in production will provide higher incomes, allowing the residents of LDCs to share in the growth of consumption, increasing their desire for consumer goods, and stimulating production yet again.

Heckscher-Ohlin theory suggests that comparative advantage will lie with goods produced by those factors of production that are abundant and accordingly cheap. In theory, at least, most LDCs will initially specialize in the export of primary products. In these countries capital, technology, and education are the scarce factors. Labor and land are relatively abundant. Hence it makes sense for such countries to eschew manufacturing for the time being, specializing in primary products. Later, the static comparative advantage for these primary products may alter. Profits can be used to finance investment. Higher incomes widen the domestic market. Large-scale manufacturing for that market becomes increasingly a reasonable proposition. Imported capital and technical assistance help in the process, and so development proceeds. Thus trade becomes, as Dennis Robertson put it, "the engine of growth."

The Critique of Trade

Today, views such as Robertson's are much challenged. The pendulum has swung so far that many economists hold that international trade itself must bear the blame for underdevelopment. "Dependency theory" and the "theory of unequal exchange" have become buzz words in the corridors of power in developing nations. Dependency theory had its origins in Latin America after World War II, and its greatest popularity may still lie in that region, although it now has many supporters in Africa and Asia as well. André Gunder Frank is perhaps the leading exponent of the idea that trade was not (and is not) an engine of growth; rather it locks underdeveloped countries into a world trading system as thralls to the rich countries, doomed to deteriorating trading conditions and sequestered from development. Hence only a revolutionary change in trading relations will allow these countries to develop.[2]

The evidence cited against international trade is varied. The arguments against trade as an engine of growth fall into two basic categories. (1) The prospects for exports from developing countries are said to be poor and their price outlook dim (summarized under the terms of trade argument), while there is little world capacity to absorb an increasing volume of exports. (2) Trade, by its nature, is said to fail to stimulate growth beyond the rather small number of people directly involved in it—the enclave argument. We begin with the first of these.

Export Pessimism and the Terms of Trade. The terms of trade, to recall our discussion in Chapter 10, refers to the exchange of physical quantitites of goods. An argument that the terms of trade are falling means that one nation must exchange more and more to obtain the same amount of foreign goods as before. This definition is that of net barter or commodity terms of trade. The proposition advanced by a good number of economists is that there is a secular long-run tendency of the terms of trade to turn against the primary product exports of the LDCs. This argument has had wide support in the United Nations, and has played a major role in the deliberations of the various sessions of UNCTAD (The United Nations Commission on Trade and Development).[3]

To find a secular decline, we look for a long-term trend covering at least several decades. It is generally agreed that yearly or cyclical price changes, no matter how severe and disruptive, are not evidence of long-term decline. Commodity terms of trade, you will recall, are figured by the index of export prices divided by the index of import prices, or P_x/P_m. This is then turned into an index by setting it equal to 100 in some base year. In subsequent years, rising export prices and/or falling import prices would give higher numbers, say 120, a so-called favorable improvement in the terms of trade.

What is the evidence? First and most famous are the United Nations figures obtained from old League of Nations data. With 1938 equaling 100, they show primary products relative to manufactured goods in world trade. It may seem that the UN should have used long-term data for the LDCs versus developed countries, rather than primary products versus manufacturing. But this could not be done, because there are no long-term statistics for the LDCs, many of which are only recently independent, and blessed with very imperfect data from their colonial heritage. Thus the UN adopted the device of considering the figures for Great Britain, which are excellent and cover a very long period. Since Britain historically exported manufactures and imported primary products, the UN believed that the inverse of Britain's terms of trade would show the terms of trade for primary producers. These figures, shown in Table 18.1, have been widely used by various UN agencies. The information is supplemented by UN figures for more recent years that compare the LDCs as a group and purport to show a continuing unfavorable trend. If 1972 = 100, we find that from this evidence, the situation does indeed appear serious. A long-term decline in the terms of trade for LDCs fairly jumps from the page.

But it is possible to cast grave doubts on both the logic of the argument

TABLE 18.1.

Terms of trade for			
Primary product exports (inverse of British terms of trade) (1938 = 100)		LDCs as a group (1972 = 100)	
1876-1880	163	1953	110
1896-1900	142	1956	107
1913	137	1960	104
1928	123	1964	102
1938	100	1968	101
		1972	100

and on the statistics themselves. If anything, this terms of trade argument is an excellent demonstration of how easy it is to "prove" something with statistics, the numbers giving the appearance of precise meaning to a question that is really very much in doubt.

The commodity terms of trade: an inadequate measure. It is actually rather difficult to draw conclusions about the impact of changing prices from the commodity terms of trade alone. Many writers imply that a higher index number for P_x/P_m is a good thing, a lower number a bad thing. Consider, though, that a rise in the index number may *not* be favorable overall if P_x rises such that the effect is to reduce the *volume* of exports enough to cut back the total revenue earned in exporting. Or consider that a *fall* in P_x/P_m may well leave a country better off if increased productivity, leading to a higher quantity of exports, caused the fall in the first place. Incomes earned through exports may rise significantly even though export prices have fallen. (This is why American and Canadian farmers prospered as their cheap grain captured many of the markets of Europe. There is also the example of Japan, which underwent a drastic decline in its terms of trade between 1910 and 1920 and again after 1930. This gave a vigorous push to exports, led to the acquisition of new markets and resulted in a multiplied impact on national income.) Unfortunately, as noted in Chapter 10, attempts to construct the "factoral" terms of trade that would capture these changes in productivity have had little success. But it is not enough to say that the commodity terms of trade are deteriorating, hence LDCs are worse off.

The doubtful evidence for a decline in the terms of trade. A serious problem with the commodity terms of trade data is that they do not reflect quality changes. Little work has been done to correct the data for quality improvement (although in theory this might be done). Few would doubt that since 1876 quality changes in manufacturing have been far greater than in primary products. Coal today is the same as coal a hundred years ago, but the motor car and the electric light did not even exist then and have improved enormously since their invention. Furthermore, the use of British statistics to show a decline of the terms of trade for primary products is fraught with peril. The British all during this period valued exports f.o.b. (not including ocean freight) but imports c.i.f. (including freight). Many countries still do the same. The result is that any major shift in transport costs would affect only the average price of imports. Several economists have estimated that the great part of the decline in P_m from 1876 to the start of World War I was due to the fall in transport costs caused by the introduction of large steam-powered cargo ships built of iron and steel, and the spread of railways abroad. Thus, says E. M. Wright, it was possible for wool prices to rise 12 percent in Buenos Aires and simultaneously to fall 8 percent in London, due to better transatlantic shipping and to the construction of the Argentine rail network. Theodore Morgan argues that in the 100 years before World War II, transport costs as a percentage of the c.i.f. costs of goods in world trade fell from 30-70 percent to only 10 percent.

Another critique has been presented by Gottfried Haberler, who has pointed out that the supply and demand for the (primary product) exports of LDCs are affected by such divergent conditions that movements in a broad, weighted index leave us with little useful information. Why expect identical or even reasonably similar behavior in the prices of such disparate commodities as food, fibres, fats and oils, minerals, and petroleum? There are many cases of completely differing trends in their prices. The British economist Alexan-

der Cairncross has written that "to average the experience [of the less developed countries] is to presume common elements that may have no real
existence."

A further problem affects the British statistics quoted by the UN. The
figures quoted in Table 18.1 give the worst possible impression that can be
drawn from the evidence. Actually, the available data go back to 1801. And if
we set 1900 equal to 100, the terms of trade showed sharp improvement for
primary products from 1801 until just before 1876, and the long downward
trend between 1876 and 1938 still left primary products in a much better
situation than they had been in at the start of the nineteenth century.

Finally, the most recent UN figures showing the terms of trade for LDCs
do not bear out a steady downward trend in the period after World War II.
Table 18.1 showed 1953 equal to 110, and 1972 equal to 100. But the years
since then do not show a continued fall. If the table is extended, we find:

1972	100
1973	110
1974	153
1975	136
1976	142

It has sometimes been argued that the improvement in the 1970s has been
due primarily to petroleum and certain minerals, and that *other* primary
products are as bad a bet as before. Here indeed is the crux of the matter. The
terms of trade cover all primary products and thus tend to conceal as much as
they reveal. Some commodities are rising in price; some falling. An overall
average does not give a country sufficient information on which to base decisions concerning primary product exports.

Possible causes for a decline in the terms of trade. Pointing out the weakness in the
statistics is not enough, however, to counter the arguments of those who still
expect an eventual decline in the terms of trade against the primary product
exports of LDCs. The logic of such arguments is also important.

The first of these arguments might be called the productivity theory.
Popularized by Hans Singer of the UN, this theory postulates that technical
progress in developed countries typically brings higher incomes in the form of
wages and profits. For exports of LDCs, on the other hand, technical progress
tends to lower prices. The reason is the greater ability of the developed world
to retain higher business and labor incomes, due to the stronger market
power of its large firms and the organized strength of its unions. With trade
unions weak in LDCs, and business enterprise often small in scale, productivity gains are dissipated to consumers abroad as competition reduces the

prices of exports. The argument actually sounds more plausible for an earlier era, as unions in recent years have grown rapidly in strength in LDCs and LDC governments often have fixed export prices. The argument is also of limited applicability to an explanation of the decline in terms of trade for primary products because it must apply to the exports of all products from LDCs and to primary products from developed nations—for example, monopoly power should raise the price of wheat from developed nations but not raise the price of clothing from LDCs.

The second argument is that of Raul Prebisch and Nicholas Kaldor, and deals with the familiar ratchet effect of economic theory. We would expect in a developed country with considerable elements of monopoly power that prices would normally rise in a boom but not fall during a slump. Unions, with their wage-push tendencies, and large firms avoid price cutting in their oligopolistic markets, joining forces in adding to the strength of the ratchet. This argument has major weaknesses. The relation of concentration to price increases is still hotly debated, with the statistics supporting both sides. Moreover, Charles Kindleberger has pointed out that labor's power alone will not raise prices unless the manufacturers have sufficient market power to pass on wage increases to buyers. This would require monopoly power in the product market as well. Otherwise, competition in the product market would result simply in reduced sales for any country with a cost-push inflation. As we argued in Chapter 15, product monopoly is uncommon nowadays. True, there was much talk of cartels before World War II, but today the impression is one of intense competition for most industrial products in world trade. LDCs can buy from many sources, as nontraditional as Japan, Italy, Czechoslovakia, and East Germany, or as traditional as the United States, Great Britain, France, the Soviet Union, or West Germany. Rather than a preponderance of *international* monopoly, market power appears largely a function of domestic protection behind tariff barriers. Hence monopoly labor power should not result in higher prices of manufactured goods.

The third theoretical argument, commonly associated with Prebisch, Ragnar Nurkse, and Edward M. Bernstein, focuses on supposed insufficient increases in the demand for primary products. A long-run decline in the terms of trade for LDCs originates in the slow rise in the demand for primary products contrasted with the rapid increase in demand for manufactured goods. There are several reasons for this. (1) Demand for food rises more slowly than income; once people have full bellies, they spend any excess on nonfood goods. This is called *Engel's Law*, after Ernst Engel (not Friedrich Engels), a nineteenth century Prussian mathematician. (2) As income shifts to higher levels, as is happening now in developed nations, demand shifts to service industries, which have a low ratio of raw material input to final output. (3) Technological improvement brings economies in the use of raw materials, as evidenced by better processing of scrap metal, electrolytic tin plating, and so forth. (4) There is also a displacement of natural raw materials by synthetics, as in the case of nitrates, cotton, and rubber. (5) Finally, there is widespread protection of domestic agriculture in developed countries. What is the support for such contentions?

Engel's Law is doubtless correct for developed countries. For example, the U.S. income elasticity of demand for food is only about 0.25, and American consumption of wheat per capita is approximately the same in the 1970s as it was in 1900. Engel's Law has yet to take effect in LDCs; there the income elasticity for food is high—nearly 1.0 in Latin America and India, and about 0.8 for LDCs as a whole. This means that sales among LDCs can grow; indeed, the vast bulk of increased sales of sugar have been to LDCs. Also note that income inelasticity is high for some foods such that the overall average can be misleading—and income inelastic foods are not heavily exported by LDCs. Coffee, tea, sugar, and pineapples are all income elastic, and are all LDC exports.

There is evidence to support points 2, 3, and 4. GATT reported that in the period 1938-1954, there was a fall in the ratio of raw material and fuel inputs to total manufacturing output in industrial countries from 25.8 percent to 20.8 percent. American figures, compared over a longer period of time, show this even more strikingly. According to the government's Paley Report, a dollar's worth of output in 1900 used $0.239 worth of raw materials, yet by 1950 a dollar's worth of output used only $0.128. We know also from the work of Theodore Schultz that real per capita income increased by about 80 percent more than real per capita consumption of raw materials between 1904 and 1950. Thus it appears that LDCs are faced with a serious problem of demand for their primary products.

Despite the impressiveness of the arguments, there are serious reservations. It is true that developed countries protect their agriculture, but with the exception of Argentina and Uruguay few LDCs produce the kinds of products that are protected. Protected crops are temperate zone, not tropical products. The tropical products that are protected are in the EEC, where the associated African members, LDCs themselves, receive the protection. Sugar, which in the form of beets is a temperate crop and as cane is a tropical crop, is also protected. There are few significant restrictions against other tropical crops. Most came into the United States free of duty even before the recent liberalization of tariffs against LDCs, and today virtually all have free access to the U.S. market.

Moreover, technical changes may increase the demand for certain raw materials; they do not always work against it. Demand has increased greatly since World War II for bauxite, copper, uranium, and petroleum, and it continues to rise, showing a high income elasticity. This will undoubtedly happen to other raw materials again. In short, the overall demand for primary products is of little interest to any specific country. What counts is the demand for what it exports.

There is yet another consideration: the ability of LDC exports to displace the exports and production of developed nations. Developed nations are important producers of primary products themselves. Indeed, at the beginning of the 1970s, 19 percent of the total value of world trade was in primary product exports from *developed* countries and only 15 percent from less developed countries. Thus developing countries could, it appears, displace developed country production of primary products, enlarging their markets that way. UN figures show the following seven items as the largest export products of the LDCs: petroleum, beverages, textiles, fibres, base metals, sugar, fats and oils, and rubber. Of these, there is direct competition between developed and less developed countries in petroleum, textiles, fibres, sugar, and fats and oils, and indirect competition in all the rest. Cairncross, for instance, feels that sluggish demand for the primary product exports of LDCs may in fact be symptomatic of the high price elasticity caused by the ready availability of primary products in the developed countries. If this is so, then the conclusion would be that high *price* elasticity for primary products might in large part offset the alleged *income* inelasticity of demand. The practical significance would be that a measure of price *reduction* might be most advantageous for the LDCs (a worsening of the commodity terms of trade). New, more efficient methods in agriculture, leading to lower prices, or lower taxes on exports could capture markets not available before.

There is, finally, the question of increasing scarcity of raw materials and primary products. Even if we accept fully the contention that the primary product exports are income inelastic, spending will rise if they become scarce. After all, price is a matter of supply as well as demand, and there may well be greatly diminishing returns in the production of primary products. If petroleum and metals become scarce; if arable land is subject to more intense use; if investment in agriculture is discouraged by the government development programs of the LDCs; then it follows that diminishing returns and higher prices will result—whether or not that demand is income inelastic. (This was the position of several noted economists, including Lord Keynes in a well-known article as long ago as 1923, and Colin Clark and Dennis Robertson.)

Kindleberger offers one final argument on the terms of trade. He suggests that a shift against LDCs will occur because their economies are less flexible than those of the developed world. It is harder in a less developed nation to move labor, land, capital, and management skills from one occupation to another. Transportation is worse, literacy lower, government abilities weak, and communication poorer—all leading to a poor ability to shift out of predictably declining industries. Hence a nation becomes locked into an export that is a loser. Very low elasticities of supply mean that it is difficult to respond to changing comparative advantage. Most economists concede a great deal of Kindleberger's argument. Inflexibility is common enough in LDCs—there are examples in nitrates, coffee, tea, jute, and bananas, to name a few. Any inflexible country suffering a decline in trade is certainly in a poor situation. The objection to Kindleberger's argument is, however, that the argument applies to any export (or any activity at all) from a developing nation. It would apply to the exporter of manufactures just as well as to the producer of primary products. It applies to producers of import substitutes (who could be driven out of business by cheaper imports) as much as to exports. It is not the nature of the product, or of trade, but underdevelopment itself that is at fault.

The issues concerning the terms of trade argument and export pessimism, in sum, are the following. (1) The case for a secular deterioration in the commodity terms of trade is really not very strong. Even staunch supporters of the argument must admit that the evidence is weak. (2) Of the theories purporting to show why a deterioration must occur, the "productivity" and "inflexibility" arguments seem logical. But they apply to all endeavors of the LDCs, both internal and external, and not just to primary product exports. (3) The "international product monopoly" argument does not seem very strong. (4) The case for declining demand for primary products, though questionable in some aspects and perhaps offset to some extent by considerations of price elasticity, remains a serious one for some products. Countries saddled with these particular primary products—income inelastic, subject to deteriorating terms of trade, and unable to capture additional markets through judicious price cutting—may well find primary product exporting a bad bet.

Balance of Payments Arguments. Closely related to the terms of trade arguments are the balance of payments arguments, popularized by Raul Prebisch of the Economic Commission for Latin America (ECLA). According to this theory, the capacity of LDCs to import, defined by the price of their exports times the quantity of their exports, is growing more slowly than is output in developed nations. This reinforces the claim that the demand for the exports of LDCs is income inelastic, and Prebisch's widely quoted statistic that the U.S. income elasticity of demand for imports is 0.66 is cited in evidence. Added to this, says Prebisch, the rate at which output can grow in LDCs without balance of payments troubles will depend on the income elasticity of demand for imports to the LDCs. This demand is assumed to be elastic, and the ECLA quotes a figure of 1.58 for Latin America. The reason for the high elasticity is said to be the international demonstration effect, whereby wants spread rapidly, and also the large import requirements of a development program.

Consider then: As income grows, LDCs want a larger amount of imports relative to their exports, compared with developed countries, which want a relatively smaller quantity of imports from the LDCs. Capital flows and foreign aid could, but are not likely to, make up the difference. The choice open to LDCs is thus (1) slower growth of output than in the developed world; (2) chronic balance of payments problems; or (3) frequent devaluation.

Earlier in the chapter we discussed the problem of income-inelastic demand for the exports of poor countries. When a country is stuck with an income-inelastic export product, the problem is serious—but note that the resources going into the export could after all be transferred to other uses, internal or external. If the transfer is difficult because transformation is limited due to specificity of the factors of production, or lack of skills and entrepreneurship, then of course the problem is doubly serious. But this is hardly a fault of *trade*, and surely any other scheme—domestic industrialization behind high tariff walls, general import substitution, or Soviet-style central planning—would perforce have to cope with exactly the same problems. Note also that the high income elasticity for imports to LDCs does not come about automatically as a rule of nature. It is due in general, as Prebisch states, to government investment programs and to the fact that labor is entering and enlarging the market economy and leaving the subsistence sector. Both these are certainly structural problems of underdevelopment, but it is difficult to argue that they are *caused* by foreign trade. Without the trade, the development plan would be starved for funds and labor would be far less likely to enter the market economy.

The Prebisch thesis is also less tenable in a world of floating exchange rates. A persistent balance of payments deficit would cause a steady downward pressure on the LDC's currency. In most situations this would increase the price of imports and thereby slow the demand for them. A price effect would counter an income effect, although a Marshall-Lerner bind or a high susceptibility to cost-push inflation would limit the use of exchange rate policy. Nonetheless, as we show in the next chapter, poor exchange rate policy has been an important factor in creating a dependence on imports. The use of a flexible exchange rate (almost invariably meaning a depreciating rate) serves as a continuing stimulus for exports, while at the same time it discourages imports.[4]

Price Fluctuations.   A last problem with dependence on exports is one figuring most importantly in contemporary discussion—the year-to-year fluctuations in price. These can be very unfavorable for a country specializing in international trade, particularly in primary products. The average fluctuation in primary product prices on a yearly basis, from 1900 to 1958, was 13 percent for a sample of fifty commodities. Experience has been worse than this in the 1970s. Some price swings seem hardly believable. At the start of 1973 the prices of all the following primary products—sugar, wheat, cocoa, lead, coffee, and copper—were lower than in August 1977. Yet in those five years wild gyrations had occurred, as shown in Table 18.2.

TABLE 18.2.

	1977 price (1973 price lower in every case)	Record high price, January 1973-August 1977
Sugar (£/tonne)	105.0	640.1 (October 1974)
Wheat ($/bushel)	2.30	6.10 (February 1974)
Cocoa (£/tonne)	3085	3465 (July 1977)
Lead (£/tonne)	304.5	416.5 (May 1977)
Coffee ($/lb)	2.07	3.265 (April 1977)
Copper (£/tonne)	655	1333 (April 1977)

Real commodity price increases, 1972-1973, were more than twice as steep as in the second worst year on record since World War II (1953-1954). Real price declines were more than twice as great in 1975 as they had been in 1971, the second worst year since that war.

This pattern of surge and collapse will, it is argued, have a serious detrimental effect on countries that export these products. Their tax revenues will gyrate sympathetically; their development plans will be left in shreds. This will be especially so when, as is commonplace, an LDC depends on just one, two, or three primary products for nearly all its export earnings. Equally serious, buyers (importers) of these commodities, plagued by uncertainty, turn to substitutes and synthetics. (In thirty LDCs, more than 80 percent of all export revenues come from no more than three primary products. In thirty-odd additional countries the figure lies between 60 percent and 80 percent.)

How is it possible that such wide fluctuations can occur? The major reasons are: worldwide price inelasticity of both supply and demand for major commodities; large changes in supply caused by the weather; and large changes in demand caused by world trade cycles. The reasons for price inelasticity have already been mentioned. Most farm crops are limited in quantity from harvest to harvest. It is impossible to plant more in the middle of the growing seasons. Tree crops (cocoa, coffee, tea, rubber, palm oil) have even greater price inelasticity of supply, as they will take several years to bear after their first planting. Mineral production can often be increased by large-scale investment in mining and drilling, an expensive and slow process. The low price elasticity of demand for foodstuffs is well documented for developed countries. Beverages such as coffee and tea are inelastic also, making up only a small percentage of consumer expenditure yet holding a warm spot in the hearts of most of us. Minerals demand is also relatively inelastic, at least in the short run, because it is difficult to substitute or switch to synthetics quickly. True, in the long run, much more price elasticity will become apparent for both demand and supply. But it is short-run fluctuations in price that we are discussing at this point, and here inelasticity is one key to a general understanding.

Weather is the second great variable. Weather killed the Brazilian coffee crop, ruined European and Russian sugar beets, and damaged the Russian wheat crop; and in this litany for the 1970s we find another key to great price fluctuations. Note from Fig. 18.1(a) that, with inelastic curves, a shift in supply causes great price changes. Finally there is the cycle in world trade. In 1972 the major industrial economies boomed. In late 1974 they slumped simultaneously. Figure 18.1(b) shows that shifts in demand can also have a great impact on prices when the curves are inelastic.

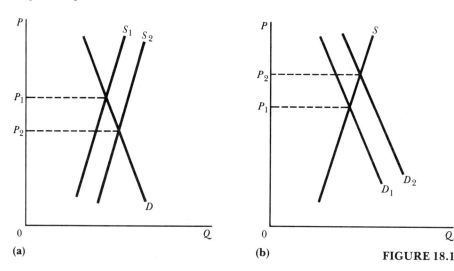

(a)   **(b)**   **FIGURE 18.1**

The Enclave Arguments

Another group of criticisms of trade as an engine of growth concerns the linkages between trading activity and the rest of the economy. The ideal export activity brings growth to the rest of the economy. The linkage may be "backward," where the export activity improves the surrounding economy by finding outlets for resources drawn from it. Or it may be "forward," where some good or service produced for export lowers costs to other domestic industry (as, for instance, the linkage between the milling of brown rice for export and the growth of a pig-raising industry, which uses the brown husks for feed). Imagine a canning factory coming into a fertile agricultural valley. To get its supplies of fruits and vegetables, it contracts with local farmers, and provides fertilizer, seed, and advice. Farmers' cooperatives, agricultural brokers, and other middlemen begin operations to more efficiently channel agricultural production to the canner. Higher farm incomes lead to demands for more products (including better food) and domestic farming and industry is further stimulated. (These are all backward linkages so far.) As activity increases, the farmers apply their freely gained knowledge to other crops, bankers lend to new cash crops (and often money used to finance one crop for four months can be used to finance others in the other eight), the cooperatives and the brokers seek new markets, and income expands further. (These are the forward linkages.)

Reality, however, may not be so rosy. Imagine another scenario. The canning factory fails to induce local supplies to be provided regularly enough or in sufficient quantity to keep its plant operating efficiently. Farmers are uninterested, fearing the risk of switching from subsistence crops. The cooperatives fail to emerge. In desperation, the canning factory purchases land and begins a plantation, hiring labor at subsistence wages and diverting water to its uses. (In the past, similar enterprises have even used imported labor if the local labor supply was limited.) The income pattern that comes about from such operations tends to be skewed, bad enough in itself, but even worse because of the resultant expenditure pattern. The newly wealthy beneficiaries of this skewing demand goods that cannot be made locally, leading to more imports but no further stimulation of domestic demand.

As an example of an enclave economy, consider Ceylon (Sri Lanka) and its tea industry, for which the capital equipment was purchased in Great Britain, transport was on British ships, and laborers were brought from India. Virtually all profits, interest, and salaries went to Great Britain, and any wages saved went to India. How could this help the Ceylonese economy? Or consider the guano exports from Peru in the mid-nineteenth century. This substance, the accumulated droppings of seabirds of many millennia on islands off the coast, was in high demand as fertilizer in Europe. Foreign boats with foreign crews and workers came to the islands, blasted away the guano (killing many birds), and left Peru with little in the way of knowledge, new market mechanisms, or domestic industry.[6]

Such absences of linkages have been noted by the Swedish Nobel Prize-winning economist Gunnar Myrdal, by the UN's Hans Singer, and by Hla Myint of the London School of Economics. Singer felt that the difficulty lay with the nature of primary product production—that it typically did not provide the additional training, the types of market mechanisms, or the capital generation in nearly the same degree as does industry. Industry, he felt, had a "dynamic radiation" that simply is not found in agriculture or mining. There is a measure of truth in these observations, as Japan in the twentieth and Germany in the nineteenth century amply demonstrate. But many economists today are less certain of the connections. There are counterexamples: Agricultural exports were key to the development of the United States, Canada, Australia, New Zealand, and Denmark, to name a few. Agriculture can be based on mechanical skill, capital intensity, and education as much as industry can. The farm boys of Iowa or the Australian Outback know a good deal more about machinery, marketing, and production methods than do many city dwellers.

Moreover, it now appears that industrialization can lead to enclaves as easily as can primary production. The complaint of many economists in the developing world today is that foreign firms come in, introduce capital-intensive technology, pay high wages and salaries, but do not by their nature hire very many workers. Those fortunate enough to get jobs in the modern industrial sector adopt a more sophisticated life style, which brings in more imports or stimulates further a rather capital intensive "enclave" industry based on import substitution. Hopeful peasants pour into the cities, trying to link up with the modern sector, generally with little success. The result is not dynamic radiation, but just another enclave. The fact of the matter is that the root causes for such enclave or dualistic development do not appear to lie in trade or the nature of exports and imports. We can cite four causes. One is the large subsistence sector in agriculture, with food produced and consumed by the family on the farm. With much subsistence production, the domestic market is small, so it is more likely that profits will be repatriated abroad and that capital, technology, and management will be imported. The second reason is the large masses of unskilled labor available for employment at low wages. With the subsistence economy important, and opportunity costs very low, only a low wage is needed to attract labor into the export enclave. Overpopulation and limited employment opportunities outside agriculture contribute to the very low opportunity costs. The result is that the export sector can become established and grow to a large size without the sort of stimulation to the economy that would be expected in a more developed nation.

A third cause is institutional—at low levels of development, financial, educational, and brokerage institutions do not develop sufficiently to provide further linkages. The banks remain highly specialized, lending only for the staple crop in the area. Foreign buyers and native brokers remain specialized—coffee buyers do not buy tobacco and vice versa. A fourth cause is also institutional. The political processes work against the building of linkages from primary products. The growing strength of the urban workers may bring them price controls on food, subsidized food imports, and high wages, but all these things work against the spread of income and employment.

A final rather bracing thought on enclave economies is that an enclave is better than nothing. Export crops or mining, with admittedly low linkages and uninspiring sales prospects, may be the only conceivable ways to raise incomes. Consider the following areas without their exports: Pacific islands without copra, northern Nigeria and Senegal without peanuts, Uganda without coffee, Sudan without cotton, Pakistan without jute, Zambia and the Peruvian Andes without mining, or Libya without oil.

The Defense of Trade: The Classical Resurgence

As can be noted above, the causes of enclave or dualistic development are independent of trade. Whatever form of development occurred, it would not spread very fast. It is interesting to note in this light the evolving thought of Hla Myint.[7] Myint first posed the question of linkages from peasant and plantation agriculture and mining in 1958. At the time, he suggested that exports came initially from surplus land and labor, previously idle because of lack of markets. Exports became a "vent for surplus." Thus coffee and cocoa were planted on previously unused land in West Africa, deserts were irrigated in Peru, and rice lands were expanded in Thailand. The labor used was often labor previously idle part of the year. Thus the initial expansion of exports was pure surplus. But after the existing idle facilities are used up, what then? Myint's first suspicion was that the pace of development would slow because few institutional changes accompanied the initial expansion of output. Thus his earlier writings contributed to the skepticism about trade. But unlike others, Myint was unwilling to abandon primary product exports as means to growth. Rather, he wanted to know what went wrong with them.

In the ensuing years, evidence accumulated that primary product exports, particularly peasant crops, could still play an important role in development. Indeed, it was often the governments themselves that were preventing the linkages. Governments in several countries set up "marketing boards" that paid a fixed (low) price to the farmer for the export crop and channeled the profits into industry or urban subsidies. Or sometimes government banks, not private banks, refused credit for the cash crop. Hence Myint has increasingly been viewing primary products as a basis for development and has been working on the institutional factors that prevent domestic linkages. Indeed, Myint today is much more positive about the contributions of peasant exports to development than he was twenty years ago.

Other economists in the 1950s and 1960s were not much interested in agricultural development. If one were to analyze the economic assumptions that most often determined or justified economic policy in developing areas in the 1950s or 1960s, one would find three main attitudes: (1) skepticism about the potential growth prospects for either manufacturing or primary product exports, (2) a belief that primary product exports could not lead to development, and (3) a belief that development was based on capital accumulation. Accordingly, policy stressed import substitution and capital accumulation. On the assumption of price inelasticity of primary product exports, these exports were sometimes squeezed mercilessly to produce surplus funds to be used for building up manufacturing capacity. The infant industry that was to be protected often became virtually the whole manufacturing sector. Unfortunately, few of these industries "grew up." Sheltered from import competition, they remained virtually as inefficient as when they began. One study of five Latin American nations showed that after the import-substitution policies began in earnest in the 1950s, there was virtually no increase in productivity for the next twenty years—a remarkably poor figure.

In addition to protecting industries, many countries penalized primary product production. Policies of cheap food for the cities, carried out through price controls, import licensing, and multiple exchange-rate manipulations (examine Chile's in Chapter 3), plus overvalued exchange rates encouraged a dependence on imported food. Encouragement of processing and assembly operations when there was an inadequate raw materials base (and its fostering through duty-free or preferential imports) further increased the dependency on imports. After twenty years of such policies, many nations (particularly in Latin America) have industrial structures that cannot use many domestic inputs.

Sometime in the late 1960s the tide began to turn. Economists became more optimistic about the markets for exports. Indeed, exports from developing nations typically rose 5 or 6 percent a year over the period 1950-1970, far above any estimates made in the early 1950s. What is more, this was despite government policies that did not actively encourage expansion. Moreover, the countries with the higher rates of export also had by far the higher rates of growth, as was demonstrated several times. One might contrast Burma with Thailand, Ghana with the Ivory Coast, or, in the 1950s, Chile with Peru. In each case the former trade-restricting nation has had a much lower growth rate than its trade-expanding neighbor with roughly the same resources. Thus, even if the cause of the correlation between exports and growth is uncertain, there was reason to give pause to anyone who previously advocated a policy of import substitution. Lastly, economists began to abandon capital accumulation theories of development and concentrate instead on the productive use of existing resources. As development theory turned away from sheer massive accumulation of capital, the stress on industrialization was seen as promoting much inefficiency in the use of capital.

In the new atmosphere, export development began to look more attractive. Even if exports were given artificial stimuli and there were some misallocations in their favor, they could never become as inefficient as the older import-substitution goods. Exports, unlike import substitutes, must face stiff international competition and the subsidy can be only a small aid. In addition, export subsidies have to come from appropriations or special tax favors, and their costs are more visible in the budget than tariff protection. Thus there is more attention to exports in most of the developing world.

Furthermore, attention is now given to the linkages themselves, and there is more optimism that agricultural development can provide economic stimuli toward growth. The vigorous development of South Korea and Taiwan, both of which stressed agricultural growth, provides two models that are being examined with increasing interest. Nearly every international agency today is promoting agricultural development—indeed, the pendulum has swung very far in that direction. Academic researchers know, for instance, that grants to do work in a developing country are overwhelmingly for rural development.

There is need for a word of caution, though. Movement toward freer trade and more realistic exchange rates, the building of more productive industries, and the stimulation of agriculture will be difficult in many nations—and particularly in those with "hothouse" economies. Politically, and perhaps even economically, it is not wise to simply turn off the heat and see which firms survive the frost—attractive as this may seem to the frustrated economist.

Notes

1. This is a point made at the start of Theodore Morgan's excellent chapter entitled "International Trade and Development" in his recent textbook, *Economic Development: Concept and Strategy* (New York: Harper & Row, 1975). This chapter is in the authors' opinion the best on the topic currently available in an undergraduate development textbook.

2. See André Gunder Frank's influential *Latin America: Underdevelopment or Revolution* (New York: Monthly Review, 1970); and also his *Lumpenbourgeoisie and Lumpendevelopment* (New York: Monthly Review, 1973). A typical title in this genre is Walter Rodney, *How Europe Underdeveloped Africa* (London: Bogle L'Overture Publications, 1972). Dependency theory has an airing in a journal of orthodox respectability in Theotonio dos Santos, "The Structure of Dependence," *American Economic Review*, LX (1970): 231-236. *Unequal exchange* was a term made popular by Arghiri Emmanuel, *L'echange inégal* (Paris: 1969), translated into English as *Unequal Exchange* (New York: Monthly Review, 1972).

3. The name most commonly associated with declining terms of trade for LDCs is Raul Prebisch, former head of the United Nations' Economic Commission for Latin America.

4. The experience of Julius Klein, an American economic adviser, is interesting in regard to floating exchange rates. Invited to Peru in the late 1940s, Klein recommended abandonment of the notably unsuccessful experiment with exchange control (discussed in Chapter 3) and the use of a floating rate. Recovery of exports was swift, while cost-push elements were held in check by a military government. Peru enjoyed more than a decade of export-led growth (brought to an end, interestingly enough, by another military government), as exports recovered quickly and expanded rapidly throughout the 1950s and early 1960s. Invited to Chile in 1956 and giving approximately the same advice, Klein was disappointed. Exports did not respond to devaluation and floating rates as they had done in Peru and cost-push pressures were intense.

   What made the difference between Chile and Peru? Peru had an export base to begin with and little hothouse industry, though like Chile it had vocal urban interests. Peru had followed policies of overvalued exchange rates and high urban subsidies for only about three or four years, however, while Chile had to recover from well over a decade of hothouse industry and weakened exports. Moreover, Peru was facing an inflation of a mere 20 percent or so a year, compared with rates in Chile of almost 100 percent. The Chilean economy was unable to respond quickly and the political support for the Klein policies rapidly waned. Hence when we note that a floating rate can be beneficial, we do not necessarily mean it is so in all situations.

5. The table is constructed from the *Economist* index of commodity prices in the issues of May 1, 1976, p. 76, and August 20, 1977, p. 92.
6. The "Guano Age" did leave two valuable legacies: (1) a partially built railway that, when completed, opened access to Peru's mineral wealth for the succeeding generation; and (2) a merchant and banking class of enough skill and acumen to rebuild the economy in short order.
7. See Hla Myint, "The Classical Theory of International Trade and the Underdeveloped Countries," *Economic Journal* (June 1958), and his "Exports and Economic Development of Less-Developed Countries," paper delivered at the Fifth World Congress of the International Economic Association, Tokyo, August 29-September 3, 1977

19

TRADE AND DEVELOPMENT: WHAT CAN BE DONE? WHAT HAS BEEN DONE?

To resolve the trade-related problems of less developed countries, in recent years there have emerged, if not solutions, at least some palliatives. This chapter will survey, critically where necessary, the major measures that have been taken or are contemplated.

New Loans and Grants

For the LDC in difficulty because of the terms of trade, the balance of payments, or extreme price swings for its exports, few solutions offer the utter simplicity of aid from abroad. Foreign aid to counter the problems of international trade is inextricably mixed with aid for other purposes—military and political assistance and aid for general economic development. But recent years have indeed seen a rapid increase in the dollar value (though not the *real* value after account is taken of inflation) of aid intended to counter the problems of trade.

In 1975, the net flow of official economic aid (grants and low-interest loans) amounted to some $17 billion, about 80 percent from the developed industrial countries, 16 percent from the newly rich OPEC oil exporters, and 4 percent from Communist countries. The figure $17 billion represents an approximate doubling in aid flows in just two years, and much of the increase can be explained by the precarious balance of payments situation of oil-importing LDCs. However, in real terms (1975 dollars) the amount of aid given in that year was actually only 12 percent greater than it had been back in 1961. In that year, developed countries were donating 0.53 percent of their GNP to the poor countries, but that figure had fallen back to 0.36 percent of GNP by 1975.

The major shift in aid patterns has been in the surge of grants from the oil-exporting countries. As a percentage of their GNP, some of these countries are taking their Koranic charitable obligations very seriously indeed—Qatar in 1975 gave 5.4 percent of GNP, United Arab Emirates 4.3 percent, Saudi Arabia (the largest OPEC gift-giver, $3 billion, over one-third of all OPEC aid) 2.55 percent, and Kuwait 2.5 percent. The other side of the coin is that the lion's share of this goes to Muslim countries, with Egypt, Jordan, and Syria the most favored recipients.

The LDCs hope that the developed countries can be persuaded to expand their aid programs substantially. Some years ago at a meeting of UNCTAD (United Nations Conference on Trade and Development), the LDCs insisted on a target, to be met by 1980, of 0.7 percent of rich-country GNP to be handed over as aid. Though many developed countries have accepted the challenge, and three (Norway, Sweden, and the Netherlands) have reached the goal, it seems impossible that aid of this magnitude will actually be forthcoming in the near future. To meet it by 1980, aid would have to expand by a third every year until then. West Germany and Japan do not in any case accept the target date, and the United States (which currently gives 0.25 percent of GNP) has not even accepted the target. Startling comparisons are sometimes made—total aid is now equal to only eighteen days' worth of world military expenditures, or two months' worth of alcohol and tobacco consumption in the rich countries—but invidious comparisons of this type do not make it politically any easier to raise the total of aid.[1]

There is even an argument that foreign aid is regressive. The tax systems of many developed nations are, as a whole, somewhat regressive, with many loopholes for the rich and a rather heavy burden on the middle classes. Foreign aid frequently appears to go mainly to the benefit of a tiny, very wealthy elite of politicians, businesspeople, landowners, and speculators in the LDCs. Hence, while aid may be transferring income from rich to poor nations, it is also transferring income from poorer to richer people. The thrust of this analysis is that increases in foreign aid should be joined to effective tax reform if the redistributive aims of foreign aid are to be realized. Why, asks plain-speaking Robert Lekachman of the City University of New York, should the assembly line worker in the United States pay higher taxes to support and enrich the entourage of the Shah of Iran?

Incidentally, most donors nowadays "tie" their aid, meaning that recipients are required to spend the funds received on goods produced in the donor country. Since the donor may not be the world's cheapest producer, sheltering behind tariff walls, and since businesspeople facing a sure sale may well jack up the price in any case, it is not surprising that tied aid is reduced in value. One current estimate is that 6 percent of the money value of aid is lost to the LDCs because of tying.[2]

The unfortunate politics of aid has led to a growing popularity for disbursements through international agencies instead of from national governments. The IMF has been the main agency making more money available for balance of payments purposes. The IMF's special oil facility of 1974-1975 ($8 billion) and the new so-called Witteveen facility ($10 billion), established in August 1977, are conduits for this assistance, as is the increase in IMF quotas permitting greater "normal" borrowing.[3] All were discussed in Chapter 9.

There is one other IMF program, the compensatory-financing facility, designed to offset balance of payments problems. Introduced in 1963, this program allows LDC members of the IMF to borrow up to 50 percent more than their normal borrowing rights when their total earnings from exports fall short of their average exports of recent years. For many years a strict interpretation of the program's rules and lack of funds meant that the compensatory-finance facility was not all that important. As late as 1975, for example, only $280 million was disbursed under the facility. But extensive liberalization of the rules was agreed on at the end of that year, and in 1976, forty-four member countries drew the equivalent of $2.6 billion from the facility, nearly twice the total of all previous loans since 1963.[4]

In spite of the international action described above, the shortfall in LDC balances of payments in the past three years would not have been covered without an enormous expansion in lending by private banks (most dealing in Eurodollars) to LDCs in deficit. Such lending was once small, with net lending averaging only $0.9 billion per year in the period 1968-1972. The takeoff came in 1973, when lending amounted to $6 billion, rising to about $9 billion in both 1974 and 1975, and by 1978 LDCs as a whole owed private creditors more than $50 billion. This expansion, hardly credible to believers in bankers' conservatism, has led to fears that private banks are now overexposed to the risks of default. In reaction, the maturities of this type of loan have been reduced drastically. In 1974, only 19 percent of private bank loans to LDCs were of short maturity (1-6 years). This figure rose to 75 percent in 1975. The sudden truncation of the repayment period meant that the next few years will see some strains as LDCs struggle to make payment. It is interesting that the best customers for private bank lending have been important and relatively well-to-do. For example, a full two-thirds of the private lending just described has gone to Argentina, Brazil, Mexico, Peru, the Philippines, South Korea, and Taiwan—but it is also true that these seven countries accounted for about half the total balance of payments deficits of all the nonoil LDCs in 1975.[5]

Recently, the World Bank has begun to explore whether private bank lending might not be joined to international aid in a consortium relationship. The first "cofinanced loan" was made in December 1975 to Brazil, $95 million from the World Bank and $55 million from two private banks, the interest on the latter to be routed through the World Bank. The idea is to increase the amount of resources available for lending, and improve the credit status of the borrowing LDC, vouched for in effect by the World Bank.

Loans and grants remain a politically volatile topic, which could easily lead to confrontation between the rich and poor countries. At the UNCTAD IV meetings in Nairobi in 1976, and again at the "North-South" conference in Paris in 1977, the LDCs were asking for immediate relief from debt problems caused by balance of payments difficulties. The demands currently range from complete cancellation of debt for the poorest, least developed countries, to debt relief for the forty-two countries designated by the UN as most affected, to widespread consolidation of debts at a standard, lower, interest rate, with repayment stretched out to twenty-five years. Though these demands in their present form may appear to be quixotic at present, it is a good guess that debtor/creditor conferences will be a fixture of the future as LDCs attempt to renegotiate their burden of debt, both with aid-giving governments and the private banks.

New Access to Markets: GSP

One outcome of the first UNCTAD meeting, at Geneva in 1964, was a proposal for preferential tariff rates (or free trade) on imports to the developed world from the LDCs. The idea soon came to be known as the Generalized System of Preferences (GSP).[6] Preferential treatment of imports to developed countries of goods manufactured and semimanufactured by LDCs spread rapidly. The first to offer such treatment were the original six members of the EEC (July 1971). The last important country to accede to the plan was the United States, with President Ford's executive order of November 1975 abolishing tariffs as of January 1, 1976, on 2,724 categories of imports from 98 LDCs and 39 colonies. Both the United States and the EEC hedged their GSP generosity with restrictions. Lobbying in Congress by vested interests resulted in exclusions for shoes, textiles, iron and steel, electronic products, glass, and that coddled beneficiary of American Selling Price protection, benzenoid chemicals. Tariffs may be reimposed whenever imports of a product to the United States exceed $33.4 million per year or make up 50 percent or more of total American imports of that product. The United States also refused to grant GSP privileges to all developing countries in UNCTAD. (Most other countries' GSP schemes did so.) The members of OPEC are excluded—and indeed it seems hard to justify tariff concessions for Saudi Arabia or Kuwait—but at the same time this means that very poor oil-producing countries such as Nigeria and Indonesia are harmed.

The EEC's restrictions on GSP are wide ranging. All primary products and base metals to the ingot stage are excluded, as is a long list of manufactured and semimanufactured goods that, in 1970, made up 62 percent of the dutiable imports from LDCs to GSP-grantors. The exclusion of most agricultural products was perhaps the most serious of the omissions.

GSP has been a popular measure among development economists. It promotes exports from LDCs and increases the return on them, very satisfying for proponents of "trade, not aid." Infant industries in LDCs receive advantages without which they might not become established. But GSP is so hedged about by restrictions that it cannot at present play a very important role. One of the major topics at the UNCTAD IV Conference in Nairobi, and at the Paris North-South talks in 1977, was how to modify GSP so that its undoubted benefits might be extended more widely. In truth, the biggest benefits to LDCs will come only when all barriers to their trade with developed countries are dismantled.

International Commodity Agreements (ICAs)

No plan of action has attracted more attention than the international commodity agreements (ICAs), designed to stabilize the swings in the prices of primary products, and also in some cases designed to increase price. As early as the Bretton Woods Conference of 1944, John Maynard Keynes was suggesting the possibility of an international commodity system, and although nothing came of it, Professor Benjamin Graham was advocating that ICAs be financed by the new International Monetary Fund. There had been relatively long experience with price-stabilizing agencies on a national level. National "buffer funds," usually called marketing boards, had in some countries long set a fixed price paid to farmers for produce, and then had sold the produce on the world market at whatever that market would bring. The farmer found the price level certain throughout the crop year, with the marketing board paying out of its cash reserves whenever world prices fell below its fixed price, or accumulating reserves when world prices rose above that level. There are today many such boards—the Ghana cocoa marketing board, the New Zealand board for dairy produce, the British egg marketing board, one for Burmese rice, one for Uganda's cotton and coffee, one for Argentine beef products, and so on around the world. Sometimes these boards are supplemented or replaced by variable export taxes, which rise or fall as the world price falls or rises, again providing price stabilization.

But it was long ago realized that there was little chance for such arrangements to have much of an effect on world prices, because each individual country almost always provided too small a portion of the supply to affect the world market to any large extent. Thus, while national efforts might have a stabilizing effect within a crop year, they could not stabilize prices effectively for a longer period.

The first attempts on an international level were crude quota arrangements where producers agreed to limit production, with the limits adjusted according to the state of the world market. In such quota agreements, national shares are assigned and the building up of new production capacity outside the agreement is prohibited. In each member country, existing producers receive a share of that country's quota. Examples include the sugar agreement of 1902 (the earliest such agreement), tin (1921), tea (1933), rubber (1934), and coffee (1962). The coffee scheme, ratified at the UNCTAD I Conference, included an International Coffee Organization that urged its members to limit production by uprooting trees. Brazil, which exported about 40 percent of the world's coffee at the time, tore up a billion trees and cut its crop by a quarter.

Then suddenly a glare of publicity lit up the whole subject of ICAs. The United Nations General Assembly called in 1974 for a "new international economic order" including stabilization schemes for primary product prices. The UNCTAD IV Conference in Nairobi in May 1976 proposed a $6 billion "common fund" to finance a whole new series of ICAs to cover eighteen commodities. These include six industrial raw materials (cotton, fibres, jute, rubber, timber, and vegetable oils), six foods (bananas, cocoa, coffee, meat, sugar, and tea), and six minerals (bauxite, copper, iron ore, manganese, phosphates, and tin). Together, these presently account for about 25 percent by value of all LDC exports. There is a great gap between representatives for the LDCs, who wish to use the new scheme to raise price, and negotiators for the developed countries, who wish to stabilize prices. One suggestion by the LDCs has been to peg commodity prices to a price index for manufactured goods, but this has been sharply criticized on the grounds that supply and demand conditions can be very different for commodities and manufactures, so that attempting to control prices would give the usual problems of shortage, surplus, and distorted incentives. Initial talks on a common fund began at Geneva in November 1977, but broke up in disagreements over finance a month later. More will be heard of the idea.

By 1978, it was clear that of all the various forms of stabilization that might be attempted, the buffer stock idea was receiving the widest acceptance. Buffer stocks have been rare historically. The International Tin Agreement is the only real example. Established in 1956, it accumulated a stockpile of tin and working cash balances through donations by member nations.[7] Thereafter the managers of the stock, based in London, sold tin from the stock whenever prices reached some ceiling level, and bought tin to add to the stockpile whenever tin prices touched some floor. Figure 19.1 shows the buffer stock in operation. The diagram looks much like that for a "dirty float" encountered in Chapter 3. The managers must sell a quantity of tin equal to AB if demand rises from D to D' and it is wished to keep prices at the ceiling $0P_c$. Conversely, to keep prices at the floor level $0P_f$, the managers must buy a quantity of tin equal to XY should demand drop from D to D''.

The tin stock keeps both cash and metal. In 1969, for example, it had 11,000 tons of tin and £30 million at its disposal. In the years directly after

1969, the managers were defending a ceiling price of £1,790 per ton and a floor of £1,450 per ton. Membership in the five successive five-year tin agreements has included all major tin exporters (Malaysia much the largest) except China, and all major consuming nations. The United States, a tin consumer, joined only the last agreement, which came into force July 1, 1976. Several consumers of tin (France, the Netherlands, Belgium, Great Britain but not the United States) contribute to the financing of the stock.

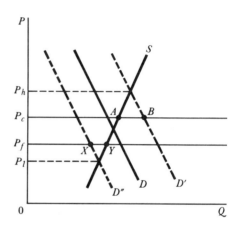

FIGURE 19.1

   The tin stock is a near-perfect textbook example of how things can and do go wrong in the management of buffer stocks. If the managers ever run out of tin defending a ceiling, or out of money when defending a floor, they will then make price fluctuations more sudden and dramatic than they ever were with no buffer stock. In Fig. 19.1, we see that prices will skyrocket to the high market equilibrium $0P_h$ when the buffer stock runs out of tin. And indeed the tin buffer stock was exhausted in April 1970, when the price bumped up dramatically. Again the stockpile ran out of tin in 1977, and the International Tin Council raised its floor/ceiling figures by 20 percent (to £4,600/£5,825 per ton) in an attempt to catch up. In July of that year, the tin price was still higher than the ceiling at £6,000 per ton, and the buffer was empty. The converse can occur when prices fall. In Fig. 19.1, should the managers run out of cash, price collapses to $0P_l$. In 1957 the Council exhausted its war chest for buffer stock purchases, could thus no longer defend a floor price, and witnessed a sudden fall through the floor. The lesson is plain enough: To succeed, a buffer stock must have both sufficient funds and sufficient quantities of the stored commodity or sharp price fluctuations will occur when the managers give up the fight. The fifth Tin Agreement has responded by raising the size of the buffer stock considerably, and if Congress approves, the United

States will reverse previous policy and contribute an extra 6,000 tons on top of the 20,000-ton stock already agreed on.

The buffer stock idea is the key to the "common fund" proposals that resulted from UNCTAD IV at Nairobi 1976, and the North-South talks at Paris in 1977. Buffer stocks have been suggested in particular for coffee, cocoa, sugar, rubber, and copper. Other methods of stabilization have also been suggested for these primary products. The background to this is discussed below.

Coffee. Coffee is the largest agricultural export from the LDCs, with Brazil supplying about one-third of the total. Ten countries account for about 75 percent of world exports. "Booms" and "busts" in coffee prices have been common, the latest boom starting in 1975. The United States and Brazil spearheaded an International Coffee Agreement in 1962 that, as noted earlier, was intended to reduce overproduction. The agreement involved export quotas for member countries, policed by prohibitions on the entry of non-quota coffee into importing countries. After renewal in 1968, this ICA eventually broke up when Brazil refused to agree to the granting of export quotas to African producers of robusta coffee (robusta is cheaper than Brazilian arabica, and African labor costs are lower). After the great 1975 frost in Brazil, which caused a spectacular 600 percent jump in coffee prices during the next two years, a new International Coffee Agreement was entered into on October 1, 1976. This too is a market-sharing quota arrangement on exports, though the quotas are now suspended because prices are so high. Market shares are determined by past export performance. The quotas will come into effect automatically when and if coffee prices fall to a level between $0.635 and $0.775 per pound. Consuming nations oppose the quota. The suggestion of a coffee buffer stock is being actively discussed.

Like any other quota on production, including the monopoly behavior of an individual firm where the "quota" is self-set, there are some clear and detrimental results. High-cost producers are protected by the prohibition on new entry into the industry. Countries may thus continue producing commodities in which they are actually losing comparative advantage, the loss being concealed by the protection. Costs of production may well be inflated because the scale of output is less than full capacity. The quotas are subject to intense political manipulation as to who gets what share, between countries (as when Brazil resisted the spread of coffee production to Africa) or within countries (the constant conflict between Malayan plantation producers of rubber and smallholder farmers). Finally, if the quotas are successful in raising prices, this will stimulate production in areas not active before (African coffee once again) and also stimulate the search for substitutes or synthetics.

Cocoa. Talk of a cocoa ICA has gone on for more than twenty years. Cocoa conventions at Geneva have had the dubious distinction of constant failure, but supporters of a cocoa ICA are nothing if not persistent. A three-year agreement constructed in 1972 expired unused. It had relied on export quotas as its principal weapon, with surplus stocks to be stored in consuming nations. The reason for the nonuse of the 1972 agreement was that cocoa prices remained well above the price targets set by the member nations, so that the quotas never came to be enforced. A new cocoa ICA was negotiated in 1975. The United States suggested a 250,000-ton buffer stock, which would have had to be located in consuming countries because cocoa is hard to store under tropical conditions. But producers rejected the idea, and the 1975 agreement was similar to that of 1972, depending on export quotas, though with some elements of a buffer stock. In protest, the United States refused to join. As with its predecessor, the 1975 agreement has not been tested because cocoa prices have remained above the target levels defended by the quotas.

Sugar. International Sugar Agreements were negotiated in 1937 (short-lived because of World War II), 1953, 1958, and 1968. Because so much sugar was produced and traded under preferential arrangements (Cuba's trade with the Soviet Union, the discriminatory U.S. Sugar Act, and the British Commonwealth Sugar Agreement) the sugar ICA actually affected only a residue of sugar in international trade, less than 50 percent of the total. The various sugar agreements have essentially been market-sharing arrangements that depended on export quotas. At one time there was an element of buffer stock, with members required to hold back from the market 12½ percent of the previous year's crop. The 1968 version was also a form of "multilateral contract" (see wheat, below) under which exporting members agreed to furnish a fixed quantity of sugar to importing members at an agreed price ceiling. There was no floor price. Attempts to renegotiate the 1968 sugar ICA failed in 1973 on the issue of price. Shortly thereafter came the great sugar boom, and the expiration of both the U.S. Sugar Act and the British Commonwealth Sugar Agreement. The free market now accounts for much more of the sugar trade than heretofore. Negotiations for a new five-year agreement were held in Geneva in April and May of 1977, and these led to a new pact in October of that year. Once more the United States was the prime proponent of a buffer stock, to be accumulated when prices are low and sold off when prices are high. 2.5 million tonnes was the size agreed on. When prices reach $0.19 per pound, one-third of the stock will be sold. Another third will be sold with each cent rise in price. In a falling market, production quotas are to be imposed when prices reach $0.14 per pound. (The big three, Cuba, Brazil, and Australia, have nearly 50 percent of the world's total of quotas.) As of July 1978, the U.S. Congress had still failed to ratify the agreement.

Rubber. There is interest on the part of both consumers and producers in a rubber buffer stock. Malaysia and Indonesia, two important exporters, have already agreed to establish a 100,000-ton stockpile on their own initiative. The "common fund" negotiations that resumed in November 1977, will take up the prospect of joint financing.

Tea. A tea export quota arrangement of 1970 successfully limited supplies for a time, but went aground on the shoals of productive capacity. Asian countries, with old tea plantations and large surpluses, want to cut production and raise prices. African producers, newly entering the market, want to expand their sales by selling at low prices. A new agreement, perhaps involving a buffer stock, has not been negotiated even though the major consuming country, Great Britain (the destination of 40 percent of all tea exports), is a firm supporter.

Bauxite. Bauxite, the major source of aluminum, has been the subject of an incipient scheme of cartelization. The eleven members of the International Bauxite Association must decide unanimously on policy changes. Thus far the association has denied that it intends to boost prices as OPEC did. But its study groups have given careful consideration to export taxes and the indexing of the bauxite price to the price of finished aluminum. Unfortunately for the member countries, there are substitutes both for aluminum and for bauxite, since aluminum is found in other ores as well. Aluminum is the most abundant metal in the earth's crust, and exists in large quantities in the United States as well as in numerous other consuming countries. Stringent export quotas and successful engineering of price increases are doubtful.

Copper. Copper is the world's most important (nonfuel) mineral export in international trade. There is an "Intergovernmental Council of Copper Exporting Countries" (CIPEC, the French acronym) that has dabbled with plans for a cartel, though little has been achieved. Agreement was reached in 1976 to set up a permanent producer-consumer forum for copper, but specific plans for price stabilization are not yet agreed upon. For copper, a buffer stock would be a difficult proposition because of expense. Estimates running upward of $3 billion have been made for a stock large enough to defend a floor and ceiling within 10 percent of the average level. This would make copper much the most expensive candidate for stabilization, even though the magnitude of metal traded makes instability more serious for both producers and consumers than it is for many of the products just discussed.

Buffer stocks are generally thought to be far superior to cartel/quota arrangements for stabilizing price. But they are expensive, and some studies indicate that the $6 billion proposed by UNCTAD to finance the common fund proposals will not be sufficient. Attitudes change rapidly, however, in the face of the political reality of resource shortages engineered by LDC cartelization. The United States originally opposed the common fund idea when it surfaced in 1974, but by 1977 its stance was one of support. The UNCTAD timetable currently calls for completion of the common fund discussions by February 1978, to be followed by negotiations on the actual implementation.

Wheat. International efforts to stabilize world wheat prices were initiated in 1933 with the formation of the first International Wheat Agreement. Members were to reduce exports and take land out of wheat farming, but the Great Depression scuttled the pact. In 1949, a new agreement was ratified, this best exemplifying the so-called multilateral long-term contract form of price stabilization. This involved guaranteed prices between exporters and importers. Here, both buyers and sellers agreed to conduct a part of their commerce, say 60 percent, at prices within a band between a ceiling and a floor. Only 40 percent of the wheat traded could be marketed at prices above that ceiling or below that floor. In 1967, in connection with the Kennedy Round, a similar successor, the International Grains Agreement, was negotiated. But belying the name, floor and ceiling prices could be agreed on only for wheat. When the new pact came into effect in 1968, it ran immediately into a growing oversupply of wheat, stimulated in part by the "miracle wheat" developed by Dr. Norman Borlaug of Iowa State University, the Nobel Price winner. The rigid price structure and the narrow band between floor and ceiling proved unrealistic, and the agreement fell apart at its first use. Attempts to revive it in 1971 led only to ongoing exchanges of information and consultation. With the great swings in wheat supply during the 1970s (very scarce in 1972-1973, huge surpluses in 1977), it is hard to see how any multilateral contract arrangement could have survived the resulting gyrations of price. In July 1978, negotiations for a new agreement were underway, but fruition was still far in the future. The principle of a wheat buffer stock had, however, been agreed on.

Stabilization May Destabilize

All schemes for commodity stabilization share a set of connected problems. With the best will in the world, stabilization may turn out to destabilize. Planners must consider whether they should be stabilizing prices of commodity exports or the incomes earned from those exports. It is simple to show, as in Fig. 19.2, that a decision to stabilize price may well cause violent fluctuations in income (and vice versa). See on the diagram how some agency (perhaps the Western Nigeria Marketing Board setting a fixed price for cocoa, to quote a real-world example from the 1960s) defends a fixed price, $0P_f$. Now say the crop year is a bad one, so that supply declines from S_1 to S_2. In a free, unstabilized market, price would rise along the demand curve to $0P_h$. But here, with the price fixed at $0P_f$, the normal reaction of higher prices does not occur. The higher prices would have had the effect of partly compensating for the fall in supply, maintaining income to a large extent. The initial level of income earned is $0P_fE_1Q_1$. After the crop failure in a free market, income earned is $0P_hE_2Q_2$. But with a price stabilization scheme in operation, and price fixed at $0P_f$, income plummets to $0P_fAQ_3$. A large amount of income is lost, as indicated by the hatched area in the diagram. One year in the 1960s, Nigerian cocoa farmers suffered an estimated 43 percent loss of income. The upshot: Stabilizing prices can destabilize income. This is a major reason why some economists oppose the common fund buffer stock plan, and advocate

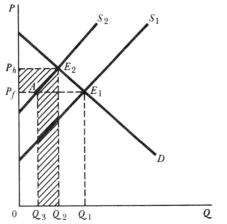

FIGURE 19.2

instead greater expansion in the IMF's program of compensatory finance and similar agreements such as the EEC's STABEX scheme mentioned earlier.[8]

Similarly, price (or income) stabilization runs up against the difficulty in detecting the direction of long-term movements in demand and supply. Any first-year economics student appreciates that fixing a price without reference to underlying demand and supply and their changes leads inevitably to serious shortages or surpluses. For the managers of a buffer stock or other stabilizing ICA, the omnipresent task is the identification of long-term trends within a welter of short-term price movements. Who can tell what the long-term trends are? The wrong choice will make the situation worse, for then the buffer stock managers must eventually exhaust their cash reserves or their stock, resulting in a rapid climb or slump in prices—and an unstabilized free market could have avoided this, though of course it will suffer from the same old problem of short-run instability. Thus, in all commodity ICAs, the international fixed-price ceilings and floors are difficult to set.[9]

Finally, there is a danger of destabilization whenever one commodity is covered by an ICA but closely related substitute commodities are not. For example, on the demand side, if copper is stabilized in a business slump while the price of unstabilized aluminum falls, buyers will switch from the former to the latter, and producer incomes fluctuate widely. Consider also the supply side. If the wheat price is stabilized, but corn and soybeans fall in price, then many farmers will increase their production of wheat. Thus, from the standpoint of both demand and supply, an ICA must include the close substitutes or trouble is sure to occur.

Import Substitution Policy

There is one final policy that can be adopted as a response by LDCs to the problems of international trade. For some countries, this policy is actually a gesture of defiance. It is called "import substitution," and although in application it can be mild or severe, we will here consider import substitution as a complete and overriding policy goal. Sometimes the model is called "autarkic," from autarky, self-sufficiency, with the implication of no dependence on outsiders. Any single import will be set up as a target, with a main goal of national planning being the elimination of that and all other imports.

Now, of course, *some* import substitution is eminently logical, because some imports if produced at home will be subject to natural protection due to transport costs. Recall from our earlier discussion in Chapter 10 that market-oriented goods such as beer and soft-drink bottling, or supply-oriented production as with the great weight-and-bulk adders, may be obvious candidates for an import substitution policy because they will need no tariff or quota protection. Beyond these, it will also be rational to pursue import substitution in the production of manufactured goods where a comparative advantage exists or can be achieved with a dose of infant-industry protection—textiles being a good example for several LDCs.

Beyond these stages, however, comes import substitution, where there is no present comparative advantage and little hope for developing it. Such an inward-looking, or autarkic, policy is not uncommon nowadays. All around the Third World are an intelligentsia of impatient planners—politicians, home-grown economists, military officers—longing for direct action that can raise a country by its bootstraps to faster development. This attitude means concrete projects, and concrete projects often involve widespread, pervasive import substitution.

In general, tariffs and foreign exchange controls are so adjusted that it becomes profitable to manufacture imported products. This means a stiff levy on the import, combined with relatively free entry for the capital goods, raw materials, and other inputs into production. Recalling our discussion of "effective protection" in Chapter 12, the reader will note that this policy understates the actual rate of protection on the finished product. Effective protection for import substitutes with a high degree of imported inputs (which are subject to low rates of duty and may even be subsidized) and with little value added at home is thus much more stringent than appears from simply comparing domestic prices to world prices.

Several results are predictable. First, since for balance of payments reasons it is common to place the most strict limits on imports considered least essential, there will then be a bias in favor of starting up these very same least essential industries. Second, the industries so protected will potentially be highly profitable for their owners. But their efficiency is likely to be lessened, as is usual when competition is lessened. At its outer limit, import substitution approaches a situation of "absolute protection," wherein the aim seems to be to protect the whole economy against any imports whatsoever. Here, sheltering behind high tariff walls, some business pursuits become "hothouse activities," turning out such things as very high-cost iron and steel (Egypt), modern jet aircraft (Argentina, Egypt, India), automobiles (Turkey, Nigeria), and many other products in many other settings, where comparative advantage would seem hopeless of attainment for many years into the future. To make matters worse, there is often no competition behind the tariff barriers, and the quality of the finished product is not as good as the import.

A further effect is that hasty expansion of industry will draw factors of production, perhaps especially scarce capital and entrepreneurial talent, away from areas with a comparative advantage and to areas where protection has artificially stimulated profits. As the Turkish economist Oktay Yenal has written, "Soon they reach a precocious 'maturity' when the substitution . . . is completed, and can continue to expand only on the basis of an increase in domestic demand, at the peak of which they lapse into monopolistic indolence, with lower rates of profit, little investment and aging plant and equipment." Most distressing of all, the "thin layer of industrialization in the shape of assembly plants and packing industries" (quoting Yenal) has often increased, rather than reduced, the dependence on imports, as we noted in our last chapter. Some industries actually import more in value terms per unit of output than the value of the finished good imported before a policy of protection was imposed.

Fairly obvious side effects include losses suffered by export industries, which must now switch from importing some of their inputs to buying them from inefficient local producers. Meanwhile, industries that *could* become efficient exporters are allowed to stagnate into inefficiency behind high tariff barriers.

In view of these detrimental results from a general policy of import substitution, the authors advocate a simple-sounding policy with the full knowledge that it is not easy to implement: namely, careful attention both to present comparative advantage and to the changes occurring in it. General import substitution, in their opinion, is far too likely to retard growth and reduce income in the LDCs, when—as everyone will agree—the goal is to do just the opposite.

Conclusion

As the reader may have gathered from the last two chapters, the authors are skeptical of development policies that are based on the restriction of trade— whether this is done through tariffs, import licensing, multiple exchange rates, export taxes, or anything else. Although we do recognize that a very selective use of tariffs or export subsidies can effectively stimulate development, we are cautious lest the process get out of hand. We feel that the use of capital is more important than its accumulation and accordingly are quite concerned with microeconomic distortions that occur under hothouse conditions. Along with many development economists, we are optimistic about the linkages that arise from agricultural development and we believe that agricultural exports are a key element in the progress of the farm sector.

Naturally we are concerned about the fluctuations in income and receipts from LDC exports, but remain skeptical about the feasibility of price-fixing schemes. A more practical solution may be to diversify export structure to achieve a "portfolio effect"—where products whose prices move up balance those that move down. This can be achieved through a judicious mixture of export incentives and disincentives. Indeed, the experiences of fairly open economies such as Thailand's and Peru's suggest that export diversification may tend to occur without any specific governmental policy toward that end.

To facilitate diversification and development of exports, developed nations should allow the import of both raw materials and finished goods from less developed nations without any restrictions. Present restrictions on textile and other imports should be abolished. This may not be politically expedient in the short run, but it is wise in the context of the development of a more stable and prosperous world.

Notes

1. See Joris J. C. Voorhoeve, "Trends in Official Development Aid," *Finance and Development* 14, No. 2 (June 1977): 10-14, for a recent survey of aid flows. One sign of progress was an undertaking in March 1978, by the rich countries to cancel all debts owed by the poorest LDCs as a result of earlier loans. Since 1972, all aid to this poorest group of 29 countries has been in the form of grants.
2. In addition, some scholars such as P. T. Bauer of the London School of Economics criticize aid because of its adverse side effects (see especially his *Dissent on Development,* Cambridge: Harvard University Press, 1972). Such effects might arguably include the politicization of economic life, as effort and trained manpower is thrown into the search for grants rather than the struggle for economic development; a "world-owes-us-a-living" attitude of reliance on others; and a maldistribution of income with the proceeds of aid going largely to the politician, the city-dweller, the educated elite, and the civil service. Some of these problems have indeed been serious in a good many recipient countries.

3. The balance of payments problems to which the new IMF facilities are intended to be a response have meant that some LDCs have had difficulty in making interest payments on their outstanding loans for economic development. The World Bank (IBRD), which makes many such loans, has thus instituted its so-called third window scheme (the name stemming from the term "discount window" in central bank lending) to subsidize interest payments on past World Bank loans. $600 million was allocated for this in 1976-1977, far less than hoped because the United States, France, Germany, Japan, and Belgium would not agree to participate.

4. The liberalization of the rules came in December 1975. Before then, countries could not draw on the facility if the cash value of its export earnings in the current year had increased by 5 percent or more over the average of the previous two years. In an era of high inflation, this figure was often exceeded, even by countries whose real earnings from primary product exports were sharply declining. This clause was scrapped. At the same time, the shortfall in export earnings that could be financed was raised from 25 percent of a country's IMF quota annually to 50 percent, and the ceiling on total drawings was raised from 50 percent of quota to 75 percent. The result was that the $2.7 billion actually borrowed in 1976 was very much higher than the $0.6 billion that would have been permitted under the old rules.

   There is also a compensatory finance scheme administered and funded by the member nations of the EEC. Under the Lome Convention, signed in the Republic of Togo in 1975, the Common Market's Export Stability scheme (STABEX for short) was agreed on with forty-six (now fifty-two) developing countries. These may receive grants or interest-free loans to cover shortfalls in earnings from primary product exports to the EEC. In the first year of STABEX operation, 1976, the EEC paid out $84 million to seventeen countries. For a review of the compensatory facilities, see Louis M. Goreux, "The Use of Compensatory Financing," *Finance and Development* 14, No. 3 (September 1977): 20-24.

   There are several other international sources of funds for development. The United Nations Development Program (UNDP), the biggest international organization for technical assistance, had a 1976 budget of $370 million. The International Finance Corporation (IFC), an arm of the World Bank that makes loans in the private sector, was expected to have a 1976 budget of $480 million. The soft-loan International Development Agency (IDA), another arm of the World Bank that lends to governments on easy terms, was seeking $7 to $9 billion in 1976 to cover a three-year period. Its budget for 1974-1977 was $4.5 billion. At the same time, the parent World Bank was seeking an increase of $8 billion-$10 billion in its own lendable capital. (It lent $5.8 billion in 1977, almost all of it going to LDCs.)

5. There is a concise, up-to-date account of the debt crisis in the *Economist*, October 2, 1976, pp. 78-79.

6. See Zubair Iqbal, "The Generalized System of Preferences Examined," *Finance and Development* 12, No. 3 (September 1975): 34-39.

7. There is a comprehensive survey article by G. V. Smith and G. R. Schink, "The International Tin Agreement: A Reassessment," in *Economic Journal* 86, No. 344 (December 1976): 715-728.

8. Recent theoretical work by Ezriel M. Brook and Enzo R. Grilli, contained in a World Bank Staff Working Paper, "Commodity Price Stabilization and the Developing World," has attempted to identify the main sources of prices and income instability. The two authors show that the source of the price fluctuation, demand or supply, is the critical factor in determining whether ICAs result in a welfare gain for producers and consumers, and whether income will fluctuate widely. In their model, demand shifts were seen to destabilize exporter income, while supply shifts tended to have the opposite effect. The greater the elasticities of demand and supply, the greater stabilizing effect on income of a price ICA when demand shifts are the original cause of the fluctuation. When supply shifts are the cause of the problem, however, the authors predict that stabilization of price also stabilizes income only when demand and supply are inelastic. They conclude that the greatest benefits to LDCs will come in ICAs for wheat, sugar, coffee, cocoa, cotton, and jute; but that stabilizing the prices of other products will have a negative effect for LDCs.

9. In the 1950s, Professors P. T. Bauer and B. S. Yamey of the London School of Economics demonstrated that a chain-index linking mechanism could be relied on for determination of the fixed floor and ceiling prices. The floor and ceiling would automatically change depending on the price trends of recent years. But the managers of ICAs have not been willing, on the whole, to lose the power of setting prices through negotiation, and countries, too, enmeshed in political tradeoffs, have been unwilling to let prices be set by a rote formula. However, the IMF's compensatory finance scheme does use a moving five-year average to determine eligibility for benefits, and thus accords with the Bauer/Yamey suggestions.

ENVOI

Economic models can, as we have noted at several points in the text, only suggest questions to ask. They do not in themselves give answers. The simplifying assumptions we must make to understand underlying forces and mechanisms move us far away from "reality." Two centuries of economic thought, often by some of the greatest minds of the time, have indeed given a series of marvelous frameworks into which fit the economic processes of the world. We would be shirking our duty as educated citizens if we failed to employ such frameworks as we struggle with practical decisions. At the same time, we will be led to grievous errors if we fail to realize how the specifics of each problem differ from our model. One becomes humble before this vast, exciting, confusing, and often frightening world.

REVIEW QUESTIONS

Chapter 2

1. Describe briefly the foreign exchange market, explaining the way bank customers buy and sell foreign exchange, the way banks do so, and the way central banks do so.

2. What reasons would cause American banks to hold smaller than usual amounts of foreign currency—say the Swedish kroner?

3. Trace through on T-accounts the clearing of a check drawn on the Continental Bank of Illinois and deposited in Barclays Bank in London. Assume that Chase Manhattan and Barclays are correspondent banks.

4. Try the following cross-rate arbitrage. (To see if you would be a good arbitrageur, try to solve them in fifteen seconds!)

   a) US$1.00 = DM4.00 b) US$1.00 = C$1.05

   US$1.00 = Fr5.00   £1.00 = US$1.85

   DM1.00 = Fr1.10;   £1.00 = C$1.90

   C$ means Canadian dollar, Fr means franc, and DM means Deutsche mark, the German currency.

5. Trace through the demand and supply curves of Figs. 2.6 and 2.7. Why do we just not move the demand or supply curves to show government intervention?

6. With upward pressure on the £ sterling, the British government decides to ____ (buy or sell) £100,000 to stem the rise. Decide whether it buys or sells, diagram this with D and S curves, and show on T-accounts between the United States and Britain.

7. Why do individuals wish to acquire foreign exchange?

Chapter 3

1. What political and economic features do you think contributed to the stability of the gold standard?

2. Trace the evolution of foreign exchange systems from the gold standard to the present mixed system, describing briefly the main forces causing each change.

3. The gold-exchange standard was formalized by the Bretton Woods Agreement. When did it really start?

4. Describe gold points.

5. Exchange control gives rise to a great number of administrative problems. What are they? Why do they occur?

6. After an experiment with exchange controls in the late 1940s, Peru moved to a freer system, reducing the value of the *sol* to nearly half its old rate. Yet the prices on the market of most imports did not rise dramatically. How can the concept of a "hidden devaluation" under exchange control explain what happened?

7. Why does exchange control generally hurt exports?

8. Examine the Chilean exchange rates in Fig. 3.6. What would their effect be on the allocation of resources?

9. Why is dirty floating dirty?

10. Compare the exchange rates under the gold standard with modern floating rates. Which could encourage more trade? How can the level of trade still be high today?

Chapter 4

1. Examine the chart on the next page. It gives enough information to predict, on an interest-rate basis, where the three-month forward exchange rates should be in relation to the dollar. Fill in the blanks in lines 1-6. The Belgian example is done for you.

2. Lines 7-9 of the chart show the actual premium or discount on a 90-day forward rate on an annual basis. Thus line 3 and line 7 can be compared. The difference is in line 8. For line 9, figure the actual 90-day forward rate from the annual premium or discount. Lastly, tell whether an arbitrageur holding forward exchange of the currency in question should sell it or buy more.

   Explanation of example: using the Belgian franc

   Line 3. The difference between interest rates is 2.63 percent. These interest rates are on comparable 90-day investments.

   Line 5. Converting the annual interest-rate difference to a 90-day rate we divide by 4. Then we multiply that times the spot rate to get 0.23.
   $$0.263/4 \times 35.93 = 0.23$$
   Line 6. Since borrowing is more expensive in Belgium than in the United States, we find the Belgian franc at a discount. This means more francs to the dollar so we add the 0.23 to the 35.93 to get 36.16.

   Lines 7-8. The actual discount is 2.00 per annum, or 0.5 percent for 90 days. This gives an interest rate arbitrage opportunity of 0.63 percent a year. (If line 7 or 8 is not given, see below.)

   Line 9. The actual forward rate is 0.5 percent below spot, or 36.11. To figure lines 7 and 8 from line 9, take the difference between spot and forward (lines 9 and 6), figure it as a percentage of the spot, and annualize it.
   $$(.18/35.93 \times 4 = .02)$$
   Line 10. Since the Belgian franc should be discounted more than the market is so doing, the arbitrageur can sell forward Belgian francs and invest in Belgian securities, and come out slightly ahead. The arbitrage opportunity is rather small, however.

3. Some months later, the situation had changed as follows: interest rates are US 6.5 percent; Britain, 4.81 percent; France 9.56 percent; Germany 4.15 percent; Japan 4.125 percent.

   Actual cost of forward in percentage per year against the dollar is Britain, Premium 2.02 percent; France, Discount 5.93 percent; Germany, Premium 3.24 percent; Japan, Premium 3.25 percent.

   What would explain the changes from premium to discount since May of the same year?

   Why is there considerably larger premium on the mark and yen than interest rate arbitrage would suggest?

4. Assume you are exporting tobacco from a nation whose currency may very likely fall in value soon. How do you handle your leads and lags to protect yourself?

5. Many governments intervene in the forward market as well as in the spot. By purchasing pounds forward, the British government raises the price of forward pounds. This encourages arbitrageurs to sell pounds forward and buy pounds spot. Because it buys in the forward market, Britain does not need the foreign exchange to cover until the contracts are due. Demonstrate the above with an example. What might be the dangers of such a policy?

6. You are convinced that you have three six-packs in the refrigerator so you and your friends one warm night drink away happily. At 10 P.M. you go to get pack number 3, and find you really had only two. Your disappointment is not only that you didn't have three, but that you could have done OK with two. How would proper speculation have improved your welfare?

Category	Belgium	Britain	France	Germany	Japan
1. Annual interest rate (90 day prime paper)	7.5	7.78	9.375	4.60	4.87
2. U.S. interest rate	4.87	4.87	4.87	4.87	4.87
3. Difference per year per quarter	2.63 .65				
4. Spot rate (currency unit per dollar)	35.93	.5814	4.948	2.4375	276.60
5. Predicted discount or premium on 90-day forward (in units/dollar)	0.23				
6. Predicted forward rate	36.18				
7. Actual premium or discount on 90-day forward (% per year)	2.00	D3.25	D4.75		
8. Arbitrage opportunity (% per year)	0.63				
9. Actual forward rate	36.11			2.4300	276.69
10. Interest rate at which arbitrageur should buy (B) or sell (S) currency	S				

Chapter 5

1. If there can be Eurodollars, why are there no Ameromarks?
2. Banks can lend 100 percent of their Eurodollars, yet there can be little multiple expansion of Eurodollar deposits. Why?
3. In what ways do Eurodollars thwart national monetary policies? In what ways could they aid monetary policy?
4. What factors gave rise to the Eurodollar market?

5. Distinguish Eurodollars from Eurobonds. What are the differences and similarities?

6. Why would people use the Eurobond market rather than New York for lending and borrowing today?

7. What are the disadvantages of Eurobond and medium-term Eurodollar markets?

Chapter 6

1. A definition of the balance of payments often seen in the press is: "A balance of payments deficit indicates Americans have been spending abroad more than foreigners have been spending in the United States." Is this a meaningful statement? (The fuzzy words are *Americans, spending,* and *deficit.*) How can there be a deficit in an account that by definition is a balance? How might you modify the statement to make it fit the balance of payments on an official settlements basis?

2. What produces "errors" in balance of payments figures? Answer both according to data limitations and the presentation of information. Why should there be unusually large or small errors in some years?

3. Handle the following items of this year's U.S. balance of payments.

a) A payment for $500,000 worth of corn exported last year.

b) A gift of six tractors to the people of Mexico from the Future Farmers of America.

c) Default on a $50,000 debt by a foreigner.

d) $20,000 paid by the Ford Foundation to an American adviser in Turkey.

e) The salary of a U.S. diplomat abroad.

f) Expenditures on prostitution by U.S. soldiers abroad.

g) Imports of heroin.

h) Earnings of American companies abroad, reinvested there and not brought back to the United States.

i) Payment for textile imports from Puerto Rico.

j) New York Federal Reserve purchases of German marks.

(The answers are, we think, (a) lower net loans (short-term investment); (b) export +, unilateral transfer − ; (c) item moves from trade credits (under short-term investment) to unilateral transfer, which will alter the balance on current account, but not payments; (d) services +, unilateral transfer − ; (e) U. S. government expenditures −; (f) either errors or military −, probably the former; (g) errors −; (h) until 1978 it did not show, but now it is a receipt under services and a payment under direct investment; (i) doesn't show either; (j) monetary +.)

4. How does the American role of world banker increase the liquidity deficit?

5. What are the limitations of the liquidity deficit concept?

6. How do the Canadian and Thai balance of payments statements reflect their own specific interests?

Chapter 7

1. Trace through the T-accounts the purchase of $500,000 worth of Canadian dollars from the Chase Manhattan Bank (which works with the Bank of Nova Scotia) by the Federal Reserve Bank. What effect does this have on Chase's ability to lend? What is the maximum amount of new money it could create?

2. Show on T-accounts how the Fed could sterilize the $500,000.

3. Why do countries other than the United States have trouble sterilizing inflows of foreign exchange?

4. One reason the U.S. dollar remains the leading currency is because the U.S. allows large inflows and outflows of foreign deposits. What monetary factors allow the United States to operate this way, yet do not allow Switzerland, Germany, or Japan to do so?

5. Draw a diagram similar to that of Fig. 7.10, using the following data. At an income of 200, $S = 20$, $M = 40$, $I = 30$, $X = 40$. I and X are autonomous. MPS = 0.20, MPM = 0.25. What is the equilibrium level of income? Assume exports were to rise by 20, what is the new income?

6. Use the same data as in the previous model with one exception. Assume that $X = 40$ only at the income of 200, and that it slopes downward at a slope of 0.10. What is your new conclusion?

7. As the new Mexican oil discoveries come into production, many U.S. purchases of oil will shift there from the Middle East. This would not depress U.S. national income as far as before, even given that oil imports may be the same in value. Why?

8. In 1977 the United States attempted to recover from a recession. Interest rates fell and the government stimulated the economy. Results domestically were fairly satisfactory with a higher level of economic growth and little inflation. The U.S. balance of trade, however, worsened greatly, falling from a record surplus in 1975 to two years of record deficits.

   a) Demonstrate this using the $X - M = S - I$ framework.

   b) Most people in the Carter cabinet agreed the tail shouldn't wag the dog, but by late 1977 there was considerable concern about how far this logic could be pushed. Why? (The dog won.)

   c) How did the continued sluggish growth in Germany and Japan contribute to the size of the U.S. deficit? Demonstrate with the $X - M = S - I$ model how Japan could pile up billions of dollars in trade surpluses.

   d) Using a Swan-Mundell diagram, locate the zone of Germany and Japan.

9. Consider the position of the United States on a Swan-Mundell diagram. With a budget deficit and moderate interest rates, the United States was close to internal balance, so for simplicity, assume the United States is on the internal balance line. Now, considering this same position produced a large external imbalance, suggest the location of the external balance line. What factors might move it in a more satisfactory direction?

10. Why do economists generally dislike selective monetary and fiscal policies as means for ending deficits?

Chapter 8

1. Why is it difficult to compare per capita income between nations with any precision?

2. In the years 1975-1977, the United States had less inflation than many of its trading partners, yet the value of the dollar declined. Why did purchasing power parity theory not work?

3. Why are the slopes of import demand and export supply curves generally greater than their domestic equivalents? Why cannot individual curves be summed to give the nation's import demand or export supply?

4. Why can we be sure a dollar devaluation will reduce the foreign exchange value of dollars entering the foreign exchange market (except under very extreme cases), but we cannot be sure what will happen to foreign exchange offerings?

5. Why are supply curves not considered in defining the Marshall-Lerner condition?

6. What is the Marshall-Lerner condition?

7. What are some reasons for feeling that the Marshall-Lerner bind is unlikely to occur?

8. What are some possible effects of imperfect competition on the response of the United States to a dollar devaluation?

9. In constructing demand and supply curves for foreign currency based on import and export elasticities, why does only the demand curve bend backward?

10. Demonstrate the Marshall-Lerner condition on currency demand and supply curves.

11. The American position in 1976-1977 was described in the questions at the end of the last chapter, where the information was put on a Swan-Mundell diagram. Now place the same information on the Meade tables (Tables 8.2-8.4). Assume the United States is in a period of mild recession, its principle trading partners in stronger recessions. What exchange rates and income policies should the United States follow? Germany? Japan?

12. In the Great Depression, the United States had a surplus while Britain and France had deficits. All were in depressions and all were holding fixed rates as best they could. Using the Meade tables, sketch out the policy options.

13. Sik Lee Pehl, ailing premier of Paludia, realizes his currency is seriously overvalued. To correct this situation, his government initiates a "currency reform" whose essence is this: The following Monday a new currency, the New Dollar (N\$); will come into effect. All old currency will be brought to the banks and changed to new dollars at the rate of \$1.50 = N\$1.00; all bank accounts, all debts, all wages, and so on will be rendered in New Dollars. Everything, indeed, would be changed with the exception of the exchange rate, which would remain as it was before. A day after the change is completed, Paludian authorities announce that the New Dollar will henceforth be called the "dollar," and that the whole scheme was just a way of removing purchasing power from the economy. They are heralded by certain economists as having effected "the world's most perfect deflation." The leader of the opposition, the Radical Intransigents, simply describe it as "a terribly awkward devaluation." Which was it?

14. Discuss in the context of the Thai balance of payments: "Sensible international behavior calls for recipients of long-term capital inflows to expand their economies far enough to use the body of that inflow."

15. "Considering the heavy American investments in Canada in the 1950s, the Canadian trade deficit of that period was a natural counterpart for the American surplus." Explain.

16. Because of the cheapness of capital in New York, a Finnish firm borrows $10 million there. Although a heavy importer; Finland imports little from the United States, so American exports do not rise to cover any of the $10 million. If Finland has not provided her own savings, who has?

Chapter 9

1. Why does the Hume specie-flow mechanism not work in modern economies?

2. Trace the history of gold's decline from a sole reserve to a secondary reserve. What were the major factors causing the changes?

3. How do "swap" arrangements help defend currencies?

4. "Borrowing from other nations through swap agreements or ad hoc measures is a bit like borrowing from relatives. Borrowing from the IMF is more like borrowing from a bank." Comment.

5. More than half the IMF's holdings of currency are useless. Why?

6. If swap lines and the IMF buttress a nation's reserves, what buttresses the IMF's reserves?

7. Explain the tranche system.

8. Explain the Triffin and Stamp plans.

9. Is it accurate to call SDRs "Paper gold"? Why or why not?

10. "Floating rates have done more than SDRs to improve nations' reserve positions." Explain.

11. How could floating rates increase inflation? How could they decrease it?

12. What kind of environment is necessary to have fixed rates like those of the gold standard?

13. We say on one level that a surplus can be created by restrictive monetary and fiscal policy; on another level we say that such a surplus is costly. Are these not basically the same idea?

14. Would the balance of payments figured on a liquidity basis give a good idea of the proper amount of reserves to be held as precautionary balances?

Chapter 10

1. "The pure theory of trade is abstract to such a degree that it is useless for any practical economic analysis." Comment.

2. "There can be no such thing as 'absolute advantage'. Cost must be rendered in terms of opportunities forgone, not in resources used. If the cloth-exporting nation can indeed make both cloth and wine with fewer resources than its trading partner, it still must face the fact that the opportunity cost of producing wine is the high amount of cloth it must forgo." Comment.

3. Why is international microeconomics important?

4. What are the limitations of Ricardo's model and how does modern theory take these into account?

5. In a constant-cost comparative advantage model, why does the ultimate equilibrium price end up between the prices of the trading partners? Why will countries with identical price ratios not trade?

6. In increasing-cost models, why will specialization normally be incomplete? Under what circumstances would it be complete?

7. A community indifference curve differs from an individual indifference curve in what respect and with what implication for trade theory?

8. "The gain from trade is, in essence, the ability to consume beyond one's own production possibility curve through the use of trade. It is the ability to move to a higher indifference curve." Explain.

9. Why should nations trade if their production possibilities curves are the same?

10. What is the effect of scale economies on the gains from trade?

11. "Offer curves are a curious sidebranch of economic theory; they help us tell with precision what would happen in the very unlikely event that two nations traded two commodities. The gains from studying them are most marginal." Comment.

12. Ocean freight rates have not risen as fast as land rates, such that in many instances it is cheaper to get goods to California from Japan than it is to get them there from New York. Demonstrate this on a set of diagrams similar to those in Fig. 10.20. (Treat New York as a separate country.)

13. What types of goods are "naturally protected"? Give some examples.

14. Examine the following list of products. Indicate which you think tend to be supply oriented, market oriented, or footloose. Explain why you think so.

calculators	refrigerators
candy bars	aluminum refining
standard clothing	pineapple canning
fashion clothing	sugar refining

15. Can you use factor proportions to show why the United States imports textiles and exports machinery?

16. "It is not the *absolute* amount of capital or labor a good uses that determines its exportability, but its ranking compared with other goods." Explain.

17. What are the principal limitations of the Heckscher-Ohlin theory?

18. As the next chapter indicates, many U.S. exports are more labor intensive than U.S. imports—for example, computers, industrial machinery, textbooks. What are some possible reasons for this? (Consider the ranking of goods according to capital intensity, the role of demand, or additional factors.)

19. Protection of labor through controlling immigration can never be fully effective if there is free trade. Why?

20. Following ten years of an aggressive export drive in which exports have trebled, the developing nation of Aumentia finds its commodity terms of trade have declined to 80 from a base of 100 ten years before. Has it been following the wrong policies?

21. "Low wages do not exist in industries under heavy import competition because of that competition. Rather, they are low there because domestic competition for labor makes them look low." Explain.

Chapter 11

1. What is the Leontief Paradox? How might it be explained so as to keep the Heckscher-Ohlin theory intact?

2. What is intraindustrial trade? Why does it make Heckscher-Ohlin difficult to use?

3. Explain learning curve analysis. How does it introduce a dynamic into a static theory?

4. "Trade is not necessarily a static thing, determined by fixed endowments. Rather it is determined largely by technological leads and lags and production experience." Comment.

5. Linder's model suggests trade arises between similar, not different, economies. How can this be?

6. Explain the process of maturation in a product life-cycle model. What are the stages of a "typical" product life cycle?

7. Explain the Wells-Vernon model and discuss its limitations.

8. What causes trade in differentiated goods? What are the costs involved in manufacturing and selling differentiated goods?

9. It is felt that virtually all the gains from trade between the United States and Canada in automobiles arises because of increased specialization within the industry. How does this come about?

10. Two nations enter trade with identical cost and demand configurations, and accordingly have identical prices. Market segmentation, however, has led to a great variety of models and brands in each nation, and consequently high production costs. Can trade still occur? What will happen to the pattern of costs after trade?

11. Intraindustrial specialization, the text suggests, is less disruptive of labor than classical interindustrial specialization. Why?

Chapter 12

1. Construct demand and supply curves and tariffs showing the following situations:
   a) High revenue effect, little protection. (What is terms of trade effect?)
   b) High protective effect, no terms of trade effect, and little revenue effect.
   c) High deadweight loss effect, no terms of trade, and little revenue effect.
   d) Low consumption effect, high protective effect.

2. The essentially revenue tariffs of the First World War were turned into protective tariffs afterward. Both aims of protection and revenue cannot, however, be pursued simultaneously. Why?

3. "Unlike tariffs, quotas do not raise domestic prices." Comment.

4. What happens to the "revenue" effect if quotas replace tariffs?

5. Why do most economists dislike quotas?

6. Voluntary export quotas restrict Japanese exports to the United States. Alternatives would be (1) higher tariffs or (2) revaluation of the yen against the dollar. Which method would you advocate? And why?

7. "The only logic behind Buy Domestic acts is political." Comment.

8. Where does a domestic subsidy to aid a poor region end and an export subsidy begin?

9. "DISC is the biggest ripoff ever perpetrated on the American taxpayer." Comment.

10. "In a world of floating exchange rates, the border tax question is really rather academic." Explain.

Chapter 13

1. Why was the bargain between American farm state senators and manufacturing state senators over tariffs in the early 1920s a poor one?

2. Why was the Smoot-Hawley Act a tariff of abominations? What political and social changes had happened in the 100 years since the first Tariff of Abominations to make the Smoot Act pass so easily?

3. What were the main differences between the Reciprocal Trade Act and previous tariff law? How did Roosevelt try to solve the agricultural issue presented in the 1920s tariffs?

4. "Since the Trade Expansion Act put virtually all U.S. tariffs on an ad valorem basis, free traders have lost their greatest ally in cutting tariffs—inflation." Explain.

5. What are the functions of GATT?

6. Roosevelt separated agricultural problems from tariffs. Should the problems of industrial maladjustment also be separated from tariffs? How have the TEA and the TRA handled such problems?

7. Contrast the major provisions of (1) the tariffs of 1920-1930; (2) the RTA Acts; (3) the TEA act; and (4) the TRA act.

8. "The Generalized System of Preferences goes part of the way toward ameliorating the harm done by high effective tariffs." Comment and explain, showing what is meant by GSP and effective tariffs.

9. Thailand has been moving toward increasing protection of its automobile industry. At present it requires local assembly and is considering laws requiring local content. The population of Thailand is about 42 million, with a per capita income of around $300. There are ten assembly plants assembling over twenty automobile

models. The total sales in 1977 for all cars were 72,000. World-scale auto assembly plants should be nearly 100,000 a year. Thailand's largest is 20,000. Evaluate automobile production as an infant industry in Thailand.

10. What are the weaknesses of the cheap labor argument?

11. "The vast majority of America's work force is foolish to think it needs protection from imports; it should strive to lower the price of consumer goods through more imports." Comment.

12. "So what's wrong with dumping? If some Japanese company wants to subsidize my consumption, I'll let it." Comment.

Chapter 14

1. "The tolerance of the United States for some of the EEC's abuses must be understood in the context of a long term political-economic strategy." What are some EEC "abuses" and what long-term strategy does the quotation refer to?

2. Explain the difference between a Customs Union and a Free Trade Association.

3. Draw diagrams demonstrating the case that the EEC's industrial trade was largely trade creating; its agricultural trade, trade diverting.

4. The more ambitious student may wish to try to draw the customs union effect diagrams with the foreign and partner supply curves sloped upward. What difference does this make to the conclusions?

5. Larger customs unions have small trade diversion effects, but larger customs unions are also quite dangerous to outside nations. Why?

6. Why is there more growth of trade between complementary economies than competitive ones?

7. The authors appear unhappy over the EEC's agricultural policy. Why?

8. "In the end, the reduction of NTBs in the EEC may be as significant as the tariff cuts." Comment.

9. Why is it difficult to analyze Comecon according to standard economic analysis?

10. Explain the types of bi-lateral arrangements frequently necessary to engage in East-West trade.

11. "East-West trade is not necessarily beneficial because prices are often only remotely related to costs." Explain.

12. "East-West trade can never be more than a rather marginal activity. The dynamics of Communist planning, the lack of free markets, and the often-justified complaints of dumping by Western firms, will allow trade on only a small scale." Comment.

Chapter 15

1. Demonstrate the misallocative effect of a monopolist or monopsonist.

2. "The countervailing power in a bilateral monopoly may establish a fair price to participants, but the economic equilibrium so established is hardly optimal or fair." Explain.

3. Why doesn't Saudi Arabia drive the marginal oil producers out of business? (Answer in economic terms.)

4. How did the Oil Cartel work through the middle years of this century?

5. Generally, oligopolies and cartels are poorer users of resources than monopolies. Why?

6. What conditions allow "successful" cartelization?

7. Is a U.S. company's foreign subsidiary free of U.S. antitrust law? Explain.

8. "Monopolistic competition (particularly that following Chamberlin's price-rigid model) serves to explain why trade in differentiated goods can bring large saving." Explain.

9. "The increased competition in the airline industry, favored by the Carter administration, should test the validity of Chamberlin's models." Comment.

10. In what sense does imperfect competition strengthen the argument for freer trade? How does it weaken it?

11. Why are the authors fairly confident that, even with imperfect competition, the goods traded tend to follow true comparative advantages? How do they cover themselves for an expected list of exceptions?

Chapter 16

1. What evidence is there that the multinational firm is not a post-World War II phenomenon?

2. "The idea that firms are not even trying to maximize profits rather throws our economic theories awry." Comment, evaluating the reasons for the statement and the validity of the idea.

3. "MNCs are generally oligopolists. There appears to be a direct link between oligopolistic behavior and the establishment of foreign subsidiaries." Evaluate, indicating what the linkages are and evaluating the explanatory power of this statement.

4. Why do not MNFs simply sell their unique assets to foreign firms?

5. What is the connection of the internalization process with market imperfection?

6. How could an MNF allocate resources differently from the way trade theory would predict? (Consider that imperfect competition theories as developed in Chapter 15 are part of trade theory.)

7. "If the Coasian theory holds, it is the difficulty of discovering the 'correctness' of prices that brings the firm into existence in the first place." Explain and comment in regard to transfer prices.

8. Assess American labor's case against the MNF.

9. "Host nations are rightly cautious about MNFs. In most situations, they are more trouble than they are worth." Assess this statement in economic terms.

Chapter 17

1. What economic conditions allowed the establishment of the "Majors' " oil cartel in the middle years of this century?

2. What factors led to the breakdown of the Majors' cartel?

3. What economic constraints are there on the operation of the OPEC cartel?

4. Does a $15 per barrel posted price for oil mean a $15 cost to the producer?

5. How did governments handle the macroeconomic effects of the rise in oil prices? What special conditions prevailed, making standard Keynesian solutions difficult?

6. Students might test their understanding of international macroeconomics by imagining that Saudi Arabia applied for admission to the United States as the fifty-first state. If admitted, what would happen to the dollar? To the price level in the old fifty states? To employment there? Imagine yourself as president, receiving the request. On economic grounds do you accept it or reject it?

Chapter 18

1. What are the grounds for pessimism about the exports of LDCs?

2. What might have caused a decline in the terms of trade for LDCs—at least in the statistics?

3. Are there special difficulties faced by most LDCs in handling their balance of payments problems?

4. "The enclave argument is a serious one, but it is not at root a problem of international trade." Comment.

5. "The problem with export growth from LDCs lies in their own policies, not in the nature of their exports." Comment.

6. What are the causes of the recent revival of interest in exports as a means of growth?

Chapter 19

1. The GSP arrangements, if properly liberalized, will be more effective than aid in stimulating economic growth." Evaluate.

2. "Many developed countries support ICAs only because LDCs want them, not because they think they will work. History does not suggest anything hopeful." Comment.

3. What are the problems in managing buffer stocks?

4. What are the principal difficulties of growth through import substitution?

INDEX

Taussig, Frank, 127, 143
Taxes
  internal, border adjustment for, 272–274
  in international economics, 3, 225
  on oil, 393–395, 401
  as trade barriers, 272–274
Tea, 430
Terms of trade, 217, 223, 232–233, 236,
    322, 404–411, 419
  commodity terms, 232, 404–406
  double factoral terms, 236
  effect of tariff, 260–262, 279–280
  income terms, 236
  and LDCs, 404–411, 419
  and price elasticity, 410
  single factoral terms, 233, 406
Tin, 426–428
Tokyo Round (Nixon Round, "Mulilateral
    trade negotiations"), 290, 300–301
Trade creation; *see* Customs unions
Trade diversion; *see* Customs unions
Trade Expansion Act (1962), 286,
    290–292, 294, 296, 312
Trade Reform Act (1974), 286, 294–299,
    312
Trading with the Enemy Act (1917), 293
Transfer costs; *see* Transport costs
Transfer price; *see* Multinational firms
Transnational activity, 7, 359, 379
Transport costs, 5, 8, 224–228, 260–262
  and location theory, 226–228
  natural protection, 226, 305
Triffin, Robert, 192
Triffin Plan, 192
Trigger price, 297

Underdeveloped countries; *see* Less-
    developed countries

Unilateral transfers, 103, 171
  as motive for acquiring foreign currency,
    28
United Fruit Company, 341, 356–357,
    371–372
United Nations Conference on Trade and
    Development (UNCTAD), 422,
    424–426, 428, 430
United States International Trade
    Commission; *see* United States
    Tariff Commission
United States Tariff Commission
    (International Trade Commission),
    234, 287, 292, 294–296, 298, 309,
    357, 376
Upward revaluation; *see* Revaluation

Value added tax (VAT), 275–277, 282,
    326–327
Vernon, Raymond, 246–248, 254; *see also*
    Wells–Vernon Model
Viner, Jacob, 318–319, 321
Voluntary export quotas, 293–298, 311
Voluntary foreign credit restraint (VFCR),
    76, 142

Webb-Pomerene Act (1919), 350
Wells, Lewis, 246–248
Wells–Vernon Model, 246–248
Wider band proposal,
Wheat, 431
Witteveen, Johannes; *see* International
    Monetary Fund
World Bank (IBRD), 192, 195, 423–424,
    436
Wright, E. M., 406

Zenith Case, 277, 282